THE NOBLEST CRY

THE
NOBLEST
CRY

A History of the
American Civil
Liberties Union

CHARLES LAM MARKMANN

ST. MARTIN'S PRESS
New York

Published in Canada by
The Macmillan Company of Canada Limited
70 Bond Street, Toronto 2

To the Reader:

Unless specifically ascribed to named individuals or groups, all opinions expressed in this book are the responsibility of the author alone.

I did not set out to write an "anti-American" book. Americans far more than the citizens of any other nation proclaim limitless devotion to an ideal of freedom. These perennial professions of faith, against which their acts must be measured, aggravate derelictions that in a less hypocritical and self-adulatory society, where they occur quite as frequently (human nature having no national variations), would perhaps appear less contradictory.

C.L.M.

To those who have made the most significant contributions of the past quarter-century to the development of a conscience in the United States, this book is dedicated with ambivalent thanks:

Ross Barnett
Roy M. Cohn
T. Eugene Connor
Charles E. Coughlin*
James O. Eastland
Orval Faubus
Barry M. Goldwater
Billy James Hargis
William Randolph Hearst*
J. Edgar Hoover
Fulton Lewis Jr.
Albert J. Lingo
Joseph R. McCarthy*
Robert R. McCormick*
Richard M. Nixon
Joseph Medill Patterson*
Westbrook Pegler
William Dudley Pelley
Leander H. Perez
George Lincoln Rockwell
Gerald L. K. Smith
George Sokolsky*
Edwin A. Walker
George Wallace
Robert H. W. Welch

* R. I. P.

Contents

Liberalism is the supreme form of generosity; it is the right which the majority accords to minorities and hence it is the noblest cry that has ever resounded in this planet. It announces the determination to share existence with the enemy; more than that, with an enemy which is weak. It was incredible that the human species should have arrived at so noble an attitude, so paradoxical, so refined, so acrobatic, so anti-natural. Hence, it is not to be wondered at that this same humanity should soon appear anxious to get rid of it. It is a discipline too difficult and complex to take firm root on earth.

José Ortega y Gasset in
La Rebelión de las Masas, 1930

Foreword

My first lesson in the theory of civil rights and civil liberties was administered in the fall of 1932, when I was nineteen, by a man who often thought President Hoover was dangerously inclined toward radicalism. My first experience of the practice of civil rights and liberties was provided six months later by the same man.

By Thanksgiving, 1932, my father was already the most implacable opponent Franklin Delano Roosevelt was ever to have, even if Mr. Roosevelt never knew it. After a difficult day spent defending what private property was still intact in those days, my father was relaxing, according to his custom, by denouncing Roosevelt in rhetoric to be matched only by that of John L. Lewis. I, having reached the peak of the age of omniscience, was assuring my father of my regret that, when the inevitable triumph of the right—that is, the left—was celebrated, he would have to be liquidated before his reactionary ideas could undermine the new Eden.

"By the way," he interrupted himself and me: "here's a book I've been meaning to suggest you read. Let me show you one passage." Opening the book so that I could not see its title, he pointed to the paragraph that I have presumed to borrow for this study. The book, of course, was José Ortega y Gasset's *The Revolt of the Masses*. "I may be quite as much a damned fool as you think me," my father remarked equably; "but I'm not damned fool enough to believe I can kill an idea by killing its advocate, or to claim the right to suppress it even if its success means the end of me."

Not only was I impressed; I was dumfounded. The pre-Bourbon who had begot me was more of a "liberal" than I!

Six months later an old, respected university—kindness begs me not to identify it—informed my father (since he was signing the checks) and me that it would be impossible to grant me the degree duly contracted for four years earlier because of "literary opinions that cannot be countenanced by the English Department." (Not an industrious youth, I had naturally chosen—officially—to major in English in order to concentrate my energies on matters of eternal moment, whose names escape me.)

My father's habitual courtroom urbanity shattered. "No one ever denied you're a horse's ass!" he cried in outrage. "But what has that to do with your right to a degree? Common decency and the Constitution give every one of us the right to be a horse's ass and none of us the right to penalise the others for being horses' asses."

He spent the next three days—vainly, of course—attempting to impart this truism to the leaders who governed that university and to persuade them that *what to think* was not a proper element of the curriculum of any institution that pretended to educate. But those men were like diplomats: they forgot nothing and they learned nothing.

Having had all his education from a private tutor—himself—my father had lived forty-six years in a reverent deference for those who, he stopped believing in June, 1933, were interested only in maturing, not in deforming, the minds of the young. What appalled him most about the whole incident—more even than the petty penalisation of a pimpled youth's literary heresies—was the final unbelieving protest of his academic antagonists: "But surely, Mr. Markmann, it is not true that you have never censored your children's reading?"

Well, it was true—my eleven-year-old sister was reading his Burton at that time (we grew up in ignorance of the existence of bowdlerisation). Perhaps because of that ruthlessly liberal upbringing by an archetype of reaction—shrewd enough, when he wanted to combat an idea, to know that an ounce of ridicule was worth a ton of repression—this book was begun thirty and more years later, while the United States was defending its democcratic principles by tapping German telephone wires in contravention of the Bonn Constitution as Christian soldiers in American and Viet Nam uniforms redeemed the heathen with water in the nostril and electrodes at the nipple.

THE NOBLEST CRY

1

"75,000 Private Attorneys General"

"It is impossible to over-estimate the stake of the true conservative in the constant strengthening of civil liberties," Whitney North Seymour, former president of the American Bar Association and for years a vice chairman of the board of directors of the American Civil Liberties Union, remarked in December, 1964, "for the whole principle and practice of liberty under law are what it is always most essential to conserve. Once either the principle or the practice is corrupted, the conservative is in as great peril as is the innovator."

Ten years earlier, Roger Nash Baldwin, founder of the ACLU in 1920 and still, forty-five years later, its symbol, declared (in a proclamation of faith repeated in 1964, when he was eighty years old, with the same virile conviction): "I think highly of reformers, revolutionists, dreamers, dissenters, disturbers of the *status quo*. I know a lot of them are proved wrong—some dangerous. But the spirit of reform that drives them has driven me, and, while I have never been fanatically sure of any cause, I am dead certain that human progress depends on those heretics, rebels and dreamers who have been my kin in spirit and whose 'holy discontent' has challenged established authority and created the expanding visions that mankind may yet realise." To this Baldwin added, in private conversation: "I am still a dissenter."

1

Between these two poles—the man who established and for thirty years ran the American Civil Liberties Union in order to refashion society and the man who for more than a decade shared his burdens in order to preserve the foundation of any decent society; men whose firmest bond was and remains their dedication to the rights of others to combat their own conflicting creeds—there stand today 75,-000 Americans (out of 193 million) of the right and left, clergymen and atheists, industrialists and workmen, millionaires and collectivists, who are busy daily in the protection of the freedoms of one another and of their 192,925,000 compatriots who know no principle but "let the other guy stick his neck out: it's better for me not to get involved." But those few who are willing to assume the risks of concern with something beyond their immediate selfish interests can point to a thick file of acknowledgment and praise of their contribution to the advancement of freedom in the United States—expressions of appreciation and esteem not only from disinterested observers of social phenomena but from such widely disparate sources as Presidents Roosevelt, Truman, Eisenhower and Kennedy and General Douglas MacArthur, in addition to scores of governors, judges, clerics and educators. By no means all were united in their political or economic philosophies but each was moved to pay public tribute to the American Civil Liberties Union by its passionate dedication to equal justice for everyone within the jurisdiction of the United States.

In the forty-five years since barely a thousand Americans deliberately chose to *get involved* even if involvement might prove bad for business, job advancement or the kind of social security that was most important to their neighbors, the American Civil Liberties Union's corps of what was once termed private attorneys general has grown to a membership of 75,000 in early 1965. As the organisation completed its forty-fifth year, operating through a national headquarters in New York, a Washington office, a newly established southern regional office with headquarters in Atlanta, and thirty-five affiliates subdivided into numerous local chapters, the private attorneys general were deeply involved in virtually every problem of civil liberties created by the day-to-day life of the United States. The involvement took many forms: direct legal action, briefs filed as a friend of the court in state and federal appeals, lobbying in Congress and the Legislatures, testimony before Congressional and legislative committees and administrative agencies, negotiation with officials, consultation with other organisations concerned both with advancing and with restricting Constitutional freedoms, public educational projects and studies of pending problems by the ACLU's national board of directors, its committees and its affiliates. (If in this history I have not always distinguished between the Union and an affiliate, between direct counsel and activity *amicus curiae,* it has been only in order to avoid wearying the reader.)

In every instance (as has been the case since its first intervention almost a half-century ago), the American Civil Liberties Union is totally unconcerned with the merits or fallacies of a political, social or religious philosophy; with the guilt or innocence of a man accused of a crime; with the "morality" of private conduct between compe- tent, consenting adults. Its sole interest is the enforcement of the rights guaranteed by state and federal constitutions: the right to speak, publish and associate freely, the right to a fair trial, the right to the equal protection of the laws, the right to personal safety—in a word, liberty under law. The Union's "clients", when this compila- tion was made, included real and alleged Communists, homosexu- als, authors, publishers, union leaders, dissident union members, em- ployers, criminal defendants, policemen, Negroes, students, teachers, Fascists, avowed bigots, newspaper proprietors, lawyers, television reporters, farm-hands, merchant seamen, religious fanatics, unbe- lievers, letter-carriers, welfare recipients, social workers—one could catalogue indefinitely.

"No fight for civil liberty ever stays won," Baldwin has often said. The list of cases and problems on the agenda of the ACLU and its affiliates at the beginning of 1965 represents dozens of instances in which the organisation is constrained to go back into court to com- pel the recognition of earlier victories—some of them forty years ago —on identical issues. Even the Supreme Court of the United States has been known to ignore its own rulings; as one descends the judi- cial scale, the flouting of its authority, whether by design or by the natural growth of ignorance and stupidity in direct ratio to the dis- tance from the top, becomes appalling. The administrative agen- cies of government, in particular, in love with their own powers, must constantly be haled before the courts to be enjoined from repeating the same tyrannical abuses for which they have again and again been disciplined. Even worse recidivists are state courts and legislatures that compound the inherently pernicious doctrine of states' rights for the further contumacy not only of law and the Constitution but of justice and fundamental morality, no matter how often the Supreme Court calls them to heel. (While the orthodoxy of that philosophical anarchy to which experience drives every intelligent being deplores a strong central government, even the most rigid anarchist is compelled to prefer a strong national régime to a so-called federal government forever threatened with emasculation by the jealous rivalries of fifty would-be parallel sovereignties.)

Hence, at the end of its forty-fifth year, the American Civil Liberties Union and its affiliates stood before the Supreme Court to defend for the nth time, against the terrors and the blindnesses of the mob and the demagogues dependent on it for their tenure of satrapy, such causes as these:

—An appeal to the Supreme Court of the United States to take the historic step of instructing the lower federal courts to adhere to its judgments and enforce the law regardless of any unpopularity, instead of either disregarding the clear precedents of the highest court or refusing to exercise their jurisdiction and thus shifting their responsibility to the Supreme Court and at the same time obstructing justice, particularly in civil-rights matters. This appeal was embodied in the ACLU's brief *amicus curiæ* in a challenge to the validity of Louisiana's Communist Control Law and Subversive Activities Law and to the application of these laws against the Southern Conference Educational Fund and the National Lawyers' Guild — both of which are extremely active on behalf of Louisiana citizens of the wrong color.

—The unconstitutionality of the detention of mail by the Post Office on the ground that it is Communist propaganda, and its destruction unless the addressee requests its delivery. A Federal District Court in New York City had upheld the 1962 statute — the enactment of which had been opposed by the late President Kennedy, the State Department, the Justice Department and the Post Office Department itself—calling for such action, while a similar court in California had ruled the statute unconstitutional on the ground that, as the ACLU contended, it violated the First, Fourth and Fifth Amendments to the Constitution. These amendments protect, respectively, the right of freedom of speech, publication and association; the right to be secure against search and seizure without the issuance of a warrant therefor on a showing of probable cause; and the right not to incriminate oneself (in this case, by requesting the delivery of mail deemed "subversive" and thus exposing oneself to the danger of being named in a blacklist). In May, 1965, the Supreme Court ruled the law unconstitutional.

—The unconstitutionality of the seizure of 2,000 pieces of literature from a bookseller's home under Texas' Suppression of the Communist Party Act. The Supreme Court voided the warrant on the ground that it did not comply with the Fourth Amendment's requirement that things to be seized must be described with particularity; and the court emphasized "the Constitutional impossibility of leaving the protection of those freedoms [guaranteed by the First Amendment] to the whim of the officers charged with executing the warrant."

—The unconstitutionality of a Louisiana law forbidding so-called "crimes against nature" on the ground that its excessive vagueness opens the way to widely divergent interpretations.

—The unconstitutionality of summary contempt-of-court convictions of two civil-rights lawyers, imposed solely because they sought a change of venue from the Virginia court that thereupon promptly found them in contempt.

—Whether live television coverage of the trial of Billie Sol Estes for swindling, despite his repeated objections to such circus proceedings, deprived him of a fair hearing and due process of law. In June, 1965, the court ruled that it did.

—The right of a labor-union member to challenge the validity of a union election before it has actually been held.

—The unconstitutionality of Connecticut's statutory ban on the sale of contraceptive equipment and on the dissemination of contraceptive information by physicians to patients, married or sinful. The law was voided in June, 1965.

—The illegality of a search made without a warrant when there was ample time to obtain one; and the obligation of the arresting policeman to disclose the identity of his stool-pigeon in order to enable the court to determine whether there is probable cause for a search.

—The unconstitutionality of the "Communist-front" provisions of the Subversive Activities Control Act of 1950, which professes to outlaw all totalitarian activity from both the Right and the Left. —The unconstitutionality of various Mississippi statutes designed to restrict the right of voting to whites by means of a state poll tax, a literacy and constitutional-interpretation test and a test of "good moral character."

And, in various circuits of the United States Court of Appeals, the ACLU was resisting these further invasions of Constitutional and moral rights:

—An order to deport a merchant seaman to a country where he is certain to be imprisoned solely for his adherence to the tenets of Jehovah's Witnesses, despite legal provision for withholding deportation of persons facing persecution. Deportation was sought because the seaman, having married an American during his authorised time in this country, overstayed his permitted sojourn.

—The cutting off of aid to dependent children, otherwise eligible, when their divorced father exercises his right of frequent visitation.

—A conviction for robbery obtained when there had been a six-month hiatus between arrest and trial.

—The refusal of a Civil Service job solely because the applicant was alleged, without proof, to be a homosexual.

—Maryland's state and county residence requirements for voting in presidential elections.

—The jury-tampering conviction of James R. Hoffa, president of the Teamsters' Union, through the Government's use of evidence illegally obtained by the employment of an informer to spy on Hoffa and his lawyers.

—A group of Louisiana rape convictions, carrying the death penalty, on verdicts rendered by juries from which Negroes were systematically excluded.

—A Louisiana life sentence of an alleged habitual criminal, based on Louisiana's refusal to recognise a pardon granted in another state having appropriate jurisdiction.

—Louisiana regulations cutting off much of the incoming and outgoing mail of prisoners condemned to death. "Correspondence [with prisoners] is not permitted unless the correspondents are of the same race," under Louisiana law.

—Violation of the Federal Civil Rights Act by a Los Angeles police officer charged with unlawful search and seizure in compelling a woman to disrobe in a police station and submit to searches of all bodily orifices.

—A criminal conviction for traveling to Cuba without a passport specifically validated for that country.

"Acts, not words, created our most effective public relations" Baldwin said of the early years of the ACLU. That the truth of this principle has grown more convincing throughout the years is manifest in these instances and in a further sampling of ACLU court work in state and lower federal tribunals, most of it pending but some recently successfully concluded, in which the Union has opposed:

—The dismissal of a teacher solely because he refused to remove his beard, in California, and, in Maryland, the dismissal of another solely for instructing a social-studies class to read Aldous Huxley's *Brave New World*.

—The commitment of a member of the American Nazi Party to a hospital for mental observation on the sole basis of a policeman's affidavit stating that the Nazi had shouted in the Senate Gallery in Washington (the hospital released the Nazi before the ACLU's court challenge of the commitment came to trial).

—The constitutionality of Virginia and California laws forbidding intermarriage between whites and non-whites.

—Racial segregation and the barring of Black Muslim clergymen in a reformatory.

—A decision by a United States District Court in California that a woman had no right to a damage action under the Federal Civil Rights Act when police promiscuously circulated nude photographs of her, taken by them when she lodged an assault charge (the decision was reversed by the Ninth Circuit).

—The termination of a former Government employe's retirement annuity without a hearing after he had been accused of making false statements as to Communist affiliations.

—The discharge of a member of the faculty of Texas State University for activity on behalf of civil rights.

—The constitutionality of an Alabama law prohibiting newspapers from "electioneering" on election day.

—Conviction on a plea of guilty without counsel, entered by a defendant never told that he had the right to be represented by a lawyer.

—The constitutionality of prayers in public nursery schools, led by teachers (in Long Beach, California, as in many other parts of the United States, the Supreme Court's outlawry of such practices is consistently flouted by local authorities).

And the Union is currently supporting:

—A damage action against the municipal officials of Dearborn, Michigan, for refusing to provide equal protection of the law when police allowed a mob to damage the property of a Dearborn house owner suspected of intending to sell to a Negro family.

—Challenges to municipal restrictions in all parts of the country on the use of public or publicly licensed premises by individuals and organisations of a controversial nature (this battle is fought and won over and over as it has been almost weekly since 1920).

—A suit to void California's Proposition 14, which restores racially restrictive covenants in land deeds, as a violation of the 14th Amendment to the Constitution, guaranteeing "equal protection of the laws" to all citizens. (The invidious distinctions still made between citizens and aliens, and between native-born and naturalised citizens, will be discussed in a later chapter.)

—An action to compel the Police Commissioner and the Criminal Court of New York City to expunge the records of six Hunter College students unjustly arrested during a "round-up" of pickets at the New York World's Fair. This is the first step in a campaign to abolish the preservation of arrest records of persons found not guilty or obtaining dismissals of charges against them.

—A motion for summary judgment reversing the decision of the Veterans' Administration to cut off the disability pension of Robert G. Thompson, a Communist veteran of the Second World War, because he had criticised American policies during the Korean War, using standard Communist jargon that the VA, in defiance of earlier court decisions and of the First Amendment to the Constitution, chose to construe as "assistance to the enemy."

—Court action to void Delaware's law providing for the flogging of criminals as a violation of the Eighth Amendment's prohibition of cruel and unusual punishment.

—An appeal from the practice of the Pennsylvania courts in assessing costs of prosecution against acquitted defendants.

These random samplings represent only a small percentage of the litigation case-load of the ACLU and its affiliates when the writing of this book was begun. Work in the courts, though it is the most dramatic aspect of the American Civil Liberties Union's unremitting battle for the rights of man, represents, however, only that part of the iceberg that is always visible above the surface of the water. The national board of directors, its various committees, the affiliates and their chapters are constantly engaged in an innumerable variety of studies of problems, as well as negotiations with elected and appointed officials that range from informal discussions to officially recognised lobbying. Some of the negotiations under way at the beginning of 1965 may seem on their face to be of lesser importance than the grave philosophical issues of conscience involved in, say, the right of non-religious opponents of conscription to be exempted as objectors; but, to quote Roger Baldwin once more, the police station and the magistrate's court are the places where most injustice begins and where rights are most often infringed. There is after all no moral difference between the third-degree frame-up and the conviction in the court of public opinion obtained by the irresponsible pseudo-factual allegations of the House Un-American Activities Committee.

—Affiliates and chapters throughout the country, backed by the national office, were exerting every effort to obtain the establishment of civilian review boards in municipalities so that persons deprived of rights by policemen (whether through mistaken zeal or for the pleasure of brutalising) may prefer and prosecute charges before impartial tribunals—an effort spurred by the generally successful experience of Rochester, New York, and Philadelphia, Pennsylvania, where such independent boards have been set up (the Philadelphia police commissioner has publicly paid tribute to the value of the city's board in terms of better police work and greater community cooperation). In Newark, New Jersey, negotiations between the New Jersey ACLU and the police department have led to an agreement under which volunteer civilian observers will be riding in police cars and attending not only on-the-street questioning and arrests but also interrogations in police stations after arrests.

In New York City, the ACLU affiliate finally won in 1964 its long battle to compel the police to advise suspects, orally and in writing, of their rights to make telephone calls, to have legal representation and to refuse to answer questions: the police department had publicly and officially defended its practice of withholding notice of these rights to arrested persons on the ground that "giving them their rights makes our work harder."

—Informal and sometimes formal protests, short of litigation, but often turning into protracted negotiation, are constantly being initiated to further individual rights abridged out of either malice or ignorance, such as the successful fight by the National Capital affiliate on behalf of a man threatened with the loss of his right to vote because he had been convicted of the "infamous crime" of violating the draft law by reason of being a conscientious objector.

—In public statements as well as letters and conferences, both the national office and affiliates have pressed the right of policemen to belong to the John Birch Society or any other political group, left or right, and to be judged by their superiors solely on the basis of their performance of their duties on the job.

—In Massachusetts, following a practice that has become annual, the affiliate was circulating to its members, to other organisations and to public officials a complete digest of all proposed state legislation touching on civil liberties, with its own recommendations.

—Requests were made to the Justice Department for greater activity by the Federal Bureau of Investigation in civil-rights cases, citing the FBI's long record of aloofness, its occupational affinity with local police forces in areas where these are indistinguishable from the violators of law and Constitution, and the claim of human rights to parity with property rights.

—A major campaign of lobbying, pamphleteering and public education has been launched by the national ACLU and its affiliates to effect the abolition of the House Un-American Activities Committee.

—New rules for court commitments of alleged mental patients have been drafted and submitted to the courts of Illinois with a view to assuring that such persons are deprived of none of the rights of due process and equal protection of the laws.

—The Justice Department finally ordered the Immigration Service, after protracted negotiations by the ACLU, to strike the name of James Peck, CORE editor and pacifist author, from the list of "persons suspected of traveling or known to have traveled to Cuba" in violation of the American ban on such travel. Peck had been listed because, as a matter of principle, he refused to say whether he had gone to Cuba.

—A California woman's successful defiance of a local ordinance banning political signs on residential property—she had mounted a Goldwater sticker on a post on her lawn—was supported by the ACLU on constitutional grounds.

—Studies and negotiations were under way virtually everywhere with a view to assuring full protection of the rights of indigent defendants in criminal cases, both at trial and on appeal, without rigid allegiance to any one exclusive system such as that of paid public defenders, panels of court-appointed attorneys or any other panacea.

Every such intervention, like the ACLU's participation in litigation, stems from a deliberately taken policy position. These determinations are made in the final instance by the national board of directors for the ACLU as a whole and, within the broad national policy definitions, by affiliates' respective boards; but the study and debate out of which they evolve may be conducted by the national board, by one or more of its committees, by an affiliate or affiliates or by any combination of these. Thus, at the beginning of 1965, studies in various stages of progress, looking toward formulations or revisions of policy, included these major problems:

—Official and industry censorship in broadcasting and the furtherance of optimal diversity of programming as an essential of freedom of speech. The national board of directors of the ACLU, late in 1964, endorsed the "fairness doctrine" of the Federal Communications Commission, under which a broadcaster permitting an attack on an individual or organisation or a presentation of views on important issues must allow similar opportunities to the victim of the attack or the opponents of the views. Policy on FCC regulation of program content to further diversity, on the political "equal time" provisions of the Communications Act, on the preponderance of one-sided broadcasts and defamatory attacks, on community-antenna systems, on the networks' option-time regulations of their associated stations and on the efforts of the United States Information Agency to prevent private international broadcasters from presenting material offering an "unfavorable image" of the United States is in process of formulation: a problem in paradox for those seeking the greatest freedom of speech and the minimum of government control.

—Proliferating facets of academic freedom: the extent of civil liberties to be advocated for high-school students, legal protections for collegians engaged in protest and political activity and the obligation of their institutions to protect their civil liberties, special questions of academic freedom pertaining to new colleges, standards of academic freedom in international cultural exchanges.

—The extent to which the ACLU should concern itself with the civil-liberties issues inherent in the nature and functioning of corporations—for example, stockholder democracy, or penalisation of employes for private lawful conduct on their own time that may be unpleasing to their employers: a new source of tyranny, petty or other, as the American community becomes increasingly a confederation of interlocking corporate fiefs.

—The condemnation of capital punishment as "cruel and unusual punishment" outlawed by the Eighth Amendment.

—Arrest records—their disposition in case of acquittal or dismissal, questions relating to them in connection with private and public employment, the possibility of distinction between arrests for common-law crimes and those for political or social protest. Final policy formulation awaits further study, a statistical survey embracing arrest-reporting procedure in local jurisdictions and examples of specific abuses of arrest records, and consultation with the appropriate committee of the American Bar Association.

—Congressional investigating committees and their procedures: intrusions into private areas of belief and action protected by the First Amendment, arrogation of adjudicative functions, pertinence of questions, assurance of the rights to counsel, to a hearing, to confront and cross-examine accusers, to avoid public sessions, to obtain transcripts, to protect one's reputation; and the propriety of broadcasting such proceedings from the standpoint of the civil liberties of witnesses.

—A clear declaration condemning all forms of wiretapping and electronic eavesdropping.

—Government surveillance of individuals' and organisations' mail.

—The legalisation of all forms of private sexual behavior between competent consenting adults; abortion as a constitutional and civil-liberties problem of private conduct: condemnation of all restrictions on birth-control information and devices and of compulsory practice of contraception.

—Whether peacetime conscription is an unwarranted invasion of civil liberties; and a restudy of wartime measures repressive of civil liberties.

—Civil disobedience based on conscience, the defense of those arrested for such disobedience and recommendations for legislation relating to such disobedience.

—A court challenge to the 1964 California referendum vote outlawing pay-television, on the ground that such a prohibition is an unconstitutional limitation on freedom of expression and an unconstitutional deprivation of property without due process.

—Pennsylvania prison rules denying inmates the right to buy law books and limiting their religious reading matter to the Bible and the Koran.

—Fingerprinting as a condition of employment for teachers.

—Appeals to all advertising media not to reject material on the ground of its controversial nature.

—Government aid to church-related educational institutions, the continuance of tax exemption for property or income devoted to religious purposes (all questions on which division of opinion was marked, in some instances for substantive reasons, in others because of the fear that procedural problems might produce more injury to civil liberties than would the continuance of the *status quo*) and the discriminatory granting of tax benefits to religious bodies but not to similar classes of associations.

It should be obvious from these examples that the American Civil Liberties Union is unique in that it grinds no axe. It does not concern itself with the merits of Communism, Fascism, homosexuality, continence, unionism, "free enterprise," pacifism, militarism, racial purity, inter-breeding, religious worship, atheism, Sunday baseball, Hollywood pap, "intellectual" indecent exposure: it does concern itself, and solely, with the protection of the fundamental rights of everyone to speak, meet, read and write about these or any other subjects and, in his private life, to enjoy what the late Justice Brandeis called the greatest civil liberty of all: the right to be let alone.

How did anything so basically "un-American" ever come into being? how has it managed to survive and even grow in the age of the Fifth or Bourgeois International, whose only slogan round the world is: "Let's all be liked—and alike"?

2

"Jails Are Waiting for Them"

The struggle for human decency and dignity is always a losing battle but never a wholly lost cause. Both elements of the paradox arise from the complications of one infuriating nexus: the human psyche. Like infinity, the ultimate defeat is always approached but never attained.

That is the secret of the birth and survival of the American Civil Liberties Union against the whole basic tendency of the race. The United States is a country of several traditions, but only two are dominant, coupling again and again to beget the same spawn—the tradition of lawlessness embraces the tradition of repression and in nine seconds vigilantism is born. Because the world belongs to the god whose ineffable name is Irony, it is always unaccountably endowed with a random few who have both the wit and the will to brave the horde for a principle that can protect their enemies as well as themselves and that may (at least in theory) make better men of both.

It is from this intellectual and moral aristocracy—the involuntary monopolist of genuine liberalism—that the American Civil Liberties Union emerged to forge what may one day become in actuality the American tradition that is most loudly touted and most assiduously flouted: the freedom of every man to be, think, say and do what he believes right. Such a tradition has always been falsely called part of what is denominated with shabby grandiloquence "the American dream"; but the most cursory review of the history of the country and of the records of its colonist founders themselves demonstrates overwhelmingly that each successive wave of settlers sought purely and simply freedom only for those who accepted its dogmas. The way of him who dissented from these dissenters was as perilous in this hemisphere as theirs had been in their homelands.

The record of the United States as an independent nation is no better than the history of the colonies. When, in 1929, Ortega y Gasset wrote: "As they say in the United States, 'to be different is to be indecent,' " he was merely taking note of what had almost invariably been the unwritten law for more than three hundred years in the country that gave every language in the world the verb *to lynch*. The average man needs someone to hate—all the more when he has been the object of hate—and no one is easier or safer to hate than the less numerous non-average.

In Puritan Salem the average man persecuted witches, Papists, Anglicans, Jews and pagans; but this was before America as a civilisation had furnished Negroes, Communists, pornographers, pacifists, internationalists and other liege-men of Satan. All that has changed is the labels and, in some cases, the identities of persecutor and persecuted.

Probably the worst effect of the First World War on the United States was its official and unofficial legitimisation of persecution of the different. Consciously or not, Woodrow Wilson was gulled by the comforting fallacy that has seduced almost all governors since the primal father: *Better injustice than disorder.* It is only after they have irrevocably given their benison to injustice that these well intentioned men recognise that they have endorsed and enforced, in the name of whatever ideal, only the geometrical progression of disorder.

"Few people," Donald Johnson notes in *The Challenge to American Freedoms*, "have ever been so intolerant of their fellow-men as Americans in the First World War." Whips, clubs, stones, tar and feathers and the rope enforced on the opponents of war that tyranny of the majority predicted by Tocqueville. Patriotism may indeed have been then (and may remain today) the last refuge of the scoundrel; but in the First World War it became as well the first resort of the sadist, the frustrate and the fool, for all of whom, as any day's newspaper demonstrates, it has retained its full value.

The first targets of the bully-boys were the Industrial Workers of the World, the Christian Pacifists, the Socialists, the Friends of Irish Freedom, the International Bible Students' Association (later to be known and mobbed again as Jehovah's Witnesses), the Farmers' Non-Partisan League, and any individual *naïf* enough to question the holiness of the war or to refuse to buy Liberty Bonds. Congress adopted a Selective Service Act intended to make exemption impossible and an Espionage Act purposing to silence all dissent against the *jehad*. Thus Congress and President Wilson, who signed both measures gladly and who was soon to sign a Sedition Act that could have served as a model for the most absolute totalitarianism, made inevitable the American Civil Liberties Union. For, despite the rampaging gangs of patriots and the uncountable mass of respectable citizens who pretended not to know about them (as another generation in another country was not to know it was breathing the smell of corpses every day), a handful of men and women, who often did not know one another and who would have quarreled endlessly among themselves on capitalism, Marxism, war, religion and private sexual morality, were unanimously outraged by the savagery and the suppression with which the world was to be made safe for democracy.

As early as the autumn of 1914 some of them, fearing American participation in the war, had created the nucleus for the American League for the Limitation of Armaments on the insistence of Paul Kellogg, editor of *The Survey,* a magazine for social workers; Jane Addams, founder of Hull House, a Chicago settlement, and Lillian Wald, who established the Henry Street Settlement in New York. They were soon joined by Frederic C. Howe, Commissioner of Immigration; Oswald Garrison Villard, editor of *The New York Evening Post* and *The Nation,* and Nicholas Murray Butler, president of Columbia University. When, by the end of 1915, it was obvious where Wilson's course was leading, the ALLA called on other pacifist groups to unite in an Anti-Preparedness Committee, the leadership of which reached out to include a mixture of clerics, religious pacifists, social workers and Socialists. Their original aims were few: to lobby for the defeat of the pending National Defense Bill, to outlaw armament profits, and to bring into being a League of Neutral American Nations.

The new leaders included the Rev. John Haynes Holmes, a socially aware Unitarian minister; Rabbi Stephen S. Wise of the Free Synagogue of New York; Crystal Eastman Benedict, lawyer, expert on industrial accidents (she was a member of the New York State Liability Commission) and Socialist; her brother, Max Eastman, also a Socialist and editor of *The Masses;* L. Hollingsworth Wood, a Quaker lawyer with a thriving estate practice; Louis P. Lochner, at that time a pacifist directing Henry Ford's futile peace mission to Europe; Alice Lewisohn, heiress and social worker, and Florence Kelley of the National Consumers' League. Within a few months the Anti-Preparedness Committee forthrightly changed its name, becoming the American Union Against Militarism; within a year it had fifteen hundred members in the nation. It could claim the sympathy of William Jennings Bryan, once Secretary of State; of William Howard Taft, then on the board of the League to Enforce Peace; of James Maurer of the Pennsylvania Federation of Labor.

When the National Defense Act was finally passed on June 3, 1916, the AUAM felt that it had gained a limited victory: though the law called for the expansion of the army, it provided no draft and it omitted the compulsory training that Wilson had sought. Furthermore, Germany had pledged herself—and was keeping her promise—not to sink merchant ships without warning, and this had deprived the advocates of American military action of one of their principal arguments. The remainder of 1916 was so barren of militaristic activity in the United States that the AUAM was considering dissolution.

In Februrary of 1917, however, with that sure gift for foreign policy that has no rival except in Washington, Germany announced that she was resuming unrestricted submarine warfare, and the United States immediately broke off diplomatic relations with her. The AUAM was revitalised and its board, which by now included Amos Pinchot, a liberal New York lawyer, was convoked to an emergency meeting. Rabbi Wise offered to resign: he was convinced not only that the United States was about to enter the war but that it must do so in order to uproot German militarism. Wise had no support among his colleagues, though Villard wavered, uncertain whether he should support this war. All the others knew—and refused to hide from the knowledge—that any war would solve nothing.

A month later, Crystal Eastman Benedict, who had married Walter G. Fuller, a fellow-member of the AUAM, had to give up her work as executive director because of her approaching confinement (her son, Jeffrey, is today a staff associate of the American Civil Liberties Union), and a special assistant joined the group—a St. Louis social worker virtually unknown outside his profession. For the rest of his life he has been the incarnation of the American Civil Liberties Union.

Roger Nash Baldwin, like most of the founders of the AUAM, came from the solid comfort of the upper middle class. He was born in Wellesley Hills, Massachusetts; his father was a prosperous shoe manufacturer and a paternal uncle, William, was president of the Long Island Rail Road. Roger Baldwin held two Harvard degrees (including a master's in anthropology); as a student he had belonged to the better clubs, considered radicals "nutty," avoided politics, and pleasured himself with music and bird-watching and teaching adult classes for working people at the Cambridge Social Union. He had, however, grown up with one passionate belief: equal rights for Negroes. His railroad-president uncle, an admirer of Robert Ingersoll, like Roger's father, had been for years chairman of the board of Tuskegee Institute, and Booker T. Washington, its president, had frequently stayed in the homes of both the elder Baldwins.

From Harvard, Roger Baldwin had gone vacationing in Europe; on his return, he sought from various of his father's associates guidance on the choice of a career, and he thought, he said many years later, of entering "some of the more human aspects of business." One of these advisers was his father's lawyer, Louis Dembitz Brandeis, and the future Justice of the United States Supreme Court told the young man that he was obviously cut out for public service, a career hardly alien to the family. Roger Baldwin's grandfather had given up his business in order to found the

Boston Young Men's Christian Union in 1870, antedating the YMCA, and become a Unitarian lay preacher. Uncle William Baldwin, the railroad president, was also president of the New York City Club and a director of the National Child Labor Committee; his wife, Ruth, was one of the founders of the National Urban League. Roger's mother in her later years was a pacifist, though her husband vigorously backed the First World War, and an agnostic.

Roger Baldwin himself has said that his relatives "were all free-thinking and independent, moderately well-to-do, Unitarians and respectable Republicans. My Uncle William was the only Democratic backslider . . . I suppose that from the beginning my slant inclined me to the underdog. It was not a far jump from doing good to the poor—as we were brought up to do as good Unitarians—to figuring that there should be no poor. That notion made me a radical, the supporter in spirit if not in fact of every force I thought headed for the abolition of poverty, the achievement of equality and the triumph of justice. I was no sectarian; any or all of the forces that seemed headed that way gripped me . . . I have been a man of action to whom almost any evil needing reform appealed; to whom any little service was an ego-satisfaction."

Not too difficultly persuaded by Brandeis, young Baldwin accepted as his first job the management of a settlement house in St. Louis, where he was to meet many future associates in civil liberties, notably Lucile B. Milner, for twenty-five years active secretary of the ACLU, and Louis F. Budenz, who was to desert the ACLU for the Communist Party and the Party for the rôle of professional penitent and stool-pigeon. The ideological baggage that Baldwin took to St. Louis was what had accompanied him to Harvard: respectable New England liberalism. His new job was combined with teaching sociology at Washington University (one of his students, Barney Gallant, was later to find Baldwin in New York as second cook in a restaurant helping his employes to form a union). But even these two jobs could not absorb his energy: simultaneously he became Chief Probation Officer for the Juvenile Court of St. Louis and was designated to reorganise its new probation service. Soon he dropped the teaching and the settlement house. As a co-founder and volunteer unpaid secretary of the National Probation Association, he was co-author, with Bernard

Flexner, of *Juvenile Courts and Probation,* long the outstanding work in its field.

It was in St. Louis that Baldwin first entered the arena of civil liberties. Though it was a generally liberal and easy-going city in 1912, Margaret Sanger found it impossible to hire a hall in St. Louis for a lecture on birth control. This censorship by prior restraint shocked Baldwin, and he offered to lead a public meeting of protest. It was held, with full police protection, and there was no disturbance; the ensuing publicity was wide and favorable. But a fresh shock awaited Baldwin in the same year, when the police forbade a meeting of the unemployed on the steps of the Old Court House, lest it provoke disorder. Again Baldwin led the protests, and he won permission for the meeting to proceed. It was his introduction to the Industrial Workers of the World, which was to exercise a strong influence on him for years afterward.

But in effect it was the teasing of friends that led to Baldwin's excommunication (undoubtedly with his entire consent) from the ranks of the *bien-pensants.* He went one day to hear a lecture by Emma Goldman, the anarchist, and he was lost to orthodoxy thenceforth. Much later he said of this experience: "I knew that here was a champion for the things which mattered most to me. The more I saw of poverty and distress—and, believe me, I saw plenty of it—the more I became convinced that social work alone was not enough." He began to study Socialist and anarchist literature but he found Socialism alien "because of its dogmatism and stolid German leadership." He found himself much more in sympathy with the anarchism of Tolstoi and Kropotkin and Thoreau (Baldwin in his youth was particularly influenced by Bradford Torrey, Thoreau's literary executor).

Baldwin's political philosophy is admirably summed up by Johnson in his book cited earlier. Baldwin, Johnson says, "might be called a philosophical anarchist, but he never argued for the elimination of government. He tended to follow the New England transcendentalists in their emphasis upon the goodness and perfectibility of man and the right of each individual to exercise his free will. Like Thoreau, he placed the dictates of man's own conscience above the law. Unlike Thoreau . . . Baldwin could not countenance violence in any form, although he defended the right of anyone to advocate violence. A properly organized government, Baldwin believed, could be a useful thing. It could protect the rights of individuals to meet and speak freely. It could defend labor's right to organise. But it could not interfere with an individual's right to follow his conscience unless the individual transgressed the rights of others."

By the time Baldwin joined the American Union Against Militarism he had traveled long and errant roads that had no visible link to the Wellesley Hills of his boyhood. It was not only Emma Goldman but also the labor organisers with whom his St. Louis work had acquainted him that roused an almost hero-worshipping admiration. He was especially stirred by the syndicalists of the IWW, men who risked their lives—and did not always win—for their beliefs; Baldwin felt he was accomplishing too little. In 1910 he had abandoned his probation work to become secretary of the St. Louis Civic League, a progressive group that he led into a seven-year battle to reform the city, winning a modern city charter, the initiative and the referendum. His articles in *The Survey* and *The National Municipal Review* were read with respect.

The beginning of the war in 1914 had not immediately made him a pacifist, though he wanted America to stay out. It was the news stories of the British conscientious objectors that made him aware that he was one of them, and in 1916 he joined the St. Louis chapter of the AUAM. At the onset of the crisis in February, 1917, he wrote to the national office to urge that it sponsor nation-wide mass meetings against participation in the war. Kellogg replied that Baldwin should become a "local cooperator"—a term that was later to be frequently used by the American Civil Liberties Union. But to Baldwin this seemed too little for him to contribute. He had been living frugally on what was at that time a large salary—$5,000 a year—and he could afford to work without pay for a cause that was his in a real as well as an ideal sense. He attended his first AUAM board meeting on April 2, 1917; on April 4 he was Associate Director in command of the battle against the new conscription bills. On April 6 the United States declared war.

The existence of a state of war made it impossible for the AUAM to oppose conscription; its goal became a law that would protect liberty of conscience. But the Selective Service bill sent to

Congress by Secretary of War Newton D. Baker provided only that a conscientious objector belonging to a "well recognised religious sect or organization" might be "exempted" only from "combat" service—an exemption that the AUAM contested because it would still compel some form of active support of war from those whose principles opposed war and because it recognised in this category only objectors on the ground of religion and ignored men who, though they might pay no pew rental and cast their burdens on no myth, refused on pure philosophic and moral grounds to kill or to abet in killing.

Norman Thomas, a leading Socialist who had joined the AUAM, explained its position in an article called *War's Heretics.* Though Thomas himself was a religious objector, and a Presbyterian minister, he demanded that Congress recognise the non-religious objector; he pointed out, too, that among all objectors, religious or other, individual conscience would determine individual interpretation. Some, he predicted, would go to prison rather than enter the army; some who entered would then refuse all obedience; some—probably most—would cooperate in varying degree without carrying arms or directly participating in homicide, and would perform certain tasks while rejecting others as being "combatant." Baldwin, in a memorandum to Baker, instanced political or religious conscience that might ground an objection to a particular war without barring participation in another: Socialists would not fight for capitalism; German-Americans balked at killing their ethnic kin; Jehovah's Witnesses refused to fight in any war but Armageddon. These scruples, Baldwin contended, were as legitimate as those of any Quaker or Mennonite, and were entitled to the same consideration in the law.

Baker refused to endorse these views. With such rare exceptions as Senator Robert La Follette, members of Congress could not be bothered about justice or principle when there were voters' sentiments to be reckoned with. Baldwin distributed copies of British legislation accepting political objectors; the effort was wasted. On May 18 the inadequate bill was enacted into law; on that same day, Baldwin wrote to Major Allen W. Gullion at the War Department, asking Gullion to outline the steps that one would undergo in registering for the draft, and offering the assistance of the

AUAM in dealing with conscientious objectors (the AUAM had already authorised the publication of a pamphlet on free speech). On May 19, Baldwin organised a Bureau for Conscientious Objectors. He envisaged this as a subdivision of the AUAM to provide legal and economic assistance to objectors and possibly to challenge the constitutionality of the draft law or to lobby for its amendment, while negotiating with the Government for favorable interpretations of the present act.

Work was already under way on a pamphlet for conscientious objectors and on May 27 a draft was submitted to Frederick P. Keppel, third Assistant Secretary of War, for his comments. This was the inauguration of a technique that was to prove highly embarrassing to government officials: by commenting, they would be giving (or denying) their *imprimatur,* but by remaining silent they would be implying their *nihil obstat.*

But this direct activity on behalf of the objectors was not so welcome within the AUAM as it was among the pacifist organizations in general. Though a majority of the AUAM board approved it, and Baldwin as its director, the social workers' group thought the objectors' bureau should be independent of the AUAM lest its activities be construed as opposition to the Government and the war. Only Alice Lewisohn among the social workers was willing to serve on the new group's directing committee, which also included two Socialists, Joseph D. Cannon and Scott Nearing; Edmund C. Evans, a Philadelphia architect; Wood, Holmes, Thomas and Villard. Unfortunately Baldwin was unable to find a supporter of the war who would serve on the committee.

Lillian Wald and Paul Kellogg would not give up the battle against the objectors' bureau and threatened to resign from the AUAM unless the two groups were divorced. Crystal Eastman (though she was now Mrs. Fuller, back at work after the birth of her son, she was always known publicly by her maiden name) offered a compromise: retitle the newer group the Bureau for the Maintenance of Civil Liberties and direct it to the assistance of all whose rights might be violated by wartime laws or their application. Thus there would be no stigma in the name and the AUAM's honor would be unsullied. Everyone agreed and on July 2 Baldwin changed the name to the more manageable Civil Liberties Bureau, which was welcomed on the editorial page of *The· New York Times* two days later by a column headed: *Jails Are Waiting for Them.*

This kind of press reaction combined with a decision by the AUAM board for participation in the People's Council for Democracy and Peace to bring on a far worse crisis a month later. The People's Council was an anti-war group, predominantly Socialist, whose members included many directors of the AUAM: Thomas, Maurer, Miss Eastman, Rabbi Judah L. Magnes (a noted Jewish scholar and the outstanding pacifist in the rabbinate); its program was close to that of the AUAM and called for a referendum on war and the repeal of the draft law. To Thomas, the only difference between the organisations was that the People's Council was "working-class" and the AUAM was middle-class.

Lillian Wald, whom everyone was desperately striving to keep in the AUAM, was furious. She had already found Miss Eastman, Baldwin and Charles Hallinan, a labor journalist, "more than I can manage single-handed" (an interesting attitude, perhaps professionally engendered, in a social worker who was chairman of the AUAM). Now she threatened again to resign; if she went, the other social workers would probably follow *en bloc*——Alice Lewisohn was already turning her back on the Civil Liberties Bureau. Miss Wald, in a letter to Jane Addams, professed considerable concern for "my reputation for good judgment." The AUAM board opted for Miss Wald and her reputation, and the Civil Liberties Bureau was cast adrift.

On October 1, 1917, it became the National Civil Liberties Bureau under Baldwin's direction. Freed of niggling concerns about "respectability," he need no longer waste his time and energy in efforts to conform that could only emasculate the NCLB. He knew that the course he had chosen would be unpopular, and he was prepared for accusations that had no substance.

So too were others, some of them retaining membership in the AUAM for varying periods (it was dissolved in February, 1922), who became the directing committee of the NCLB. Its chairman was L. Hollingsworth Wood and Norman Thomas was vice chairman. Helen Phelps Stokes, the Socialist daughter of a rich family with a liberal tradition, was the treasurer. Walter Nelles, a Harvard classmate of Baldwin who became a professor of law at Yale, was the NCLB's counsel. The committee included two indubitable pro-war conservatives: John Codman, a Boston engineer, and Albert DeSilver, a rich New York lawyer who had been outraged by the attempt to suppress *The Masses,* a publication inimical to all his beliefs and material interests. Crystal Eastman joined the committee, serving with John Lovejoy Elliott, leader of the Ethical Society and head of the Hudson Guild, a settlement house; Holmes; Mrs. Agnes Brown Leach, a rich Philadelphia Quaker interested in liberal causes and married to the editor of *The Forum;* John Nevin Sayre, an Episcopalian rector whose brother had married President Wilson's daughter, Jessie; and Dr. James P. Warbasse, an eminent surgeon who was president of the Cooperative League of America.

Little by little those members of the NCLB's directing committee who had remained in the AUAM began to leave it. Other AUAM adherents also began to defect, most of them winding up sooner or later with the NCLB. By the time the AUAM was formally scuttled in 1922, only Villard and Hallinan (so feared by Miss Wald) were still aboard the derelict ship.

3

The Pattern Forms

If proof of the need for the National Civil Liberties Bureau had not already existed, it would have been amply supplied by the reactions of the press and the powers to the announcement of the Bureau's creation. The Independence Day denunciation in *The New York Times* was a restrained example of press comment. To the military, *conscientious objector* meant traitor, and obviously the label applied equally to those who would defend the traitors. The civil arm of government took no different view, essentially, and Postmaster General Albert Sidney Burleson forbade the mailing of Thomas' pamphlet, *War's Heretics*, though it was no more than an exposition of conscientious objection. As soon as the Espionage Act became law in June, 1917, arrests were made on a wholesale basis, often on the instance of volunteer patriots who gathered their "evidence" by impersonating federal agents—not infrequently with the tacit consent of the Department of Justice. Aliens and radicals—"dangerous" by definition—had in practice none of the theoretical rights and defenses pledged by law and Constitution; worse, after the war state legislatures were vying with one another in the manufacture of statutes against criminal syndicalism and red flags to round up those enemies of the people who tumbled out of the overburdened federal dragnets.

The three major areas of NCLB operation for the duration of the war were thus set out for it by government, the military and the mob: the persecution of conscientious objectors and pacifists, prosecutions under the Espionage Act and the concomitant deportations of alien radicals, and postal censorship of opposition publications. For years after the Armistice, in fact, these enormities of policy were to continue to occupy almost as much of the ACLU's attention as they had done during the actual war; the hard core of them was indeed to persist until the next war brought a new proliferation of fear and bigotry. In every category the NCLB had to battle, as did its successor, the ACLU, not only the invasion of basic rights but the calculated violation of law by government itself

Yet at the same time government, or certain of its many arms, professed at least a willingness to entertain the views of the NCLB. The War Department not only accepted Baldwin's offer of cooperation to Major Gullion but even commended him. Villard and Baldwin drafted a proposal that would permit all genuine conscientious objectors, religious or political, the same opportunity to choose non-combatant service and the same assurance of humane treatment, while "absolutists"—those opposed to any furtherance of the war effort—would be furloughed from the army, provided they took "essential" jobs in agriculture or hospitals. Baldwin sent a memorandum to this effect to Secretary Baker, whose generous sympathy was made plain, and Villard sent a similar draft to Wilson. Assistant Secretary Keppel declared the proposals would violate the draft law; Wilson thought them sensible. But Baker was strongly influenced by Gen. Enoch H. Crowder, provost marshal general, whose military mind had no room for conscientious objectors. Baker himself did not know how to define non-combatant service nor who would be entitled to it.

After conferring with him, Baldwin and Villard adopted a compromise, under which absolutists refusing non-combatant work might be court-martialed and sent to special detention camps under civilian guard, while other objectors would be segregated in cantonments where they could have non-combatant work if they wished it. Crowder was amenable to the cantonments provided they were limited to religious objectors: in his view, the political objector had no rights. Baker, who unquestionably meant well, dissuaded the President from insisting on an immediate definition of non-combatant service lest this increase the number of objectors. In September the Secretary published his first instructions concerning objectors, deliberately making them vague in the ingenuous trust that commanding officers would blend justice with mercy in the execution of policy. They were told to segregate the objectors in their camps, find work for them but not punish any who refused to perform duty, without distinction between religious and non-religious conscience. In principle, the NCLB was largely satisfied. But no guide for practice had been set forth.

No such high-minded, if ineffectual, good will was demonstrated by either the Justice Department or the Post Office Department when the Espionage Act took effect. One section of the law proclaimed that any written or printed matter "in violation of any of the provisions of this act is hereby declared to be non-mailable, and shall not be offered in the mails or delivered from any post office nor by any carrier." The purpose of the law, according to its draftsman, Attorney General Thomas W. Gregory, was to punish "willful" attempts to obstruct or hamper the conduct of the war and to prevent the publication of vital information or its transmission to the enemy. "It is not necessary to Prussianise ourselves in order to destroy Prussianism in Europe," Senator William E. Borah of Idaho protested; but no one paid attention.

The President's signature of the act was to his Postmaster General, Burleson, like the trigger to the bullet. At once Burleson ordered his men to turn in all publications "containing matter which is calculated to interfere with the success of any federal loan . . . or to cause insubordination, disloyalty, mutiny or refusal of duty in the military or naval service, or to obstruct the recruiting, draft or enlistment services . . . or otherwise to embarrass or hamper the Government in conducting the war." Within a month fifteen major publications, most of them Socialist, had been excluded from the mails by Burleson and the Post Office Solicitor, William H. Lamar; among the dangerous mailings intercepted was the AUAM's announcement of the formation of the Civil Liberties Bureau.

Max Eastman's *Masses,* which denounced the motivation of the

war and the propaganda supporting it, was the major target. Burleson held up various issues, then revoked second-class mailing
privileges on the ground that *The Masses* was not a "continuous"
publication because those issues had been found—without hearing
—to be non-mailable. The CLB went into action at once, sending a
delegation of four lawyers—Clarence Darrow, Frank Walsh, a labor lawyer associated with the AUAM; Morris Hillquit, a Socialist,
and Seymour Stedman—to ask Burleson for a more reasonable
policy; Burleson refused categorically and suggested that publishers who disliked his rulings go to court. Wilson defended him, telling Villard that only publications containing "matter explicitly forbidden by law" had been barred from the mails. But Lamar had
for weeks been holding *War's Heretics,* refusing either to clear it or
to declare it non-mailable: his first attention, he told Baldwin
after two months, was "naturally" given "to people whose loyalty
to the Government was unquestionable." As a result, the NCLB
made its first appearance in court—and won.

Two of the chief techniques to be relied on by the NCLB and
the ACLU were thus established at the very beginning: quiet negotiation on a high level of government, and litigation. The third,
publicity, was for a long time to have the most gingerly handling,
generally taking the form of pamphlets. For the most part these
were simple expositions, like *War's Heretics,* or unassailably "official" material—pamphlets whose basic content had already been
safely published or that had been submitted before publication to
appropriate government officials who, if they disapproved, could
be accused of suppression or censorship or, if they stood mute,
could be construed to have found nothing objectionable. Publicity,
however, offered an almost even balance of assets and liabilities.

In 1917, as is true to a lesser extent today, only a minuscule
part of the press was really receptive to the mere concept, let
alone the practice, of civil liberties: partly because the mass press
subsists by carefully pandering to the mass mind, partly because it
effortlessly and naturally reflects the mass mind from which, in most
cases, it springs. Hence the activities as well as the releases of the
NCLB, when they were not ignored (as the activities and the releases of the ACLU too often are today), were treated with hostility and distortion. Its material resources for publicity were ludi-

crously incomparable to those of dominant sentiment and of government; it had no standing of authority; above all it had openly
offered aid and comfort to rebels, so it was itself a pariah. Nonetheless it was sometimes to find, when it caught government out on
particularly shaky ground, that the threat of publicity could be surprisingly effective. This was a lesson that Baldwin was to learn as
quickly as he was to grasp what was soon to be illustrated in the
controversy over the objectors: indifference or hostility to the
basic principles of decency and law is to be found in government
not so much at the top as in the middle levels, where—as in society
at large—short-sighted self-interest and concern for position are so
strong as to be virtually the only motivation of any decision, any
act.

What Baldwin learned the NCLB learned; in effect he *was* the
NCLB as for thirty years he was to be the ACLU. In an unpublished doctoral dissertation as remarkable for its prose as for its
incisiveness, setting an admirable standard for scholars in the social
and other studies, Barton Bean has provided invaluable insights
into the formative years of the NCLB and the growth of the
ACLU, and it is only just at this point to acknowledge a debt to
his *Pressure for Freedoms: The American Civil Liberties Union* as
great as my debt to Dr. Johnson's book mentioned in the previous
chapter. Dr. Bean (without once, in more than four hundred pages,
polarising or extrapolating, structuring or generating or feeding
back—without any of the seminal *clichés*) shows how Baldwin was
to imbue his creation with his own character. Baldwin, Bean says,
combines the glorious idealist determined to die for his principle
with the shrewdly maneuvering politician capable of accepting an
incomplete success as the alternative to heroic failure because of
principle. "A relativist who expresses himself in absolute terms,"
Baldwin, Bean implies, represents the perfect twinning of conscience and politics.

Certainly Baldwin's work in St. Louis, where, in addition to his
other functions, he had served as a member of the Children's Commission and as president of the Missouri Conference of Char-
ities and Corrections, had equipped him with the organisational
and negotiating experience necessary to the realisation of his ideals.
In the midst of the internal battle with the more timorous of the

AUAM directors, his delicate *démarches* to the War Department, and his probes of the outposts of the Post Office Department, he had already begun to marshal a combat force of lawyers for the inevitable court tests. From Major Gullion he had got ten thousand copies of a circular on the workings of the Selective Service Act, to be distributed with NCLB literature in the effort to enlist lawyers who would serve as volunteer defenders for objectors; and in fact many lawyers who themselves whole-heartedly backed the war were to offer their services to defend the rights of those who differed with them.

Baldwin in those days, Dr. Bean points out, even handled all the correspondence himself, establishing a tradition, which persists, of open, courteous replies and frank answers to criticism and even abuse. From the beginning the government of the NCLB and the ACLU was what Bean calls "oligarchy tempered by advice"; he raises—though he is careful not obviously to answer—the question whether indeed such an organisation should be run "democratically" and he permits himself the observation that the smooth internal functioning of the ACLU and "most" of its victories in the arena have been the product of what he calls "aristocratic" methods, all of which began to emerge at the very start.

Without them it would have been impossible for the NCLB to withstand, let alone to combat, the paranoia into which it was born. A mock-judicial assembly line of judges and juries was jailing "enemy agents" for denouncing the Liberty Loans, threatening Wilson, calling for the repeal of the draft, making a film about the American Revolution (entitled *The Spirit of '76,* it was branded anti-British propaganda), calling the Government a tool of Wall Street. Not all the evidence presented by eager prosecutors was gathered by authorised law-enforcement officers. "Several hundred thousand private citizens," Attorney General Gregory boasted, "most of them as members of patriotic bodies," were working for him for nothing, "keeping an eye on disloyal individuals and making reports of disloyal utterances, and seeing that the people of the country are not deceived." Gregory himself helped to set up one of these patriot businesses, the American Protective League, every member of which carried a card identifying him as a "Secret Service Division" operative. (President Wilson did not much like this, but he accepted Gregory's assurances that the League was a fine body of men.) One platoon of APL sentinels descended on the NCLB in the guise of agents of the Department of Justice but, when Baldwin insisted on seeing their credentials, he ordered them out and protested formally to the Bureau of Investigation (later the FBI), whose then chief, Bruce Bielaski, admitted the illegality of the raid. But hundreds of other victims round the country, less astute or more awed than Baldwin, were actually arrested by the patriots in their assaults on suspect meetings, and the Government of the United States ratified these unlawful abductions by bringing the quarry to trial. Neither the patriots nor the real enforcement officers, however, could (would?) check mob violence, which finally outraged too many people when a formerly pacifist minister, Herbert S. Bigelow, was kidnapped by masked horsemen in Cincinnati, carried off to Kentucky and lashed with a blacksnake whip—most probably because, though he now supported the war, he was still denouncing sweatshops. President Wilson became so indignant that he made no secret of "my earnest protest."

So loud and almost universal was the outcry that Baldwin was deluded into believing that all liberals, pro- and anti-war, could now be fused in protest against censorship, violence and invasions of civil liberties. But his attempts to organise a liberal mass meeting came to virtually nothing. The National Single Tax Association and the National Association for the Advancement of Colored People, for example—and they were by no means alone—refused to be associated with a "pacifist" organization, and individual liberals (it is time for that word to be set within quotation marks) took the same brave line, despite Baldwin's assurances that the NCLB was not pacifist. Nonetheless a somewhat less than mass meeting was held by the NCLB in January, 1918, when two supporters of the war were among the speakers. It was the only public meeting attempted during the war by the NCLB, which went back to its prime tactic of negotiation. The *fiasco* is its own commentary on American "liberalism."

Despite all the evidence, the random arrests, the censorship, the land of the free and the home of the brave remained terror-stricken: the Socialist Party and the IWW were still abroad in the land and patriots thundered that, if the Government did not act, its liberty-loving citizens would. Baldwin, somewhat more reasonable, suggested to the President's *éminence grise,* Col. Edward M. House, that the fearsome radicals might be more readily persuaded to support the war if the Government would stop persecuting them at the instance of employers who did not wish to raise wages—the NCLB had already involved itself in the defense of the hundreds of Wobblies seized in a nationwide dragnet in September, 1917, and could prove that they had been responsible for exactly three of the 521 labor disputes reported in the preceding six months. House agreed with Baldwin, and told the President as much; but in matters of what was later to be called national security the Attorney General carried more influence, and he was already drafting an amended Espionage and Sedition Act that would make it a crime to obstruct the sale of Liberty Bonds, to utter "disloyal, profane, scurrilous or abusive language" about the Government, the Constitution (nothing was said, however, to encourage complying with it), the armed forces, the uniform or the flag, or to make fun of any of these. In addition, an amendment made it possible to cut off all mail to and from any violator. Even Senator Borah supported the bill, which, as Baldwin pointed out, would outlaw the Republican Party, since criticism of the Democratic administration would be criminal. Woodrow Wilson signed the bill on May 23, 1918.

Naturally, Baldwin wondered whether the NCLB was still legal. The Justice Department admitted it did not know; it had no standards of enforcement for the guidance of local United States Attorneys, though Gregory went through the ritual of warning them that "protection of loyal persons from unjust suspicion and prosecution is quite as important as the suppression of actual disloyalty." How much that meant was soon illustrated: Eugene V. Debs was sentenced to ten years for saying to an audience he was trying to recruit for the Socialist Party: "You need to know that you are fit for something better than slavery and cannon fodder." Rose Pastor Stokes wrote to a St. Louis newspaper:"I am for the people and the Government is for the profiteers," and she too was sentenced to ten years for the protection of her fellow citizens. (Both her sentence and Debs' were later commuted.) "The public," Johnson says in *The Challenge to American Freedoms,* "was so hysterical about traitors and spies that the Justice Department felt obligated, in part at least, to give the people what they wanted."

What they wanted is set forth in a National Civil Liberties Bureau pamphlet, *War-Time Prosecutions and Mob Violence,* covering the two years ended in March, 1919. Besides innumerable mass attacks on parades and meetings and the destruction of property, patriotic Americans carried the faith to the heretics by forcing twenty-two of them to kiss the flag in public and painting a half-dozen in various colors, of which yellow was preferred. Three men —one of whom compounded treason with membership in the IWW —were fatally hanged; others were hanged for a while and then cut down before they had quite died. Sixty-four were tarred and feathered; fifty-five were kidnapped and whipped. Eleven hundred were forcibly ejected from cities, counties or states (one of these deportations consisted of one thousand miners in Bisbee, Arizona, and another included seventy miners in another part of the same state). Some of these figures overlap, because often the same person would receive several of the patriotic therapies; and they represent only the major reported instances of the period.

Government was doing its part shoulder to shoulder with the rabble to which it owed election. A sampling of federal prosecutions under the Espionage and Sedition Act, based in each case on stool-pigeons' reports of private conversation and correspondence, shows sentences of fifteen years for talking against the draft; of ten years and a thousand-dollar fine for opposing the Liberty Loans; of twenty years and a $10,000 fine for calling the Government a liar, approving the Lusitania sinking and predicting a German victory. Similar sentences were regularly imposed for public utterance, by speech or publication, of such sentiments or of criticism of Allied intervention in Russia. State and local courts did their best to match, though generally they could find no basis for such long sentences.

Wilson's signature of the new sedition law coincided roughly with the opening of the trial of IWW leaders in Chicago under the earlier Espionage Act and with the issuance of a pamphlet that the NCLB had been preparing for four months, *The Truth About the IWW*. The pamphlet contended that the IWW was a legitimate labor organisation and had not obstructed the war. The Justice Department was so enraged that it ordered the Committee on Express Transportation to refuse its shipment by express. The Post Office Department barred it from the mail, began to investigate the

NCLB's other pamphlets and, naturally, since it was looking for them, found elements of disloyalty in each. The War Department broke off its relations with the NCLB. Concurrently with the postal probe, the Justice Department ordered a complete investigation of the NCLB, from which Baldwin had just resigned in anticipation of a prison term: he was about to resist induction into the army.

Lamar, the Post Office Solicitor, admitted privately to the Justice Department that none of the NCLB's pamphlets violated the Espionage Act, but he ruled them all non-mailable anyway because, he decided single-handed, the NCLB was engaging in the illegal activity of defending the IWW. Nelles asked the District Court in New York for injunctive relief. Two weeks later, when he went to the NCLB office, Nelles found an agent of the Bureau of Investigation awaiting him with a posse of dollar-a-year security police from the Union League Club. Nelles examined the federal agent's search warrant and challenged it for lack of a showing of probable cause in the supporting affidavit and, in the case of his own files in the office, as an invasion of his clients' right of private communication. Justice replied by drawing its revolver, and Nelles yielded.

Both he and the directing committee of the NCLB expected to be indicted, probably for conspiring to obstruct recruiting and enlistment. They knew that Military Intelligence had filed a report accusing the NCLB of encouraging objectors. Despite the fears of one member, the committee decided to cooperate with the Justice Department but to sue to vacate the search warrant, while pushing the injunction against the Post Office. The cooperation with the investigating agents was something out of a comic opera. They succeeded almost immediately in so disordering the files that nothing made sense, and they had to have Baldwin, by now a federal prisoner on a draft charge, to take them by the hand. Every day, then, he was taken to the BI's office so that he could restore order.

The Justice Department in Washington had apparently not expected the raid to be made, and one official, John Lord O'Brian, urged the utmost care in the investigation of an organisation engaged in the protection of civil liberties. Part of the utmost care included tapping the NCLB's telephone. Meanwhile an eminently conservative Tammany lawyer, George Gordon Battle, was retained in the hope that his friendships with the Justice Department attorneys might keep the NCLB out of court. Some six weeks after the raid, the United States Attorney for the Southern District of New York informed the NCLB that, while it was irredeemably undesirable, he had been unable to find any illegality in its activities. But to his superior, the Attorney General, the local prosecutor suggested an indictment of the NCLB for defending the IWW, encouraging objectors and advocating unlimited free speech. O'Brian reined the enthusiast by pointing out that anyone had a right to advise objectors of their rights and the NCLB had attempted no proselytisation; that free speech was guaranteed by the Constitution and that "the organisation of defense of persons accused of crime is not in and of itself a crime."

Nelles' action to enjoin Lamar, meanwhile, was so well based that the Government sought an adjournment in the hope of an out-of-court settlement that would save the federal face. The Justice Department believed all the seized literature mailable; but Lamar refused to yield. In spite of his obduracy the Justice Department agreed to the issuance of the injunction and Judge Augustus Hand ordered the Post Office Department to deliver the seized pamphlets.

When Baldwin registered for the draft in September, he declared himself an absolutist objector and he refused to allow his friends to post bail pending his trial, which was postponed at the request of the Justice Department so that he could undo the damage its agents had inflicted on the NCLB's files (occasionally, he and his special guard went to a party together). When his trial began on October 30, he pleaded guilty, and concisely stated his opposition to all war as well as the current one. Justice Julius M. Mayer, who knew of Baldwin's juvenile-court work in St. Louis, exercised his discretion not to surrender the prisoner to the military and imposed the maximum sentence of one year in a civil penitentiary in Newark, N.J. During Baldwin's sentence DeSilver served as director of the NCLB, to which he was a constant and generous financial contributor despite his support of the war and his political conservatism.

Baldwin enjoyed his Newark stay; the Irish warden was sympathetic toward objectors, Baldwin wrote to his friends, and, when Baldwin insisted on working, gave him a job in the kitchen. Baldwin quashed his friends' efforts to obtain a pardon for him in the absence of a general amnesty; with other prisoners he formed a welfare league that retained counsel for those who had none, organised a glee club, helped prisoners' families with funds raised from the wealthier inmates and from philanthropists outside, "and in general conducted a service agency." While the warden approved, the Essex County Sheriff did not: he wanted the trouble-maker out of his jail, and Baldwin's request to be sent to a prison farm nearby in Caldwell was quickly granted. He liked the farm and the outdoor work. Good-behavior allowance and a typo-graphical error in the date of his sentence got him out of jail on June 19, 1919, and he was welcomed home with a party at Norman Thomas' residence, where Baldwin cheerfully disclosed that prison had not reformed him at all.

The NCLB wanted to reinstate him at once as director; but Baldwin wanted to learn more about the labor movement and the concerted efforts by business and government to destroy it. He planned a tour of the country as a manual worker: "I am going to do what a so-called intellectual can do in the labor movement and aid in the struggle of the workers to control society in the interests of the mass." (One cannot help the question posed by all history: what gains would the mass have ever enjoyed, material or other, if it had not from time to time had the providential, though often resisted, intervention of the eccentrics among its rulers?)

Baldwin was not going to return to civil-liberties work unless the NCLB revised its orientation. What he wanted was concentration on "the cause of freedom of expression in the industrial struggle . . . The Bureau is bound to serve partisan causes though standing on a general principle. The cause we now serve is labor," he said at the end of the year, when he had returned to New York. In the interval he had joined the IWW and the Cooks' and Waiters' Union, ridden the rods to Chicago and, after a restaurant job there, farther west, taking odd laboring jobs; heading back east, he had arrived in Pittsburgh at the height of the post-war steel strike and, after two days' talking, convinced William Z. Foster, then an AFL leader, that he was not a company spy, whereupon Foster hired him to spy for the union as a strikebreaker in the Homestead plant. A week later Homestead fired him for being a union spy. Back in New York, he was ready to outline the reorganisation of the NCLB.

His memorandum to the board proposed that work be directed by "those directly engaged in the labor struggle who know the facts first-hand and who represent large constituencies, those who by their writing and speaking are close to labor problems, and those who stand on general principle for freedom of expression." All policy questions, he suggested, should be decided by a large national committee and policy should be carried out by a small directing committee like the existing one. He proposed that it work through a network of local cooperators and volunteers strung on a skeleton of a few major branches in important areas. It was his intention that at least two-thirds of the committee members represent labor: "it would be absurd," he commented "to expect opponents of the cause of labor to join with us." The memorandum did not mention political pressure as a means of action, Bean says; it "slighted legal activity and emphasised the kind of direct intervention and 'test-case' technique that later became so important." In Bean's view, the new emphasis focused on social ends rather than on "the process of freedom."

The memorandum was approved at the end of 1919 and in January, 1920, the American Civil Liberties Union came formally into being as an unincorporated association. Despite Baldwin's stated preference for the composition of its national and executive committees, only twelve of their sixty-four members were labor leaders, fifteen could be called partisans of labor and the thirty-seven others, both conservatives and progressives, were "those who stand on general principle for freedom of expression." The directing committee, composed of national committeemen who lived in the New York area and could meet frequently, was almost immediately to become the real policy-maker, enjoying the consistent ratification of the larger group.

Three paid employes were contemplated: Baldwin and DeSilver as co-directors, at $125 and $75 per month respectively, and a full-time publicity director. This last post became a nightmare, for it was many years before the ACLU could pay a competent man a living wage (to say nothing of a competitive one), and the turnover was to be spectacular. Baldwin and DeSilver, the two directors, retained all the old board members on both the new committees, to which they found it possible to add men who had been afraid of the NCLB stigma during the war, some who were as reserved about the labor movement as DeSilver (he had at one time championed the use of the injunction by employers in labor disputes) and even a representative or two from the Old Guard of the AUAM, such as Jane Addams and Maurer. Among the other members of the National Committee, some of whom in the next few decades were to find themselves in unforeseeable company elsewhere, were two Harvard professors, Felix Frankfurter and Harold J. Laski; the completely apolitical Helen Keller; a brace of reporters, Lincoln Colcord and Robert M. Bruere; Bigelow, the kidnapped minister; Elizabeth Gurley Flynn of the Workers' Defense League (twenty years later she would be asked to resign in a major policy schism), A. B. Gilbert of the Farmers' Non-Partisan League, Robert M. Buck, editor of *The New Majority;* James Weldon Johnson of the NAACP, Crystal Eastman and a mixed clutch of union officials: Henry R. Linville, president of the Teachers' Union of New York City; Duncan McDonald, president of the Illinois Federation of Labor; A. J. Muste, national organiser for the Amalgamated Textile Workers, who was to be read out, when he did not read himself out, of one organisation after another; Julia O'Connor, national organiser for the Telephone Operators' Union, and Joseph Schlossberg, secretary of the Amalgamated Clothing Workers.

As variegated as this excerpt from the roster is, it did not mean that the whole "liberal" movement had welcomed back the prodigal—or, to put it more bluntly, had become liberal without qualification.

4

The Right Not to Kill

It was not until 1923 that the truth about the United States' treatment of conscientious objectors and pacifists became generally known. In that year B. W. Huebsch, Inc., whose president was a member of the Executive Committee of the ACLU, published Norman Thomas' book, *The Conscientious Objector in America*, with an introduction by Robert La Follette, Senator from Wisconsin. To those few who read it, the book was an incredible shock.

In the first place, no claim of conscientious objection was recognised unless it was founded on some theistic-religious basis; preferably the objector had to belong to one of the few sects long recognised as pacifist. Among the recognised classes of objectors, the absolutists—those who refused any war-connected service of any kind—were the most persecuted. The War Department contended that only 3989 persons in its camps claimed conscientious objection, but this number took no account of the thousands who refused to register for the draft or to be examined for induction and who were sentenced by the courts as violators of the draft law. Of its 3989, the War Department said, 1300 accepted or were assigned to non-combat service, 1200 were furloughed to farm

41

work, ninety-nine were sent to France to serve with the Friends' Reconstruction Unit, 450 were imprisoned by courts-martial and the remainder were in objectors' camps at the time of the armistice.

Even after the armistice, the medievally illegal practices of the authorities continued unabated. In an effort to prove that all of them were mentally unfit, objectors as well as other prisoners in the Disciplinary Barracks in Leavenworth were subjected to intelligence tests that disconcertingly demonstrated the average of all objectors to be considerably higher not only than that of the other prisoners but also than the intelligence level of the army as a whole. The religious objectors (and one forbears to comment on the phenomenon) made the lowest scores, frequently below those of sergeants and members of the Officers' Training Corps; the political objectors were excelled only by officers; and the absolutist objectors averaged far higher than anyone in or out of uniform. These were the men who shared Baldwin's motivation for refusing service: "uncompromising opposition to the principle of conscription of life by the state for any purpose whatever, in time of war or peace . . . I am opposed to this and all other wars." But 90 per cent were merely religious objectors. At most 33 per cent of all objectors were of German extraction, and 90 per cent were native Americans.   The first object of the National Civil Liberties Bureau was to protect their right to refuse service and to utter their views; very soon it had also to concern itself with their right to be treated as human beings in the camps and prisons among which they were distributed and in which the ending of the war made no difference to the indignities and brutalities imposed on them by the Government of the United States.

Camp commanders frequently disregarded orders to segregate objectors from others and at least tacitly encouraged the patriots among their underlings to engage in such persecutions as their dull wits could contrive. The commanders themselves, when objectors refused orders to cook their own food, pick up trash, clean latrines, etc., court-martialed them and imposed heavy sentences for "disobeying army orders in time of war." Though here and there a commander and, even more remarkably, a subordinate showed kindness, sympathy and even some ideological affinity with objectors, "rough treatment" was more generally the rule. This consisted, in its more humane forms, of assigning objectors to unheated cells and refusing to give them blankets, compelling them to stand at attention for hours in all weathers, forcing them into uniform through the moral suasion of injection by bayonet or variations on the classic water torture. Recalcitrants were occasionally hung head down in reservoirs of human excrement, compelled to do heavy physical work in arm and leg shackles, subjected to eye-gouging, deprived of food, hanged until not quite dead, exposed to fire-hose attacks (the alternative to this was the unremitting cold-shower treatment), thrown into solitary confinement on a daily diet of eighteen ounces of bread and one pitcher of water, or remanded to a cage in which one could only stand. From time to time, those non-religious objectors who refused to go to divine service were beaten by YMCA workers and cross-wearing chaplains, but the Government did not approve of this.

None of these punishments was ostensibly imposed for conscientious objection. The objector was always tried and convicted on a legitimate charge—refusing to sign his induction papers, or to peel potatoes—and an eighteen-minute trial often led to a twenty-five-year sentence. Of 504 recorded trials, only one ended in acquittal; only three men were sentenced to less than a year. Seventeen were condemned to death (all were later commuted), 142 to life imprisonment, 266 to ten to twenty-five years —whereas an army captain convicted of profiteering was sentenced to two years. In contrast, the severest British sentence of an objector was two years, and even Karl Liebknecht, the militant Socialist objector who defied the Kaiser, was sentenced to only four years, and part of that term was remitted.

Solitary-confinement prisoners in the United States, fighting to make the world safe for democracy, were often manacled erect to their bars all day in cells lacking not only toilets but even buckets, and receiving air and light only through grills in the doors or ceilings; this was alternated with two-week periods of wood-chopping in the open, on a diet of uncooked food. Refractory prisoners were deprived of mail; all were forbidden to speak to one another. Those who spoke little English or who, like the Russian Molokans, were strict sectarians, got the harshest treatment. It was only in 1919, after repeated *démarches* by the National Civil

Liberties Bureau and other organisations interested in the fate of the conscientious objector, that these men began to be moved to special stockades. But requests for a general amnesty for objectors were firmly rejected; sentences were then reviewed, however, and releases began as the Government was compelled to concede that all the penalties were outrageous and many were totally groundless.

Though these enormities were not revealed until 1923, an NCLB pamphlet of 1919, *War-Time Prosecutions and Mob Violence*, reported state and federal court sentences of civilians to fifteen years for talking against the draft; $1500 fines conditioned on the purchase of $1000 worth of Liberty Bonds; ten days for laughing at recruits drilling in a park; $50 fines for refusing to stand up when the national anthem was played; and ninety days and a $300 fine for disturbing the peace by being publicly beaten, tarred and feathered for alleged disloyalty!

One of the first objector cases to be pursued by the new American Civil Liberties Union after its foundation in 1920 was that of Anton Karachun, a Russian national living in the United States who was drafted illegally for service in Siberia against his compatriots. Ignorant of his few rights under the law, Karachun, when he learned that he would be expected to shoot to kill against other Russians, deserted; he was soon picked up and was sentenced to twenty years, reduced from the original penalty of death. It was to take the ACLU five years to win the Government's grudging, conditioned recognition of its crime: ultimately Karachun was released on his promise to return at once to Russia, and the ACLU arranged his passage.

Meanwhile the wartime hysteria survived into the postwar decade. Victor Saff of St. Louis was arrested in 1926 for saying that he would never again be a soldier, and a police-court judge compelled him to kiss the flag in public! A year later the College of the City of New York suspended two students who voiced anti-militarist sentiments, and the University of Minnesota expelled thirty-six who opposed compulsory military training; the University of Georgia attempted to oust a YMCA secretary on the same ground but yielded to a student protest. It was at this time, too, that the issue of conscientious objection as a bar to naturalisation was first raised and that the ACLU suffered the first of many defeats on the point on which it ultimately won.

Mme. Roszika Schwimmer, a famous Hungarian pacifist who had been one of the leaders of Henry Ford's 1915 Peace Ship voyage to Europe in a futile attempt to end the First World War, applied for American citizenship but refused to swear to bear arms in defense of her adopted country. (The fact of her sex was ignored by the Government and the courts—and, for that matter, by her own counsel and the ACLU: though it was relevant to her case, the principle involved was what mattered.) Her naturalisation petition was therefore rejected and she appealed, with ACLU aid, to the courts, which consistently ruled that her refusal to bear arms made her ineligible for citizenship—a classic instance of the discrimination against aliens and naturalised citizens that will be more fully investigated presently. The ACLU carried the case to the Supreme Court, but uselessly, though it evoked a classic dissent by Holmes and Brandeis. (Later Mme. Schwimmer won a handsome libel judgment against Fred Marvin, a professional patriot who denounced her as a Bolshevik agent doubling as a German spy; this defeat put Marvin out of the patriot business and he founded the New York Chamber of Commerce.)

The Schwimmer case was only the first of its kind, and its blatant injustice outraged Americans of many political allegiances. In 1930 John W. Davis of the ultra-respectable Wall Street law firm of Davis, Polk, Wardwell, Gardner & Reed offered his services to the ACLU to appeal a similar case to the Supreme Court, where it might be assumed that Davis' professional reputation and the fact that in 1924 he had been the Democratic Presidential nominee would carry considerable weight. His client was Professor Douglas C. Macintosh of the Yale Divinity School, a Canadian who refused to bear arms in a war that he did not consider morally justified—a less rigorous stand than Mme. Schwimmer's, which barred service in any and all wars. But in 1931 the highest court ruled against him, citing its ruling in the Schwimmer case: "That it is the duty of citizens by force of arms to defend our government against all enemies whenever the necessity arises is a fundamental principle of the Constitution." Admitting that Professor Macintosh put the will of God above the laws of man, the court countered that the nation "must go forward upon the assumption, and safely can proceed on no other, that unqualified allegiance to the nation and submission and obedience to the laws of the land, as well those made for war as those made for peace, are not inconsistent with the will of God." No analogy with the alleged right of the native-born citizen to be a conscientious objector existed, the court held, because the citizen objector is exempted by grace, not by right.

In a notable dissent, Justice Hughes upheld the view of the ACLU and of the Circuit Court of Appeals. He pointed out that nothing in the naturalisation law passed by Congress exacted a promise to bear arms as a condition of citizenship; he quoted the oath of naturalisation, embodying the pledge to support and defend the Constitution and the laws of the United States against all enemies and to bear true faith and allegiance to the Constitution and the laws; and he concluded that the long practice of granting exemption to conscientious objectors (dating back to the Civil War) warranted the interpretation that Congress did not intend to require any promise of armed service as a condition of citizenship. Holmes, Brandeis and Stone concurred with Hughes, as they did in the equally unsuccessful appeal (also conducted by the ACLU) of Mrs. Marie Bland, a Canadian-born nurse who took the same position as Mme. Schwimmer. It was to be many years before the court minority's and the ACLU's view was to become the law, and then only in a diluted form that limited the right of naturalisation to those alien objectors whose basis was religious rather than merely moral, political or humanitarian. Ultimately the requirement of bearing arms was eliminated.

Compulsory military training at so-called land-grant colleges had long been opposed by a handful of students, both religious and nonreligious objectors, and the world-wide circulation of the Oxford Oath in 1933 brought their opposition into the open. The Oxford Oath pledged its original British signatories never to fight for King and country (in the Second World War millions of signers throughout the world allowed the emotional surge of anti-Fascism to sweep away all their principled antipathy to armed conflict) and, with the elimination of the reference to the king, was enthusiastically subscribed to by young men and women everywhere. It was logical for those in public colleges to seek to implement their beliefs by resisting required service in the Reserve Officers' Training Corps, and in most cases the resistants were promptly expelled from their institutions. Some, however, went to court, and invariably lost; but one case involving the University of California was carried with ACLU help to the Supreme Court on the ground that the denial of a student's conscientious objections to such training amounted to a violation of religious freedom without due process of law and to a state's unconstitutional abridgment of the privileges and immunities protected by the Fourteenth Amendment. In an opinion of many pages and little logic, Justice Butler rejected all such arguments, and this time Hughes stood with the majority. Only Stone, Brandeis and the usually conservative Cardozo dissented. But a hopeful note was sounded when Wisconsin's Legislature voted to make such training optional in the state university.

Other areas of the country were less enlightened. Everywhere students were staging anti-war rallies, and on April 12, 1934, a national student strike against war was called by the National Student League (immediately, of course, branded Communist) and the Student League for Industrial Democracy, which had admitted Socialist ties. Not only the nation-wide strike but the local pacifist meetings were inevitably the targets of other, more numerous students who generally enjoyed the overt support of the public authorities and not seldom that of their academic mentors as well. But, in general, questions of pacifism and conscientious objection were relatively rarely raised until the outbreak of the Second World War in late 1939 and, even more, the enactment of a new American draft law in 1940, when it was apparent to the slowest mind that sooner or later the United States must be drawn into a war that it might, had it and its Allies had a modicum of courage, have been able to prevent. This new national emergency produced a double crisis for the American Civil Liberties Union.

Obviously the Union would have to defend far more cases of conscientious objection under a conscription act than had been the case in the twenty interwar years when the question was largely academic, except when what the commonalty called "some kind of a nut" brought it to irritating if temporary actuality. But this foreseeable external crisis was accompanied by an unanticipated internal tension within the ACLU. Its membership was almost overwhelmingly anti-Fascist; a large proportion, too, was Jewish. The inevitable enemy in the coming war was both Fascist and anti-Jewish; its destruction was of paramount importance to all who believed in the rights of man, and especially to those who felt any bond of kinship to the enemy's victims in Europe. The philosophical resistance of a Baldwin to any form of conscription in any circumstances could hardly be expected to be shared by men and women whose emotions were so deeply involved in the events of Europe—whether for reasons of political principle or of real or fancied kinship—that the ACLU's traditional endorsement of pacifism and opposition to conscription were automatically forgot by all but a handful of authentic civil-libertarians who put the absolute of freedom above all other ideals and goals and who refused to accept the questionable thesis that freedom could best be defended by its temporary abandonment.

To such an extent were the few apostles outnumbered that the Union's 1930-40 annual report, entitled *In the Shadow of War,* bore a prefatory note warning the reader that nothing in this title "is to be construed as opposition to the national defense program or conscription, with which the Union is not concerned, except at points where freedom of opinion or conscience is involved." But the American Civil Liberties Union implied all too plainly that, even in defending the rights of the opponents of this new conflict, it too condemned their heresy. And yet, when the Union's critics, especially after the German military successes of early 1940, declared that all civil liberties should be restricted, if not suspended, in such emergencies, the Union replied by quoting the *dictum* of the Supreme Court in the Milligan case that arose in the Civil War:

"The Constitution of the United States is a law for the rulers and the people, equally in war and in peace, and covers with the shield of its protection all classes of men, at all times, and under all circumstances. No doctrine involving more pernicious consequences was ever invented by the wit of man than that any of its provisions can be suspended during any of the great exigencies of government."

As in the earlier war, the ACLU was involved at once with absolutist objectors who simply refused to register under the new draft law and who, on conviction, were subjected to excessive sentences dictated by "patriotic" emotion or by the groundless hope of creating deterrents. The Union refused to defend the non-registrants, advising objectors instead to register but to state their positions when so doing; and, though it refused to defend the absolutists, it did endeavor to obtain equal treatment for them in the courts. The thorniest of the immediate problems was that of members of Jehovah's Witnesses, who were often refused recognition as religious objectors because their faith required them to declare their willingness to fight in one war: Armageddon, when, as and if. Another of the rules peculiar to their sect created a further problem; since every Witness is considered a minister of religion, each claimed exemption on this ground as well as that of conscience, and the Government recognised as ministers of religion only those duly licensed by a recognised manufactory of clerics. Nonetheless the American Civil Liberties Union was able to win the release of one Witness from the army after he had been inducted by physical force into the crusade against dictatorship. But, even in the height of hysteria that followed Pearl Harbor, such outrages were rare and in general, the Union reported in mid-1942, objectors were being much better treated than in 1917-18: even those whose objector claims were unrecognised and who were imprisoned for resisting induction were often treated in prison as the objectors they really were, and many were paroled to civilian service camps.

A National Committee on Conscientious Objectors was created by the ACLU to keep the national office and the affiliates abreast of any cases that might arise and to maintain *liaison* with the appropriate public authorities, which for the most part showed every disposition to cooperate and to assure objectors of fair treatment. But, as the war continued, work loads mounted, the hyperemotional *togetherness* of the first months of American participation began to dissolve in the acid of rational analysis, and tempers shortened noticeably. The new committee found itself with an unexpected number of cases as successive court rulings and administrative orders narrowed the criteria for the exemption of objectors and, consequently, more and more of them were ordered to jail.

In August, 1943, the ACLU distributed a sixteen-page pamphlet, *The Conscientious Objector Under the Selective Training and Service Act of 1940*, prepared in 1941 and recently revised by the National Service Board for Religious Objectors, whose Consultative Council represented thirty-six organisations concerned with the problem: Catholic, Jewish, Protestant (including a variety of denominations, of which Jehovah's Witnesses was one), as well as the YMCA and the Women's International League for Peace and Freedom. Under the new law, the pamphlet pointed out, membership in a recognised "peace" church—the Mennonites or the Friends, for example—was no longer required: it was enough to claim conscientious objection by reason of religious training or belief. Those to whom exemption was granted might be assigned to non-combatant service as defined by the President or, if this too violated their principles, to work of national importance under civilian direction. Objectors might appeal from their draft boards through intermediate bodies and ultimately to the Justice Department, whose findings, however, were not binding on the intermediate appellate bodies. Within ten days of notice to report for induction the objector could file his appeal with his local draft board, but the Board of Appeal would not act until the Justice Department, through the FBI, had investigated his case and held an informal hearing in which he could ask to see the FBI's report; time would be granted for the filing of affidavits to correct or refute any inaccuracies. The Justice Department then made its non-binding recommendation to the Board of Appeal, from which there could be no appeal as a matter of right to the President unless there had been a division within the Board of Appeal. Once imprisoned, the objector might seek any of four types of parole: to military service, to non-combatant work, to civilian activity and to special types of service that might be established.

The required religious training or belief was variously interpreted. It might mean indoctrination received in the home, in church or in some other organisation with religious influence, even if the organisation did not profess a religious character. Or it might cover what one had come to believe from one's schooling or from one's own religious experience and conduct of life. But in March of 1942 Brig. Gen. Lewis B. Hershey, the director of selective service, narrowed this by order to require "recognition of some source of all existence, which, whatever the type of recognition, is

Divine because it is the Source of all things." A year later Judge Augustus Hand of the Circuit Court of Appeals specifically excluded exemption for conscientious objection based on political beliefs. Both these restrictions were consistently battled by the ACLU.

Civilian service meant a choice between a government camp and one operated by the Mennonites, the Brethren Service Committee or the American Friends' Service Committee. Once basic training had been completed by an objector choosing non-combatant service (basic training meant all normal military discipline and training except that entailing weapons), he might also seek a transfer to a camp operated by the Association of Catholic Conscientious Objectors or by the Methodist Church's Commission on World Peace. Any camp, it was stipulated, must be 100 miles from the objector's local board (on the West Coast, 200 miles); those in government camps received their keep and $3 a month in pay, while inmates of church camps who had means had to pay $30 a month. The law forbade any compensation beyond maintenance costs to those objectors employed in designated federal and state agencies such as forest services, hospitals, farms, medical research or meteorology. Transfers to such duty might also be requested by ordinary soldiers who, on becoming objectors, applied to their commanding officers. From the first, the ACLU sought to obtain for objectors electing some form of service the same compensation paid to enlisted men in the ranks.

The Union's own publication, *Conscience and the War*, followed the Service Board's publication by a month and was signed by eighteen distinguished lawyers, educators, writers, clergymen and other notables, "none of whom are [*sic*] pacifists, some of whom are veterans of World War I and all of whom support wartime military conscription." In some respects they noted decided improvements over the handling of conscientious objectors in the earlier war: all except those electing non-combatant service were removed from military camps; conscience was recognised in persons not affiliated with the few sects traditionally opposed to war; special hearing officers gave personal hearings to each applicant for exemption; religious agencies provided for the care of their own communicants assigned to civilian service; and the general public attitude was much more understanding.

Yet, the ACLU's report found, some administrative aspects evidenced marked retrogression. For example, by July of 1943 there were 1600 objectors, mostly Jehovah's Witnesses, in prisons (a year later the figure was 3000), against 500 in the First World War; in practice, as opposed to theory, the basis of recognition of objectors' claims was narrower; and civilian service was less satisfactorily handled, having been put on a group rather than an individual basis, without compensation. In addition, 500 members of Jehovah's Witnesses had been imprisoned because they had refused civilian camps, though either the courts or the Selective Service Administration could have assigned them to other services. Since the Witnesses recognised no other religions, the Government's requirement that the camps be run only by religious agencies automatically excluded them, as well as unbelievers. The ACLU demanded that this be rectified, that the military pay, dependency allotments and compensation for injury allowed to objectors in non-combatant service be extended to all and that, as in the first war, those on "detached service" be allowed to retain their earnings. The ACLU also protested, with equal unsuccess, the procedure under which a man whose claim of conscience was rejected had to submit to induction before he could obtain a review.

In a battle that was still being fought before the Supreme Court in 1965, the ACLU called also for a change in the law to extend the exemption on the ground of conscience to those who had no belief in the possibility of a so-called Supreme Being and, as in Britain, to include those who objected only to some wars and to allow total exemption from all kinds of service; but this was bitterly resisted lest the godless Communists take advantage of such looseness —and this at a time when the party line called for all-out collaboration in a war in which Russia was an Ally of the United States! The Union also called attention to a number of deliberate violations of the law by the Government, such as the appointment of military officers to the Presidential Appeal Board despite a clear statutory requirement that its members be civilians—to this Washington replied that the officers were serving in a civilian capacity. Other objections focused on the nature of the questions asked to verify religious beliefs and practices (including the name and address of the objector's ghostly *Gruppenführer*), the virtual monopoly of intermediate appeals boards by lawyers, and the clear pronouncement that those in civilian camps had no rights but only revocable privileges and could be sent anywhere, even overseas, without their consent: the whole philosophy of administration was branded a planned deterrent to conscientious objection, and the Union quoted General Hershey's approving statement that it had succeeded in keeping the number of objectors well below what had been anticipated. The Selective Service Administration made it plain that it would continue to occupy the objectors' time with made work, exerting no effort to provide any training for post-war occupations that might benefit both the objector and society, and that the civilian camps would continue under military direction despite the statutory proviso that civilians must run them. Court rulings that religious belief is not susceptible of definition were ignored by the draft administrators, who lived in fear of denunciation by the American Legion every time they released an objector to "detached service" in mental hospitals, farm work or public health, as well as private industry, at a special bonus of $15 a month above his maintenance.

Procedurally, the ACLU pointed out to the public and to potential objectors, review in the courts was difficult. The most practical method was the writ of *habeas corpus* after induction, but many objectors refused to be inducted. One Federal Judge, Leon Yankwich of Los Angeles, ruled, however, that *habeas* might issue at any stage before induction at which the objector was deprived of liberty by the arbitrary act of his draft board. Black Muslims, second to Jehovah's Witnesses in the number of refusals to register because their creed forbade participation in international wars, were automatically jailed; but men who notified their draft boards in writing that they would refuse to register because of principle were treated as having registered anyway, in order to avoid the embarrassment of prosecuting them. Jail terms were short at first, when the draft was only for a year, but they became longer as the draft was extended to cover the duration of the war; parole was possible on condition that the parolee worked in public or quasi-public service and retained from his salary only the equivalent of basic army pay, which was $50 a month. Men who served their full terms were frequently re-arrested for again refusing to serve in the armed forces, though all other ex-convicts were automatically classified 4-F and hence exempt.

Those who claimed exemption because of their race were ignored, except Indians, who could prove their exemption by tribal treaties. Puerto Rican Nationalists were treated as evaders, as was a Negro who wrote to a United States Attorney that he would be glad to fight the enemies of the Four Freedoms and "I can fight them best, it seems to me, by doing what I can, in my own person, to protest the policies of race discrimination that beset me as a citizen. I cannot fight Fascism in any army where I am treated as an inferior citizen." The army, navy and air force of the Four Freedoms, of course, were rigidly segregated.

An ACLU delegation waited on President Roosevelt to present the case against the flaws in the law and its administration and to seek some amelioration of the more flagrant. Headed by Ernest Angell, later chairman of the Union's board of directors and formerly a regional administrator of the Securities and Exchange Commission, the delegation included Dr. Rufus M. Jones of Haverford College, an internationally famous Quaker educator, and the Right Reverend William Appletown Lawrence, Episcopal Bishop of Western Massachusetts. Roosevelt listened politely, referred everything to the Selective Service Administration, which rejected the lot, and left no doubt in his visitors' minds that the Government was obviously afraid of public criticism of any leniency—an attitude that, however craven, seemed well founded: Roosevelt could have cited not only the chronic outcries of the professional patriots but the action of the Illinois Supreme Court, which refused to admit a conscientious objector to the state bar. But the United States Supreme Court, somewhat more bravely, ruled that the forced induction of Arthur G. Billings, formerly of the faculty of the University of Texas, was illegal and that the oath of induction must be taken voluntarily. The ACLU had been advised by counsel that no hope of success existed in Billings' case and hence it had not participated, but it had at least helped to defray the costs of his appeals.

Government's implied (and sometimes expressed) plea of excuse for inaction on the objector question—the fear of public reaction—was not without some exceptions: Governor Earl Warren of California did not hesitate in 1944 to veto a bill that would have required all prospective state employes to state their views on the war. It was, he said, nothing but an incentive to witch-hunters. Independent surveys of the press and of public opinion indicated rather strongly that the official fear of a hostile public had little factual basis; but on the whole Government and the courts barely faltered in their repressions. Perhaps astonished by its own boldness in the Billings case, the United States Supreme Court upheld not only the refusal of Illinois to let a pacifist practice law but also the convictions of objectors who rebelled at forced labor under military direction in civilian camps. Despite the law's provisions, the court rejected an attack on military control of Selective Service, and Congress promptly amended the law to stipulate that military men administering the draft were serving in a civilian capacity. A court-martial invoked the death penalty for one Henry Weber, an objector and a member of the Socialist Labor Party, on his conviction of disobedience of military orders after his request for non-combatant army service was denied. Prompt ACLU intervention won successive commutations to twenty and then to five years and action was then instituted to obtain a total reversal of the judgment and the assignment of Weber to the non-combatant service he had originally sought. But hundreds of other objectors imprisoned because they rejected both military and civil service could not convince the Federal Board of Parole and the Bureau of Prisons that their regulations should be modified to allow the parole of these men.

By the time the war ended in 1945, the number of objectors in prison was seven times the First World War figure; their release was agonisingly slow after V-E Day and among the last to be freed were the much hated Jehovah's Witnesses, whose open contempt for all other faiths had won them no friends. The end of the war posed for the Union a problem that had never been more than academic in the years between the wars: peacetime conscription; for it was evident that the draft law, under whatever sweetened title, would survive the war. Now that the emergency had ended and the emotions of the crusade against Fascism had cooled off in the merciless light of the truths about that and all other crusades, those who had never quite stomached the ACLU's acceptance of wartime conscription led the successful campaign for a firm declaration of policy in opposition to any peacetime draft. Unexpected recognition of Union views that had previously been dismissed came now from the Supreme Court, which, overruling its Schwimmer, Macintosh and Bland rulings, held that a pacifist was entitled to naturalisation, basing its changed view on the statement of a Canadian-born Seventh-Day Adventist that he would perform non-combatant service but would not bear arms in the event of war. No valid distinction could be made between these two forms of service, the court declared, since Congress did not intend to require more of the alien than of the citizen. The decision, enlightened though it was, evaded the logical question that arose: what if the alien would refuse non-combatant service?

The return of "peace" did not, however, mean a real cessation of the persecution of the objector. Many of those still unreleased went on strike in protest against their continued detention. The ACLU, in a curious quibble, defended their moral but not their legal right to strike and, what was more important, provided bail and counsel for them. Appeals from wartime litigation were still pending: the Supreme Court affirmed the right of objectors assigned to civilian service camps to challenge their classifications when they were brought to trial for refusing to report for induction; but the court refused to review the action of the draft authorities in denying objector's status to opponents of war on none but humanitarian grounds. Similarly, it would not entertain appeals on the legality of holding objectors beyond the twelve-month term provided in the original 1940 draft act. Nor did release from prison after the war mean that objectors had been restored to their rightful place in society: many states refused to issue professional or vocational licenses to them on the basis that they had been convicted of a felony. The Union began a campaign of pressure on President Truman to restore their civil rights by proclamation; but the President's Amnesty Commission recommended only limited pardons for 1500 of the 5000 imprisoned objectors and specifically discriminated against those who were Jehovah's Witnesses. Congress, in 1947, two years after the end of the war, behaved no better and enacted a peacetime draft law that pointedly omitted to prohibit segregation or to provide for recognition of conscientious objection. A year later the operation of the law was suspended, but objectors who had refused to register under it went on being prosecuted and those who had urged them to live up to their principles were also brought into court. In vain the Civil Liberties Union sought some victim of such harassment who would be willing to test the constitutionality of the peacetime draft.

The outbreak of the conflict in Korea, which everyone refused to admit officially was a war, terminated the suspension of the draft law. In the changed circumstances—neither war nor peace—the Union no longer viewed the statute as an invasion of civil liberties and did not attack prosecutions for refusals to register under it. In February, 1951, the Union went on record with the view that the law was justified as an emergency measure by the new threats to the nation's security, despite its continued opposition in principle to a universal military training law. But, then or, in retrospect, now, it is more than difficult for the keenest naked eye to discern precisely what or where these threats were, and one is constrained to ask whether the ACLU's uncomfortable straddle was not largely a defensive measure in the interest of its own security. Truman had proclaimed an emergency, which Congress had ratified, but neither the Executive nor the Legislative would brook the designation of "war" for what both termed a "police action." Truman's "emergency" is still legally in effect though Korea is long since a dead issue, and the ACLU has again found the necessary strength to reconsider its position on the 1947 draft law and its successors.

The abuses of the Second World War were repeated on a smaller scale during the Korean period, and again, for the most part, they were upheld by the courts. The Supreme Court found nothing illegal in the Justice Department's practice of using FBI reports as the basis of its recommendations in objector cases even though the contents were forbidden to the men whom they concerned. A District Court in Kansas sentenced an objector for refusing to fill out his draft questionnaire and report for induction despite the fact that he had already served a prison term on the same charge. Sixty-eight objectors were prosecuted in 1953, and forty-eight went to jail. The sixty-eight trials, however, produced a few significant defeats for entrenched bigotry. The United States Supreme Court threw out a refusal of objector status based entirely on the draft board's simple disbelief of the objector's sincerity despite the total lack of any evidence to ground such skepticism. It ruled too that, when the Government admits error in questioning the genuineness of the pacifist convictions of an applicant for citizenship, the Naturalisation Court judge is estopped from gratifying his own prejudices by denying the applicant's uncontroverted testimony as to his principles of conscience. This latter case, that of Arthur Jost of the Mennonite Church, seemingly established a further point: the position of one's sect on war was not governing, but what counted was one's own religious training and belief. The highest court reversed itself again, or at any rate swung round better than ninety degrees, by holding that the objector investigated by the FBI was entitled at least to a summary of the contents of its reports, and a District Court construed this to mean the entire contents except the names of the FBI's stoolpigeons. The Immigration Service lost another round to an objector when, on appeal, it was held that violation of the draft law did not constitute moral turpitude or undesirability rendering an alien subject to deportation.

In the dozen years since the Korean truce the Supreme Court has taken to heart the lesson it taught itself in 1953, and even the lower courts and the administrative agencies seem to have learned, if only by being beaten increasingly often. The Supreme Court has put an end to the denial of objector exemption to those who, like Jehovah's Witnesses, refuse to fight in any but a theocratic war; it has strengthened the requirements for information to an objector as to the FBI's reports on him; it has ordered the draft administration to furnish the objector with a copy of the Justice Department's recommendation on his claim. A laughable attempt to deprive a draft registrant of objector exemption because of one conviction for speeding and another for drunkenness collapsed.

But what happened at the highest level of the judiciary, as is so often the case in this country of fifty-one rival sovereignties, did nothing to cut the case-load of the ACLU. Throughout the past twelve years it has had to be constantly alert to protect, for example, women whose naturalisation applications have been imperiled by their objection on principle to making munitions; state university students seeking exemption from the ROTC; teachers ousted for pacifism; soldiers who become objectors during their enlistments and are court-martialed for insubordination. In 1958 the late Patrick Murphy Malin, then executive director of the Union, wrote to President Eisenhower to urge him to recommend the amendment of the draft law to give non-religious objectors equal status with those relying on their faiths, but the White House did not even acknowledge the letter. A year later Malin sought the reinstatement of William R. Martin, discharged from his post as assistant to the Senate Republican minority when he urged students called in the draft to register as objectors; but Malin's citation of the First Amendment's protection of freedom of speech went unanswered. Yet here and there the ACLU was able to score a victory: in San Francisco, for example, the schools exempted all objectors, without reference to religion, from saluting the flag and pledging allegiance to it after the Union had cited the 1943 ruling of the Supreme Court that no citizen may be required to affirm any belief for any reason; and Iowa repealed its 1917 law barring conscientious objectors from state employment.

But thus far, despite the ACLU's testimony before the Senate Armed Services Committee in 1962, when the draft law was being revised, Congress has refused to eliminate the theistic test for objectors, even though the Supreme Court, upholding the right to atheism, ruled that "neither a state nor the Federal Government can constitutionally force a person 'to profess a belief or a disbelief in any religion.' " The revised draft law still provides for deferment as a conscientious objector only on the ground of religious training or belief defined as "an individual's belief in relation to a Supreme Being involving duties superior to those arising from any human relation, but [this] does not include essentially political, sociological or philosophical views or merely [*sic*] a personal moral code." In March of 1965 the Supreme Court ruled in effect for the contention of the ACLU that Arno Sascha Jakobson, Forest Britt Peter and Daniel Andrew Seeger are *bona fide* conscientious objectors and hence entitled under the law to exemption from the draft even though they deny or question the existence of a deity and base their religious beliefs on more reasoned grounds. The attempt of Congress to define and specify what constitutes religious belief, the three men and the ACLU, in its brief *amicus,* contend, contravenes the First Amendment's statement that "Congress shall make no law respecting an establishment of religion, or prohibiting the free exercise thereof . . ." The court, in characteristic contemporary American fashion, evaded a clear ruling on the constitutionality of the draft law's attempt to establish theism; it preferred to twist fact, logic and principle into a finding that in essence the three objectors somehow accepted the possibility of a supreme being. Once more justice had tainted itself with injustice to achieve a desirable result in an individual case and left a bad law standing unscathed in contravention of the Constitution and of the court's own prior rulings.

5

"Every Idea Is An Incitement"

To maintain throughout the United States and its possessions the rights of free speech, free press, free assemblage and other civil rights, and to take all legitimate action in furtherance of such purposes—so the aims of the American Civil Liberties Union are stated in its charter.

Free trade in ideas—the phrase is that of the late Justice Oliver Wendell Holmes—is the root of all civil liberty, and the unremitting war that the ACLU has been waging for almost a half-century to preserve that free trade is the foundation of all its work, paramount even to its equally relentless struggle for freedom of lawful action and restraint of lawless invasion. If the foundation of freedom of expression is sapped, no right, of property or of person, public or private, remains secure. No more convincing recognition of the might of thought and expression can be imagined than the obsessive determination of every power system in history to shackle it.

In every period and every country, thoughtful men of unimpugnable good faith have sought to establish a balance between the absolute freedom of trade in ideas and the safety of society, while less thoughtful men of more questionable integrity have

61

striven to establish categorically the *status quo* as the highest good and have sought to extirpate impartially all that questioned it. Both kinds of men, whatever their motives, have been seduced by a fallacy, for absolute security is no more possible to the nation than to the individual. Even if it were either possible or as desirable as anxiety makes it appear, safety, any more than any other end, can never ennoble a base means.

In a 1919 dissent in Abrams v. the United States, Holmes epitomised (with the sole concurrence of Brandeis) what is meant by freedom of speech. Abrams, after the Armistice of the First World War, was ordered deported to his native Russia because he had protested the continued presence of American troops there. The majority of the Supreme Court rejected his appeal, but Holmes rejected emotionalism and expediency. He wrote:

"When men have realised that time has upset many fighting faiths, they may come to believe, even more than they believe the very foundations of their own conduct, that the ultimate good to be desired is better reached by free trade in ideas—that the best test of truth is the power of the thought to get itself accepted in the competition of the market; and that truth is the only ground upon which their wishes safely can be carried out. That, at any rate, is the theory of our Constitution. It is an experiment, as all life is an experiment. Every year, if not every day, we have to wager our salvation upon some prophecy based upon imperfect knowledge."

In 1919, as in 1000 B.C. or in 1965, this was too high a demand of courage for society and most of its individual components to meet, for nothing is so much to be dreaded as experiment and uncertainty. Perhaps the least challengeable compromise between this virile embrace of the natural rights of man, within the immutable conditions of life, and the artificial and apprehensive claims of society was embodied in the formula that Holmes, in the same year, evolved for the unanimous court in Schenck v. the United States. Schenck was appealing a conviction under the Espionage Act: he had "impeded recruiting" during the war by public utterance of Socialist Party condemnation of the war. Holmes chose these terms for the test he devised to determine the degree of freedom to be permitted to expression:

"The question in every case is whether the words used are used in such circumstances and are of such a nature as to create a *clear and present danger* [italics added] that they will bring about the substantive evils that Congress has a right to prevent. It is a question of proximity and degree. When a nation is at war, many things that might be said in time of peace are such a hindrance to its effort that their utterance will not be endured as long as men fight, and that no court could regard them as protected by any constitutional right."

This was the birth of the "clear and present danger" doctrine that has become a major guide of the American Civil Liberties Union and the target of forty-five years of attack, misunderstanding and often quite conscious distortion. On its face the doctrine appears eminently reasonable in principle—provided one accepts the postulates concerning what Congress has a right to prevent and admitting circumstances of war as an exception to the rule of law—even when one recognises the calculated risk it implies: interpretation and application by courts composed of men no more immune to prejudice and emotion than any others. There are, after all, still many Germans and others foolish enough to believe that it was the civil-liberties protections of the Weimar Constitution that made possible the triumph of National Socialism, and hence to insist that freedom is to be defended only by selectively allocating its exercise.

The career of the "clear and present danger" doctrine has been exemplary in the hands of the ACLU and rather less so in those of the courts, which have been more easily intimidated by hysteria and bigotry (because they are less accustomed to and far more afraid of unpopularity). But, even though the ACLU has so admirably employed Holmes' test to defend the morally inalienable right to preach even the most repugnant idiocy, one must respectfully submit that by accepting this criterion to such an extent, however critically, the ACLU has bowed to an unwarrantable restriction of civil liberty, as Holmes had made clear in the Abrams case and as he was to do again, by implication, six years afterward.

Benjamin Gitlow (later to see the blinding light on that one-way road to Damascus that became so congested—and so profitable—during and after the Second World War) was appealing his conviction for criminal anarchy under a New York law specifically making mere advocacy a crime. Discussing that portion of the appeal that relied on the First Amendment's guaranty of the right of free speech, Holmes did not pause to weigh the likelihood that the toiling masses, Gitlow's *Left Wing Manifesto* clutched in their teeth, might rush forthwith to tear Wall Street brick from brick and girder from girder: it was irrelevant. Holmes said (and the italics are mine):

"Every idea is an incitement . . . *If, in the long run, the beliefs expressed in proletarian dictatorship are destined to be accepted by the dominant forces of the community, the only meaning of free speech is that they should be given their chance and have their way.*"

But this was Holmes' view alone; even his equally courageous colleague in dissent, Justice Brandeis, could not quite accept the implications of Holmes' view, though in his apparent retreat in 1927 to the original "clear and present danger" doctrine Brandeis attempted to arm it with some standard of measurement. Refusing to join the majority in what the ACLU at the time called a revival of the medieval concept of guilt by association at the sacrifice of the Anglo-American common-law theory that all guilt is personal, Brandeis protested the conviction of Charlotte Anita Whitney, a social worker, for violating California's criminal-syndicalism law by mere membership in a proscribed left-wing organisation. Rejecting the rigidity of "security," Brandeis declared:

"Those who won our independence by revolution were not cowards. They did not fear political change. They did not exalt order at the cost of liberty. To courageous, self-reliant men, with confidence in the power of free and fearless reasoning applied through the processes of popular government, no danger flowing from speech can be deemed clear and present unless the incidence of the evil apprehended is so imminent that it may befall before there is opportunity for full discussion. If there be time to expose through discussion the falsehood and fallacies, to avert the evil by the processes of education, the remedy to be applied is more speech, not enforced silence."

These were brave men—never numerous in public or private

life. It has been no less courageous for the American Civil Liberties Union to copy their words out of unread case reports and repeat them broadcast to the rednecks of the intellect who know no Mason-Dixon Line. Yet, of the few accusations that can be drawn against the ACLU, probably the gravest is its formal refusal to progress beyond Brandeis' refinement of the "clear and present danger" doctrine to Holmes' protection of absolute freedom of expression. Anything less, however well intentioned and however pragmatically justified, is in the end a mockery of freedom of utterance: for the purpose of all advocacy is to produce action. If it is to be shut off as soon as action seems imminent (and who is to measure imminence? by what infallible standards?), then it becomes no more than an empty plaything of the intellect. If utterance actually grows into unlawful conduct—political, economic, sexual—then and only then may government honorably and rightfully intervene; and, if its intervention fails and a new *régime* emerges, the unlawful may become the lawful. To flee the risk of change is to negate life; to profess freedom only as long as it remains an academic exercise is to snap its sword at the hilt. Fortunately, the ACLU's own interpretation of the doctrine has been so truly liberal as to nullify all but the formality of the indictment.

But the danger of the doctrine does not lie in its moral inadequacy alone. Even if one could accept it as a principle, no criteria are—or can be, despite Brandeis' effort—established for ascertaining when a danger becomes "clear and present," when a speech will so carry away its hearers that they will rush out of the hall to launch the revolution (or kill the Jews), when *Fanny Hill* will send teen-aged females to pound on the doors of the employment offices of the white-slave cartel (or *One* will convert all their clients to pederasty). The Supreme Court, to its credit, was quick enough to strike down one perversion of the "clear and present danger" doctrine by the ultra-orthodox: the argument that the test is met when an utterance "provokes" or is likely to "provoke" violent reaction by those who oppose it. From the time when this casuistry was first offered by the authorities, the ACLU has emphasised in its *amicus* briefs, its pamphlets and its news releases that the same authorities are bound by their oaths of office to protect the utterers and to prevent such outbreaks, and even the Supreme Court at its most reactionary has not wholly ruled *contra.*

In 1949 the court reversed the conviction of a collaborator of the Reverend Gerald L. K. Smith, one Father Terminiello, for inciting to riot because, as a result of his inflammatory Fascist speech at an indoor meeting in Chicago, persons outside the hall had attempted by violence to break up the meeting. "A function of free speech under our system," Justice Douglas said for the majority, "is to invite dispute. It may indeed best serve its high purpose when it induces a condition of unrest, creates dissatisfaction with conditions as they are, or even stirs people to anger . . . as it presses for acceptance of an idea. That is why freedom of speech . . . is . . . protected against censorship or punishment." Two years later, it is true, the court upheld a disorderly-conduct conviction of a Progressive Party speaker who ignored the order of a New York City policeman to desist because the speaker had allegedly urged Negroes to "rise up in arms and fight for their rights" and because a member of the audience had protested. But Douglas, Minton and Black strongly dissented from the majority's departure from the Terminiello rule, Douglas stating specifically that the record (in Feiner v. New York) "shows an unsympathetic audience and the threat of one man to haul the speaker from the stage. It is against that kind of threat that speakers need police protection. If they do not receive it and instead the police throw their weight on the side of those who would break up the meeting, the police become the new censors of speech. Police censorship has all the vices of the censorship from city halls which we have repeatedly struck down."

True freedom, then, must comprehend the freedom to change the existing order, even for the worse. If suppression, even only to a degree, is the price of security—so-called—then security costs more than it is worth. For the mass of mankind, indifferent—to put it kindly—to abstractions, to truly moral and intellectual considerations, one may state the blunt ugly corollary: no idea, no program that really appeals to a basic need, however speciously or impracticably, can ever be totally suppressed. It can be—it is immediately—made more attractive, in an infinite variety of ways, by being driven underground, where obviously it can only become more dangerous. The sole hope—when there is any—of defeating it is to make it risk exposure to all the normal hazards, including not only rebuttal but ridicule. If the otherwise admirably civilised pagans of Greece and their Roman successors had had the wit to laugh Judaism into desuetude, the world would have been spared the 2000-year sickness of Christendom. (Even so desirable an end, however, did not justify attempts at suppression.) But the undoing of paganism was not only its theological ludicrousness (if one may be permitted the redundancy) but also the mental mediocrity of Rome, that earlier America that also knew no remedy for fear other than brute force.

* * *

During and after the First World War almost three-quarters of the states enacted laws aimed at the IWW and banning "criminal syndicalism," which operated alongside the federal Sedition and Espionage Acts. California's criminal-syndicalism statute, which was one of the most infamous, is fairly representative of all such legislation. It defined criminal syndicalism as "any doctrine or precept advocating, teaching or aiding and abetting the commission of crime, sabotage or unlawful acts of force and violence or unlawful methods of terrorism as a means of accomplishing a change in industrial ownership or control or effecting any political change." Such legislation was exceeded in its intrinsic viciousness only by the deliberate dishonesty with which it was interpreted and enforced. *A Survey of the Workings of the Criminal-Syndicalism Law of California* by former Dean George W. Kirchwey of the Columbia Law School, published by the ACLU in 1925, documented the hundreds of prosecutions based solely on allegations of speeches made outside California, of disrespect for the flag, of unmarried cohabitation and of mere membership in organisations alleged to be committed to those objectives specified in the statute: in effect, the IWW and the Communist Labor Party.

No indictment under the California law—and few in other jurisdictions—specified alleged offenses, but rather merely repeated the statutory definitions without instancing individual utterances or advocacies (no acts were ever charged). Hence courts did not restrict the admissibility of prosecutors' evidence, and the conduct and vengefulness of district attorneys were excoriated by Dean Roscoe Pound of the Harvard Law School. On appeal, the higher courts tended to uphold the legislatures and to impute to members of proscribed organisations full knowledge of the unlawful nature of such groups merely by reason of membership, the statutes having generally omitted to require such knowledge as a condition of guilt.

Wherever possible, the American Civil Liberties Union contested such prosecutions. But they added difficulties also to another goal that the Union set itself from its foundation in 1920 and that took years to accomplish: the release of 100 wartime political prisoners of the Federal Government, as well as similar victims of state prosecutions. The Union raised $5000—half of it from a New Yorker named Robertson Trowbridge, who was incensed by imprisonments for opinion—opened an office in Washington in November, 1921, and presented to President Harding a petition signed by winners of the Congressional Medal and other war veterans, who also, with many other groups, picketed the Washington Arms Conference to call attention to the continued detention of those who had spoken against the war to make the world safe for speaking against things. The President twice received ACLU delegations; lobbying in Congress was intensive; *The New York World* mounted a special publicity campaign. As a result, twenty-five men were set free for Christmas, including Eugene V. Debs. Six of those amnestied were IWW leaders. But widespread criticism of this elementary act of justice came so violently from the press and the American Legion that the Administration stopped in its tracks.

From the first the ACLU had such powerful supporters as Senator Borah, the Idaho independent, who relied heavily on the Union for documentation of his efforts. The Union prepared a special brief on defects in the federal pardon system (such as procedural hindrances, like those requiring reports from trial judges and prosecutors, hardly cordial to any effort to undo their work) for Harding and the Justice Department; but the Attorney General, Harry Daugherty, was too concerned with Teapot Dome to heed any tempest over malcontents without money. Albert DeSilver, the rich conservative lawyer who was associate director of the ACLU, presented the case for amnesty to a hostile House Judiciary Committee in March, 1922; fifty-one members of Congress signed the ACLU's petition. But the final blow to the ACLU's hopes for the moment was delivered by Harding's conviction that the coal and railway strikes of 1922 made it unwise to set any more dangerous radicals loose. At the end of 1922 there were still sixty-three political prisoners in federal custody. But one notable ACLU victory was the release of Mrs. Mary Hunt and her two sons from the Colorado State Insane Asylum, to which they had been committed during the war for preaching the pacifism of Seventh-Day Adventism.

But the pattern set by the Federal Government remained throughout the next decade the model for most state and local action. Philadelphia—Pennsylvania, not Mississippi—led the nation in the 1920's in police censorship of speech, leaflets and meetings, though every ACLU effort to test these suppressions in court was thwarted by the refusal of the police to make arrests or raids when they had any reason to expect court tests, as well as by the tendency of minor courts to dismiss charges when an unexpected challenge was offered by the Union. The targets were not only radicals and labor; in New York City the police cut short a Town Hall lecture on birth control by Margaret Sanger. In San Francisco the police regularly raided the Marine Transport Hall and arrested all present on vagrancy charges, which were as uniformly dismissed when the men were arraigned. An action for damages against the Denver police for raiding the Labor Forum, however, won a considerable respite in that city.

One suppression of speech that was to keep the ACLU occupied for years occurred when the Bureau of Investigation, then headed by William J. Burns, who had groomed himself for his work in the Department of Justice by running a nation-wide private-detective agency that took no heed of the law but much of the profits, illegally used federal funds and power to enforce Michigan's state syndicalism law, since no federal statute would

have enabled him to raid a secret Communist meeting in Bridgman, Michigan, where William Z. Foster and twenty-two others
were arrested. Foster, an AFL organiser, had only recently become a Communist and was also a member of the national committee of the ACLU. Frank Walsh, a labor lawyer and ACLU national committeeman, won a dismissal of the charges against Foster when the jury deadlocked; another defendant, Charles J.
Ruthenberg, was convicted and lost his appeal to the United
States Supreme Court; but the cases against the rest were
dropped when the ACLU announced its intention of challenging
the statute under which the arrests had been made. The indictments were not formally dismissed until 1932.

At the same time the Union was defending the right of the Ku
Klux Klan to meet and propagandise and, while condemning the
Klan's violence against its enemies, was equally harsh with those
who would fight back illegally. In its annual report the ACLU
found it necessary, too, to explain in detail why it was going to
such lengths on behalf of an organisation with whose every objective it so violently disagreed: even among dedicated civil liber-
tarians, it appeared, there was not always such Olympian de-
tachment as their philosophy required. Yet no dispassionate an-
alyst could have found fault with the Union's defense of the Klan
then, or its support of the constitutional rights of Fascists twenty
years later, if it was to adhere to its own ideals. But at no time
was the Union faced, in the Klan cases of this period, with the
situation imposed on its radical "clients"—Charlotte Anita Whitney,
for example, the California social worker convicted of criminal
syndicalism in California solely for membership in the Communist Labor Party—for membership in the Klan was not even given
judicial notice.

The major problems, however, remained, even into the time of
Franklin Roosevelt's New Deal, those of political prisoners and of
interference with meetings and utterances. Besides amnesties and
pardons for those politicals still held—President Coolidge released
the last at Christmas, 1923—the ACLU was concerned with winning the restoration of civil rights to some 1800 persons who had
been jailed on political charges during the war and with the elimination of the onerous limitations—such as restrictions on political

activity—attached to the paroles and conditional pardons of those few prisoners who every so often were inconspicuously turned out of the federal prisons. (The case of the IWW workers convicted *en bloc* during the mass trials of 1919 is described later.) In addition the Union was constantly occupied with the treatment of those still detained, especially with respect to physical abuse and to continuing inquisitions relative to their opinions and beliefs.

Interference with speech and assemblage was sometimes founded, as in the famous Paterson silk-strike case in which Roger Baldwin was arrested under a law never before invoked since its passage in 1796, on statute, more often on whim—the Mayor of McKeesport, Pennsylvania, for instance, testified in an ACLU litigation that he had the right to forbid or break up any meeting he disliked; the Mayor of Wilkes-Barre telegraphed (collect) to the ACLU that "I shall not tolerate any meeting in this community that is opposed by the American Legion"; the chief of police of San Francisco made it known that "I will not allow any man to deny the existence of God down there on the Plaza" (whether the denial would be permitted elsewhere was not made clear); refusing to enjoin violence against ACLU representatives in Harlan County, Kentucky, Federal Judge A. M. J. Cochran ruled that the county had the right to be "protected from free speech." In San Pedro hundreds of IWW members were herded into stockades solely because of their membership; when Upton Sinclair, the novelist and social critic, led an ACLU protest, he and three aides were arrested. But the institution of unlawful-arrest suits ended the persecution, and a subsequent protest meeting drew 15,000 persons. This was the birth of the Southern California Branch of the ACLU, now the largest of all its affiliates and one of the most successful.

The most popular means of preventing meetings was through the exercise of the police licensing power. In most cities, premises available for rental for meetings had to be licensed by the municipality, which usually delegated this function to the police; in many places no meetings could be held in such privately owned premises without prior approval by the licensing authority, which in practice meant the police. Cities that lacked such legal provisions found other means to prevent the rental of halls for disapproved

meetings: they merely threatened to suspend or revoke the required licenses. In city after city the ACLU fought these license
censorships in the courts, predominantly without success in the
lower tribunals but gradually gaining ground with every appeal,
despite the howls of patriots and the violence of mobs, all of
which will be discussed presently.

The fight for the use of private halls was particularly significant in the early years of the ACLU, when very often publicly
owned property and the streets and sidewalks and parks were arbitrarily refused to every individual and organisation that dis-
pleased this or that functionary and, while these unconstitutional
bans were being fought in the courts, no other facilities were
available to unions, radicals, atheists, free-love advocates, racists
and anti-racists (depending on the locale) and, above all, free
speakers. In Newark, New Jersey, interference with the rental of
halls was ended only by the filing of two $30,000 damage suits
against the city for the arrests of Foster and Bishop Paul Jones,
and threats of similar suits after Ludwig Lore and Alexander
Trachtenberg of the Communist Party were similarly arrested—like
the first two, in halls properly rented for the meetings. The Paterson silk-strike case was a classic illustration of the consequences
of prior censorship of indoor meetings.

On October 6, 1924, the ACLU called a protest meeting in
front of the Paterson City Hall after the chief of police had suddenly forbidden the strikers' daily meetings in their own hall because of remarks made by H. M. Wicks of the Workers' (later
Communist) Party. The City Hall protest meeting was violently
broken up by the police when one of the protestants began reading the Bill of Rights to the audience. Almost immediately, as the
prosecution admitted at the trial, fifty policemen charged, wielding
their night-sticks indiscriminately, and arrested eleven persons on
charges of disorderly conduct, obstructing traffic, resisting the police and meeting without a permit. Baldwin and five strikers who
led the procession to the City Hall were charged under the ancient
law prohibiting "unlawful assembly and rout" and the indictment
accused them of employing "force of arms." At the trial it was
conceded that the only force used was that of the police and that
the purpose of the meeting—to protest the censorship of the chief

of police—was lawful; the unlawfulness consisted of the violence to which the police were compelled to resort in order to disperse the assemblage. In a trial marked by the absence not only of a jury but even of a stenographer, Baldwin and several others were convicted after the judge had held the case under advisement for almost four months.

Samuel Untermyer, a leading conservative New York lawyer who had already volunteered to prosecute Miss Whitney's appeal in the United States Supreme Court, undertook Baldwin's appeal in New Jersey but was rejected by the first appellate court there. He was succeeded by Arthur T. Vanderbilt of New Jersey, later to head the American Bar Association, who won a unanimous reversal in the Court of Errors and Appeals, which held that the protest had been a lawful one in no way satisfying the requirement of the law, which forbade only assembly to commit a crime or such as to give a "firm and courageous" man ground to believe the peace would be breached: "these constitutional mandates [for free assembly], being in favor of the liberty of the people, must be given the most liberal and comprehensive construction." Citing the trial record to the effect that the only resistance to the police had been oral protests at their orders and at their confiscation of the assemblage's American flag, that the only visible weapons had been the police night-sticks and that only two of the defenders of the law had felt the slightest apprehension of a breach of the public peace, the court found neither purpose nor action toward so vile an end.

Though the highest court of the state interpreted the law, this was to prove insufficient for Mayor Frank Hague of Jersey City, whose firm belief that "I am the law" could not be shaken until, over a decade later, the ACLU took him before the Supreme Court of the United States in a case that became a free-speech milestone. Hague claimed the right to forbid meetings and shut off speech by all whom he deemed radical or otherwise undesirable: his police intimidated the owners of halls, set up roadblocks and searched out-of-town automobiles, and escorted the unworthy to the railway station if they had entered his fief by public transportation; local subversives were dealt with *in situ*. Arthur Garfield Hays, general counsel of the ACLU with Morris L. Ernst, was the target of eggs and tomatoes when he attempted to speak in Jersey City, as was Norman Thomas, whom a young policeman escorted to the Hudson Tubes station and put on a train when Thomas attempted to address a CIO organising rally. "What you're doin' may be moral, Mr. Thomas," the policeman said amicably, "but it ain't legal here. Lotsa things that are moral ain't legal, and lotsa things that are legal ain't moral." In 1939, the 150th anniversary of the Bill of Rights, the Supreme Court extended the jurisdiction of the Constitution to Jersey City in a major victory for the ACLU and the CIO, represented by Morris Ernst, which had been joined by the new national committee on civil rights of the American Bar Association —a short-lived body emulated by a few state and local bar associations. To celebrate the victory, the ACLU, the CIO and others long banned by Hague held an open-air meeting that was not only unmolested but protected by the same police who had so often clubbed down such demonstrations. Once more Norman Thomas was escorted—this time by a chief of police asking anxiously: "Is everything all right, Mr. Thomas?"

During the whole period between the wars, the Union's intervention in court actions on behalf of freedom to meet, to speak and, less often, to publish was generally successful. Slowly, too, press sentiment began to favor the ACLU, which originally was denounced out of hand by virtually all sectors of the press as an arm of the dreaded Communists. "Sometimes we win," Hays remarked in 1932, "but we never lose." Every ACLU move on behalf of the freedoms of the First Amendment—even the steps that failed—was publicly reported, and even the defeats made new adherents and new prestige: at least the principles for which the ACLU fought were kept constantly before the public, however indifferent most of it might remain. Eminently conservative lawyers—two future presidents of the American Bar Association, Vanderbilt and Seymour, for instance; Untermyer; Wendell Willkie, head of a utility company and Republican nominee for the Presidency, who did not hesitate to serve without fee in the cause of Communists—and such progressives as Walter Nelles, Walter Pollak and Albert DeSilver, who carried to the Supreme Court the appeal of Gitlow from a conviction under New York's crim-

inal-anarchy statute, volunteered their services on behalf of the
fundamental freedoms guaranteed by the Constitution.

Even the defeats were distinguished, as in the case of Gitlow
that evoked Holmes' dissent quoted earlier. Here the law was no
less vague than the general run of criminal-syndicalism statutes:
the New York ban on criminal anarchy—which is still on the
books and was invoked in 1964 against Harlem Negroes seeking first-class citizenship: one wonders whether it would be upheld today—made it a crime to "advocate . . . the necessity or propriety of overthrowing . . . the government by force." Faithful
to Mr. Dooley, the majority of the court found that a statute pro-
scribing specific utterances did not violate the First Amendment
when it was a "reasonable" effort by the state to protect itself
against violent overthrow and that this reasonableness obviated
the applicability of the "clear and present danger" doctrine.

Most of the Union's work for the First Amendment rights in
this period, however, was less spectacular but no less effective.
Again and again, in municipalities and states, it campaigned
against repressive legislation, frequently contributing to the defeat
of new bills and the repeal of old laws; incessantly, in local courts
and in hard-fought negotiations with local officials, it established
and expanded beach-heads for the right to hire a hall, to distribute literature in the streets, to hold public meetings on sidewalks
and in parks without obstructing the normal pursuits of the citizenry, to rent publicly owned premises for controversial assem-
blages, including its own meetings. Unperturbed by the attacks
on it from those who had the greatest stake in its success, the Union shrugged off the newspaper editorials, the denunciations by
Samuel Gompers, president of the American Federation of Labor, the libels of the United Mine Workers and of Burns in his
capacity as head of the Bureau of Investigation. One of Burns'
tirades was broadcast in 1923 by a radio station that refused rebuttal time to the Union on two grounds that were to set the precedent for the pusillanimity that has ever since remained an outstanding characteristic (second only to its vulgarity) of the medium: first of all, the subject was controversial (though it must
have been equally so when Burns first broached it) and, second,
the station did not approve the Union's subject: *What Is Liberty?*

From the time of the Palmer raids on alien radicals in 1919, the Bureau of Investigation had been a major enemy of the Union, which in 1924 ingenuously assumed that the era of good feeling had arrived when Daugherty was forced out of office by the Teapot Dome scandal and took the egregious Burns with him; Harlan Fiske Stone, dean of the Columbia Law School, became Attorney General and promptly terminated the Bureau's anti-radical propaganda and, more importantly, its illegal abuses and violations of due process. Or, more correctly, he ordered these things done; and, as long as he remained Attorney General, his orders were obeyed, however reluctantly, by what was now called the Federal Bureau of Investigation. Its new head, since 1919 assistant director and in that year one of the major principals in the illegal alien round-ups (which are treated separately later), was J. Edgar Hoover, a dedicated young bachelor who for forty-five years was to be consistently identified with the conscientious flouting, often by order of Congress, of that Bill of Rights that quadrennially he swore to sustain and enforce. Under Stone, however, Hoover's subversion of the right of speech and assemblage was held to a minimum; and it must be conceded that few substantiated complaints against the FBI appear in the Union's records.

Primarily, such violations in the between-wars decades became state and local matters, in which all too often, as we shall see, the forces of self-styled law and order countenanced, when they did not seek or welcome, mob vigilantism. By protest occasionally, by court challenge most frequently, by damage actions or the threat of them quite often, the ACLU steadily strengthened the security of those who dared to dissent. Indications of the future sometimes showed: in 1927, for example, the conviction of Harold Fiske under Kansas' criminal-syndicalism statute was reversed by the Supreme Court because the only evidence offered against him was a copy of the preamble of the constitution of the IWW, of which he was a member, and this class-struggle document contained no hint of unlawful ends or means. Yet this victory for free speech was granted by the court under the due-process clause of the Fourteenth Amendment, the court finding no evidence to warrant the sinister attributions made by Kansas to Fiske and hence an unconstitutional exercise of the state's police power.

Similarly, state courts were persuaded that the delivery of a speech to a Workers' Party meeting was not criminal simply because the speaker used Russian when there was no evidence as to what he actually said. A Pennsylvania mayor was forced to rescind his ban on anti-Fascist speakers. A magnificent hoax made fools of the Dallas City Commissioners who refused to permit the Royalist League of America to meet in the municipal auditorium in order to campaign for a monarchy: ACLU intervention won a reversal of the ban and it then became known that the "Royalist League," whose choice for the throne of the United States was George Bernard Shaw, was the prankish creation of Maury Maverick, who spent his life living up to his name. Courts sometimes dared to hold that mere membership in a suspect organisation was not conclusive proof of violation of syndicalism and sedition laws.

The advent of the depression, however, undid many of the gains for freedom. Pressure for new repressive legislation increased; in the first three months of 1930 there were throughout the country 920 free-speech prosecutions, as opposed to only thirty-six in the first quarter of 1929. The ACLU's continuing efforts for the restoration of citizenship to wartime political offenders were rebuffed by President Hoover, and bills to this end in Congress died in committees. For the first time since twenty-eight states passed "red flag" laws in the hysteria of 1919, prosecution under such a statute was brought. In California, where the Better American Federation instigated a police raid on a Communist camp for children that displayed a red flag, the leader of the camp, Yetta Stromberg, was sentenced to a maximum of ten years and five other girls and a man got five years each. (A year later the Supreme Court voided the convictions and the law.) In New York City the Board of Education decided that it was improper for an advocate of civil liberties to address high-school students. Though by the end of 1930 free-speech prosecutions totaled 1630, several cities were nevertheless restricting or abolishing police censorship of meetings in rented premises, spurred by Mayor Harry A. Mackey of Philadelphia, who ended the procedure when two socially prominent women were arrested for distributing pamphlets on behalf of the North Carolina strikers held for murder. The palm for repression passed from Philadelphia to New York, which, though it had no ordinance requiring permits for street meetings, dispersed them on such pretexts as disorderly conduct, breach of the peace, obstruction of traffic, etc., and was closely followed by Los Angeles. Newark, in third place, finally made a deal with the Union and agreed not to molest meetings held without permits, provided specified locales were used. Mayor Frank Murphy of Detroit, later to be a Supreme Court justice, went farther and allocated a park area to be used with impunity, like Hyde Park Corner in London. But, as some cities barred Communist marches, others forbade Klan parades; only when the Klan insisted on marching masked did the ACLU not fight for its freedom to demonstrate.

While Seymour was preparing to carry to the Supreme Court the case of Angelo Herndon, sentenced to eighteen to twenty years under an 1866 Georgia statute for "incitement to insurrection" because he was found to possess a Communist Party card, party literature and a black skin (though none of these was specifically illegal under the state's laws), the ACLU, already concerned by the occasional invasions of the rights of the Klan, was faced with a growing list of other potential clients whose programs represented everything it opposed. The imitation Fascists got their real start with Father Charles E. Coughlin, whose early adherence to Roosevelt's New Deal soured when Saint Franklin began to discard the corporative-state models he had imported from Italy for his National Recovery Administration and to appoint to public office more Jews (and therefore international-banking Communists, by Coughlin's reasoning) than the reverend commissar of the Kingdom of Heaven thought proper. Italian pro-Fascist groups had long existed in this country, exerting considerable influence; after the emergence of Adolf Hitler in Germany they were joined by the Friends of the New Germany and the Deutsch-Amerikanischer Volksbund, which made no secret of their Naziism. Appropriating the ideologies of these and cloaking them in pure Americanism, a dozen or so similar ventures, trumpeting the perils of the Catholics, the Jews, the Negroes, the foreigners and the Communists, began in the early 1930's to compete for adherents and dues: the League for the Liberation, the Foundation for Christian Economics, Galahad College and the Galahad Fellowship Extension, the Galahad Press, the Christian

Militia, the Christian Front, the Silver Legion, the Silver Rangers, the White Legion, the Black (but lily-white) Legion, the United States Union of Fascists, the Order of '76, the American Coalition, the American Christian Defenders, the Sentinels of the Republic, the Allied Patriotic Societies, the Constitutional Education League, the National Security League, the American Vigilante Intelligence Federation, the Paul Reveres, the National Civic Federation and a bundle of Shirts—Silver, White, Gray and Khaki (the Gray were officially denominated the Pioneer American Home Protective Association). The ACLU despised them all and stood ready to defend every one against the first infringement of its right to exist, to meet and to propagandise, as it was to continue to do during and after the war, when the splinters and leftovers became such latter-day saviors as the Christian Nationalist Crusade, the Minutemen, the White Citizens' Councils, the John Birch Society, the American Nazi Party and lesser rag, tag and bobtail. In most instances the bully-boys of the 1930's never made enough headway to incur repression; some of those that did get into trouble had just enough principle to refuse the aid of such an avowed enemy as the American Civil Liberties Union; but a few, such as the Reverend Gerald L. K. Smith's pre- and post-war enterprises, accepted the Union's help provided they did not have to traffic with Jews, blacks and other radicals to be found in the ACLU's ranks.

The same bigotry that abetted the growth of these organisations flourished on the left. When Communist-led anti-Nazis broke up a pro-Hitler meeting in Boston and the prosecution of their action led to civil-liberties invasions, the International Labor Defense rejected the ACLU's offer to help because the Union had upheld the Nazis' right to meet unmolested. Neither the Communists, who were to be delighted with Herndon's ultimate victory in the Supreme Court, nor the Fascists, who were outraged by it, allowed themselves to recognise the fundamental truth that freedom can never be one-sided and survive. The ACLU, then as later, lost a few members every time its two Jewish general counsels defended a Communist or a Nazi; but every such loss was actually a profitable spontaneous purge. Adherents of both extremes opposed even as much freedom for their opponents as the "clear and present danger" doctrine allowed; but that was the standard by which the conservative Justice Owen D. Roberts struck down Herndon's conviction and the statute on which it was based as an unconstitutional infringement of the freedoms of speech and assembly. A similar Alabama law, making it illegal to pos- sess more than one copy of a radical publication, was overthrown in the first ACLU court test and was never heard of again. Crim- inal syndicalism shook its gory locks in triumph when Osmond K. Fraenkel, for the Union, won a critical victory in a Supreme Court decision (De Jonge v. Oregon) that the mere making of an admittedly lawful speech at a Communist meeting violated no constitutional law. In general, the excesses that made 1934 the worst year for repressions since the First World War were taper- ing off as the decade ended, even in states and municipalities stirred to new excesses of gag rule by the Spanish Civil War and the growth of anti-militarist sentiment, particularly among stu- dents who often found it difficult to reconcile the love of peace with the hatred of the Falange.

Other emotional conflicts—and perhaps considerations of "or- der" and of political careers—beset certain so-called liberal office- holders, notably Mayor LaGuardia of New York, who had achiev- ed progressive adulation for his fight on labor injunctions. Paying voluble tribute all his life to all forward-looking principles, he was ruthless in suppressing picketing outside foreign consulates and, even more, outside churches: "You can't picket God," he pontificated. LaGuardia's limited concept of freedom, like those of many of his admirers, was to be demonstrated again in his sanctification of academic repression and of police brutality to- ward persons of whom he did not approve. Others of like mind called on the ACLU from within and without, as passions mounted with the obvious approach of the Second World War, to declare itself against all enemies of democracy though it would continue to defend their rights; but the Union refused, as it has always done, to take any political positions on the ground that this was "outside the province of an organisation committed to the de- fense of everybody's rights without distinction." As one will see, however, the actual outbreak of war and the United States' par- ticipation in it, as well as the national paranoia that followed, were to bring serious charges that, though it had not abandoned its apolitical stand, the Union had wavered perceptibly in the universality of its commitment.

6

Danger — Ideas in Transit

What frightened the backbone of the nation and its representatives in authority even more than did the corner radical was the black-and-white magic of the printed word, augmented, as American know-how now and then got the better of American no-how, by the fearful forces of the motion picture and wireless communication. In the early years of the ACLU, the champions of things as they are did not quite dare to proceed directly against dangerous publications; instead, they mounted an oblique attack by way of the mails and the postal laws and regulations, widened later to include the customs laws; only rarely at first were they sufficiently emboldened to launch frontal assaults on the organs of communication themselves.

The successes of wartime interference with the mailing of "seditious" and pacifist literature provided the needed precedent when the road to "normalcy" was opened. One of the earliest victims was Carlo Tresca, an Italian anarchist and anti-Fascist living in New York whose fearless denunciations of Mussolini, *viva voce* and in his newspaper, *II Martello,* had earned him the enmity of every right-thinking American impressed by the value of a *régime* that made trains run on time. The Italian Embassy in Washington hated Tresca (who was finally murdered on the street in a crime that has never been officially solved) and prevailed on the State Department in 1923 to persuade the Post Office Department to lodge a criminal complaint against him, as publisher of *Il Martello,* for running a one-inch birth-control advertisement. Convicted and sentenced over the vigorous protests of the ACLU against a foreign government's interference with the rights of residents of the United States, Tresca won a commutation from President Coolidge within a year (and, on his way to New York from the Atlanta penitentiary, joined a White House reception line and shook hands with the President). Five years later a single issue of *Il Martello* was barred from the mails because it attacked the Italian delegate to an international aviation conference in Washington.

Even stickers on envelopes—like postage-meter legends since— were subject to suppression on political and personal grounds. The Anti-Imperialist League was forbidden to use labels reading *Protest Against Marine Rule in Nicaragua* (where the United States Marine Corps was in effect the major means of installing and sustaining Somoza's dictatorship); the ACLU sued for an injunction to compel the Post Office to permit the use of the labels, but the court denied the petition on the pretext that the League had initiated an equity action with hands that were unclean by reason of its "lying" exposures of the truth about Nicaragua. But, when the Fellowship of Reconciliation, a predominantly pacifist organisation, revised the stickers to read *Protest Against Marines in Nicaragua,* the Post Office did not interfere. Perhaps it was chastened by the order of the Circuit Court of Appeals that it must permit the use of labels calling for the release of Tom Mooney and Warren Billings, labor leaders serving life terms in California on a bombing charge proved false. Ten years later, under the New Deal, the Post Office prohibited Republican stickers attacking Roosevelt, as well as others saying *I Don't Read Hearst—League Against Yellow Journalism;* these were forbidden on the supposition that the late William Randolph Hearst Sr. might be offended by them. The ACLU offered its aid in both cases, but the Republicans were not interested because, the party said, it was "only [*sic*] a matter of principle."

The power of the Post Office was also invoked against the Haldeman-Julius Company's magazine, *American Freedom,* for an article entitled "Why Don't the Workers Raise Hell?" Instead, the Government did, barring it from the mails; similarly, one issue of *Revolt,* the organ of the Revolutionary Workers' League, was withheld because it quoted a single sentence from *The Communist Manifesto* of 1848! As a result, subsequent issues were delayed while postal experts on revolution pored over them. But the ACLU did succeed in compelling second-class-mailing privileges for *The Workers' Age,* published by the Communist Opposition (there were once as many Communist as Protestant sects in the United States). On the eve of this country's entry into the Second World War, the Post Office began examining all publications entering this country from abroad, not for possible subversion of the Anglo-Saxon sexual code—this was jealously guarded against foreign poison by the Customs, the Post Office protecting it only from malice domestic—but for content inimical to the postal concept of the public interest: that is, foreign anti-democratic propaganda. "While the evil should be checked," the ACLU declared, "the method by which it is done seems indefensible." Only the charitable reflection that this was a time of all-but-warlike ecstasy, however, moderates one's angry disappointment in the Union's seeming abdication of its principles at the national boundaries. It is difficult to see how the Union could continue upholding the right to propagandise from within while apparently approving efforts to throttle the same propaganda when it originated beyond the frontiers; indeed, when the hysteria of the hot war had progressed to the paranoia of the cold one, the ACLU rediscovered its properly absolutist position.

As dreaded as the mailed menace was the leaflet handed out on the street or shoved under the door. The Federal Government had prosecuted distributors of anti-draft literature in the First World War and in 1921 it convicted Joseph Baltrusaitis for handing out Communist pamphlets; his appeal to the Supreme Court was fruitless but the ACLU sought a Presidential pardon and in 1924 Coolidge quietly commuted his sentence. Three years later, in the Fiske case, as we have seen, the Supreme Court edged cautiously forward, holding that a state could not punish mere language that it had not specifically prohibited—but this grudging limitation, recalling the Gitlow case, still left a vast range for legal muzzling. Foreshadowing a problem that was later to plague the Supreme Court—whether publications distributed gratis could be distinguished, in terms of press freedom, from those sold for a price—the ACLU defeated a California prosecution for the sale of birth-control literature, contending that this freedom was indeed thus violated. The issue was to arise again and again, particularly in the case of Jehovah's Witnesses, whose publications were doubly supercharged with issues of religion and "patriotism."

Against the Witnesses, as against political radicals, states and municipalities sought to invoke laws forbidding peddling without a license, littering the streets, disturbing the peace and other antisocial actions, since they could not directly forbid the distribution of printed matter without inevitably incurring challenge on Constitutional ground. The ACLU, however, as well as the various targets of such subterfuge, joined battle on precisely the Constitutional issue that had supposedly been avoided, and the combined legal talents of Fraenkel, for the Union, and Judge Rutherford and Hayden Covington (who enjoyed the highest esteem of the Supreme Court), for the Witnesses, caused Baldwin to observe in 1964 that, of all the Union's Bill of Rights clients, "I think Jehovah's Witnesses contributed most in law," though Baldwin himself observed that he was never able to establish whole-hearted relations with this "remote sort of people wrapped up in their other-worldliness but determined to get their rights." Surprisingly numerous victories, for the Witnesses as for the Communists, were won by the Union in minor courts, where magistrates held frequently, in the words of one Newark court acquitting three men who had distributed Communist pamphlets, that "leaflets containing matter of public interest are not subject to permit regulations." But in other instances resistance was firm throughout the whole range of appellate courts; it was not until 1939 that Fraenkel won from the Supreme Court, in three Witness literature cases (Kim Young v. California, Nichols v. Massachusetts and Schneider v. Irvington, New Jersey), a decision voiding, as unconstitutional violations of the First Amendment, all local ordinances banning the distribution of literature on the pretext of preventing or punishing the littering of the streets.

Generally, courts tended to follow this view and to limit the control of content to advertising matter, but even this was rightly opposed by the ACLU. The Union did seem to turn round on itself in 1934, however, when, after Communists had broken up a Socialist rally in Madison Square Garden protesting Austrian Fascism, it excoriated them for distributing leaflets inciting pro-Communists to disrupt their rivals' rally. In condemning the actual violence employed by the Communists the ACLU's position was impregnable; but its condemnation of the exhortations hardly squared with its unremitting efforts to protect similar exhortations from prosecution.

The Union's position otherwise was broad enough to include opposition to all forms of group-libel prohibitions and advocacy of the right of anonymous publication for all individuals and organisations except those who were foreign agents or who distributed foreign propaganda. Both stands were based, like the ACLU's whole position on utterances, on the First Amendment. In dealing with so-called group libels—defamations of Negroes as a race, for example, or of Catholics, or of atheists—the Union rightly contended that to forbid or curb the publication of even false statements about a race, a religion or a class was not only to invade the protected freedom but to provide an indefeasible precedent for further restrictions that in the end would deprive one or more segments of the population of all freedom to express their views; at the same time, the Union pointed out, any natural or legal person defamed retained the common-law right of redress by an action for damages. The defense of the right of anonymity was by no means unanimous: Morris Ernst, for example, contended thirty years ago, as he does today, that everyone who makes a public utterance should be compelled to identify himself and his sponsors, whether alien or native. But the proponents of the doctrine for limited anonymity, defending the discrimination against foreign agents on the tenuous ground of "national security"—the issue was sharpest during the Second World War and its cold successor—contended that the deprivation of the right of anonymity, by exposing the protagonist of an unpopular viewpoint to persecution both official and unofficial, operated effectively to negate the Constitutional guaranty of free speech and press. The position was and remains valid, but only if stripped of its mildly xenophobic security preoccupation.

Local political censorship, lacking the power to intercept the United States mails and gradually inhibited by the watchdogs of the ACLU in its attacks on the printed word, flexed its muscles rather more in the direction of the film and the play. Heartened by the ten-year sentence imposed during the First World War on the producer of *The Spirit of '76,* the police of Providence, Rhode Island, forbade the showing of *The Fifth Year,* a film made by the Friends of Soviet Russia, in 1921 on the pretext that the proceeds might not after all, as advertised, be devoted to Russian famine relief, and this example was widely emulated. In many cities revivals of *The Birth of a Nation* were banned at the instigation of the National Association for the Advancement of Colored People, which alleged the possibility that its Klan scenes might stir racial disorders. Both the NAACP's initiative and the local surrenders to it were strongly attacked by the ACLU, which was to have to repeat the performance after the next war, when Jewish individuals and organisations as blindly sought to prevent performances of *Oliver Twist* and *The Merchant of Venice.* A major victory against ideological (as distinct from "moral") censorship of films was to be accomplished in 1952 with ACLU help, when the massed forces of the Roman Catholic Church, lay and clerical, were routed in the Supreme Court after compelling New York to ban *The Miracle* because it offended the Cardinal-Archbishop identified by Roger Peyrefitte as "chairman of the board of God, Incorporated."

The nature of the American motion-picture industry is such, however, that its products have rarely roused political apprehensions in the good burghers. Occasionally such a sport of the craft as *Salt of the Earth,* produced by a union generally denounced as Communist, has been the target of bans that the ACLU has opposed, in general with success, under the protection of the First Amendment; but the amendment's application to films was won only in repeated battles in which so-called obscenity was the *casus belli.* There was always sporadic action against Russian films because they were Russian, whether *Ten Days That Shook the World* or *Ivan the Terrible*; in the years immediately before the Second World War, a number of foreign films (and a handful of American ones) engaged the censors' and the ACLU's attention because of ideological and political considerations—*Spain in Flames, Spanish Earth, Inside Nazi Germany* (made by that dangerous radical *Apparat*, The March of Time), *Professor Mamlock,* for example, or what most infuriated the censors, *Hitler, the Beast of Berlin*—the film, that is (it was also known as *Goose Step* and *Nation in Chains*). *Spain in Flames* got by in some localities because it was held to be a newsreel and hence exempt from censorship—though Chicago, Detroit and other cities that vested censorship powers in the police regularly deleted material relating to "industrial unrest" from all newsreels. In Chicago the ACLU compelled the police to restore deletions from *Professor Mamlock* and other anti-Nazi films. *Spanish Earth* was attacked variously because of Ernest Hemingway's narration, which criticised Germany and Italy, and because of its "scenes of horror" (perfectly licit, apparently, in the contemporary blood-curdlers warranted cleansed of any stimulus to intellection). Southern cities forbade *Brewster's Millions* for "too much social equality" and *Curley, Pinky* and *Lost Boundaries* for showing blacks with whites.

The Mayor of Philadelphia banned Langston Hughes' play, *Mulatto,* as an incitement to racial prejudice (which race was not specified). Clifford Odets' *Waiting for Lefty* was always waiting for the cops as well, but they never quite pounced despite manifold threats. Strong representations by the Union prevented the Works Progress Administration's efforts to censor the first all-Negro play by its Living Theatre, *Big White Fog,* which dealt realistically with the depression's eviction riots in Chicago. But the Union could not prevent Harry Hopkins, WPA Administrator, from barring any future Living Theatre productions that might create abroad what was later to be called an unfavorable "image" of the Land of the Free; and, in protest against such gags, Elmer Rice, already active in the ACLU as well as the theatre, severed his connections with the WPA's venture into dramaturgy. Kansas, which had no theatres but was just as afraid of books, tried in vain to extradite John L. Spivak from another state because his book, *Secret Armies*, had circulated in Kansas to the detriment of the peace and dignity of the commonwealth.

Censorship of radio began with the first commercial broadcasts and one of its earliest victims, as noted, was the ACLU itself. Congress soon created the Federal Radio Commission to regulate what was to prove a perpetually infant industry; the theory underlying federal licensing of broadcasting facilities, in contrast to the freedom of the press from licensing requirements, was grounded on the finite limitations of air channels and frequencies available and hence the necessity for Government allocations in the interests of fair and free competition. That the power to license is the power to silence was soon demonstrated when the Commission threatened to refuse a license renewal to WEVD, a New York station owned and operated by the Eugene V. Debs Memorial Foundation, for purely political reasons: the Commission disapproved the Foundation's Socialist philosophy. But the attempt was aborted by a protest led by the American Civil Liberties Union, which began to turn more of its attenttion to the new medium. Censorship in the early days of broadcasting was much more unofficial than official, and against private gags the ACLU was most often helpless. Station owners' fear of public antagonism was far stronger than any principle any of them might have had, and the Union got nowhere when it protested stations' refusal to broadcast programs dealing with birth control, private industrial police, taxation, unemployment, criticisms of government on any level, or indeed any subject deemed by a station management too touchy to handle. Shortly before the end of the Hoover Administration, Congress did pass a bill to guarantee equal radio time to all political parties, but the outgoing President vetoed it.

"The enormous increase of the power of the Federal Government under New Deal policies," the Union warned in its 1933 report, "carries with it inevitable fears of inroads on the right of agitation." The NRA "voluntary codes" for the press and motion pictures rightfully alarmed the ACLU, which feared their extension to broadcasting. But the Federal Communications Act of 1934, which renamed the Federal Radio Commission the Federal Communications Commission, did not justify the fears aroused by the proto-Fascist regulations imposed on the other media: censorship of radio continued, but it was still exercised only by the industry, fearful of antagonising the Government by allowing its audiences to hear even the slightest criticism of an Administration with which radio itself was far from wholly satisfied. The new Act, supported by the ACLU, specifically excluded Government censorship and made license approvals and renewals dependent on broadcasters' meeting of the public interest. The two major networks, the National Broadcasting Co. and the Columbia Broadcasting System, gave the Union four programs that must have caused sleepless nights before and after——two dealt with mob and police terrorism in California, one was a memorial to Justice Holmes and one dealt with a two-day Washington conference on civil liberties in which a number of "questionable" organisations (the *front* designation had not yet been coined) took part.

But the new Act did not yet provide the freedom of dissent that the Union sought; and many stations simply ignored the rules. Just as the cowardice of the newsreel distributors and producers had prevented the ACLU from fighting police invasions of freedom of visual communication, the bigotry and arrogance of New York's "liberal" Mayor LaGuardia kept viewpoints off the municipally owned and operated radio station, WNYC: LaGuardia not only refused to set aside time periods for uncensored discussion (though the station was supported by the taxes of his enemies as well as his friends) but made it plain that WNYC would always pre-censor any and all "controversial" program content. The Union had better luck with the capitalist-owned WHN, which it persuaded to allow Representative Hamilton Fish Jr. to utter his baroque criticisms of the New Deal. Fish, who saw Communists under every stone, hated the Union but was delighted to have its help. But every attempt to win legislation depriving the broadcasters of their censorship power was defeated; each victory was to be local, limited to the case in hand, and no precedent was allowed to be established.

The FCC itself openly assumed the censor's *rôle* as propaganda of all kinds mounted with the approach of the Second World War: Chairman Frank R. McNinch, a Roosevelt appointee, announced that the air was closed to programs that might stir racial and religious controversy or that embodied "indecency." Big Daddy—or Big Brother, if one prefers—laid down his law and, in true paternal fashion, offered neither justification nor definition: instead, he arbitrarily gagged. "Indecency" was really not an issue, even if the term was susceptible of objective definition; but "controversy" proved a most encyclopedic word. Father Coughlin was silenced and so was his enemy, Judge Rutherford of Jehovah's Witnesses. So were the protests of the ACLU, which was equally ignored when McNinch, proving the adage about the corrupting properties of power, extended his jurisdiction to the rest of the world, decreeing that all short-wave programs originating in the United States must convey to lesser breeds only the "culture" of the United States and good will to all nations and governments (perhaps it was the short-wavers' adherence to the first requirement that was responsible for the civilised world's condescension to the "culture" of the United States), but in 1940, prodded by the Union, the FCC withdrew again within the national frontiers.

The broadcasters themselves began to grow up here and there, and the National Association of Broadcasters—membership in which was by no means universal—drew up a code of conduct, broadening opportunities for free discussion without financial cost, that heartened every civil libertarian despite continuing imperfections and despite such stations as WNEW in New York, which broke a contract with a speaker solely because he was a Communist, and WSW in Akron, which tried but failed to follow suit in order to avoid presenting a program of the Congress of Industrial Organisations. Laboratory experiments had developed the new system of frequency modulation to commercial capacity and, as both existing and new broadcasters began to envisage its use, the Union championed their cause before the FCC as providing further vehicles for freedom of speech and for that diversity of program content that was increasingly to occupy the attention of the ACLU. Even WGN, the property of *The Chicago Tribune—World's Greatest Newspaper,* which barely a decade earlier had denounced the ACLU as a made-in-Moscow hand tool wielded by an unnamed New York lawyer, broadcast a program marking—favorably!—

Civil Liberties Week, which had been proclaimed by the Mayor of Chicago.

McNinch's departure from the FCC brought about an almost revolutionary progress in freedom of speech on the air. The new chairman was James Lawrence Fly (later to be a director of the ACLU), and he shared none of his predecessor's views. From negative prohibitions the FCC's rules moved to positive requirements, all of them fully endorsed years earlier by the Union. A radio station could be construed as operating in the public interest, the FCC declared, only if it offered equal opportunity for the discussion of every side of every question; candidates in national elections were to have equal access to radio facilities even in states in which their parties did not appear on the ballot; monopoly practices in the ownership and control of the national networks were to be investigated and eliminated. The ACLU refused to subscribe blindly to the proposition that newspapers should not be allowed to own broadcasting facilities, which was being urged on the FCC; but the Union took the position that each application by a newspaper should be examined, in order to prevent a monopoly of the means of communication in any area, in terms of the availability of other organs of news and opinion in the region to be served.

Little by little, it appeared, Holmes' ideal of *free trade in ideas,* embraced from the first by the American Civil Liberties Union, was making inching gains. But the Japanese bombs of December 7, 1941, fell as damagingly on the market-place of ideas as on the ships of Pearl Harbor, and Holmes' truth that *every idea is an incitement* became a weapon for two decades of darkness instead of enlightenment. Like the American Government and the American public, the American Civil Liberties Union was caught off balance when there was no excuse, as there was none for the Government or the public; like the Government and the public, the Union was trapped by its confusion into mistakes; unlike the Government and the public, the Union learned from its own and others' errors. In the next two decades neither the Government nor public opinion saved the world from anything; but it may well be that the Union saved the nation from making even more of a collective damned fool of itself than it has thus far done.

7

"...For Our Cause It Is Just..."

For the average American and the rulers whose tenure depended on pleasing him (or bamboozling him), everything was terribly simple at the outbreak of war in September, 1939. Nazi Germany and Communist Russia were joined together against our glorious but unhelped Allies, and therefore, even though "this was not our war," all Nazis and Communists in the United States were Lucifer's legionaries *ipso facto*. The obvious way to keep it from becoming "our war" was, of course, to get rid of these elements or, if that was not feasible, to shut them up and starve them into limbo. In the wave of fifth-column hysteria that followed the German successes of the spring of 1940, they were barred by law from the WPA, public employment and even private industry in interstate commerce. Congress passed and Roosevelt signed a bill compelling the registration and fingerprinting of every alien in the country, though the Supreme Court had voided similar state and local laws; the Legislative and the Executive teamed again to produce a new Sedition Act penalising any utterance or publication that might cause disaffection in the armed forces or advocate "the overthrow of the Government by force and violence." State and local laws and orders and widespread vigilantism to the same end proliferated again as they had done in 1917: Governor E. D. Rivers of Georgia went so far as to revoke the professional and business licenses of *all* aliens in his state.

Vigorously opposed by the ACLU, the Smith Act went triumphantly through Congress and the White House, and the states as well tumbled over one another to outlaw the Communist Party. The Party, the Volksbund and the Christian Front went on trial: the prosecutions, the ACLU found, were not based on prejudice— there was enough evidence to warrant indictments—but they were studded with Government appeals to public prejudice, demands for excessive bail and unjustly long sentences. Even the Union was not immune to the national purge fever: on February 5, 1940, years of resentment of the presence of fellow-travelers in its directorate and National Committee culminated in a narrowly won resolution by the board to bar from office or employment in the American Civil Liberties Union all adherents of any kind of totalitarianism; this was followed by the bitterly contested ouster of the lone Communist director, Elizabeth Gurley Flynn, when she refused to resign. The wounds of this civil war had not wholly healed twenty-five years later—the American Civil Liberties Union of Northern California, which in practice has always been the most stringently anti-Communist of the affiliates, is still, paradoxically, the most contemptuously vocal against the formal policy of anti-Communism—despite the obvious anomaly of the presence of advocates of authoritarianism in the policy-making or -executing levels of an organisation dedicated to civil liberties. Essentially the policy is sound; one is tempted to believe that much of the opposition was and is based not so much on its substance as on the belief that any test of opinion or association is out of place in a civil-liberties organisation.

At a time when an ostensibly liberal President had ordered the FBI, which never needed the encouragement, to investigate all "subversive activities" and when the Supreme Court was upholding the so-called educators who expelled pupils for refusing to salute the flag, the Union's action is perhaps less surprising than it might otherwise have been. John Dos Passos, already embarked on the road to the right, left the National Committee because of what he viewed as continuing Communist participation in the Union's direction through the presence of such "fellow-travelers" as Corliss Lamont on the board, and DeSilver's widow, Margaret (by then the widow of Carlo Tresca as well), followed him for the same reasons, though she continued until her death to contribute $1200 a year to the Union. The Reverend Harry Ward, on the other hand, abandoned the ACLU after years as chairman of the board because he opposed the anti-Communist policy. He promptly became head of the left-wing Civil Rights Congress.

Civil liberties became an increasingly subjective concept among the key personnel of the ACLU as the war developed, changing Russia from Germany's ally to her enemy and then, after Pearl Harbor, to our staunch co-defender of democracy as well. When the Government began its round-ups of enemy aliens and the evacuation of all of Japanese origin from the West Coast, Norman Thomas came very near resigning from the Union because of what he then rightfully, and Baldwin later ruefully, called its dereliction of duty toward these new victims of persecution. Freda Kirchwey of *The Nation* left because the Union did defend Fascists; others, like Lucille Milner, long its secretary and already troubled by the 1940 resolution and the Flynn ouster, protested the Union's refusal to put the winning of the war above the fundamental rights of individuals, and resigned because they thought the ACLU should not lift a finger for what they considered enemy agents. To a degree these divisions within the Union reflected fairly accurately what was going on in a nation as self-convinced that it was going to make the world safe for democracy again as if it had never heard of the egregious *fiasco* of the earlier war and the Treaty of Versailles. What democracy meant to most Americans, apparently, was what Henry Ford had said, in another connection, a quarter-century earlier: "Any customer can have any car painted any color he wants, as long as it's black."

The Justice Department, to which control of the nation's 3,500,000 aliens was transferred in 1940 on the ground that aliens were especially given to subversion, was in general sound, the ACLU thought at the time, despite the FBI's revival of an old index of persons deemed hostile to the national interest. Frank Murphy, Attorney General until his appointment to the Supreme Court, had set up a permanent Civil Liberties Unit with investigative, though not prosecutory, powers, and his successor, Robert H. Jackson, Solicitor General Francis Biddle (long an ACLU member) and O. John Rogge, Assistant Attorney General in charge of the criminal division, had established solid reputations as men dedicated to respecting basic rights. Such men, it was believed, could be counted on to resist the FBI's demands for unprecedented powers and for the legalisation of wiretapping "for the emergency only." Roosevelt had partly restored his "liberal" standing with his rebuke to the Dies Committee (later the House Committee on un-American Activities) for publishing the membership and mailing lists of the Washington branch of the American League for Peace and Democracy, *geb.* the American League Against War and Fascism and loosely branded an instrument of Union Square if not of Moscow. The Union—independently of the fact that Ward, while its chairman, had also been chairman of the League—battled, throughout the war as it had done before and since, every effort to obtain names for the purpose of creating blacklists, and it offered its services to defend anyone defying orders to submit such information. Dies himself, after years of denunciation of the Union by innuendo, was finally compelled to make one of his rare public surrenders to reality and to admit that the ACLU was not part of any Red Menace.

But the Union's faith in the top tenants of the Justice Department proved not wholly sound. The Department sponsored the interception of foreign mail for propaganda, recommended the creation of concentration camps for aliens whose deportation was made impossible by the war, as well as the listing of organisations membership in which would ground deportation, and called for "limited" wiretapping for the duration of a war that the nation had not yet entered. Once the United States was a belligerent, Justice's troops swallowed every rumor of sabotage by Japanese-Americans and easily persuaded that great democrat, Franklin D. Roosevelt, to proclaim on February 19, 1942, the unprecedented right of the Government, without legislation or judicial determination, to remove from such areas as he might designate any and all persons, citizens or aliens, whose transfer he considered necessary for the national defense. Test cases were begun at once; the Government was reminded that the thousands of anti-Fascist refugees were hardly likely to be aiding their persecutors.

Biddle, who had become Attorney General when Jackson joined Murphy in the Supreme Court, yielded to public and political pressure and persuaded the solicitor general of the Post Office Department to bar Coughlin's *Social Justice* from the mails, whereupon it suspended publication. Three other periodicals were censored immediately after Pearl Harbor and nine persons were indicted for sedition, but the Union, beginning to recover its internal balance, questioned seriously whether in any of these cases there had been that "direct and dangerous interference with the conduct of the war" that Biddle had proclaimed as his criterion for intervention. The Union took no part in the sedition trials, awaiting the trial of each on its merits and watching for any deprivation of due process; it urged that each be judged by the "clear and present danger" doctrine. Its protest against the vesting of the power of suppression in the postal solicitor alone led Biddle to appoint an advisory board to review the *Social Justice* case, but nothing substantive was altered thereby. To the credit of the Justice Department, it did its best, under the limitations of the states'-rights doctrine, to prosecute violators of the rights of minorities.

The concentration camp so righteously denounced on alien soil made its appearance early in 1942 when Japanese-Americans were removed in wholesale lots from the West Coast—ultimately 116,-000, of whom only 46,000 were aliens, were "interned"—and the martial-law authorities in Hawaii began shipping naturalised Americans to Camp McCoy, Wisconsin, without charges or hearings. On these matters, in deference to the strong division within its Northern and Southern California affiliates, the American Civil Liberties Union was silent far too long, despite its launching of a comprehensive educational campaign for the preservation of civil rights in war time, treating a number of specific issues:

—The Union opposed all proceedings against opinions and utterances except those inciting to illegal acts (a questionable retreat from its position on peacetime utterance, raising once more the question whether civil liberties may justifiably be abridged because of war or whether they may not be even more important, if that is possible, by reason of the existence of the state of war).

—All restraints on criticism of and debate on public policies under the pretext of wartime necessity for superficial unity were also opposed.

—The ACLU supported legislation for the registration of all foreign agents and the identification of their propaganda.

—It called for an end to dismissals without hearings on vague grounds of "national security."

—It called for the maintenance of full religious liberty and of the separation of church and state, especially in the schools, and opposed all forms of compulsion on religious conscience, including salutes to the flag (but it said nothing about the right to scorn such mummery on purely philosophical non-religious grounds).

—The Union denounced all interference by the FBI and military intelligence with political expression.

—It opposed government ownership or censorship of the radio except in areas under military control or as required in international commerce.

—Censorship of domestic mail, radio and press was condemned but the Union recognised the necessity for censoring purely military information at its source.

—Curbs on strikes were opposed; voluntary mediation and arbitration were recommended. As a corollary, the Union condemned discrimination by unions for reasons of race, religion, politics or opposition to union leaders, and it opposed closed-shop contracts for unions practicing such discrimination or otherwise unreasonably restricting membership.

—The right of employers to freedom of expression was upheld except where, coupled with affirmative acts, such expression amounted to coercion of workers.

—The Union denounced all racial and religious discrimination.

—It called for unconditional asylum for genuine political refugees and opposed deportations based on opinion and any unreasonable treatment of aliens because of their opinions or origins.

—The ACLU called for the end of the poll tax as a voting prerequisite and opposed any restriction on minority parties by reason of their beliefs or advocacies.

—All rights of criminal defendants to due process of law must be enforced and defendants must be protected against the third degree, excessive bail, wiretapping, deprivation of counsel or of jury trial, etc. Compensation for wrongful arrest was demanded.

Practically, the Union had plenty of work on its hands in addition to the inevitable conscientious-objection matters. It protested —vainly—the War Department's ban on discussion of the extension of the draft by soldiers, and, with practical if not *de jure* success, a base commander's order forbidding his men to attend meetings of America First or of any other organisation, lay or religious, at which war and peace were discussed: the War Department said the commander had been misquoted with respect to religious meetings, and the order was allowed to lapse. The denial of the right of *habeas corpus* in Hawaii under martial law was taken to higher courts (the transplanted citizens were meanwhile quietly set free) but victory did not come until after the war. In deplorable acceptance of the American tradition that makes the alien a kind of missing link or lower primate, the ACLU protested Saint Franklin's evacuation proclamation as a deprivation of the citizen's right to due process, saying nothing of the alien's right to the same fundamental protections: though it demanded individual hearings for citizens designated for removal, the Union requested for aliens only examination of their records—overlooking not only the clear discrimination but the obvious fact that people who behave themselves are virtually never made the subjects of records. To find a transplanted citizen of Japanese ancestry willing to make a test case was not easy, for obvious reasons, and no Government employee fired on allegations of Communist Party membership would admit to it in order to challenge his dismissal.

Yet, in the first year after Pearl Harbor, there were only two cases of refusal of meeting space. "In San Francisco," the ACLU's annual report noted, "the War Memorial Building was denied for a debate between Sinclair Lewis and Lewis Browne on *It Can't Happen Here*, possibly just to help demonstrate that it could [Lewis wrote this novel about a Fascist *Putsch* in America; Browne was a rabbi who had lost his pulpit ten years earlier for defending Carlo Tresca's right to speak]." And, in Brooklyn, Supreme Court Justice McGeehan upheld the refusal of a meeting place to a Communist Party group. Elsewhere the Union was instrumental in assuring the rights of Socialists, America Firsters and other unlikely bedfellows in the anti-war sheets to speak their pieces on both public and private property. The Union could do nothing for pacifist teachers dismissed in California for refusing to sell "defense" stamps to their pupils (both the Treasury and the Office of Education had held teachers need not peddle these stamps if they did not wish to) because the victims refused to appeal.

Conflicts existed too within Government at all levels. The War Labor Board insisted on equal pay for equal work regardless of race; but at the same time War Manpower Commissioner Paul V. McNutt hamstrung the Fair Employment Practices Commission wherever he could. The Senate killed a bill to intern all citizens of Japanese ancestry—the Nisei—for the duration; Arkansas forbade them to own land. Despite McNutt, the FEPC ordered industry to rehire Jehovah's Witnesses dismissed because their fellows in the ranks of labor refused to work with them; the unions to which the Witnesses paid dues sat on their hands and did nothing for them. The Native Sons of the Golden West, Inc., filed and lost a taxpayers' suit to void the citizenship of all Nisei; the ACLU and Roosevelt finally won them the right to volunteer to be shot at in the army—the navy remained pure—while their families stayed in Camp Concentration. Revising its initial myopic view on the evacuations, the Union demanded—over the opposition of one-third of its directors and National Committeemen—that evacuations be conducted by civilian authorities except in the gravest emergencies, that aliens as well as citizens affected should have prior hearings for determination on the individual merits and that those evacuated be helped to resettle wherever they chose outside the zones that, the ACLU admitted, the Government had the right to delineate within the strict limits of direct necessity to the prosecution of the war or the defense of national security. Its test cases did not get far: some plaintiffs withdrew in fear of reprisals from their fellow-prisoners; and the courts were hostile. All evacuations were secret, to the disgust of the Union, which refused to endorse star-chamber procedures, and the Justice Department itself was apparently so unsure that it refused to prosecute those who defied it.

Sedition prosecutions were limited for the most part to top leaders of Left and Right organisations (after Pearl Harbor, the Left had easier going, since Soviet Russia was now by fiat a fighter for democracy), of obscure religious sects and of admittedly anti-Semitic and anti-Administration groups, as well as such malfeasants as the Negro, trapped in a military police raid on a brothel, who asked a Negro M. P. why he was "fighting for the whites" and the naturalised citizen who, in a bar, shouted: "*Viva Mussolini!*"—both of whom the ACLU helped to free.

In general, aside from the questions of aliens, sedition and opposition to the war, issues of freedom arose more from normal conflicts, though these were often aggravated by wartime pressures; this was particularly true of strikes and of racialism. Labor and management had made any number of pretty pronouncements on their common interest in winning the war to the subordination of all other interests; every strike or threat of a strike, therefore, regardless of its causes, became tainted with "lack of patriotism" and the ACLU had often to defend basic labor rights that had nothing to do with the prosecution of the crusade. The mob prejudice against the Japanese-Americans—which did not abate when the Government, in 1943, began to ease its restrictions, or later, when it lifted the ban on their returning to the West Coast and the requirement for army clearance on their attendance at colleges—easily slopped over to include Mexican-Americans; anti-Negro sentiment intensified whenever a black man took exception to segregation from the master race in camp and battlefield, or was presumptuous enough to suggest that the necessities of life cost him as much as anyone else. Though the United States Supreme Court ruled in 1944 that it was unlawful to detain "loyal" American citizens in concentration camps (saying nothing about "loyal" non-citizens), the Nisei for whom this victory was gained found it largely a paper one when they tried to return to homes and businesses that had often been bought out from under them at ridiculously low prices and with unchallengeable "legality"; nor did they find their former neighbors impressed with what nine men in Washington had said. The original evacuations *en masse* were upheld by the court, despite notable dissents by Murphy, Jackson and Roberts, on the ground of military necessity. Toward the end of the war the Negro too made token gains, when the army began to curb segregation and the navy recognised that black-skinned sailors—provided they did not bunk or work with whites—could do something besides cook, wait on table and swab decks.

Continuing its efforts to ameliorate these and other injustices of the here and now, the ACLU was already looking to the ultimate end of the war and the old and new problems of peace. Official and unofficial advocacy of the continuation of conscription after the end of the war brought a Union declaration against any peacetime draft. Federal action during the war to bar monopolies in the press (an anti-trust action against The Associated Press), the motion pictures (a similar proceeding against the producers' association) and broadcasting (curbs on the networks' monopolistic practices) opened a totally new field for the Union, which had always envisaged only government as the real menace to civil liberties; it began now to contest the restraints on freedom of communication created by private monopolies and concentrations of private power.

Largely influenced by Baldwin, whose interest in the international aspects of human rights was rapidly mounting, the ACLU began to concern itself with civil liberties beyond the continental United States. It had always occupied itself with the enforcement of constitutional and moral rights in the American colonies — Guam, Samoa, the Philippines, the Virgin Islands, Puerto Rico—and territories; it had already involved itself in the problems of refugees in the United States. The progress of the war brought forward the prospect of new American colonies, of more refugees here and elsewhere, of military occupation of conquered areas. In addition, working with the State Department and with delegates to the organising conference of the United Nations in San Francisco, the Union began to advance proposals for what it called an "international bill of rights" intended to safeguard everywhere those rights guaranteed to Americans by the Constitution and its amendments; much of this was later to be embodied in the UN's Universal Declaration of the Rights of Man, to which the world's champions of democracy on both sides of both oceans show no unseemly haste to adhere. The Union's insistence on the inclusion of world-wide guaranties of freedom of all communications media and of freedom of travel for all journalists and students was particularly opposed at home when the need for such guaranties was most emphasised by the exclusion or censorship of American reporters in Yugoslavia, Eastern Europe, Chiang Kai-shek's China (he was really in China then) and parts of the British Empire—curbs vigorously protested by the Union to the State Department, which shrugged.

The end of the war did not abate the civil-liberties problems raised by its beginning. The ACLU—which had been shocked to hear Mayor LaGuardia howl against any proposals to resettle Nisei in his city; which had had to fight to prevent the mass ouster of Germans and Italians from the East Coast, and which had had to defeat Arizona's effort to ban Nisei from forming business associations with pure Caucasians—had now to combat the most virulent discrimination, to say nothing of outright terrorism, against Japanese returning to their West Coast homes, though violence was stemmed in part through the cooperation of California sheriffs in publicising the ACLU's offer of $1000 rewards for the convictions of offenders. The Union also backed bills in Congress and the states to compensate the Japanese for the property losses suffered while they were in the concentration camps, one of which, at Tule Lake, still held 5500 persons. Some were aliens; some had renounced American citizenship out of resentment at their treatment or under duress from the American Government or from other inmates; some had the ill luck to be related to renunciants. Some 1500 private lawsuits for the restoration of their rights were backed by the ACLU; the Justice Department began to review each case and in the end only 450 were held for court action.

But probably the biggest civil-liberties issue to follow the war resulted from the revulsion against Government controls and from the hysterical fear of "our Soviet ally" that rolled in waves across the nation even before the German surrender and that branded virtually all foreigners Communists. Aggravated by a foreign policy that trumpeted its intention of stemming the growth of Russian influence in other countries—as if the United States had a right to interfere in their affairs—the hysteria degenerated rapidly into a paranoia that was to present the ACLU with a whole new set of problems.

8

Foreign Devils

"A kike," my father explained to me when, as a small boy, I asked him why one of my congeners in the synagogue had thus addressed me, "is any Jew but oneself." Similarly, one supposes, a foreigner, in this country established entirely of the immigrant, by the immigrant and for the immigrant, is any American but oneself. It is a curious law that xenophobia flourishes most in those who have most to fear from other xenophobes; the most recent arrival in the United States is almost invariably the loudest advocate of keeping the (other) foreigners out, the shrillest to attribute every new castastrophe to the influx of un-American aliens. Hence, despite NCLB opposition, it was easy to enact in 1917 the first laws setting quotas and barring aliens for their views.

That aliens were by their nature un-American was proved by the First World War (launched by Germans), the October Revolution (carried out by Russians and Jews, considered by the unlettered a separate race or nation), Texas border raids (the work of Mexicans), strikes (instigated by Irish, Germans, Italians, Russians, Poles, Czechs, Hungarians—oh, yes, and Jews), pacifism (practiced by Quakers, Amish, Mennonites and

so on) and Socialism and anarchism (preached by all the preceding). Hence the end of the First World War, during which
aliens had been the victims of a two-year open season, brought
a flood of state and federal bills to prevent and punish sedition, treason and revolution in peacetime, for all of which, under the currently prevalent article of faith, aliens must be responsible. While the National Civil Liberties Bureau was seeking
funds and allies to combat these bills, an epidemic of bombing broke out across the country. The targets were, uniformly,
high officials, including the Quaker Attorney General of the
United States, A. Mitchell Palmer, who had opposed virtually
all the repressive legislation being shoveled into Congress. The
bomb planted on his Washington porch on June 2, 1919, did
not injure Palmer but it did disintegrate the bomber; parts of
him, insufficient for identification, were hurled across the street
on to the steps of Assistant Secretary of the Navy Franklin
D. Roosevelt.

Neither Palmer's attacker nor any of the other bombers was
ever identified; the Justice Department could not even precisely
ascertain their motives, though a leaflet found near Palmer's
house indicated an anarchist plot. Palmer concluded immediately
that *anarchist* meant *alien*—both, after all, begin with *a*. The
NCLB was inclined to agree with Max Eastman that the bomb
attacks were "a frame-up by those who are interested in 'getting' the leaders of radicalism." Palmer brushed aside such in-
sinuations and, having no law at his command but the deportation statute and being still opposed to a sedition law, he asked
Congress for $500,000 to establish a "General Intelligence Di-
vision" or "radical squad" in his department. He got the money
at once, to the applause of the public, which clamored more
loudly than ever for harsh legislation. With his new money, Palmer quickly "determined" that there were 60,000 revolutionists
in the country and virtually all of them, of course, were foreigners. Palmer wanted a law that would enable him to deport them
without exception, but he opposed most of the sedition bills,
which were drastic enough to outlaw all strikes, make it a crime
for a Republican to vote against a Democrat and penalise any
expression of hatred for a janitor in a public building.

Even after Palmer began fulminating, the Labor Department was reluctant to deport aliens merely for their opinions; Secretary of Labor William B. Wilson (not related to the President) ruled specifically that membership in the IWW, the biggest radical organisation (neither the Communist Party nor the Communist Labor Party was so strong then), was not a deportable offense. But the great American public scorned such lenity, and the resignation of Frederic Howe, Commissioner of Immigration, gave Palmer his chance. In October he told Secretary Wilson that his radical squad had found that the Union of Russian Workers advocated violent revolution; Palmer urged the deportation of the entire membership and Wilson, no longer restrained by Howe, granted the required warrants in November, 1919.

On November 7, J. Edgar Hoover led the first of what were to become infamous as the Palmer raids. Hundreds of URW members in several cities were seized in simultaneous bloody assaults protested by Isaac Shorr, an immigration lawyer and partner of Walter Nelles, counsel to the NCLB, who itemised to Hoover the destruction of property and the physical brutalities inflicted by his agents. Instead of even offering *pro forma* to investigate, Hoover, characteristically, countered by charging that Shorr should "be disbarred from further practice before the immigration authorities"; nor did Hoover shift ground when even *The New York Times*, which thoroughly approved the raids, reported without qualification the record of the savageries of Justice.

On December 21 the S. S. Buford sailed out of New York with a complement of 249 "undesirables"—184 members of the Union of Russian Workers, fifty-one anarchists, including Emma Goldman and Alexander Berkman, and fourteen miscellaneous. Wilson had ordered the deportations of men with families stayed, but he had done nothing to enforce the order. Later Louis F. Post, Assistant Secretary of Labor, admitted that the order had been totally flouted, separating dozens of families from husbands and fathers. Since the United States was then invading Soviet Russia, it was a simple matter to ship the entire cargo of the Buford there. The public was delighted, and fan mail poured in on Palmer, who promised repeat performances. "Shoot them or ship them—either will cure." one admirer wrote, and Palmer, in reply, called the support of such "substantial citizens" a "source of great encouragement."

So it must have been, for in that same December Hoover asked for 3000 more arrest warrants against members of the Communist and Communist Labor Parties, both of which had left the Socialists and supported international revolution. Wilson granted the request despite the practical difficulties of handling so much merchandise at once; he urged Palmer to deal in retail lots but Palmer insisted he was going to pick up the whole cargo on the night of January 2, 1920, before any could flee. Hoover was the field commander, and he gave orders to his stool-pigeons "to have meetings of the Communist Party and the Communist Labor Party held on the night set." Mere membership was relied on as sufficient ground for deportation, and the same Hoover who was to swear a dozen times to enforce the laws and the Constitution instructed his men to search meeting places and homes for documentary proof of membership but not to use warrants unless "absolutely necessary." (At this writing, J. Edgar Hoover still heads the Federal Bureau of Investigation, having ostensibly enjoyed the misplaced confidence of the protection-hungry American people and of Presidents Wilson, Harding, Coolidge, Hoover, Roosevelt, Truman, Eisenhower, Kennedy and Johnson—a remarkable tribute to the devotion of these assorted statesmen to the rights of man.)

Palmer and Hoover did even better than they had promised. In two weeks they harvested 6000 persons, citizens and aliens, Communists and non-Communists, raiding all kinds of meeting-places and then destroying them. IWW members caught up in the reaping machine were curtly turned loose a week later, as were citizens and non-Communist aliens. Those detained were denied counsel. Letters describing beatings and unsanitary conditions—800 persons in Detroit were held for days in a windowless corridor with one toilet and no sinks or bathtubs—were indignantly denied by Hoover; Palmer later defended the deprivation of counsel on the ground that, if the aliens were allowed their rights, he could "get nowhere." Hence he had felt justified in holding his victims *incommunicado* for weeks. Swinburne Hale, Nelles' law partner, conscripted twelve lawyers led by Professors Zechariah Chafee Jr. and Felix Frankfurter of Harvard Law School, as well as Dean Roscoe Pound; they issued a courageous pamphlet itemising the illegalities committed by the Government. Post, acting for Secretary Wilson in the latter's illness, began canceling deportation warrants by the bale after releasing Thomas Truss, who had been arrested without a warrant, who was never told that his testimony would be used against him and who did not know the full aims of the Communist Party or the fact that it was a forbidden organisation. Post ruled that no alien could be deported unless he knew he was a member of a prohibited group. Wilson, back on the job and thoroughly embarrassed, ordered a hearing for Carl Miller of the Communist Labor Party and freed him on the ground that no alien could be deported for CLP membership because, unlike the CP, the CLP had not required its members to swear allegiance to the revolutionary principles of the Third International though the party itself was an adherent.

Palmer tried to have Post ousted because of his "tender solicitude for social revolution and perverted sympathy for the criminal anarchists." The Attorney General also denounced the twelve lawyers who had believed aliens' affidavits and their own knowledge rather than the perjured testimony of Hoover's men. "I should prefer," Palmer declaimed, "to take the word . . . of these splendid men, these real Americans . . . rather than the statements of these aliens." DeSilver, a real American whose ancestry went back to the American Revolution, helped to prove the charges against Palmer, which, ignored by the House Rules Committee in its investigation, included not only searches and seizures without warrants but also forced self-incrimination without counsel and cruel and unusual punishments, thus violating the Fourth, Fifth, Sixth and Eighth Amendments. The NCLB had now become the ACLU and, providing associate counsel and arranging for newspaper coverage, overthrew Palmer in the first major court test, Colyer v. Skeffington. Federal Judge George W. Anderson freed fourteen alien CP members and ruled that CP membership alone was not sufficient ground for deportation. In addition, Judge Anderson found that Palmer's and Hoover's men had committed not only all the crimes charged to them by the twelve lawyers but some others as well: Hoover's henchmen had infiltrated the Communist Party (this was 1920, not 1965, when FBI men account for about half the total CP membership) and often written the policy declarations on the basis of which the Government built its case! Even Senator Thomas J. Walsh, a Montana Democrat who had been tempted to see alien radicals on every corner, was appalled and, in his report to the Senate on *Illegal Practices of the Justice Department*, he said: "If the constitutional guaranties which are the fundamentals of our liberties are not available in times of hysteria or public excitement, or when passions run riot, they are useless to us."

The ACLU was determined to see to it that these guaranties did not become useless, and hence Hoover's boss, Burns, considered the Union one of the most dangerous radical organisations in the country and one on which it was his duty to keep an eye (though there is no record of successful FBI infiltration into the ACLU). Despite Judge Anderson and Senator Walsh, Burns and Hoover, retained in office when President Harding took office and replaced Palmer with Daugherty, continued all their illegal practices, attending every "radical" meeting possible and circulating reports on each to all the Bureau of Investigation offices. While it was to be two years before any new mass action was initiated against "alien radicals" (the Bridgman raid, described earlier), the ACLU found plenty of work on behalf of aliens already persecuted. One such, who had committed the crime of joining a labor union, was not even an alien, the ACLU proved after his deportation: it won his re-entry to the United States by showing that, under the law as it then stood, he had derived citizenship through the naturalisation of his stepfather while the so-called alien was still a minor. Another, held for deportation for more than a year because he had once belonged to the IWW, was finally freed because he had not been deported, as the law required, within a reasonable time of his arrest. Meanwhile the Union continued its campaign to end all political deportations and raised funds for the help of aliens in detention and awaiting shipment abroad as the result of their wartime convictions; it failed to dissuade Secretary of State Charles Evans Hughes from forbidding the re-entry of the Russian-born radical wife of an American citizen.

To a degree the ACLU succeeded in its battle to extend the rights of human beings to foreigners. In 1924 it won the elimination of a rider to a new immigration bill that would have upset the whole tradition of Anglo-American law by requiring an alien held for deportation to prove that he had the right to remain here, rather than compelling the Government to prove its charge that he had none. The new law also reversed the State Department by allowing foreign-born wives of citizens to enter the country. While there was no hope of eliminating the principle of political deportation, one success was scored when the Government was prevented from deporting a number of Ukrainians under the cover of false passports issued by a self-styled Ukrainian Mission in Washington: one of the Ukrainians had been sent to Europe three times with one of these unasked documents and returned here each time because the country of destination refused to honor the fake paper. Circumstances provided another gain for common decency when the Teapot Dome scandals forced Daugherty out of office and Harlan Fiske Stone, Dean of Columbia Law School, became Attorney General. Stone, a man of principle, at once ordered Burns and Hoover to stop their propaganda against "radicals" and to abandon their wanton violations of the law and the Constitution. That Hoover, who succeeded Burns in 1925 as head of the renamed FBI, paid no attention to his superior was to be amply demonstrated six years later in the so-called Wickersham Report of the National Commission on Law Observance and Enforcement, appointed by President Hoover.

The Justice Department, however, was not alone in its inglorious mockery of American pretensions of freedom for all to enter. In 1925 the State Department, under pressure from local patriots and foreign governments, barred the Earl and Countess of Carnarvon—the Earl, an archeologist, had discovered the tomb of King Tutankhamen in Egypt—for "moral turpitude" because one of them had been involved in a British divorce (at that time Britain allowed divorce only for adultery); it refused to admit Arthur Henderson of Britain because he had been elected to Parliament as a Communist and it barred Shapurji Saklatvala on the same ground. Count Michael Karolyi of Hungary sought to join his Countess in New York, where she had become ill on the eve of a lecture tour, and the State Department banned his entry, totally without explanation, unless the first President of the Hungarian Republic agreed to abstain from all speech-making and political activity in this country. When the Karolyis had gone on to Canada, the Count declared that the State Department had acted on the plea of Admiral Horthy, the Hungarian Regent who had overthrown the Republic and who feared that Karolyi's disclosures of the truth about Hungary would imperil American financial aid to Horthy's dictatorship (which was later to expire in the arms of Hitler's). Arthur Garfield Hays, general counsel, won the Carnarvon case by proving that the adultery was not a crime in South Africa, where it had occurred. The ACLU delegated Ernst to seek to win admission for Henderson, Saklatvala and the Karolyis without strings. At the same time, and with equal unsuccess, Senator Borah introduced a bill to strip the State Department of its wartime jurisdiction over entry visas and restore the power to Labor.

Naturalisation of aliens safely within the country was also hedged with political obstructions. Though one court had found no violation of law in IWW membership, another decreed that such allegiance made naturalisation impossible. An IWW member naturalised in 1907 was denaturalised twenty years later because of his membership, but the Union won a reversal of the order on appeal to the courts. A Quaker woman was barred from citizenship for refusing, if she ever changed sex, to bear arms. Yet a Federal Judge in Michigan refused to void the naturalisation of a man accused of lack of attachment to the principles of the Constitution, evidenced by speeches against Government policies: the court held it to be the right of every citizen to agitate lawfully for the revision of Government aims and procedures.

Loss of citizenship for political reasons frequently meant deportation, which, in the case of natives of Russia, was impracticable, since this country maintained no diplomatic relations with the Soviet Union. Russians held for deportation, or under bail pending shipment, were therefore so continued indefinitely, and the Union fought for the release of their persons or their bonds, as circumstances indicated. But it was 1928 before the first such battle was won, after the bail had been maintained for four years. Other victories were scored piecemeal, on behalf of aliens facing physical persecution or death in their native countries: the Union gained permission for some to remain and for others to be sent to countries, other than their own, that were not afraid to allow dissidents to cross their borders. In one case the Union had to be called in to bar the deportation of a British subject, who happened to be a bishop and black, solely because he had spoken out for the rights of labor and criticised the continuing American naval rule of the Virgin Islands.

In 1931, almost simultaneously with the issuance of the Wickersham Report, the Government resumed its round-ups of aliens, allegedly limiting its targets to those illegally in the country. Few were to be deported solely on the basis of their opinions; in those few cases the Union did not contest the deportation of Communists for being Communists because that fight was foredoomed, but confined itself to those instances in which the deportee faced shipment to a country where he would be imprisoned or executed for his views. The Labor Department refused to let Communists try to go to Russia. The federal round-up received state assistance as Michigan pioneered in the state alien-registration legislation that was to be voided by the Supreme Court, and turned over the illegal entrants to the Federal Government. Former Attorney General George W. Wickersham's report on the administration of the whole alien program was damning.

Methods of arrest and examination, it stated with documentation, were often unconstitutional, tyrannical and oppressive. Deportation was frequently precipitate, ordered and carried out despite the fact that further investigation would have shown the alien's right to remain; families were arbitrarily broken up in violation of all humanity. The immigration machinery was over-centralised and over-burdened; the lack of public findings made it impossible to build up a body of administrative law. Immigration inspectors, Wickersham concluded, were as a rule totally unqualified for their work, particularly since the bureau was a government agency that sat in judgment on its own acts and agents. Finally, the economic position of most of its victims was such that counsel and the proper protection of their rights were automatically precluded; and furthermore the Labor Department, even when it might wish to do so, lacked the legal discretion to prevent unnecessary hardship. Wickersham's recommendations for the correction of these evils (not all were to be adopted, of course) emphasised not only better personnel and adherence to the law but also the creation of an independent Presidential board of appeals, the provision of adequate defense facilities to protect the rights of all suspects and permission for deportees facing persecution in their own countries to elect to go elsewhere at their own expense (though why they should be made to pay for being thrown out escapes comprehension: it is as grotesque as billing prisoners for their rent and food).

The last provision took effect *de facto*, if not *de jure*, almost immediately. In a number of cases the ACLU won Communist deportees the right to go to Russia instead of Spain, Italy or China. One of these enlisted the interest of William J. Donovan, former Assistant Attorney General and later head of the Office of Strategic Services, who offered to serve the ACLU without charge. His appearance in the case shocked the Labor Department into reviewing its whole policy and voluntarily instituting alternate destinations for deportees facing persecution. The Union won again when it compelled the release of all facing deportation to Russia itself; and it made rather a fool of the Government when it assisted Mohammed al Raschid of New York to prove, after a number of trans-ocean trips to countries that refused to accept him, that he was a true-blue red-blooded native of the United States: a Turkish royal prince, he had been born in Brooklyn when his parents were living there.

ACLU attempts to test the depression-born ban on working permits for aliens here as students were thwarted in every instance by the Labor Department's making a special exception. But Secretary of Labor Wilbur Doak loudly endorsed the campaign by the American Federation of Labor to force foreigners out of employment and hand over their jobs to good native stock, yelled equally loudly at the presumably alien-dominated left-wing unions to which the brotherhood of labor meant somewhat more than it did to the monopolists of the AFL, and then had to go out of office when Roosevelt was inaugurated and replaced Doak with Frances Perkins, a member of the ACLU. All pending cases were reviewed with her; she put an end to the fingerprinting of incoming aliens, abolished her department's secret-service division and announced that Wickersham's recommendations would be adopted and agents violating them would be dismissed. The law, however, remained unchanged; among the cases under it inherited by Miss Perkins was the arrest of forty-two persons in White Plains, New York, on suspicion of illegal entry as the result of a raid made without warrants on spectators at a court hearing. This had spurred the Union to create, under LaGuardia's then law partner, the late Vito Marcantonio, a Committee on Aliens' Civil Rights. Similar actions without warrants had been taken against a textile-union local in Providence and, aided by the customary stool-pigeon, an organisation of aliens in San Antonio.

Roosevelt and Hitler took office in the same week of 1933. Almost immediately the efflux of refugees from Germany began, and the ACLU added them to the Russian and Italian *émigrés* with whose rights it was already occupied. But, despite the Union's activities on behalf of all refugees, Roosevelt signed a bill severely limiting political asylum in this country: in practical effect, the legislation opened the door only to White Russians. But this did not prevent Roosevelt, a few years later, from sanctimoniously calling on all the other democracies (to use a convenient catchword) to welcome any and all refugees—presumably including those whom the United States would not admit because of its infamous immigration quotas. But in the first afterglow of Roosevelt's accession to power there was some easing of curbs on those who could be relied on to be mere birds of passage. Holders of student visas were allowed to work; known radicals received visitors' visas even when it was certain that they would utter their pernicious views. So Tom Mann, a British Communist, and Henri Barbusse, chairman of the French section of the International League Against War and Fascism (a largely but by no means dominantly Communist united front with such national offshoots as the American League Against War and Fascism), moved and spoke freely through such of the United States as dared to listen. Even Emma Goldman, once deported for her fearsome anarchism, was allowed to come back to see her relatives and deliver lectures.

The middle years of Roosevelt's first term were in general the worst period of local repression of rights and liberties since the war, but the alien, on the whole, came off relatively lightly. In part this must be credited to the report made by the Commissioner General of Immigration, Colonel Daniel W. MacCormack, who made it his business to analyse exhaustively all data available on the wave of strikes that marked the period and who informed the nation that an infinitesimal number of the "agitators" were in fact foreigners; he suggested that those alarmed by "agitation" would do well to examine their fellow-natives. MacCormack was incensed when his agents in Hackensack allowed struck employers to accompany them along a picket line, single out all "alien" pickets and supply trucks in which to cart them off for questioning. On this as on all substantiated charges by the Union the Immigration Service acted promptly and fairly. Spurred by Hearst and other professional patriots, the Labor Department tried to deport John Strachey when the British M.P., generally branded a Communist, arrived for a lecture tour, but the whole American press, except Hearst and Bernarr Macfadden, upheld his right to speak. The ACLU defended him, but Strachey abandoned his project.

Denials of citizenship took on a new aspect when naturalisation was arbitrarily refused by a federal court to any alien receiving relief benefits—a denial that did not long stand up. Pacifists here and there were being admitted to citizenship; but two members of the International Workers' Order were refused on the ground that the group was Communist-led, even after the Labor Department's solicitor had ruled that it was not. In a more or less academic echo of the Strachey case, the Circuit Court of Appeals held that a United States consul could not revoke an entry visa once it had been granted. At the same time when Roosevelt, by proclamation, was indefinitely extending the visitors' visas of refugees, the same imminence of war that motivated the President caused the tribunes of the people in the House of Representatives to pass a bill (which died in the Senate) providing for the deportation of any alien advocating any change at all in the American form of government.

Such sentiment, while it may not always have solidified itself into statute, was responsible for the eight-year fight to deport Harry Bridges, Australian-born president of the West Coast longshore union, who could never be proved to be a Communist or other species of "subversive" but who was generally so deemed by all the right-thinkers. Bridges was so feared, and therefore hated, that a bill was introduced in Congress with the sole aim of deporting him. The battle began before the Second World War and ended when the war did: Bridges was accused of having been a Communist, even if he no longer held a card, and of having aided and abetted various so-called Communist-front organisations and causes. Bridges, if he was not a Communist, was therefore guilty by association, and the lives and fortunes of 140,000,000 Americans were jeopardised by every day of his sojourn here. While it was advising the defense in the Bridges case, the Union won a major triumph in a citizenship battle that was closely related: the Schneiderman case, in which Wendell Willkie served without fee to argue in the Supreme Court.

Schneiderman's naturalisation was attacked on the ground that at the time of its issuance he had been a member of the Communist Party and therefore he must be an advocate of the overthrow of the Government by force. The Justice Department argued, and the trial court found, that this advocacy must be imputed to him by reason of his membership; but the Supreme Court held that citizenship could not be revoked without proof that a defendant had personally advocated illegal doctrines. The Court ruled similarly for one Baumgartner, who voiced mere pro-Hitler statements before and after naturalisation but who uttered no actual advocacy. In both these cases relating to naturalisation the court rejected guilt by association.

In effect it did so once more in 1945 in the Bridges appeal. Though the court avoided the issue of Congressional power over deportation by concluding that the Justice Department was estopped from deporting him by reason of having denied him a fair hearing at which he could confront and cross-examine his accusers and inspect the evidence against him, Justice Murphy's concurring opinion voiced the Union's view that Congress' exercise of the power to deport was limited by the Bill of Rights and that the proceedings against Bridges violated the Constitution because he had done nothing except to "exercise his personal right to free speech and association." Deportation even for membership in an organisation advocating the overthrow of the Government, Murphy declared, was inadmissible except on proof of a "clear and present danger" that the organisation's activities might produce the overthrow. Of Bridges' alleged danger to the nation Murphy said:

"Deportation, with all its grave consequences, should not be sanctioned on such weak and unconvincing proof of a real and imminent threat to our national security. Congress has ample power to protect the United States from internal revolution and anarchy without abandoning the ideals of freedom and tolerance. We as a nation lose part of our greatness whenever we deport or punish those who merely exercise their freedoms in an unpopular though innocuous manner. The strength of this nation is weakened more by those who suppress the freedom of others than by those who are allowed freely to think and act as their consciences dictate."

Aliens less influential and less dramatic than Bridges and Schneiderman had troubles no less grave, and they too found help in the ACLU. During the war many Latin-American countries had sent internees of German and Italian origin here for storage; when the war ended the State Department insisted these people should go back not to their homes but to the countries in which they had been born, on the ground that they had entered the United States illegally! The Union's protests and publicity aborted this injustice, as earlier it had prevented the deportation of an anti-Nazi refugee accused of "moral turpitude" consisting of a sentence in a concentration camp for violation of food-rationing rules. In western states ACLU pressure helped to gain the repeal of land-transfer and -use laws barring "aliens ineligible for citizenship"—i.e., Orientals—and of similar laws depriving them of hunting and fishing licenses. A California hotel keeper became the only man ever to claim—and receive—a reward offered by the Union when his information to a sheriff resulted in a twelve-month sentence for a Caucasian who fired shots into the houses of two Japanese.

This gunman's mentality, in only slightly more refined form, was fairly representative: not only did the Government indict eleven Communist Party leaders under the Smith Act, on the basis of the party's traditional doctrines, but it rounded up more than forty alien Communists who had lived here many years and who now faced deportation for their opinions just as if the Bridges case had never been appealed or Murphy had written his opinion on snow. The Internal Security Act of 1950—the McCarran Act— was in the womb of Congress; the Justice Department was refusing visitors' visas to presumed Communists—without hearings—even when they were on official missions for the United Nations; the Supreme Court refused to review the Attorney General's order to deport 530 German enemy aliens—after the war—under a 1798 law vesting such power in the Executive and attacked by the Union as unconstitutional; a Circuit Court of Appeals was denying citizenship to an alien who did not believe in capitalism, though no native-born citizen could be penalised for this heresy. But native Americans closely related to aliens, regardless of the foreigners' beliefs, were classified as security risks if such ill-advised Americans worked for the Departments of State, the Army or the Navy or for the Atomic Energy Commission.

"The imagined insecurity of the strongest democracy in the world in the face of the cold war with Communism," the Union declared in 1949, "has created an atomosphere in which fear makes the maintenance of civil liberties precarious." Unofficial delegates to a peace conference in the Waldorf-Astoria were refused visas; the official delegates were forbidden to make a nation-wide tour under the auspices of the National Association of Manufacturers. Two aliens planning to make a speaking tour with former Vice President Henry Wallace, 1948 Presidential candidate of the Progressive Party, were stopped at the border; Walter Gieseking was not allowed to play Debussy because Gieseking had a Nazi record. Congress was considering a bill for the permanent detention of deportees whom no country would accept. A naturalised citizen who had spent more than five years abroad was denaturalised and the Union's challenge failed in court: the Union contended that the Constitution forbade distinctions between native and naturalised citizens. More than a decade later, the ACLU was at last to win the Supreme Court's recognition of the equality of all citizenship, whether acquired by the accident of birth or by the exercise of choice and effort.

The outbreak of fighting in Korea was in effect the Caesarean section that brought the McCarran Act into the world, despite the vigorous opposition of the ACLU, which called it the worst invasion of individual rights since the Alien and Sedition Acts of 1798. Its provisions with respect to aliens already here or seeking entry were incredible. First of all, it barred visas for everyone who had ever belonged to any "totalitarian" organization anywhere (a special bill passed in 1951 modified this ban to permit the issuance of visas to "nominal" totalitarians—interpreted in practice to admit, properly, those who had more or less had to be members of Fascist parties but, improperly, not to apply the same exception to those who held Communist cards under the same conditions). Any alien already in residence who had at any time in his life belonged to an organization now required to register as subversive was subject to deportation, and any alien seeking entry who might be expected (how and on what ground and by whom was not provided for) to join such a group must be rejected. Citizens of countries refusing to accept America's deportees were ineligible for even visitors' visas. Any alien who, within ten years of the enactment of the law, had been in any prohibited category could never be naturalised; members of "front" organisations could not be naturalised unless they could overcome the statutory presumption that they were hostile to the Constitution; joining a "front" within five years after naturalisation created a presumption of fraud and citizenship could be revoked unless the defendant could prove himself innocent. President Truman vetoed the entire bill (whose other provisions against malice domestic are discussed in another chapter) and it was re-enacted over his veto.

Specifically, the law ruled out any recantations of past sins. The Secretary of State was stripped of his discretion to waive visa requirements with respect to aliens in any excludable categories. The Attorney General was not merely empowered but directed to deport every alien who at any time and in any country fell, however briefly, within any excludable category, regardless when he may have entered the United States, unless he could prove that he had not known he was joining a forbidden organisation and that he had left it immediately on learning the truth about it. The Union commented that the law could not be attacked under the Constitutional ban on *ex post facto* legislation, since the Supreme Court had held the ban applicable only to criminal matters and deportation is not a criminal proceeding; but the ACLU found hope in the court's voiding of bills of attainder for past offenses by persons now purged of them, and it saw further assistance in the Schneiderman decision.

In addition to these provisions, all of which the Union properly denounced, it opposed the denial of the right of asylum to diplomats and others renouncing totalitarianism (a word that was always, in this connection, to be translated as *Communism*), and it attacked other savageries. One of these repealed the old law limiting deportation to a country or countries with which the alien had some personal connection; now he could be sent to any country that would accept him without physical persecution. If the deportation order was not carried out within six months, he was subject to surveillance and obligations to report worthy of the MVD. A fragment out of the discarded Hobbs Bill provided that every alien, under further penalty, was responsible for getting himself out of the country when he had been ordered deported and for applying himself for the execution of the order! Any aliens left were required to register annually.

New restrictions on naturalisation not only incorporated all the old taboos against Communists, anarchists and God knew what but also included members of "action" (as distinguished from "front"—but how distinguished was another mystery) organisations. Formerly the courts had held that, when a naturalisation proceeding was pending, a deportation action must await its outcome; the new law reversed the rules. It also specifically barred non-religious conscientious objectors from citizenship and unnecessarily tightened the education and literacy requirements for the rare alien who might remain eligible.

This masterpiece was the work of Senator Pat McCarran, a member of President Truman's Democratic Party, chairman of the Senate Internal Security Subcommittee and a blood brother of the Honorable Joseph McCarthy, the Wisconsin Republican who founded mccarthyism, a word that, like *lynch*, has now become part of every major language in the world. In 1952 McCarran was joined by another Democrat, Chairman Francis D. Walter of the House un-American Activities Committee, in the spawning of the McCarran-Walter Immigration Act, which, retaining virtually every objectionable provision of its predecessor, added a few new inhumanities vainly protested by the ACLU.

Deportation was made possible if an alien had become a public charge within five years of his arrival or if he had not fulfilled a marital agreement made in contemplation of entry: in either case the Attorney General was given sole discretion to find the facts and all due-process protections were removed. The Attorney General was given sole discretion to suspend deportation proceedings, but only where he found "exceptional and extremely unusual hardship." On the other hand, he had full discretion to nullify the act's protection against deportation to a country where the alien faced persecution. The act ordered the deportation of all aliens who had ever been Communists and made no provision for those who had proved to be staunchly anti-Communist: Arthur Koestler, the distinguished author, had to be stamped *kosher* by a special Act of Congress. On the other hand, former totalitarians (that is, Fascists, Nazis, Falangists, but, in practice, not Communists) might enter the United States on proof that for five years they had been actively anti-totalitarian— a term not defined by the statute.

In addition, naturalisation could now be revoked for "concealment of a material fact or willful misrepresentation"—standards not in force previously and hence clearly retroactive. Revocation was also possible if lawful admission as a permanent resident was created through an adjustment of status for which the alien was in fact ineligible and if his former status was resumed within five years. In the only move ever made to give naturalised and native citizens true equality, both were subjected to treatment as aliens, subject to admission or exclusion on the Attorney General's terms, if their status should be questioned during their absences from the country: they might thus be barred, without a hearing, from returning, and without the former right to enter in order to sue for certificates of nationality. *Give me your poor, your suffering,* indeed!

One of them, Mrs. Ellen Knauff, the wife of an American soldier, had been barred for two years without hearing or explanation other than the allegation that she was a poor security risk. She was not allowed to know the nature of the charges or the identity of her accuser. A special bill in Congress won clearance by the House Judiciary Committee, whereupon the Government revealed that her accuser (whom it would not identify, lest he be damaged and American counter-espionage be injured) was safely here and had never met Mrs. Knauff. A new hearing was ordered and she was barred again. In 1952 the ACLU won a new hearing for her, the Board of Immigration Appeals dismissed all the charges against her as mere hearsay and Attorney General J. Howard McGrath ordered her admitted. None of this prevented all the disproved allegations from being repeated against her when she sought citizenship a year later.

The studied denial of due process of law was not the only sin of the new laws and their administration; official sabotage of individual rights is inherent, after all, in all government. Their substantive provisions were invoked, for example, to issue a ban on the entry of Stuart Denton Morris, a British pacifist, lest he lecture against war and against some American policies—a ban speedily overthrown by the ACLU. The Government, defeated by a San Francisco Federal Court's ruling voiding the new power of the Attorney General to refuse to suspend the deportation of an alien facing physical persecution without disproving the alien's allegation of such peril, appealed and then asked for the dismissal of its own appeal. Facing an ACLU appeal coupled with a private bill in Congress for a resident-alien merchant seaman who jumped ship in Japan and stowed away to return to his pregnant wife, the immigration authorities abruptly reversed their order barring him from re-entry under the 1952 act without a hearing. The ACLU tried also, with a private bill and injunction proceedings, to help a Hungarian who, after twenty-five years' residence here, went abroad and was barred from returning on the ground that his re-entry would prejudice the national interest; his request for a hearing was refused on the ground that disclosure of confidential evidence against him would equally jeopardise the safety of the United States (*how* was not stated but, in the light of the thousands of deportation, "security" and criminal cases in which this specious plea was raised to deprive a defendant of his right to know the identity of his accusers and the nature of his supposed acts, it is apparent that the peril consisted in exposing the illegal stool-pigeon and entrapment methods used by the Government to frame its cases).

Taking the new immigration laws at face value, the Supreme Court, with some notable dissents, abandoned its earlier concern with constitutionality and justice. It upheld a deportation based on former CP membership, though there was no proof that the alien knew the party's aims and though, at the time he joined it, the party was a legal organisation: Black dissented on this ground and Douglas held that deportation should be based solely on proof of what one is and does, not what one believes. In another deportation proceeding alleging present active membership, the court held that bail might be denied; then it approved the refusal of bail, without a hearing or a disclosure of charges, to a returning alien denied re-entry "for security reasons" and detained on Ellis Island because no country would accept him. Finally, with a straight face, the court sustained the McCarran Act provision making it a crime for an alien ordered deported not to apply for the necessary papers to get himself out! One wondered when the court would find a convicted criminal in contempt if he did not petition for his own imprisonment.

Even the Justice Department began to be appalled at its own oppressions, and it asked Congress to give aliens at least some of the rights of white folks. Ernest Angell, for the Union, testified vigorously in support of these proposals. An alien facing deportation, it was argued, should have the right to seek a judicial dermination whether there was substantial evidence to support the charges against him. He should be entitled to seek judicial review of Immigration Service proceedings before being taken into custody, to have this review held in the same jurisdiction where he was originally heard and to be relieved of the huge financial burden of providing a transcript of the entire record. Angell, furthermore, urged that hearings be made matters of right for aliens abroad who are refused visas and for foreign residents claiming American citizenship and refused certificates of identity. Congress paid little attention to either Angell or the Justice Department: aliens have no votes and not too many voting relatives. But here and there a lower federal court found a way to get round some of the more barbarous invasions of fundamental rights, ruling, for example, that the suspension of a deportation order against an alien legally resident here might not be refused on the basis of confidential "evidence" undisclosed to the alien affected.

Until the 1958 revision of the immigration laws, the Union had to fight piecemeal for every claim by a foreigner to be a human being. Nor did it always win: it failed to prevent the passage of a law, requested by President Eisenhower, to deprive of citizenship all persons conspiring to advocate the overthrow of the Government. Congress rejected the Union's contention that only those conspiring actually to achieve the overthrow should be penalised and its argument that Congress could not legally impair citizenship incidental to birth. One may justly question the limitations imposed by the ACLU on its objections to the law: Is not the right of revolution inherent in any society (the United States, one was taught in childhood, was founded through a glorious revolution)? Is not the attack on the penalty against native citizens itself an act of that discrimination between them and the naturalised that the ACLU has always opposed? The Union correctly maintained that no one should be deported for past or present CP membership at least until the Supreme Court had determined whether the Communist Party was indeed, as stated in various statutes, a criminal conspiracy: otherwise, the Union pointed out, the alien was punished for behavior that could not be denied to a citizen, and he was found guilty by association alone. But the Union's own civil-liberties principles seemed contravened by its acquiescense in the denial of immigrants' (though not of visitors') visas to current members because of the party's objectives, and by its acceptance of the refusal of citizenship to aliens who are Communist Party members when they seek naturalisation. CP members, the Union contends, are necessarily under a dual loyalty and party allegiance inevitably conflicts with fealty to this country.

Protesting the imprisonment of aliens pending disposition of their cases, since they were accused of no crimes, the Union urged specific changes in the law, some of which were adopted in the 1958 amendment. The ACLU called for a mandatory Board of Visa and Immigration Appeals, to be appointed by the President, with Senate approval, from outside the ranks of the service; the conduct of hearings by independent examiners subject to supervision by the service; the right to judicial review, and, when neither the national health nor the national security was involved, to bail; a 15 to 25 per cent preference for victims of any kind of persecution seeking asylum; more definite standards governing the exclusion of "persons prejudicial to the national interest"; the abolition of citizenship revocation as applied only to naturalised citizens —on the ground of prolonged residence abroad, for example, or of membership in proscribed organisations; and the establishment of a statute of limitations governing fraudulent or illegal procurement of citizenship, on the adverse force of convictions of crime in deportation proceedings and, especially, restricting the time for initiating deportation action in the light of decisions permitting such proceedings to be based on acts that, when committed, were not illegal. This last has not yet been conceded by a Government and Congress still frightened by the black-magic words *alien* and *Communist*.

Loss of citizenship by both native-born and naturalized citizens particularly plagued the Union. Its clients included native-born Nisei who had been conscripted into the Japanese army, an American of Mexican ancestry who, taken to Mexico as a child, had remained there to escape the draft and had voted in Mexican elections, another American who had served three years for fleeing to Mexico to evade army service, a soldier convicted of desertion in Morocco after fleeing a military prison and then surrendering. In every case the Union contended that neither a native-born nor a naturalised citizen can constitutionally be deprived of American nationality unless he has committed a voluntary act clearly renouncing his allegiance. The Supreme Court rejected the principle but, on other grounds, found for most of the citizens. Forced service in the Japanese army was found to be the result of duress, not a voluntary act warranting the deprivation of citizenship. The American who fled to Mexico had similarly not renounced, and, as a citizen, could not be barred from entering the country. The soldier who had served time for desertion could not in addition be punished by being made to lose his citizenship: this was cruel and unusual punishment barred by the Eighth Amendment. The American whose original entry into Mexico had been accomplished by his parents retained his citizenship because the court avoided constitutional issues and merely found the Government's case against him inadequate: at any rate, the burden of proof was clearly put on the Government in such cases. Without having to go to the Supreme Court the Union was able to save the American citizenship of a woman who had been unable to leave Rumania and, according to immigration officials, had lost her citizenship by accepting government employment there: all work in Rumania, the ACLU showed, is government work. In 1958, thirteen years after the end of the Second World War, the Justice Department restored the citizenship of 4978 Nisei who had renounced it in 1945 after having spent three years in American concentration camps.

Deportation and asylum cases handled by the ACLU were meanwhile mounting. The Union was troubled, but impotent, when Russian seamen seeking asylum here were apparently returned home under pressure from their Government, which cooperated with ours in depriving them of adequate opportunity to let the immigration service know their wishes: a classic instance of the basic confraternity that exists between governments as against the governed, regardless of conflicts of ideology or interest in other fields. In another instance, the United States Government ordered the deportation of a Korean facing certain punishment and possible execution at home because of the American puppet *régime* there, but the Board of Immigration Appeals, by some miracle of perception, decided that an anti-Communist Marxist was no threat to the American way of life. An Italian who had won a new trial for murder was ordered deported as a convicted felon. But the Government finally, in 1955, abandoned its persecution of Harry Bridges; and the Immigration Service won some praise from the Union when it announced that it would not exploit the Supreme Court's permission to deny discretionary relief on the ground of confidential information. While debate continued in Congress on statutory changes, the courts and the service confused the nation and themselves in a cluster of deportation and asylum matters.

For ten years the United States had sought to deport, for Communist associations, William Heikkila, a Finn brought here in infancy. One day the Immigration Service simply picked him up on a San Francisco street and, without letting him telephone his wife or his lawyer or get his clothes, flew him to Vancouver, Amsterdam and Helsinki. The Union backed his fight, and, when he returned to prosecute it, made the service back down on its contention that he had thus made a new and illegal entry into the country. The Union based its appeal on a Supreme Court ruling, early in 1958, that only "meaningful association" with the CP would ground a deportation: the court voided the deportation of Charles Rowoldt, who had entered the United States in 1914 and spent a year (1935) in the Party "because we had to fight for something to eat and clothes and shelter." In Heikkila's case, instead of trying to prove a "meaningful association," the service sought to defeat his appeal on the ground that it had not been filed within the mandatory sixty-day period, but the Circuit Court of Appeals threw out the entire deportation proceeding against him and the Government took no appeal. The "meaningful association" rule was applied to save three Mexican-Americans, against whom, the Union pointed out, the only evidence was that of Government-paid stool-pigeons.

The ramifications of the Left Wing confused the Government too. It dropped proceedings against some alien members of the Socialist Workers' Party and persisted against others, though this organisation claiming 600 members in the whole country had never been placed on the Attorney General's list of subversive organisations. The ACLU won a court order for the naturalisation of a member of the Socialist Labor Party despite his advocacy of drastic changes in the Constitution by peaceful means, citing such precedents as the Emancipation Proclamation, the Prohibition Amendment and social security. Social security for aliens deported as former Communists, however, was cut off, with the Supreme Court's approval, on the ground that it was not a property right and that there was a "rational" justification for discriminating among various classes of deportees who might or might not be entitled to receive what they had been compelled to buy. But this perversion of reason and right was in line with the contention that aliens, because they were aliens, necessarily lacked some of the due-process-of-law rights that citizens enjoyed, despite the Fifth Amendment's declaration that "no person"—not "no citizen"—should be deprived of any of them.

In line with the prevailing philosophy, too, immigration dragnets in San Francisco swept through factories, offices and shops to compel all Chinese present to identify themselves. The service refused to allow a Peruvian seeking permanent residence to cross-examine the Public Health Service doctors who found her tubercular or to offer confuting evidence. Its agents held a New Orleans gangster *incommunicado* and flew him to Guatemala after convincing that country—untruthfully—that he had been born there; though he had not been given the required three-day notice that he would be deported, radio and television reporters had been, and they were on hand to record the triumph of justice for posterity. A denaturalised former Communist born in Canada was deported to England, where she had never been and where she had no connections of any kind. An Israeli editor legally living in New Jersey was questioned on his political beliefs in an effort to substantiate a false charge against him. A British scientist studying here was ordered deported for picketing the House un-American Activities Committee. A seaman on immigration parole status was deprived of it in the midst of his medical treatment, for which it had been granted. All these ACLU cases—in most of which the courts connived at or collaborated in the violation of law—occurred not at the turn of the century but between 1957 and 1962.

Between 1957 and 1963 the right of asylum was made a mockery of again and again. Each time the Union intervened; often it succeeded but as often it failed. After the "flood" of Hungarian refugees—36,000—that followed the 1956 revolt, many were picked up for deportation as subversives without hearings. Immigration denied the vile charge but contradicted its own denial by seeking *habeas corpus* in each case as quickly as the writs could be signed. A Polish seaman seeking asylum was denied an interview, on the ground that Poland did not bar emigration (demonstrably false), then was granted it—on the ship that he was trying to flee, intimidated by the proximity of his officers and deprived of due process (the ACLU won this one). Another Polish seaman was refused asylum because he did not request it the moment he hit the beach but thought the matter over for three days (the ACLU also won this one). The Union failed in its plea to Secretary of State Rusk to grant asylum to General Marcos Perez Jimenez, former dictator of Venezuela, because of the probability of physical persecution if he was returned.

The passage of the 1958 immigration amendments provided some gains for refugees from totalitarian *régimes,* review proceedings and somewhat easier quotas; but the law did not include the ten-year statute of limitation on deportable offenses or the abolition of national-origin quotas that the Union had sought and still seeks. Nor did it repeal the statute under which citizenship could be revoked for draft evasion. Worse, it did set up a "conclusive presumption" that residence by a citizen in a foreign country and service in its army were voluntary and hence cost him his American nationality—a clause fought hard in the courts by the Union and not yet resolved. The Union also fought a statutory proviso automatically rendering stateless any American who served in a foreign armed force without specific approval from this Government: Herman Marks fought for Castro and, when he sought to return here, was held for deportation as an illegal alien. The ACLU's fight against his deportation succeeded, but, despite its evidence showing he had never renounced his nationality, the court upheld the order depriving him of it as not violating any of the Constitutional guaranties of due process or against cruel and unusual punishment. This and several other cases of the next few years merited all the attention that could be given to them; and yet it was still necessary to fight the pettiest kinds of harassment: rulings that the flouting of parking tickets warranted refusal of naturalisation since it showed the applicant to be "poorly disposed to the good order and happiness of the United States," or that what is known as *living in sin* demonstrates "bad moral character" sufficient to bar naturalisation. Both these lower-court astigmatisms were corrected; yet, though it was acknowledged that an alien had the right to take the Fifth Amendment, he was still required, the Supreme Court held, to prove that he was of good moral character and had never been a Communist. One asks oneself whether the presumption of innocence had been legislated out of existence under cover of all the other hysteria.

In the past three or four years the American Civil Liberties Union has won perhaps the most important of all its litigations concerning citizenship. The first victory, in 1961, was the Supreme Court's ruling that a native American deprived of citizenship during his absence abroad need not, in order to contest the matter, seek entry as an alien and then apply for *habeas* to settle the legality of his detention by the Attorney General: the Union argued and the court held that the Administrative Procedures Act guaranteed the judicial review of any action by an agency and that due process was violated in applying alien status and detention to a native judged by an administrative agency to have lost his citizenship by remaining outside the country in order to avoid the draft. Such forfeiture had been enacted by Congress: in two historic ACLU cases for which the 1961 action paved the road, the Supreme Court voided the forfeiture statute as a cruel and unusual punishment.

A year later, in the 1963-4 term of the Supreme Court, the Union finally compelled the recognition of one-class American citizenship. For years it had been battling up and down the appellate ladder on behalf of Angelika Schneider, a naturalised American who had returned to Germany, married and had children there and remained beyond the three-year period allowed by statute to naturalised citizens without forfeiture—no such limitation of absence exists for Americans born. Striking down the law, the Supreme Court said:

"We start from the premise that the rights of citizenship of the native-born and the naturalised person are of the same dignity and are co-extensive."

The nation was at last committed, at least *de jure,* to the proposition that the foreign-born are equally members of the human race. By the end of 1964 the news had reached at least New York State, where, in a case brought by the New York Civil Liberties Union, the state law forbidding a naturalised alien to vote within ninety days of his acquisition of citizenship was struck down by judicial decision.

9

Faith by Fiat and Fear

Lebanon, Pennsylvania, is the archetype of the God-fearing, law-abiding, wholesome small American community so often pointed to with pride as the heart and soul of the nation. The 30,000 people of Lebanon are proud of its low crime record, its cleanliness, its prosperity, its progress, its neighborliness.

One of the Lebanon neighbors is James N. Snavely, the forty-two-year-old father of four children, whose job is repairing parking meters. One night in February, 1964, other Lebanon neighbors—policemen—dragged Snavely out of his house to a justice of the peace, who fined him $53 for not having licensed his dog. Within the week, an old Christian neighbor lady on a bus snarled at him: "You son of a bitch!" and a wholesome neighbor gentleman who forgot to give his name telephoned Mrs. Snavely to say: "I'm going to kill your little boy and I'm going to cut your heart out."

Why are the Lebanese so neighborly to Mr. Snavely? Because they are God-fearing, law-abiding, wholesome Christian Americans and because Neighbor Snavely not only protested the refusal of the school board to obey the Supreme Court's decision on Bible-reading in the schools but, when his protests were ig-

132

nored, asked the help of the American Civil Liberties Union to go to court to compel the Lebanon school board to abide by the law. So Mr. Snavely learned that, when the Lebanon *Daily News,* like its huge namesake, threatened that any dissenter would lead a miserable life, it knew what it was talking about. After all, for four years before the Supreme Court decision, Mr. Snavely had refused to allow his children to be dragooned into religious exercises in the schools. Some 230 years earlier, the founders of Lebanon had included Isaac Snavely the Elder, who had left Germany in order to escape religious persecution.

Basically, *l'homme moyen sensuel* is too much *l'homme moyen lâche* not to envy—and hence to fear and therefore to hate—those few who can tranquilly accept the irrefutable truth of what has never received its proper recognition as Fitzgerald's Law: "Life is a cheat and its conditions are essentially those of defeat." Man in general needs myths to try to pretend the truth out of existence, and he will never tolerate those who, having outgrown the need for both myth and crutch, set thus a frightening and humiliating example to their fellows. This emotional desperation counts even more in the survival of religion and its gods than does their obvious usefulness to every ruling class in every age and every society—from Zeus and the other Olympians in Greece to Marx and Lenin in Russia. And, since every religion is by its own account the one true faith, its sheep cannot afford to acknowledge the existence of other flocks, to say nothing of those beasts that flaunt their heels at shepherds.

In the early years of the ACLU the various competing religious enterprises and their mockers provided little activity. The Supreme Court of Oregon voided a Klan-backed law banning parochial schools in 1924; in 1925 the Governor of Ohio routinely vetoed a bill to require Bible-reading in the schools; Boston, like New York and other cities earlier and later, obliged the Holy Roman Church by forbidding all birth-control meetings. For years Massachusetts, Connecticut and other states dominated by spiritual subjects of the Vatican had had statutes banning all distribution of contraceptive equipment, advice and literature, even by physicians to heretics and infidels. California, the forcing-bed of so many esoteric sects, allowed criticism of none of them, and its example began to bear fruit. In Boston one Anthony Bimba was arrested in 1926 for blasphemy and sedition, and Mayor Malcolm Nichols forbade discussion of the case in any licensed hall, but, when Dean Pound led a rousing protest, Nichols permitted one meeting in Faneuil Hall, owned by the city. Bimba admitted to blasphemy, under a 1698 law, and was acquitted; he denied sedition, of which he was convicted. The fever spread to Georgia, where Charles E. Falloon was arrested for challenging the Biblical "proofs" of the existence of Jesus Christ.

The Union's first religious-freedom case arose in Washington State in the same year, after Denver had suspended fifty school children abstaining on religious grounds from some prescribed patriotic mummery. In Washington, nine-year-old Russell Tremain was told by his parents, who belonged to an obscure sect called the Elijah's Voice Society, that he must not salute the flag in school. The educators promptly brought suit and the court ordered Russell permanently separated from his parents and offered for adoption; since the elder Tremains did not recognise what they termed "earthly courts," they refused at first to accept the Union's offer of assistance, but normal parental love got the better of them. It took the Union eighteen months to win a new hearing in which Russell was restored to his unpatriotic parents.

From then on, religion appeared more often on the ACLU's agenda. In 1927 it appealed the six-month sentence of Warner G. Williams in Massachusetts for a book containing the sentence: "Jesus Christ was immoral," and the prosecution was dropped before the appeal could be argued. In New York in the same year the first challenge to the state's released-time law—under which public-school children were excused for religious instruction during the school day—was defeated; but the Attorney General of Illinois ruled that all religious instruction in the public schools was unconstitutional, and even Chattanooga abandoned Bible instruction and credit for religious studies. The generally urbane atmosphere of the 1920's, however, never penetrated the intellectual fog of Boston, where Professor Horace M. Kallen was indicted (unsuccessfully) for blasphemy because

he likened the beliefs of Sacco and Vanzetti, whom Massachusetts was determined to execute, to those of two felons executed
earlier: Jesus and Socrates. Public protest and ridicule put a
quick end to this. In Reading, Pennsylvania, Albert Phifer, called as a witness in court and told to swear on the Bible, replied:
"To hell with all that," but he was acquitted of blasphemy. In
Arkansas, where he was making propaganda against the Fundamentalists' bill to forbid the teaching of evolution, Charles
Smith of New York was not allowed to testify in his own behalf
because he was an atheist and the Arkansas constitution forbade courts to accept the testimony of the godless. Six other
states had laws barring them not only from the witness stand
but also from all public office, but a decision in Alabama (!)
permitted them to testify.

In contrast, New York City sought in 1931 to prevent atheistic
street meetings on the ground that, as religious gatherings, they
required the issuance of permits. The ACLU reacted at once
and won a decision by the Court of Appeals that no permits were
required because atheist meetings were not religious—a sound
decision despite the reasoning behind it. The Board of Aldermen
at once changed the permit law to embrace the atheists. The same
year brought before the Supreme Court the first Bible-reading
case, but the court refused to review a Washington State decision
that had voided the legislature's ban on Bible-reading in the
schools. A year later a New Jersey court upheld the state's
ban on court testimony by atheists—a defeat for the Union—but,
without explanation, reversed a conviction because the atheist
witness had not been permitted to affirm instead of swearing.
In 1935 a New Jersey divorce judgment deprived a mother of
custody of her three children because not only her political but
her religious views were not those of the community; the Union's
efforts to obtain a reversal were ultimately defeated by the woman's changes of counsel. At the same time, in New York State,
ACLU lobbying and publicity helped to defeat bills that would
have prohibited the utterance of "racial and religious hatred"—
not because the Union approved the procreation of bigotry but
because such a ban, however well intentioned, was obviously susceptible of corruption to further precisely what it sought to

oppose: no clear standard could be set that would not unconstitutionally silence legitimate religious discussion and debate. The state of Washington, which only a few years before had sought to wrest a child from his parents because their religion forbade salutes, grew up enough to exempt children of Jehovah's Witnesses from that ritual without penalty. Defying the influence of the Vatican in New York, Morris Ernst led the Union's successful court battle for the right of physicians to import and distribute birth-control materials.

Despite the rise in propaganda against religious minorities as Naziism grew stronger abroad and the threat of war increased, there was little overt action to occupy the Union in the late 1930's except the restrictions on Jehovah's Witnesses. This sect was even more positive than the Catholic Church in its claim to the monopoly on divine revelation; it was also much more aggressive in its proselytising. Besides offering its literature on street corners—when it did not thrust the gospel at every pedestrian— it sent (and still sends) its evangelists on door-to-door missions that understandably irritated the unwilling hosts. The Witnesses are persistent; they are also generally offensive in their blunt attacks on all the rivals for superstitious allegiance. Few Americans were or are polite enough merely to refuse the Witnesses' offer of salvation; hardly more were content to slam the door in the martyrs' faces. As we shall see when we examine the fundamental threat to civil liberties—the mob and its subdivisions, the gratification of whose passions and prejudices is essential to the survival of all elected officials—the Witnesses were to suffer more than any other denomination: and the chief authors of their sufferings were their competitors, notably Roman Catholicism. The traditional butt, the Jews, was almost neglected, except as propagandists warned and imbeciles repeated that the war that menaced the nation was "only a Jewish war." And God found an opportune, if not an opportunist, defender in Fiorello LaGuardia, who decreed the deity's immunity to picketing.

The actuality of war won for the Witnesses a monopoly they had not claimed: exclusivity of persecution both popular and official. Their refusal to salute the flag, which they considered a secular image and hence an idol, now made their patriotism suspect; so did their conscientious objection to rendering any aid to the war. The duly constituted authorities of Charleston, West Virginia, decreed—and saw to it that the decree was executed—that all Witnesses within their jurisdiction should be force-fed with castor oil and then put out of town—for which the authorities were convicted of violating the Civil Rights Act of 1866. In the South, of course, the position of the Witnesses was further complicated by the fact that their deity was color-blind, in contrast to the local one. Even the Supreme Court, which ruled against them when it held that a permit could be required for the distribution of literature for which a contribution was sought (the Witnesses frequently asked for gifts, a practice protected in the more enlightened states), may well have been influenced by passions of patriotism as well as by the hyper-sensitivity of Justice Jackson, a devout Catholic, to the Witnesses' insistence on being quite frank about the money and power drives of the Vatican and of the other major faiths.

Jehovah's Witnesses and the War, a thirty-six-page pamphlet issued in January, 1943, by the ACLU over the signatures of twenty-two Protestant and Jewish clerics, summarised their beliefs and the price that had to be paid for them. The Witnesses' first loyalty was to what they called God's commandments, their second to man's: they believed in "the Theocracy." They had their own pledge to the secular arm: "I respect the flag of the United States and acknowledge it as a symbol of freedom and justice for all. I pledge allegiance and obedience to all the laws of the United States that are consistent with God's law as set forth in the Bible." It was hardly a sophisticated standard, but it was far from unadmirable. The record of both local and federal authorities in extending to the Witnesses the protection of the laws to which the votaries pledged allegiance, however, was almost wholly unadmirable. The Supreme Court had by now affirmed their right to distribute leaflets and play records in the streets, though it would not protect the sale of literature; but in March, 1942, the police of West Jefferson, Ohio, reminded of this, replied: "We don't care for the Supreme Court and the Constitution don't [*sic*] apply here." (In sum, this remains an excellent epitome of too much of the general American attitude—and of the philosophy of police everywhere in the world.)

The Justice Department always—except in the West Virginia

case—found no federal question in the refusal of anyone to include the Witnesses in Constitutional protections and the uniform opposition of local law-enforcement bodies to any prosecution of outrages in which they had or had not connived. Even when the Supreme Court, reversing itself, voided laws compelling school children to salute the flag or be expelled, and Congress enacted a law (backed, amazingly, by the American Legion) permitting respect for the flag to be shown merely by standing at attention, there was no enforcement against states and school boards that, like the police of West Jefferson, suspended the Constitution in their jurisdictions. Witnesses had no protection by their labor unions; American Legion requests were sufficient to bring about their dismissals from Post Office jobs. ACLU representations to the Justice Department did finally bring about orders to treat the Witnesses as people; these orders, the Union's own offers of rewards for the conviction of violators and, according to the pamphlet, the rationing of gasoline began at last to make some inroads on the incidence of violence. Surprisingly, much of the press began to take up the cause of the Witnesses, and this may have influenced the Supreme Court to decide that a Witness might not be deprived of public employment for refusing to salute the flag—thus extending the rights of children to adults.

The tribulations of the Witnesses and the fears of other minorities led again to misguided campaigns for state and federal laws to ban not merely discrimination but prejudice—an undertaking about as practical as prohibiting lust or thirst. The drives were supported by many Jewish organisations, whose members should really have known better, but they were successfully opposed by others, assisted by the ACLU, the NAACP, various Protestant minorities themselves targets of bias, the Union for Democratic Action and the Workers' Defense League. The right to prejudice, the Union properly believed, was as valid as the right to combat it; what was not entitled to protection was only overt illegal acts of discrimination. Hence the Union properly conceived it as its duty to assist the Reverend Gerald L. K. Smith against prosecutions based on his anti-Jewish propaganda even though some Jewish members of the Union thereupon proved the flaw in their devotion to civil liberties by becoming non-members.

Religion in the schools, which had sporadically occupied the attention of the Union and the public until the war had naturally thrust aside the question, became much more of an issue as complaints came in from widely distant parts of the country. In 1945 the Union persuaded the schools of Maine to desist from including fundamentalist religious teaching in their curricula; in the area along the border with Quebec, heavily populated by former *habitants,* there was much more resistance to the Union's attack on Catholic indoctrination in the public schools. In the Southwest too this was to become an issue, linked to the problem of hiring nuns as public-school teachers and to the demands of parochial schools for the same free bus service provided by the taxpayers to public schools, upheld by the Supreme Court in 1947 as benefiting the child, not the school! The Union's opposition to any encroachment of religion in the schools and to any public support to religion is founded, of course, on the ban in the First Amendment on any "law respecting an establishment of religion, or prohibiting the free exercise thereof." The intrusion of even non-sectarian religion in the schools, the Union rightly contended, was manifestly an interference with the free exercise of the right to have no religion; financial aid to any religion was essentially a step in furtherance of establishment, not only of the sect aided but of formal religion in general as against irreligion. The controversies over religion that flourished in the two decades after the war incited a venomous bitterness exceeded only by that over the Negro's claim to human rank.

The minor aspect was that of the orthodox Jews and, by implication, the Seventh-Day Adventists, who also observe Saturday as their Sabbath. Most states had Sunday-closing laws long before the five- or even the six-day week became customary: these laws had nothing to do with the rights of labor but were enacted to give a helping hand to the power of God to compel the adoration of his supposititious creatures. But only the Sunday deity was recognized; hence it was possible for an Ohio court to deny unemployment relief to a Jew who refused a job entailing work on Saturday; presumably, if there had been a Moslem in Ohio who would not work on Friday, he would have suffered comparably. Corollarily, persons who insisted on opening their shops on

Sunday—except in those occupations deemed necessary to the public health and welfare—were subject to arrest, and such harassment by the police was common even in such heavily Jewish cities as New York. Attempts by the Union to end these so-called blue laws have never, unfortunately, been either consistent or particularly successful; in view of the gravity of its other problems one finds it difficult to castigate the Union for having given so little of its badly limited time and resources to the matter. In practice, relaxation of public attitudes, the demands of a more leisured society and the age-old panacea of *Schmiergeld*—one of the most sacred of all perquisites of the enforcers of law—have combined to make such prosecutions almost noteworthy by their rarity. Jews may possibly be the largest single identifiable minority group among ACLU members, but they have probably occasioned fewer issues on its agenda than any other. One notable exception at the end of the war was the public statement by the counsel of the House un-American Activities Committee, Ernie Adamson, who warned a Jewish witness not unduly impressed by the committee: "The Jews in Germany stuck their necks out too far and Hitler took good care of them; and the same thing will happen here unless they watch their step."

The battle against the cohabitation of church and state had for years to be conducted on a local level by the Union and its affiliates: the Federal Government was simply, for the most part, in no way involved, and federal courts for a long time sought uncomfortably to see no federal questions in the various state and local efforts to couple the sacred and the profane. In state courts, as in lobbying efforts with legislatures, the Union was more often than not defeated in its efforts to preserve the separation: released time was upheld; Catholics won the use of Protestants', Jews' and unbelievers' money to build their schools, supply textbooks and transport the young faithful; the dissenters and the godless were penalised for their independence in a variety of ways. Sometimes, when the minority complaining was large enough, the authorities quietly yielded to it and the Union, as New York did when Jews protested the recital of the Lord's Prayer in the schools and the practice was halted; New Jersey, on the contrary, insisted on the prayer and the Bible. Sometimes, as in North Dakota in 1948, laws were adopted to forbid public-school teachers to wear religious garb: in some localities public-school faculties had to be augmented by part-time help from religious institutions but the Union fought constantly to confine their teaching to clearly non-religious matter.

While as a rule what was most to be feared was the domination of state by church, there were in the early 1950's notable instances of an equally dangerous contrary tendency. The Supreme Court outlawed a Maryland city park's practice of requiring permits for religious meetings in the absence of any law to this effect and of any standards by which to grant or deny applications. The court also voided a Pawtucket ordinance permitting church services in a park but forbidding less formal religious meetings there. But the most important of such cases was Kedroff v. St. Nicholas' Cathedral of the Russian Orthodox Church in North America, in which political panic and religion were stirred into a real witches' brew. The suit was an action in ejectment based on a New York statute that undertook to transfer control of all Russian Orthodox churches in the state from the central governing hierarchy, the Patriarch of Moscow and the Holy Synod, to the governing authorities of the Russian Church in the United States. "Legislation that regulated church administration, the operation of the churches, the appointment of clergy, by requiring conformity to church statutes 'adopted at a general convention (*sobor*) held in the city of New York on or about or between October fifth to [*sic*] eighth, 1937, and any amendments thereto,' prohibits the free exercise of religion," Justice Reed declared for the majority. The statute's further requirement of conformity in all other respects to the doctrines and customs of the Eastern Confession, Reed added, established such conformity "by legislative *fiat* and subject to legislative will." Concurring, Frankfurter, Douglas and Black agreed that such a statute would affect not only the possession of church property but the actual conduct of the church. Jackson alone dissented, closing his eyes to all matters of constitutionality and principle (as the Vatican—like all other religious bodies— has done for twenty centuries when advantage or expediency dictated), and saw only the bloody hand of the godless Communists that must at all costs be hacked off.

The same stigmata were hereafter to be seen more and more

—at any rate, they were to be alleged to be seen—in every controversy involving religion. The ACLU's brief on behalf of opponents of released time was *ipso facto* Communist-inspired, even if the same Justice Jackson, dissenting from the majority's approval of such statutes, declared that under them the school "serves as a temporary jail for a pupil who will not go to church." Despite its defeat here, the Union was beginning to make some impression on courts, officials and legislators who did not view the whole world through red-colored glasses. It persuaded San Francisco schools to give up a mandatory prayer addressed to "Our Lord, Jesus Christ"; the Board of Regents in New York State framed a "non-sectarian" prayer, which the Union at once fought because it was still religious; the New York City Board of Education tried to compromise by replacing prayer with the theistic last stanza of *America*. That the Union was infinitely less rigid than its opponents was evident in its opposition to the categorical exclusion of clerical teachers from the public schools of New Mexico: the Union found it improper to assume that a teacher would be a doctrinarian evangelist solely because of his membership in a religious organisation. Laws banning adoptions across religious lines were fought when it appeared that both real and foster parents wanted the adoptions and the children's best interests would be served. An alien whose petition for naturalisation had been denied because of his atheism was finally accepted. Michigan and Illinois abolished sectarian teaching, celebrations and materials in their schools. Released time began to encounter local opposition—much of it resulting from ACLU educational drives—and the Union prevented two California cities from making religious censuses of their schools.

Braving the anticipated wrath of Catholics, including those few who were among its members, the ACLU took the position that state laws prohibiting the sale and use of contraceptive devices violated the Fourteenth Amendment, which extends the guarantees of the Bill of Rights to the states, and the Ninth and Tenth Amendments, reserving private rights to the people. But attempts to get the issue before the Supreme Court by challenging such statutes were to take almost ten years: in 1965 the court finally agreed to entertain a challenge to the Connecticut law. Those Catholics outraged by this ACLU policy might have been somewhat consoled when in 1957 Patrick Murphy Malin, executive director of the Union, excoriated the superintendent of schools in Moundsville, West Virginia, for refusing diplomas to Roman Catholic graduates who would not attend a Protestant baccalaureate service. The Union, in short, was determined to preserve the liberty of every communicant and of every non-communicant as well. Too often, however, the same Catholics who rejoiced in the Union's victories for them against a Protestant tyranny turned on the ACLU when it sought to protect the heretic and the infidel from the Catholic *Diktat.* Most Jewish organisations and individuals in this country tended, in refreshing opposition to the religious dictatorship in Israel, to support the Union's fight for the right to believe or disbelieve as one chose. The support of the Jews may have much to do with their traditional ban on seeking converts, whereas the Christian tradition of the duty of carrying salvation to the unredeemed may well account for the last-ditch resistance to true religious freedom. The shrewdness of the human unconscious must also be busily at work: much of the aid thrust upon the putative deity by his ostensible followers must be motivated by the fear that he may prove less omnipotent in his own defense than they profess him to be.

It is hard otherwise—even with allowance, of course, for the perennial "Communist conspiracy"—to account for the almost superhuman resistance to the Union's ultimately successful campaign to outlaw *de jure*—since so much of the country ignores the Constitution and the Supreme Court, one must qualify—the compulsory Bible-reading and prayer so long established in the public schools. Nor can anything else account for the venomous counter-attacks and the fanatic efforts to re-establish the forbidden practices. How otherwise is one to explain the Christian neighborliness of the people of Lebanon, founded by men and women seeking religious liberty? On what other basis can one explain the ordinance of Bensalem Township, Pennsylvania— overthrown in an ACLU challenge—that forbade the issuance of house numbers to persons who did not disclose religious affiliations?

"It is proper to take alarm at the first experiment on our liberties," President James Madison observed more than a century ago, and Justice Black repeated the quotation when, in June, 1962, the Supreme Court finally outlawed compulsory prayer of any sort in public schools. The decision was rendered in the Union's fight on the New York Regents' "non-sectarian" prayer, which began by apostrophising "Almighty God." While the fundamentalists thundered (since their deity did not), the official publication of the Methodist Church remarked that perhaps "God can finally climb off the coins and into the hearts of the American people." That these organs were beyond his reach was amply demonstrated a year later when the Supreme Court categorically outlawed Bible reading in the schools: the mob and its demagogues howled *Communists!* and Congress was flooded with bills to amend the Constitution and legislate a supreme being into existence. An honest God, as Tom Paine noted almost two centuries ago, is indeed the noblest work of man.

By these two victories the American Civil Liberties Union established in principle the recognition of that true religious liberty envisaged in the Constitution. To cause the recognition to be put into practice will probably require at least a generation: the Lebanon incident is only one of hundreds, and the Union has now to devote as much energy to combatting renewed efforts to overturn or defy the prayer and Bible decisions as it had to give to achieving them. The decisions by the Supreme Court are not to be derogated. But the true worth of the American Civil Liberties Union is demonstrated not only in its contribution to these decisions but in its continuing day-to-day policing of their observance, through both its national organisation and its thirty-five affiliates. Neither decision ends the continuing subversion of the separation between church and state.

Before, during and since the litigation that brought about the two rulings the Union has done battle against innumerable attempts to destroy or to restrict religious freedom. It has fought prison rules that penalise convicts who do not attend services and other rules that deny them the services of the faiths to which they belong; it has battled against religious celebrations in the public schools and against the erection of *crèches*, Decalogues and other cult symbols on public property, with or without public funds; it has had to save the job of a California teacher threatened with dismissal for objecting to the inclusion of religion ("under God") in the national pledge of allegiance. To the credit of most major religious organisations—Protestant, Catholic and Jewish—they have stood firm with the Union in its successful resistance to federal legislation to undo the decisions on prayer and the Bible. The reputable organisations have equally resisted and helped to defeat the ironically dishonest efforts to restore Bible reading on the specious argument that its purpose is not to inculcate religion but to provide "moral and spiritual values" and "moral training." Comparable integrity was demonstrated by the Military Chaplains' Association less than two years ago: the Union asked the Defense Department to bar chaplains from conducting religious classes in public-school buildings for military dependents, whereupon the association of the militant men of God adopted a resolution charging that the ACLU had "declared chaplains are in violation of the Constitution of the United States."

The Union is still fighting to prevent the use of public funds for religious schools; not only the festering school-bus question but the whole issue of federal aid to church-run institutions remain unsolved. The Union has indicated its acceptance of a distinction between church-run schools and those merely related to a church, and it sees no constitutional violation in aid to the latter, provided, and only provided, that a clear and unmistakable standard of classification can be evolved and that it is not surreptitiously breached afterward. On behalf of the religious rights of individuals the Union has been more successful in this decade: statutes and regulations barring unbelievers from witness stands and from public office have been frequently overthrown, the Supreme Court stating categorically in 1963: "We repeat and again reaffirm that neither a state nor the Federal Government can constitutionally force a person 'to profess a belief or a disbelief in any religion.' " (But the original draft of the Civil Rights Act of 1964 tried to.) The court specifically undid, too, the injustice of state denial of unemployment compensation to persons refusing jobs requiring work on their Sabbaths. Yet at the same time the army, under the guise of "character guidance," was shoving sectarian indoctrination down the throats of its men—a practice that, the army promised the Union, would be eliminated. More laughably, the legions of the Lord are now enriching the banner industry and making fools of themselves by the wholesale purchase of ONE NATION UNDER GOD pennants that they display on public buildings in an infantile defiance of the Supreme Court rulings that frighten them. These tantrums too are under court challenge by the Union.

One of its major targets was provisions in President Johnson's 1965 program for aid to education that, the Union contended, "as it is written, . . . could authorise the most dangerous subversion of the Constitutional principle of church-state separation since James Madison's famous Remonstrance set the directions of American religious liberty in 1786." What the Union fears in the new bill is not only religious control of public programs but, with equal justice, an "unprecedented control of church-related activities by the infusion of federal funds." The Union's objections were set out before the Senate Education and Welfare Committee by Lawrence Speiser, the highly competent director of the ACLU's Washington office, and George La Noue, an instructor in government at Teachers' College of Columbia University and a member of the ACLU's Church-State Committee.

Their major attack was directed against provisions for "shared time"—aid to children of low-income families, including those in parochial schools, through part-time attendance in public schools. This is an issue on which the Union itself was then divided—in April, 1965, it unequivocally condemned shared time—but Speiser and La Noue pointed out certain perils in the proposals that could not be blinked: for example, discrimination between poor and well-to-do parochial students, a violation of the equal-protection clause of the Constitution; the perversion of the program by segregationist private schools; the furtherance of religious rather than public purposes; aiding the parochial school rather than its student; diluting the public control of public expenditures. Clauses enabling the Federal Government to by-pass state laws barring taxpayer provision of books and library facilities to private schools were attacked by the Union as "indefensible . . . federal interference in the educational affairs of a state," but here, it is submitted, the Union has the wrong handle, since educational policy and its execution should be a national rather than a local matter if this is indeed a nation and no longer a loose confederation of a handful of underdeveloped former colonies.

The Union's policy calls for the exemption of *all* non-profit public-service property from taxation: this includes the property of every kind of religious, educational, charitable and welfare institution. To exempt only the property of one or several categories but not of all, the Union argues, is discriminatory and even worse than to exempt the property of none. But one wonders whether any form of tax-exemption is not discriminatory and hence an infringement of civil liberties; and, it is submitted, the logical conclusion of the Union's utterly Constitutional position on the separation of church and state would indicate that any state aid to religion—and tax exemption is unquestionably state aid—is a step toward the end of that separation. It is not saved from unconstitutionality by being extended to all religions equally: it is as unconstitutional for the Government to assist all religions as to assist one or a few. Indeed, the abolition of all tax exemption would seem far more just than the creation of any tax-privileged class of the society, clerical or lay.

10

The Rights (and Wrongs) of Labor

When the National Civil Liberties Bureau became the American Civil Liberties Union in 1920, it firmly believed, with touching *naïveté*, that capital's passionate resistance to the toiling masses was the greatest menace to the rights of man. The advent of the New Deal thirteen years later only heightened this romantic misconception: in the view of the ACLU, the New Deal was primarily devoted to saving the capitalist system as it then existed and was hence "frankly an ally of business—the struggle between capital and labor is the most vital application of the principle of civil liberties." The Union was almost as far from the truth in its appraisal of the New Deal (though this is not the place to analyse the curious amalgam of theoretical Marxism, practical Fascist corporativism, know-nothing economic nationalism and plain trial and error that so entranced the superficial intellect of Franklin Roosevelt in his earlier terms) as it was innocent of the nature of the human animal in its conclusion after the first year of the New Deal: "Despite the unparalleled power of the Federal Government, effective control over the exercise of civil liberty in the United States remains where it always has been—with the masters of property." Like all doctrinaire dogmas, the proposition was

148

much too oversimplified, even for an organisation almost all of whose "clients" had thus far come from the left because virtually no one else was being victimised, save felons.

One does not intend to imply that masters of property have not generally, as a class, been as eager to muzzle the underlings as the helots have lusted to silence their self-styled betters. Certainly in the first forty years of the twentieth century—until the National Labor Relations Act, promulgated by that same New Deal that the ACLU somehow managed to view as the bosses' instrument, took firm hold—the propertied interests, with virtually no exceptions, did their utmost to provide irrefutable evidence for the Union's thesis, and in this they had all too often the eagerly servile collaboration of too many in the ranks of the enemy. Whensoever two or more were gathered together in labor's name and one among them proclaimed the first verse of the Wobbly's Creed, "The working class has nothing in common with the employing class," some underpaid proletarian boot-licker was almost always on hand to shout *Criminal syndicalism!* There was always room for one more working-man in the prisons. Yet at the same time, then as now, the overwhelming majority of the employing class was privately stating and publicly living the identical fallacy, as if to demonstrate that, if workers and employers alike saw no confluent interest in a healthy economy and a just society, they were twinned at least in blind porcine stupidity. But words and acts that, on the street-corner or the picket-line, were criminal syndicalism became, in the living-room or the club or the board-room, keystones of the sacrosanct *American way.*

Unquestionably the most frequent and spectacular invasions of civil liberties at the time of the Union's formation were directed against the great organising drives of labor that marked the 1920's. Not only speech but, even more, the strike and the picket line were battled without scruple. Unconstitutional legislation forbidding strikes and picketing, injunctions against both, the use of force by police, troops and private militias organised and paid by industry were the most effective means, and of these the injunction and violence were the most frequent. Violation of injunctions or of anti-labor legislation meant long jail terms, like those of the thirteen Oklahoma and Texas tenant farmers whose crime was the attempt to organise a union and whose wives and children, in 1922, staged a Children's Crusade to march on Washington and picket the White House, where President Harding refused to receive them despite initial widespread press sympathy. Organised by two Socialists, Kate and Frank O'Hare, the Crusade was financed and advised throughout its brief term by the ACLU, which raised the money by solicitation.

The Union was in the thick of all the combats—not only in the courts but in the streets. Arthur Garfield Hays, then a volunteer ACLU attorney—one of a thousand across the country—was beaten and jailed in 1921 in Vintondale, Pennsylvania, when he attempted to speak on behalf of labor during the national coal strike. Alfred Bettman of Cincinnati, a former assistant to the United States Attorney General, directed the Union's legal efforts to help the AFL fight the indictment of 1800 armed miners in the same year for murder and treason when 10,000 of them marched against the private-army rule of Logan County, West Virginia, by gunmen recruited by the mine owners' association. In New York City the ACLU sought to end the police practice of violently breaking up meetings of the unemployed. In all the areas where arrests skyrocketed in the national coal and railway strikes, as well as lesser labor disputes, the ACLU supplied bail, to the limit of its resources, through the National Bail Fund, a cooperating independent body. The Union imposed one limitation on its work: it devoted itself to the defense of civil liberties, not to the condonation of overt criminal acts. Eleven hundred "local cooperators" or correspondents in the various states kept it constantly advised of day-to-day developments. From the beginning, it coupled its court and street fights for the rights of labor with public education through press releases and pamphlets and with constant agitation for the repeal of repressive laws and the passage of protective ones.

No success—and there were rather many—was long-lasting. In some areas police raids without warrants on workers' meeting places were temporarily halted by damage suits; in others protests were effective for a while. But sooner or later the authority temporarily restrained would resume its old practices, which meanwhile were springing up in a dozen other areas.

Hays, Baldwin, Norman Thomas, Robert W. Dunn (Baldwin's associate director for a year), the Reverend Harry F. Ward (the Union's national chairman), Powers Hapgood (a nationally known labor organiser) and hundreds of less well known Union members went time and again into the battlefields—and streets and mine areas and picket lines were really battle areas in those days, attacked with the clubs and tear-gas and guns of the local police, the militia, and the private legions such as the Pennsylvania coal-and-iron police—and from there to jails and hospitals. It was a commonplace for ACLU members to be physically escorted to a station and put on an outbound train (as Mayor Hague's police in Jersey City were still doing in 1937). "We took risks with the liberties, indeed the lives, of some of our best friends," Baldwin said many years later, and their "courage and convictions carried them through without a casualty."

The history of repressions of labor in the United States between the wars has been too well and too often told to be repeated in indigestible digest form. The quasi-legal means were paced by the same kidnapings and deportations of labor "agitators" that officials employed against sectarians, aliens, pacifists and others. Mob action was so commonplace and so intertwined with the forms of legality that it is often impossible to determine when the rabble was stirred by manipulators and when it was simply rooting about for a pretext for its bestiality. From the beginning of its life the Union's battle for the protection of the Constitutional rights of workers and unions—and, as it grew wiser, of employers as well—has been unreasonably snagged by the traditional conflicts between state and federal law and powers, a conflict that has invariably been exploited to defeat justice and morality, as much in labor relations as in race relations.

Before the New Deal there was virtually no federal legislation governing labor relations, and what little there was was directed against the growth of unions. The Sherman Anti-Trust Law and the companion Clayton Act were utilised to outlaw strikes whenever they could be construed to be unlawful combinations in restraint of interstate commerce. State legislation was almost equally repressive, especially since the Supreme Court had held unconstitutional, as violations of the liberty of contract, state laws outlawing "yellow dog" contracts: these were individual agreements with each worker under which he forfeited employment if he joined a union. State laws restricting the employer's use of injunction in labor disputes were outlawed by the court in 1921 in the historic case of Truax v. Corrigan, on the ground that such legislation denied the employer the equal protection of the laws—though in practice almost no court would grant workers an injunction against illegal activities by employers. For eleven years neither the ACLU nor labor succeeded in winning any federal protection for the latter's constitutional rights, until in 1932 Congress passed the Norris-LaGuardia Act, forbidding the use of the injunction by employers in labor disputes in interstate commerce. The Supreme Court upheld the federal act but persisted for years afterward in invalidating state legislation to the same end.

The Union's contribution to the recognition and enforcement of labor's rights, despite frequent opposition by the American Federation of Labor, which feared the ACLU because in principle and practice the AFL would not tolerate civil liberties for rival unions, is immeasurable. It was made through constant, heartbreaking struggle against entrenched power, political subservience (to use a polite term) and conscious and unconscious distortion of Constitution, statute and decision, to say nothing of mob emotionalism. The right to picket had to be established over and over again, in reliance on the First Amendment's protection of freedom of speech and assemblage and against constant harassment under ordinances purporting to regulate disturbance of the peace, obstruction of traffic, loitering, vagrancy and similar misdemeanors. The right to strike was denied Constitutional protection by the Supreme Court, which in 1926 asserted the power of the judiciary to pass on the legality of each strike's purpose. The objectives of unions were obscured by smokescreens of baseless charges such as inciting to riot; their quarters were raided without warrants; police brutality was a commonplace decried even by the most conservative parts of the responsible press. Each instance within its resources was combatted by the Union, and the doggedness and skill of its attorneys compelled courts to recognise the weight of evidence when charges had been framed; in some cases, which became more frequent as time passed, its counsel succeeded even in convincing courts that injunctions against peaceful picketing should be modified or withdrawn and that others, against unlawful interference, should be issued and enforced. Throughout the decade California, Pennsylvania, Kentucky, West Virginia and Illinois were constantly replacing one another in the van of repression.

Though the score of ACLU victories for the right to picket mounted, the adversary learned nothing. In one month of a New York City garment strike, 1350 pickets were arrested on trumped-up charges: the Union protested all the arrests and only five of the pickets were held for the grand jury (which did nothing about them). In St. Clairsville, Ohio, fifty-one women whose husbands had been arrested in a mine strike were held for "riotous assemblage" when they went to see their husbands on visiting day but were told the charge would be dropped if they would persuade the men to end the strike. The ACLU won the dismissal of the charges but even the publicity attendant on the outcome did nothing to discourage the continuation of such harassment. The excesses of both official and unofficial police forces, notably in Colorado and Pennsylvania, where murder and brutal beatings were routine police sports, persuaded more and more of the press to support the Union's efforts for the protection of labor. Even local courts began to listen (especially when the Union sent such nationally prominent lawyers as Hays and Clarence Darrow to defend its clients). In Pittston, Pennsylvania, Powers Hapgood and his wife, Mary Donovan, were indicted for inciting to riot and held in high bail when, after state police had machine-gunned two union leaders to death on the street, they paraded at the site of a banned protest meeting with black armbands lettered WE MOURN FREE SPEECH: Hays won a directed verdict of acquittal.

Inter-union conflicts complicated the problem, particularly as left-wing organisers entered the coal fields, setting up the National Miners' Union in Pennsylvania as a competitor of John L. Lewis' United Mine Workers (who, in Illinois, had to contend with the Progressive Miners). Thereupon the UMW men would join the same policemen who had clubbed them and both former antagonists would savage the "upstart" union. The ACLU found itself thus compelled to condemn its former clients. The only arrests in such cases, as in all others in which police and strikers clashed, were those of the men assaulted; in virtually every instance of murder or attack on union men throughout the country there were either no indictments or acquittals. Even such Southerners as former Senator Thomas W. Hardwick of Georgia were sufficiently outraged by the frame-ups of union men in their part of the country to volunteer to defend them for the Union (which Hardwick subsequently left when it insisted that the Constitution applied to Negroes). Frequent actions for damages for assault and false arrest were filed by the Union on behalf of the victims, but few judgments were won.

When on the eve of the depression the Supreme Court upheld an employer's right to discharge a worker for joining a union and sustained bans on the secondary boycott—picketing those who dealt with a struck company—the Union increased its agitation for legislation. Mrs. Carol Weiss King, a skillful labor lawyer who was later a Communist, issued its long series of law bulletins interpreting the right of workers to choose their own unions, to combat the open shop, to picket peacefully without being enjoined. In spite of the earlier Supreme Court decisions, legislatures began to pass, with active ACLU backing, new bills outlawing yellow-dog contracts and labor injunctions. Meanwhile unemployment was skyrocketing and those jobless who gathered to protest their plight were treated like strikers: in New York City their meetings were clubbed down; in Dearborn, Michigan, city and Ford Motor Company police killed four and wounded forty in a parade; Melrose Park, Illinois, police shot eight at a peaceful meeting. The Kentucky coal fields, which had been under shotgun rule by the state and the mine owners since the mid-1920's, continued in a state of siege even after the inauguration of Roosevelt, and assault, murder and framed indictments of strikers and organisers went on unchecked. It was there, as we have seen, that a federal judge refused to enjoin violence against ACLU emissaries on the ground that the area must be protected *against* free speech.

The passage of the National Industrial Recovery Act in Roosevelt's Hundred Days was the first positive indication that the Federal Government might undertake to enforce the Constitutional rights of those of its subjects who belonged or wanted to belong to labor organisations. Despite the Act's multiple borrowings from Signor Mussolini, who was even less a friend of the great middle-class and the masters of property than was the ACLU, neither the famous Section 7(a) nor its ultimate successor, the Wagner Act, threatened labor with any of the Fascist perils that at least some ACLU leaders professed to foresee; on the contrary, both pieces of legislation incorporated at least part—and a great part—of the protection of labor freedom that the ACLU had so long been seeking. But the very protection that the Federal Government hoped to provide by Section 7(a) was made a mockery by its inability or unwillingness to intervene in the renewed repressions undertaken by the states as strikes soared after the legislation took effect and workers and their leaders allowed themselves prematurely to believe that it had some practical meaning. Forty state injunctions were issued against striking, picketing and organising; fifteen strikers were killed and 200 were wounded. California's Imperial Valley was put under a *régime* Fascist in all but name in order to prevent, by any and all means, the organisation of its thousands of miserably paid fruit workers; Roosevelt refused to send in United States marshals to restore the Constitution, though there had never been any hesitation in using them against strikers. It was difficult not to remember what Huey Long, who certainly knew the subject, had said in 1931: "When Fascism comes to America, it will call itself democracy."

In 1934 the Union published a fourteen-page pamphlet of photographs. Each picture had previously been published in one or more "capitalist" newspapers and each portrayed police brutality against labor. Caption after caption—and all were reprinted as they had originally appeared in the various newspapers—stated categorically that the police had provoked violence or indeed initiated it in order to get rid of peaceful pickets. In the 1934 general strike that crippled San Francisco and in all other major strikes, the ACLU charged, the New Deal either openly aided management or so terminated the dispute through its mediation boards that labor lost—an accusation hardly borne out by fact on its economic side, though it is undeniable that both Roosevelt and his New Deal were often equivocal in the cause of civil liberty. When, as the Union rather quaintly put it, the New Deal turned "right" late in 1934 (a turn that, had it occurred, would have won back a host of enemies), Hearst, the United States Chamber of Commerce and the patriots were loud in demanding repressive legislation, but they succeeded only on the state level, at which, corollarily, hostility to the Union mounted. Governor Eugene Talmadge, the Huey Long of Georgia, set up a concentration camp for textile strikers, ignoring the ACLU's protests; but the Union won the reinstatement of John Donovan when General Hugh S. Johnson, administrator of the NRA, which was charged with enforcing labor's right to organise, fired Donovan for unionising the NRA staff in the American Federation of Government Employes. And in New York City the ACLU forced the Police Commissioner, General John Ryan, to rescind his order that all union representatives must be licensed by his department.

The work of the Union was in part responsible for the Senate's creation of a Civil Liberties Committee under Robert M. La Follette in 1936. It was charged with exposing all abuses, though its major effort was concentrated on those affecting labor activities; as is so often the case, few of its disclosures were to make any difference, though its work crippled the use of detective agencies against labor. Pennsylvania, which, despite its long record of oppression, had been one of the first states to make jury trials mandatory in labor-injunction actions, created a state Bureau of Civil Liberties (which it dissolved not too much later). For whatever reason—the Union attempted to ascribe none, and such obvious explanations as economic recovery and politics are probably superficial—all repressions began to slack after Roosevelt's second inauguration. The Federal Government was virtually permissive, except toward alien radicals; the states were still active; local governments' lawlessness in the persons of mayors, sheriffs, policemen and the lower judiciary was far more marked; and worst of all, of course, were the unofficial enforcers: vigilantes, mobs, volunteer spies, strikebreakers, professional patriots and the much accelerated anti-Communist crusade of the Catholic Church and its lay organisations. Rather significantly, the ACLU felt compelled to point out to its critics that, in conformance with its basic principles of defending equally the rights of all, it stood ready, whenever occasion demanded, to champion not only the non-union worker but the union member victimised by tyranny within labor.

The demands of occasion, however, were still almost exclusively those of all labor against its opponents. Sentiment for both state and national legislation to regulate labor's rights and conduct was rising in direct ratio to labor's own gains in membership, contracts and power: the Union opposed all such attempts for the moment on the ground that they were hasty and ill advised and that the matter required further and deeper study. Even the sit-down, newly imported in 1937 from France, was not to be precipitately outlawed as a trespass on property, the ACLU contended; and it was equally reluctant to commit itself on proposals to require unions to incorporate (which it has never accepted) and to render accountings (which it now finds desirable). That only negotiations, never violence and bloodshed, should be invoked to end sit-down strikes, as the Union argued, is incontestable; but it is difficult, even after almost thirty years of public acceptance of (or submission to) this basically unlawful and immoral technique, to find any ground on which to deem it acceptable. The occupation of the employer's property by dissatisfied workers, however just their grievance, must be clearly distinguished from the utterly licit and defensible sit-in technique of the civil-rights movements: this is in no sense a seizure of private property but, on the contrary, the acceptance of the invitation to the public to enter and do business that is implicit in the existence of any place of business soliciting customers or clients. The civil-rights demonstrators make no attempt to seize property or to prevent its lawful use by its owner; quite the contrary.

The National Labor Relations Board, created by the Wagner Act and more often than not upheld by the courts, began to cut deeply into the Union's work load in the late 1930's. The injunction, the strike-breaker, the private gunman and the militiaman were less and less frequently utilised as the NLRB and the courts ruled increasingly often against them. Even the Justice Department could no longer pretend not to have heard the ten-

or twelve-year outcries of the ACLU, the labor organisations, the Federal Council of Churches and innumerable other groups against the terrorism in Kentucky, and prosecutions of both public officials and mine owners were begun under the old civil-rights law based in essence on the Fourteenth Amendment. Strike-breaking and industrial espionage were set back when New York State refused to renew the licenses of private detectives engaging in either.

What was generally considered the Communist or pro-Communist faction in the Union's directorate—Nathan Greene, formerly an associate of Felix Frankfurter; Corliss Lamont, perhaps the classic example of the millionnaire radical, and others who could not be accused of holding party cards, as well as the only actual card-holding director, Elizabeth Gurley Flynn—persisted for some time in considering the NLRB no more than the tool of a Fascist law and hence, when the Labor Board issued a sweeping order in 1938 that in effect forbade the Ford Motor Company to express the most innocuous of views (had Ford had such) on the United Automobile Workers, the ACLU was more than laggard in reacting. Ford was one of the favorite foes of the far Left, which, like the extreme Right, rarely distinguishes itself by acting on rational bases. But these ACLU directors—including Lamont—who were really concerned with civil liberties, rather than with the advancement of a partisan cause at all costs, insisted that even Henry Ford, like the Ku Klux Klan or the Communist Party, should be assisted in asserting his right to speak. Out of a painful factional struggle within the Union a policy was evolved that has persisted: the Union will defend the right of the employer to utter anti-union sentiment provided this is not done in association with coercion of the workers.

By the time the United States entered the Second World War the basic rights of labor had been fairly firmly established despite constant forays by its enemies, who seemingly could not learn to accept defeat. The fact of war, of course, encouraged them to attempt to utilise its passions toward fresh efforts for legislation to undo what had been gained; but, outside strictly defined laws relating directly to war industry (called, with the

American insistence on evading ugly truths, *defense industry*) and limited by their terms to the duration, little was accomplished. The readiness of both labor and management to pledge themselves to a moratorium on strikes and lockouts in such industries helped to preserve the rights of labor as a whole, despite some new relaxations by the courts in what had seemed the absolute ban on labor injunctions in the Norris-LaGuardia Act and such state legislation as had emulated it. In evolving these exceptions the courts did not proceed on any theoretical basis, preferring to take each case as it arose; and both the decisions of the Supreme Court and the efforts of the ACLU were once more hamstrung by the persistent emphasis on the claimed rights of the states to equal authority with the Federal Government outside interstate commerce. No such excuse, however, existed for the ACLU's acceptance of the job- and pay-freezing provisions of emergency war legislation, which might have been vigorously contested (as indeed they should have been in any case) had this war not seemed so holy a crusade against the Prince of Darkness: even the ACLU preferred not to recognise the anomaly of invoking this typically Fascist and undemocratic (as well as Communist) technique to further the war against Fascism and for democracy.

Even today it has not become clear to what extent states may limit peaceful picketing. In 1941 Justice Frankfurter ruled for the majority that past violence justified a preventative injunction for the future; Reed, Black and Douglas rightly contended in dissent that the remedy lay "in the maintenance of order, not in the denial of free speech." A year later the court banned picketing a business dealing with a struck firm. But the use of false statements by pickets, Frankfurter said, could not be enjoined: ". . . to use loose language or undefined slogans that are part of the conventional give-and-take in our economic and political controversies—like 'unfair' or 'fascist'—is not to falsify facts." One may not like this emotionally, but one must accept it if one has any principles, particularly when one recalls one's quick outrage at injustice in 1928 when a Massachusetts court sentenced a man for libel because of a poster denouncing Governor Fuller of that state for refusing to pardon Sacco and Vanzetti: FULLER—MURDERER OF SACCO AND VANZETTI, the poster said, and the court held that *murderer* must be read literally. In the 1950's the Supreme Court extended the legality of injunctions against picketing to include support of an objective declared illegal by state law (even if valid under federal law), public policy or judicial decision. Its decisions under this rule have resulted in the condonation of racial injustice as they have protected the right to abstain from breaking the law: in the first instance, a state court forbade picketing to compel proportionate hiring of Negroes as being against public policy; in the second, a union tried to compel a firm to make its employes join the union in violation of a state law forbidding employer interference in the choice of bargaining representatives. Similarly, Frankfurter upheld an injunction against the picketing of a firm without employes, intended to compel the same working hours as those in comparable unionised places, on the argument that a state was free to choose without federal interference between the independence of self-employers and the protection of union members against non-union competition.

The confusion and random injustice inevitably growing out of the outmoded adherence to the doctrine of states' rights, even when the adherence is not tainted by the deliberate distortion of the doctrine to protect a vested interest, has affected both picketing and other freedoms, not only of the union and the employer but also of the non-union worker. In some states the closed shop is forbidden by "right-to-work" laws; in others, as in interstate commerce governed by federal law, the worker can be compelled to join a union he detests if he wants to keep his job. Injunctions to enforce both kinds of laws have been upheld, despite the declared federal policy, because, technically, they fall within states' jurisdictions only. The ACLU has here lost sight of the logic of civil liberties by upholding the principle of the closed shop, as a "voluntary civil contract," despite its professed interest in protecting the individual worker by its formulations of programs for union democracy, which will be discussed presently. Rightly, however, the ACLU has supported the Supreme Court's overthrow of an injunction against picketing by a union whose officials reject the ridiculous loyalty oath of the Taft-Hartley and subsequent laws; equally rightly the ACLU contests such laws' restrictions of the use of union funds for political purposes, which the court has evaded confronting.

The ACLU's interest in internal union democracy was spurred by the rapid growth of union power under the New Deal even before the invasion of the union business by displaced racketeers, and by the flood of complaints to the ACLU from union members. Though the ACLU never accepted the facts that unions had always relied as much as employers on violence and that labor had now won as unbalanced a domination as management had formerly held, it was keenly aware of abuses within unions, and it hoped to see them become miniature models for a free society (which, of course, is always a contradiction in terms). The discussions within the ACLU that led to its first formulation of policy on the subject would have shocked those of its critics who were always so positive about the "Communists" and "fellow-travelers" alleged to dominate it. Osmond K. Fraenkel, now general counsel with Edward J. Ennis, was branded *Red* because of his activity in the National Lawyers' Guild and his constant readiness to defend the most unpopular causes and persons. Yet it was this *Red* who was one of the strongest antagonists of union leaders in their private meetings with the ACLU that led to its first statement on the subject, in November, 1943. Fraenkel firmly believed that the labor movement needed considerable reformation, especially with respect to the right of the rank-and-file member to criticise his leaders and their policies. When Fraenkel insisted that every member of a union had the right to speak up in opposition and that the people in power could hardly be expected to like it but must accept it, Jacob Potofsky of the Amalgamated Clothing Workers took bitter exception, and many other professional unionists joined him in seeking to suppress such heresy. More detached experts on labor, from writers for *Fortune* to editors of *The Nation,* were among the twenty-six persons who signed the fifty-six-page pamphlet, *Democracy in Labor Unions.* All the signatories, from right to left, opposed the incorporation of unions, legal restrictions on the right to strike (except as it might be voluntarily surrendered in time of war), curbs on picketing, the licensing of union representatives and the outlawry of the jurisdictional strike and the closed shop. The endorsers made it clear that they favored only two legal restraints: (1) the guaranty that union membership be open to all qualified workers without discrimination of any kind, and (2) the protection of members' democratic rights under union constitutions.

The abuses dealt with in the pamphlet, the ACLU stressed (one can sense a discomfort as great as that with which the Union discussed its early *démarches* on behalf of the Constitutional right of the strip-tease), were all exceptions rather than the rule. "Although the ACLU's obligations are essentially the protection of civil rights guaranteed by the Constitution, not the denial of rights by private associations," it was explained, "it made an exception in the case of trade unions . . . [because of] the Union's conviction—long before the days of the National Labor Relations Act—that freedom of speech, press, assembly in unions and the right to criticise and oppose union officials were close to our guaranties of political liberties, and, in a field where a man's livelihood was at stake, quite as important . . . The increasing responsibilities placed on trade unions by governmental protection of their democratic rights demand that they in turn accept the responsibility for the democratic conduct of their own affairs." The principle is unassailable and it is to the credit of the ACLU that it is the only organisation that has ever attempted to obtain democracy in unions without ulterior motive. The same principle, one hopes, will ultimately bring about the success of those elements in the ACLU that are increasingly concerned with the tyranny exercised by another entity protected by the Goverment: the corporation, which so often interferes unlawfully with the private lawful conduct of its employes, if only by penalising them economically for behavior of which it disapproves, and which even more often hamstrings its stockholders' legal rights of ownership and control. The interlocking cooperation of big management has created as huge and powerful a dictatorial fief as that of the big interconnected unions, and one that is no less dangerous to the rights of the individual dependent on it for subsistence.

The ACLU's first study of the unions was restricted to their internal administration and, for obvious reasons, excluded such patent criminality as racketeering. It was concerned with union government, membership requirements, discrimination, expulsions and other disciplinary action, the distribution of authority within the organisation and especially the executive powers and the restraints on them, the frequency of conventions, tenure of office, financial reports and member participation in the determination of policy. Its findings were based on two years of hearings by the ACLU's Committee on Trade-Union Democracy, headed by Professor Eduard C. Lindeman and including Lucille B. Milner, Alfred M. Bingham, Dorothy Dunbar Bromley, Professor George S. Counts, Fraenkel, Walter Frank, Greene, Hays, Professor Karl N. Llewellyn and Thomas. They were assisted by Baldwin, who edited the report. Exhaustively examining union practices, both good and bad, the committee framed a *Bill of Rights for Union Members* that has remained a model for more than twenty years. Unfortunately, one finds it difficult to think of a single union that really meets its standards, despite all the progress imposed by the war, the various fair-employment statutes and commissions and the CIO's vast superiority to the AFL in concern for the actual well-being of those who pay the leaders' salaries. The criteria set by the ACLU for trade-union democracy included:

—The admission of every qualified worker without discrimination as to race, religion, color, nationality, ancestry or political affiliation.

—Democratic membership participation in the conduct of union affairs through regular meetings, free elections, free discussions and the control of finances by the members, with the issuance of periodic clear and authentic reports.

—Protection against arbitrary disciplinary proceedings: constitutional provisions for fair hearings before impartial tribunals with the right to appeal to separate independent bodies. (Arthur Vanderbilt, for the ACLU, was suing for the reinstatement of an AFL member fired under an employment contract forbidding employes to criticise union officials.)

—Fair and equal treatment in job placement wherever a union exercises control over employment.

—Majority approval of any special assessment and the exemption of any member from assessment for a political purpose he opposes.

—Provisions for orderly elections, trial of accused officers, full disclosure of all contracts and records to members, free expression of dissident views at meetings and in union publications, due process in disciplinary proceedings with appeal to courts under certain conditions.

The ACLU opposed any legislation beyond the minimum, preferably federal, to prevent discrimination and exempt employers from penalties for refusing closed-shop contracts to unions in which it was practiced. In 1945, 1952, 1958 and 1963 the pamphlet was reprinted, usually in conjunction with ACLU analyses of new federal labor laws and with some additions to the earlier paradigms, such as the 1945 list of *Labor's Civil Rights*. This included complete freedom to strike, federal and state protection for collective bargaining and the choice of the bargaining agent, freedom from injunction for peaceful activities, freedom to picket peacefully subject only to public order, traffic control and abstention from fraudulent statements, free speech for employers as long as it does not threaten and the attendant circumstances do not constitute coercion, the conditioning of NLRB certification on the elimination of discrimination, and the protection of union members against encroachment on their rights by union officials or undemocratic procedures. The ACLU opposed anti-trust prosecution of unions except when they engaged with employers in true restraints of trade, as it opposed compulsory arbitration. It called on public agencies to protect the right of the non-union worker, as distinguished from the strike-breaker, to have access to his job, and it emphasised the basic rights of the public at large in any labor dispute. In 1958 its analysis of the Kennedy-Ives labor legislation found fault above all with its continuation of the loyalty oath for union leaders and its extension of it to employers as a condition of eligibility for NLRB intervention, as well as the clause barring ex-convicts from union office (which, while intended to reduce racket control, was as deterrent to rehabilitation of the criminal as any other employment prejudice against former felons—a class that includes political offenders such as concientious objectors). The ACLU opposed also the requirement that officers and employes of unions report payments received from non-union sources, on the ground that this constituted wrongful self-incrimination. It also criticised limitations on recourse to the courts that would ease the expulsion of union dissidents, but it found no threat to labor's rights—how, one cannot imagine—in the appalling lack of uniformity in state labor laws. The ban on the use of union funds in local elections was also scored. All these criticisms were repeated in 1963 when the ACLU analysed the regulatory Landrum-Griffin Act; the ACLU contended that such legislation should declare and enforce essential individual rights but avoid impairing civil liberties in the effort to promote them.

All this legislation retained the grotesque non-Communist oath introduced by the Taft-Hartley Act in the post-war paranoia. The Supreme Court upheld the oath provisions of that Act on the specious ground that they did not substantially impair Constitutional freedom—as, one supposes, a woman eight months away from confinement is not seriously pregnant. Even practical considerations, otherwise paramount in this pragmatic nation, could not shake the *naïve* faith placed in the oath: critics pointed out that any good Communist would not hesitate to swear to his anti-Communism and hence the oath would at best deprive a union of NLRB assistance and perhaps ground a perjury prosecution against the affiant. It is perhaps the only occasion in American legislative history when a genuine, if panic-based, belief was impervious even to the practical.

For evident political reasons it was highly dubious whether Congress would adopt restrictive legislation seriously threatening the ACLU's position on the matter. But, during and after the war, many states enacted laws, over local ACLU opposition, that required unions to incorporate, forbade them to use their funds for political purposes and prohibited various kinds of strikes "against the public interest." Some of these laws were overthrown by the courts of the states that had adopted them. A few states prohibited racial and religious discrimination in unions, and these laws were challenged by the unions in the Supreme Court, which was mercifully silent on the limited brotherhood of labor in its decisions upholding color-blindness. The employer blacklist, which dated back to the beginnings of unionism, had long been outlawed, but that did not prevent its being used by the Roosevelt and Truman Administrations against civilian workers on navy jobs who had protested their conditions of employment:

the ACLU went directly to War Manpower Commissioner McNutt and prevailed on him to abolish it. For this the unions praised the ACLU, on which they promptly turned when it called on them not to deny access to a struck plant to its owners and maintenance personnel: labor rejected not only the ACLU's argument of the right to access but also its practical counsel that such stupid denials of access would jeopardise all the rights of labor. That the warning was sound was almost immediately demonstrated by the Taft-Hartley Act's provisions, protested by the ACLU, for injunctions against strikes "affecting the national health and safety," its curbs on union political activity and contributions and its ban on all strikes by government employes.

Neither reaction in legislatures nor ACLU strictures and exhortations had much effect on many unions. The Railroad Brotherhoods had to be haled into court and punished for refusing to admit Negroes; others had to be compelled legally to abandon their segregated Negro locals. A 1949 rebellion within the National Maritime Union, in which the New York union hall was seized by the officers and their opponents were physically routed, resulted in an ACLU study by Professor Philip Taft, who found that, under the color of barring "subversive totalitarians" from membership, the leadership was in effect outlawing all legitimate opposition to itself. Reprisals, once the revolt had been quashed, included the expulsion of a number of dissidents, many of whom won reinstatement when the ACLU took up their cause in negotiations with the union officers. The ACLU also rendered assistance in court to a man ousted from the Retail Drug Store Employes' Union for criticising its Communist leaders, but the ACLU took the view that unions had the right to bar adherents of totalitarianism from office if their loyalties to their causes were superior to their fealty to the union. It urged unions to appoint non-labor arbitration panels for the settlement of complaints. In curious contradiction to its rigid stand on the closed shop and the right to strike in private industry, it upheld the renunciation of both by unions of government employes provided adequate grievance machinery existed.

The early years of the decade of the 1950's produced many changes in the thinking and practices of the ACLU, and these extended to its activity on behalf of labor. Heartened by the action of the AFL Upholsterers' Union in accepting the ACLU's review machinery—an example that has not been overwhelmingly followed by the self-styled champions of the democracy of labor—the ACLU now called for more freedom for the union member, notably the right of dissent limited only by the clear and present danger (again!) of harm to the union—a limitation in itself a clear and present danger to the right asserted. The ACLU sought also to provide for the defendant in a union proceeding the same due-process protections that he would have—if he had money—in a court, with ultimate appeal to some independent agency to be created. At the same time the ACLU recognised "acceptable" curbs on picketing: bans on the use of libelous or fraudulent language, on violence, on the obstruction of passage. Outspokenly (despite those critics, internal and external, who now accused it of excessive concern with "respectability," whereas more than ever the Union was forwarding its proper major concern, the rights of the individual) it warned against the use of the picket line as a form of coercion, citing the 1954 New York newspaper engravers' strike, in which all the other newspaper unions honored the engravers' picket lines and prevented all the papers from publishing; but publicly it confined itself to appealing to unions and publishers to respect the public's right to be informed. Neither benevolent capital nor crusading labor, of course, paid the slightest attention; both sides reveled in an equally egocentric intransigence in the 1962-3 blackout of the New York press. Critical as it was of gangsterism in labor, the ACLU was equally opposed to both the terroristic methods of some unions—notably the International Longshoremen's Association—and the arbitrary and capricious legislation by which the elimination of the racketeers was sought: particularly the licensing of longshoremen without due-process protection for those deemed ineligible.

The ACLU has never renounced the closed shop, holding only—though, it is submitted, erroneously—that the closed shop creates no violations of civil liberties as long as a union's ranks are kept open on a reasonable, non-arbitrary and non-discriminatory basis. Corollarily it has taken no position on the so-called "right-to-work" laws, prohibiting the closed shop, as long as civil liberties are not violated in their application: yet it would seem patent that the ban on the closed shop protects a rightful liberty that is destroyed by compelling union membership as a condition of employment. But the Union contends that no civil-liberty question is automatically raised by the question of freedom of contract or association—a position that at best smells of the teleological. Strangely, during this period, when it had not abandoned its proper view that women are human even when employed and hence should not be discriminated against, it partly justified its opposition to the Equal Rights Amendment by arguing that it was better that mothers remain at home with their children and hence there might be some merit in differential-pay laws if their classification of individuals was reasonable and resulted in "true" as opposed to "mathematically exact" equality of compensation— since, in order to enable mothers to remain at home, fathers must have more pay than unmarried women doing the same work. The Union supported laws differentiating between the sexes for protective reasons—the differences in strength, the dangers to women in being compelled to be out alone late at night, etc.—but it stood firm on the principle of equal pay for equal work.

On sounder ground as the decade progressed, the ACLU was able to defeat a Maryland law to compel the fingerprinting of night-club workers, to contribute to the victory by which the Teamsters' Union was made to recognise a union of its own employes, to persuade the Sunbeam Corporation of Chicago to end periodic lie-detector tests of its workers (initiated in an effort to discourage pilferage) and to rehire one who had refused to take the test—which at this time is still thrust down the throats of thousands of employes of other companies whose managements apparently have not heard of the abolition of the chattel status of the human being. Both management and the AFL-CIO came under the ACLU's lash in this paranoid period for summarily expelling any individual who took the Fifth Amendment before the small-time Torquemadas of the House and Senate witch-hunt committees. In the Supreme Court the Union helped to defeat a Baxley, Georgia, ordinance that would have prevented labor organisation by requiring licenses at fees as high as $2000 per year per organiser.

By the end of the decade the ACLU had apparently lost some of the devotion with which, in its earlier years, it had seemingly presumed the infallibility of the labor leader. "Self-regulation" was virtually non-existent and at last the ACLU had to reverse itself and endorse, as a "necessary evil," federal legislation to further union democracy. In a more restrained modification of policy, the ACLU's directors opposed, for government employes, the ban on the union shop and on the right to strike, holding that the latter should apply only where the maintenance of uninterrupted service is essential and where adequate grievance machinery is provided. Vainly, it battled the discharge of a San Francisco postal worker who, in his free time, picketed in behalf of his union. And in the same state it was defeated in court, then victorious, when it sought to regain membership in the International Association of Machinists for two men expelled because they had defended the state's ban on the closed shop. Elsewhere it sprang to the assistance of workers in Chester, Pennsylvania, who lost their jobs because neither the Philadelphia nor the Wilmington local of the Asbestos Workers would admit them (there was no Chester local and each of the others insisted its adversary must take the men).

Recognising the labor unions' contention that the majority had the right to speak for all in political matters, the ACLU demanded that dissidents should receive a refund of dues proportioned to the ratio of the total spent on politics; but the paladins of labor were deaf in that ear. They heard hardly better when the subject of color was raised, or even when the NAACP, bored with their indifference, threatened lawsuits. But the Supreme Court began, in the current decade, to take some heed of a few rights of union members championed by the ACLU, refusing a railway union's plea for the enforcement of its union-shop contract against workers compelled to finance political activity of which they disapproved. A New Jersey court upheld the right of a member to sue a union that did not process his grievance in good faith. The NLRB, prodded specifically by the ACLU, held that racial discrimination by a union was an unfair labor practice for which the union could lose its certification as bargaining agent. But no external agency could change the sentiments of the holders of union cards who, like the New York City plumbers, walked off their jobs rather than work with Negroes and Puerto Ricans, or who, like countless members of Local Six of the International Typographical Union, have said to me and others: "If a nigger ever goes to work here, we'll all walk out."

One of the most important ACLU actions ever undertaken in behalf of the right to a livelihood is still pending. An Eastern Air Lines pilot was found guilty of an error in judgment by the Civil Aviation Board, which revoked his pilot's license but declared him qualified to remain a co-pilot. Thereupon the airline discharged him. The CAB denied having recommended such action; it had merely, it said, followed its usual policy of passing on relevant information to improve safety. But the ACLU contends, with impregnable justice, that such a practice can constitute "arbitrary government interference" with the right to earn a livelihood, in flagrant violation of the liberty and property concepts of the Fifth Amendment. It remains to be seen, in this age of friendly cooperation among big labor, big business and big government, whether the individual who must pay tribute to all of them has the right to go on earning the money with which to buy the further right to go on paying.

11

Oh, Every Day Is Loyalty Day to Me!

No government considers the governed its first responsibility: its real first responsibility is itself and its continuing power. Hence its primary concern must always be—whether in the Australian bush, the American colonies before 1776, Tanzania in 1965, Czarist or Soviet Russia, the Deutsche Bundesrepublik or the United States of America—to render its overthrow impossible. The chimera of *security* has the same disastrous fascination for governments as for individuals.

But the obsession with security that has characterised the American Government even more than many others and that brought into being the Alien and Sedition Acts of 1798, the subsequent federal legislation in the same pattern as an *obbligato* to every major war, and the weird criminal-syndicalism laws of the several states becomes a harmless clinical phenomenon in contrast with the paranoia that even before this country's entry into the Second World War began to infect almost the whole nation, resulting in the Dies Committee, the Smith Act of 1940, the infamous McCarran Internal Security Act of 1950 and the unbelievable Communist Control Act of 1954. Even the American Civil Liberties Union, until 1940 superbly above the panic,

171

has succumbed, so that today its official position on the reigning Antichrist, the Communist Party, makes of that organism a kind of Dr. Jekyll and Mr. Hyde. The Communist Party in the United States, the Union says, has a dual character: it is at once a domestic political entity and the instrument of an international conspiracy directed from a foreign headquarters. If this be so of the Communist Party, it is largely true of the Catholic Church and of the whole Zionist complex, both of which are equally divisive and equally dominated from beyond the borders—directed from, and devoted to the aggrandisement of, the Vatican and Israel, respectively. But it is only the Communist Party in which this duality is the basis for proscription. One supposes it is necessary here, in this time and society, to explain that what one is criticising is not the exemption of the other "conspiracies" but the proscription of any. It is impossible to challenge Baldwin's recognition in 1954 that one of the worst of the Union's mistakes was its refusal at the very outset to challenge the whole concept of Government *loyalty* and to battle every effort at "screening."

This position of the ACLU is of relatively recent origin; to its credit, the greater part of its history is one of defense of absolute freedom *de facto*, and even under the current dogma Union practice is far more exemplary than Union precept—a precept, by the way, that is not unquestioningly accepted by all its affiliates. Their work in behalf of the victims of *loyalty* and *security*, like that of the national organisation, has been vastly increased since the Second World War by the spate of imitations of the new federal legislation in the states, most of which has merely aped and some of which has even outstripped the barbarities of Congress. In practice if not in theory, these have been directed exclusively against the Communists and those deemed so to be: though all the legislation uses such broad terms as *subversive* and *totalitarian* and some of it, *pro forma*, does mention *Fascist* or *Nazi*, there has never been more than the merest token effort to apply the various bans to the Far Right—a fact that has its fortunate aspect in that such a compounding of unconstitutional action would only overtax the facilities of the ACLU. (One hopes one has not thus given aid and comfort to its enemies by indicating a new means by which to seek to embarrass and cripple it.)

Besides the Communist, real or otherwise, the other major victim—less numerous, perhaps, but no less unjustly purged—has been the homosexual, who is attacked not only as a security risk *ipso facto*, but, even more absurdly, on so-called moral grounds. It is a curious phenomenon that homosexuality is most excoriated in precisely those countries that most tend to produce it: Germany, Great Britain and the United States, where the view of women held by all sexes is at its lowest in the modern world. The mere fact of homosexuality argues neither special vulnerability to blackmail nor special emotional instability. The indiscreet homosexual, obviously, invites blackmail: but no more and no less than the indiscreet wencher or adulterer or horse-player. Logic and such statistics on disloyalty and betrayal as exist point together to the inescapable fact that the typically underpaid and overfamilied civil servant, obliged to maintain a *façade* beyond his means, is far more vulnerable to the blandishments of the foreign spy than is any pederast; and certainly any spy worth his pay, even on the lowest level, knows enough to choose his man from as inconspicuous a category as possible. If one elects the career of automobile theft, one does not court success by stealing rare and conspicuous vehicles. Homosexuality has exactly the same relation to loyalty and security as does a preference for ladies with prostheses.

The real preoccupation with loyalty and security, so-called, whether political or sexual, can be dated from the onset of the Second World War and the passage of the 1940 Smith Act. This statute made it unlawful to conspire to advocate bringing about the overthrow of the Government by force and violence or to organise a group for the purpose of teaching such doctrines. The major federal sedition law of its period, it was opposed before its passage by the Union, which with equal vigor and equal unsuccess attacked (while the Communist Party applauded) the indictment and trial of twenty-nine so-called Trotskyites under the act in 1941, as well as the similar prosecution of thirty alleged Nazi sympathisers in 1943 and the 1948 prosecution of eleven Communist leaders, resulting in a trial lasting from January 17, 1949, until

October 14 of that year. In the Nazi case the Union, adhering to its 1942 declaration of policy, born of the war, refused to help the defendants because many were clearly enemy agents and also because the Government indicated it planned to offer evidence going beyond speech and publication; nevertheless the ACLU deplored the Government's resort to the Smith Act as well as its dragnet use of the conspiracy statute, and ACLU observers attended the trial to be alert for civil-liberties violations.

Neither the Trotskyite nor the Nazi case provided the clear illustration of the Act and its dangers that was afforded by the 1949 trial. The Trotskyite case, which included a number of members of the CIO Teamsters' Union that had broken with its AFL original, was complicated by labor politics—David Beck, the sterling president of the AFL Teamsters, not yet in jail, insisted on the prosecution of his rivals—and by ridiculous allegations of the formation of a Workers' Defense Guard to unseat the Government, as well as proved charges of Trotskyite—i.e., Socialist Workers' Party—propaganda in print. These were in fact the only charges that stood up—the "guard" having been proved to exist only to defend union property against lawless violence—and they alone were the basis of the convictions, all of which were unsuccessfully appealed. The Nazi conspiracy trial of 1943 was, to put it kindly, a mish-mash. All the defendants were accused of conspiracy on behalf of the German Government to undermine the morale of the American armed forces. They were at first indicted under the Smith Act as well as the wartime espionage act, but the Smith Act charges included matter that had occurred, if at all, before the passage of the Act, and such charges had to be quashed. The dismissal of the espionage act charges followed, and all that was left was acts alleged to have been committed between the passage of the Smith Act and Pearl Harbor. The worst that was proved against these deadly enemy agents was that they had circulated literature to their minions advising them that they should demand tests of their Constitutional rights as a condition of accepting military service; a year later the Supreme Court voided their convictions on the ground that the distribution of such counsel did not amount to a violation of any law or aid and abet the Thousand-Year Reich. During their retrial the presiding judge died, a mistrial was declared and the proceedings were dropped.

The 1949 Communist Party trial, however, resulting in a conviction that was a foregone conclusion the moment the indictments were handed up, and that was upheld by the Supreme Court over the dissents of Black and Douglas, provided a far truer portrait of the legislation. It was obviously an uncomfortable decision for the majority of the court to have to make—not so much for Chief Justice Vinson or such associates as Burton, Minton and Reed, none of whom could claim eminence at bar or bench, but certainly for Frankfurter and Jackson, whose concurring opinions swung the balance. In sum, the court delineated a law full of vaguenesses, compromises, hypotheses and, above all, the same blind animal fear that had sired the law and the prosecutions under it. These mercantile minds made it quite clear that the narrowest construction must be put upon the determination of the time when a danger becomes clear and present (emasculating the already shaky "clear and present danger" doctrine to the "clear and probable danger"). They plainly implied that the whole Bill of Rights must be equally narrowly construed in the light of contemporary world conflicts; but, far more honorably, both Black and Douglas affirmed their belief that the framers of the Constitution intended (like so many curbstone psychoanalysts, generations of Supreme Court justices have pontificated their arcane certainties of the intentions of these long-dead men) the nation to assume the calculated risk that the world might not always be serene and that the danger of action must be accepted—a view that the ACLU, despite its lip-service to the "clear and present danger" doctrine, boldly and rightly endorsed.

"It is the existence of the conspiracy that creates the danger," Vinson argued, regardless whether the conspiracy was directed toward some overt act or toward mere speech. Jackson did not like this but he could find no way of striking it down; more courageous, Black called this view the baldest unconstitutional prior censorship, and Douglas said, since it was necessary to labor truisms, that no conspiracy to speak could transmute speech into seditious conduct. These two agreed that the existence of a clear and present danger was a question of fact, but Vinson declared it a rule of law to be judicially applied, which must have surprised every intellectually honest lawyer from Seattle to London. In essence, then, the ACLU said in its thirty-nine-page pamphlet of 1952, *The Smith Act and the Supreme Court,* the decision appeared to prohibit a group (but not an individual) from advocating (but not from discussing) under certain (but not under all) conditions the violent overthrow of the Government (but not necessarily any other end). The distinction between discussion and advocacy was left blurry, and the criterion for "what may be said" was established in terms of what some future decision might reasonably view as containing potential elements of serious danger. Even the unhappily concurring Frankfurter and Jackson could not abstain from voicing the strongest doubts as to the worth of the Smith Act and its threats to freedom. "The most frightening aspect of this decision," they said, "is that judges, legislators, executive officers of government and the public generally may take it as precedent, authority and encouragement for prohibiting the free speech of many other people besides Communist Party leaders." This was indeed the strongest argument against the Act, as the weakest of the ACLU's arguments was the probability that the Communists would exploit this discrepancy between precept and practice in the United States—as if wrong would be less wrong if no one could make propaganda of it. Right for the sake of right is indeed an un-American concept.

The dread expressed by Frankfurter and Jackson was soon enough justified by the passage of the McCarran Act, to say nothing of the encouragement given by this decision to the House un-American Activities Committee, whose outrages had contributed so much to the passage of the Smith Act and inspired the creation of the rival Senate Internal Security Subcommittee. McCarran, the earliest *vedette* of the latter, devised a law that, besides undertaking to purge the United States of the physically alien, defined sedition as an attempt to set up any dictatorship under foreign control—absolutely nothing was said about dictatorships under pure American ownership and operation—or knowingly combining with others in any effort contributing to such an imported tyranny (*Buy American* in another guise). Generously, McCarran's adoption of the definition of sedition first proposed by Karl Mundt (later a leal henchman of

Joseph McCarthy) and the chameleon turned Vice President, Richard Nixon, did not bar the advocacy of Constitutional amendments, though it seemed clearly to outlaw any campaigning for legislation. Intent to set up the dreaded foreign dictatorship was irrelevant: all that mattered to these pioneers of jurisprudence was a possible result, whether it actually occurred or was determined by soothsayers to be inevitable; but nowhere did the statute define the forbidden acts, speech, publication.

The registration provisions of the Smith Act, which merely ordered such registration but stipulated no penalty for refusal, were now given enforcement teeth: violation carried punishment for both the offending organisation and its members. All "Communist" organisations in being in the United States when the law became effective must register within thirty days; those that later turned Red must register within thirty days of changing color. (None in either category bothered.) Communist organisations were decreed to be of two types: *action* and *front* (the Communist Control Act of 1954 created a third category: *infiltrated*). An *action* group was one primarily dedicated to revolution (yet these legislators professed to revere the Boston Tea Party and the revolutionists of Bunker Hill and Independence Hall). A *front* was any organisation substantially directed, dominated or controlled by an action organisation and primarily operated to aid and support an action organisation, a foreign Communist Government or the world Communist movement. If he believed that any organisation fell into either category, the Attorney General was empowered to serve it with a petition for an order from the Subversive Activities Control Board to register; no hearing need be held but, if the Government condescended to permit one, it must be public. In reaching its decision, the SACB would ponder the degree of external control of the organisation, the extent to which it deviated from the CP, how many people it sent abroad for training and (most important) the extent to which it resisted registration and disclosure: mere refusal to register was ground to consider the objector Communist, and each day's delay in registering could incur a penalty of five years in prison and a $10,000 fine.

All members of registered organisations, like all members of groups on the Attorney General's list of subversive organisations (regardless whether listed without hearings), were to be automatically discharged from Government employment without hearings. The Attorney General was further empowered to publish the names of all such organisations and, if he could find them, the names of their members. To complete the castration of the Constitution, the Government was given power, if the President proclaimed an Internal Security Emergency (whatever that might be, and however determined), to round up and herd into concentration camps every person who it had reason to believe might participate or conspire in espionage, sabotage, etc. Each must have a hearing, but the Government could withhold such evidence as might jeopardise the national security by being made public. Appeals were possible and, in the unlikely event that any accused proved himself innocent, he might claim indemnification for loss of income. Thus was freedom to be further defended by the nation that had contributed to the defeat of (foreign) Fascism and that professed an illimitable hatred for dictatorship—by Communists.

It would be hasty to conclude that bad faith and stupid thinking had reached their zenith. The Communist Control Act of 1954 solemnly declared, in the approved mumbo-jumbo of legislative language and patriotic bombast, that the Communist Party and its successors (it assumed various names) were not political parties but instruments of a conspiracy to overthrow the Government and that the members of this conspiracy were "not members but slaves." Therefore all such organisations were proscribed and all persons who had "knowingly and willfully" become their slaves were subject to the penalties prescribed by the McCarran Act for the members of action organisations. Membership was to be established by evidence of knowledge that one was so listed, financial contributions, the acceptance of any organisation discipline, work for such an organisation, communication of its instructions by any means (including, specifically, semaphore!), preparing or mailing its literature, offering counsel or participating in any other way. Slaves of the conspiracy were barred from holding office not only in unions but also in companies embraced by federal labor legislation. Action and front organisations were required to register not only themselves but their printing equipment.

The new category of Communist-*infiltrated* organisations was defined as any group whose officers were or within the preceding three years had been Communists or employes of any entity engaged in impairing the military or industrial power of the United States. The Attorney General was empowered to file with the SACB and to serve on the accused infiltratee a petition for a determination of its infiltration; within six months of having been so branded it might petition for absolution on proof that it had purged itself. Organisations that did not appear in answer to the Attorney General's petition could be heard and condemned *in absentia*.

As early as 1948 the whole loyalty-security *pogrom* had been found to have no parallel anywhere in the world except in Vichy France, Fascist Italy and Nazi Germany. In a study of *Loyalty Among Government Employes* by Thomas I. Emerson and David M. Helfield of the Yale Law School, reprinted by the Union from the *Yale Law Journal*, this conclusion was stated without qualification. The investigators found no genuine need for any such program in this country because the existing laws were already more than adequate. If Congress lacked the courage to resist the outcries of the rabble, the authors added, it should set up the most narrowly limited of loyalty-security programs, provide full due-process safeguards for both individuals and organisations and follow the British system of discharging a clear security risk only if no non-sensitive post exists to which he can be transferred. Membership in an organisation should not *per se* justify any action, the article contended (and the Union agreed), and only organisations presenting a demonstrably real danger should raise any question. Two years later the Union's own *Restudy of the Loyalty Program*, based on the establishment of the Attorney General's list of subversive organisations, the use that had been made of it thus far and the procedures under it, resulted in conclusions like those of the Yale study, plus others that, of course, were ignored by a Government hag-ridden by the HUAC and its Senate counterpart. These further recommendations proposed:

—That the Attorney General's list should be abolished because it had more than served its purpose (which, originally, was to preserve wartime security) and because it had so easily and often been abused by Government and the press through irresponsible utterances and accusations based on it. Corollarily, that mere membership in an organisation listed by the Attorney General should not be used derogatorily against any individual.

—That every organisation on the list, if it were not abolished, should be given a formal hearing with all due-process safeguards, instead of the prevailing informal procedures, and that such hearings should be private except where no need therefor is demonstrated by a *prima-facie* showing by affidavit.

—That any loyalty-security program be limited to sensitive jobs.

—That review be granted in every case, including those in the Departments of State and Defense and the Atomic Energy Commission, which were deprived of review by Presidential order.

But the spontaneous and interminable orgasm of fright reveled in by the mob after the war and adroitly manipulated by its demagogues, as noted in the Union's 1946 pamphlet, *Post-War Hysteria*, would permit no hint of rationality, and the ostensible leaders of the nation were, as so often, led, primarily by their need for popular support. An excellent example was the refusal of a House committee to publish a Library of Congress document, *Fascism in Action*, prepared as a companion-piece to its already published *Communism in Action*: only months of pressure led by the ACLU finally prevailed on the courageous Congressmen to allow its appearance. It was no wonder that the 1947-8 report of the Union was titled *Our Uncertain Liberties*; and the nation's loss was the Union's gain: as the paranoia mounted, more and more of the few sane citizens uninfected by it began to offer their dues and their volunteer services to the ACLU as the one all-encompassing champion of civil liberties that would not serve a partisan cause or refuse to fight for an unpopular one. The Union was almost alone, for example, in demanding that the President's Loyalty Review Board (the President in question was Truman) allow accused "risks" to confront and cross-examine their accusers and to know the contents and sources of the FBI reports on the basis of which their careers might be aborted. This tradition-hallowed kind of guaranteed conviction was applied not only to Government employes but to workers in "defense" industry and, very soon, to those in jobs not even remotely linked to "defense"—for example, subway lavatory attendants—as the states and cities entered into lively competition for scalps with the Federal Government.

"The FBI's functions," the ACLU noted in 1949, "have been expanded under laws now penalising opinions and associations, risking for the first time in our history the creation of a secret political police system with its array of informers and undercover agents." The risk had become reality almost before the ink of the statement had dried, and the reality is still with us: the FBI maintains a dossier of thousands of names of individuals who have ever been imprudent enough to refuse to submit to a so-called security clearance or publicly utter the truth about its own activities or challenge the high-mindedness of their country's meddling in the internal affairs of others; telephones are tapped by Government without regard to statute and decision; private persons' mail is unlawfully opened and read, without their knowledge, before it is delivered; stool-pigeons are assured of protection regardless of the motives for or the facts of their denunciations; at least half the dues-paying membership of the pitiful remnant of the Communist Party—8,000 card holders in a frightened nation of 193,000,000—is FBI agents or stoolies working some on retainer, others by the piece. If one is rash enough to send a subscription application to *The Worker*, one may receive an FBI visit even before the first issue of the paper arrives.

The loyalty hunt was no federal monopoly, though by June of 1949 almost 2,500,000 federal employes had been investigated— and exactly eighty-three had been shown to merit discharge. The Attorney General's swelling list was grossly misused to stimulate heretic hunts in the states and local denials of basic Constitutional rights. California led the pack, but only with great effort. The Detroit police commissioner—over the opposition of the American Newspaper Guild, the ACLU and one Detroit newspaper—refused to issue press cards to reporters and photographers who would not take loyalty oaths. Many New York City newspapers insisted on loyalty oaths by all employes. Like some states, they based this on making everyone a civil-defense aide. New Jersey demanded a loyalty oath of every candidate for public office. The Rapp-Coudert Committee, New York State's version of the HUAC, unearthed Communists everywhere, even while Illinois and Washington were abolishing their HUAC imitations.   The AEC instituted a loyalty-oath requirement for all its fellowships, as well as its jobs, and applications fell off at once. Nor were all the intransigents living on Moscow gold: thousands were men whose politics were otherwise irreproachable—i.e., indistinguishable from those of their neighbors—but who would not exhibit their political maidenheads to butchers. This luxury of integrity was not available to jobless workmen who could not collect unemployment insurance until they had sworn that they were not going to overthrow the Government and did not belong to any group that the Attorney General thought might be considering such action (of the 150 such organisations on his list at the outbreak of the Korean "police action," exactly six advocated revolution). In most cases the ACLU accomplished little against entrenched stupidity; but it did win the right to challenge members of the Coast Guard review board for prejudice in clearing merchant seamen, and it compelled the Coast Guard to refuse clearance only on all the available evidence, not on mere membership in a blacklisted organisation. The Circuit Court of Appeals, charged with enforcing the Constitution, found the Attorney General blameless in enrolling organisations on his blacklist without giving them hearings. McCarthy launched his four-year war of character assassination, choosing as his first victims former Ambassador Philip K. Jessup, Owen Lattimore of the State Department and former Judge Dorothy Kenyon, a veteran anti-Communist director of the ACLU: Senator Tydings investigated McCarthy's investigation and, inevitably, since McCarthy never scrupled enough to seek for facts or refuse artifacts, Tydings found all three impeccably loyal and non-Communist. In the next two years the membership of the American Civil Liberties Union rose 150 per cent, from 8148 to 21,284.

Here and there an isolated instance of justice occurred—the Pennsylvania Supreme Court, for instance, would not countenance the State Attorney General's investigation into the political views of a county District Attorney, and it reversed the contempt conviction of a lawyer who in an ordinary civil litigation refused to say whether his soul was Red, even though the United States Supreme Court was busily upholding all varieties of loyalty oaths as conditions of employment. But in general the states behaved no better—sometimes, if possible, worse—than the Federal Government. Many declared the Communist Party a criminal organisation—only Utah resisted pressure for any kind of "sedition" statute—and state loyalty procedures were no more Constitutional than the federal. Twenty-seven states barred all "subversive" parties from the ballot. In this they were merely aping the federal legislation that outlawed the Communist Party and, in addition, deprived it of the right to institute lawsuits and the right to have bank accounts. It is notable here that, despite the traditional venomous rivalry between Socialists and Communists—to each the other is far more abhorrent than the worst Capitalist—it was Norman Thomas, the veteran Socialist who helped to found the ACLU, who pleaded eloquently before the House Judiciary Committee for the right of the Communist Party to function as a political party despite its Mr. Hyde aspect.

In general the ultimate responsibility for the enforcement of security and loyalty laws lay with the FBI, which—it said in the laws—was to collect and not to evaluate information. The FBI exhorted the citizenry to report all possible factual evidence, but not gossip or rumor, and to respect the rights of others (after all, someone had to). These FBI reports became the criterion for judging individuals' loyalty. In Truman's original 1947 loyalty order, employment was barred to any person when there was reasonable ground to believe him disloyal, even if he presented no security danger; in 1951 Truman stiffened the rule, so that now employment was barred if there was a reasonable doubt of one's loyalty: the accused was called on, as if the Code Napoléon had suddenly joined the Constitution and the common law, to prove his innocence. In May, 1953, President Eisenhower, to the plaudits of the ACLU, restored some semblance of justice by making security rather than loyalty the criterion; but the Union opposed the abolition of the old non-governmental Loyalty Review Board, contending that the judgments of Government employes and department heads serving on such a board might be colored by fear for their own jobs and by dread of public dissatisfaction in unpopular cases. Truman, the apostle of the Fair Deal, consistently flouted the Supreme Court's orders for hearings in loyalty-security cases; Eisenhower yielded to the law but the ACLU criticised his Attorney General, justly, for announcing in advance what organisations would be given hearings before they were listed: this, the Union said, was prejudicial. Other Eisenhower procedures were much worse. Clearance for employment in war industries could be denied to one in "sympathetic association" with a member of a Communist organisation even if one was totally ignorant of one's friend's membership (this was analogous to the "reasoning" of the 1952 Gwinn Amendment, bitterly fought by the ACLU, which denied leases in federally aided housing not only to members of proscribed groups but also to their close relatives, even if the relatives were at political swords' points with the *subversives*). Both the Government and war industries allowed each security board to supplement the Attorney General's blacklist with its own—but the Union persuaded the Defense Department to cancel that of the Detroit Army Ordnance District because it included even organisations mentioned in inter-office Government correspondence. Some slight concept of the effect of this reign of white terror on individuals may be had from the consideration of representative ACLU cases of the 1950's:

—In Puerto Rico, which had a Little Smith Act, Ruth Reynolds was convicted of advocating the forceful overthrow of the Government on only this evidence: When Pedro Albizu Campos, leader of the Nationalist Party, bade his audience: "Raise your right hands, all of you who are willing to sacrifice your lives and fortunes to defend our cause," she did so. The Puerto Rico Supreme Court reversed her conviction, holding that taking an oath does not constitute advocacy.

—Arthur Manning of Philadelphia was suspended by the Navy Yard there because his wife's grandmother belonged to the Communist Party and was a friend of Mother Ella Bloor, one of the Party's pioneers, and, during a period of financial constriction,

Manning lived in his grandmother-in-law's house. In addition, the Navy charged, he attended racially mixed parties. It took him eighteen months to regain his job. (This and the next four instances are taken from a publication of the Greater Philadelphia Branch of the ACLU, *The Federal Security Program*: *Some Philadelphia Episodes*.)

—David Feinberg, a Navy chemist, was an Orthodox Jew like his wife. Before his marriage he had courted a girl who may or may not have held a CP card (this was not certain), and he had signed a petition attesting to the good character of a non-Communist leftist. The accusation that Feinberg had held a card in the Young Communists' League ten years earlier was disproved; but he may have been on the mailing list of a "front." Luckier than Manning, he was reinstated after only a year.

—Adele Warren, a secretary for the Signal Corps, lived one floor above her radical brother in their mother's house; there was no allegation of any illegality in her brother's political activities. She was asked at her hearing whether she ever ate with her brother, where the family telephone was in relation to her brother's room, and then: "Suppose you were reinstated and then found your brother was a Communist: would you tell your supervisor?" Apparently Miss Warren did not know that good anti-Communists particularly loathed the Communist tenet calling on saviors of the proletariat to denounce their near and dear; rather ingenuously she countered: "Would that be part of my duties?" (*Yes, Adele*, the hearing board might have truthfully replied: *it is as patriotic for an American to denounce her Communist brother as it is reprehensible for a Russian to denounce his anti-Communist brother. Betrayal is only what the other fellow does*.) Miss Warren was cleared by the hearing board but the clearance was reversed when the Government appealed, and two and a half years later she was still awaiting justice in a federal court.

—Elmer Schwartz, Arsenal supply clerk, senior vice commander of his American Legion post and a member of the hardly less proto-Fascist Jewish War Veterans, was accused of pro-Communist criticisms of the Korean conflict and the Berlin airlift: the evidence consisted of quotations from letters obtained by the

FBI from his fellow-students in a technical school. The writers of the letters refused to appear at his hearing, and neither Schwartz nor his lawyers could win permission to see the letters. The charge of mental instability and infantilism was disproved. Schwartz was reinstated after nine months.

—Clarence Smith, a janitor for the Veterans' Administration, was an almost illiterate young Southern Negro (the product of a "separate but equal" school), who admitted having joined the YCL in 1942; he did not remain in it long. In a pitiful letter to the General Services Administration, he explained that, knowing nothing of political parties, he had joined because there were pretty girls in that club whom he wanted to meet. When he listed his membership in a job application and the employer revealed the diabolic essence of the YCL, he left it, but the *Daily Worker* went on being sent to him though he did not pay for it. His letter was ignored but he went at last to a lawyer and, after seven months of suspension, he won back his sensitive janitorship in the VA.

One of the most spectacular of the loyalty-security outrages was the dismissal of John Stewart Service, a State Department career official, in circumstances that brought down on Secretary of State Dulles the cold castigation of the Supreme Court. Like his colleague, John Paton Davies, ousted from the State Department for alleged deficiencies in character and judgment that were never specified, and J. Robert Oppenheimer, denied security clearance by the AEC under similar secrecy, Service, who had been cleared under the earlier Truman witch test, was found ineligible for continued service because he could not prove his loyalty to the Government beyond a reasonable doubt (a feat that might be beyond the powers of the most sterling patriot). Truman set up a special commission to study Service's case: it found that he was loyal but might be a security risk; this finding, based on evidence that the accused had no opportunity to examine and confute, was approved by that prominent volunteer salesman of Christian love and Godliness, the Secretary of State. He arrived at this judgment on his fellow-man without reading any of the evidence or making any independent determination, though the law permitted him to do so whenever he found it in the nation's best interests.

But Dulles had earlier promulgated loyalty-security regulations that included his pledge to safeguard the rights of every employe accused: a decision of reasonable doubt of loyalty, his regulations provided, "shall be reached after consideration of the complete file, arguments, briefs and testimony presented." Having exercised his right to subject himself to rigorous standards, Dulles was estopped from abandoning them, Justice Harlan ruled in finding for Service; Harlan added: "Regulations validly prescribed by a Government administrator are binding upon him as well as the citizen, and this principle holds even when the administrative action under review is discretionary in nature."

Such cases as these and the hundreds of less spectacular, if more laughable, instances in state courts—like the overruled attempt to increase the normal sentence of a man guilty of fraud in applying for an automobile registration because he was also a Communist—caused the ACLU, after two years of study followed by an internal referendum, to issue a statement of its own policy on loyalty-security cases. Opposing judgment by accusation, guilt by association, the invasion of the privacy of personal beliefs and opinions and the confusion of dissent with disloyalty, the Union declared that, while it would continue not to employ or elect to office anyone who did not believe in civil liberties (this was reasonable: should the College of Cardinals choose a Protestant as Pope?), it would also continue to defend the rights and liberties of all, regardless of unpopularity and of the associations and beliefs of its "clients." As for the Communists or other totalitarians, in the character of political agitation movements they should be untrammeled but, in the other character of membership in international conspiracies, they were rightly subject to legal curbs on employability. Again one is reminded: what of the Roman Church and the Zionist movement?

In specific cases the ACLU fought hard but sometimes vainly. Oppenheimer had been found to be both loyal and discreet but also to be an associate of alleged—not of proved—Communists. Ernest Angell, formerly New York regional chairman of the Loyalty Review Board, challenged the denial of information to Oppenheimer; the AEC's Special Personnel Security Board challenged the right of Oppenheimer or any scientist to give more than only technical judgment on matters of top security, ignoring

Angell's argument that "to ask that a scientist categorically divorce the whole experience and the judgment of his life from his technical service would paralyse those qualities of mind which serve his country." Malin, executive director of the Union, tried to shame Dulles into granting Davies' request to publish the charges against him: Davies, with twenty-three years of State Department service, had survived eight loyalty-security hearings with a virgin record before Dulles took a dislike to his "character"—which was that of a heretic who did not believe Dulles' foreign policy stemmed directly from heaven. Malin sought also to persuade the Federal Civil Service Commission to clarify its statistics of resignations and discharges with respect to alleged subversiveness and to indicate in how many such cases the accused had had the benefit of even the virtually *ex parte* hearings that were the only kind granted. Malin asked, too, for a clear definition of subversion. Of course he did not get one, since to attempt to define subversion clearly must of necessity stigmatise the holy Revolution of 1776.

But, though the outrages mounted, consciences began to prick. When the Loyalty Review Board decided that Dr. J. B. Peters of Yale was a security risk in the Public Health Service despite the latter's clearance of him, the Supreme Court ruled that the board had no authority to review independently the loyalty of a man already cleared by the employing agency, and it ordered the charges and findings expunged (from the record; nothing expels stigma from the public mind). Former Senator Harry Cain, a member of the Subversive Activities Control Board, to which his honesty was a constant threat of subversion, called for security officers who could distinguish between treason and heresy, between disloyalty and non-conformity. The requirement that employment of a given worker must be "clearly consistent with the interest of the United States," he said, should be modified so that dismissal would be recommended only if continued employment were "reasonably inconsistent with the national interest." Cain also denounced the practice of lumping mere drunks, pederasts, gossips and connoisseurs of low life with the actually disloyal, implying, correctly, that the former were not necessarily security risks and should be ousted only when their work was clearly encroached upon by their pleasures.

But so much reasonableness had few followers. California required a loyalty oath for any individual or organisation seeking exemption from property taxes—the first victims were a war veteran, a Protestant church, a Quaker meeting and a synagogue, all of which rightly resented the gratuitous slur of demanding proof of their purity. All were taken up by the ACLU, which found loyalty problems in the armed forces, too: a less-than-honorable discharge was issued, for non-military reasons, to a soldier guilty of consorting with his radical mother and step-father and accused (without proof) of having, before his induction, worked for the Urban League, registered as an American Labor Party voter, worked at a summer camp alleged to be Communist-run and solicited defense contributions in a Smith Act trial. Four years later the Union's help finally brought victory in the Supreme Court, but even afterward the army continued the same policy condemned by the court, insisting on less-than-honorable discharges for all men whose pre-military political activity was more leftist than the military thought fitting.

The army also distributed a pamphlet, *How to Spot a Communist*, until the Union won its withdrawal. The army's clues to Communists required no great intellectual effort in their application: a Communist was one who discussed such issues as civil rights, racial or religious discrimination, the immigration laws, anti-subversive legislation, curbs on unions, the military budget or peace. To trap the warier Reds who avoided these topics, the reader was alerted to listen for such terms as *vanguard, chauvinism, book-burning, colonialism, demagogy, witch-hunt, dialectical, reactionary* or *progressive*. The air force was no less alert to danger: it compelled Republic Aviation to fire an engineer with seven years' service because, the air force insisted, he had a psychoneurosis (if this were to become the criterion of employment, 95 per cent of the western world's population would be walking the streets). Later the air force admitted that what the man had was in fact neurodermatitis, or jungle rot, contracted while in uniform, and it allowed him to go back to work. Loyalty-security programs were getting into the hands of industry, too, and the ACLU contested every application of them by private employers, not only because of their application to such non-war work as wrapping bottles of proprietary medicines but also because of industry's refusal to provide even the rudimentary safeguards of the federal inquisitors. Even in the latter's solicitous hands, as the ACLU's brief for Peters had pointed out to the Supreme Court, complete investigation had thoroughly discredited the testimony of star-chamber witnesses, often disclosing shocking ulterior motives for their baseless accusations, and had uncovered innumerable other instances of injustices resulting from the denial of cross-examination. One of the most ironic of these was the case of a man who had earned his livelihood by spying for the California National Guard within the Communist Party: he was now barred from Government work because of his record as a former Communist!

The multiplication of state *simulacra* of the Smith Act complicated the situation. Convicted under Pennsylvania's statute, Steve Nelson of the CP enlisted the help of the ACLU, which persuaded the state Supreme Court to reverse his conviction on the ground that the federal law superseded the state statute, but Pennsylvania appealed. In the United States Supreme Court the state lost again, thus satisfying the Union that multiple prosecutions for the same act would not be tolerated; but in the case of Carl Braden, a Kentucky newspaperman whose seditiousness consisted largely of being what is so elegantly called a *nigger-lover*, a distinction was made between sedition against the Federal Government and sedition against a state, thus permitting both to get the same man. In the 1956-7 term, however, the court began to narrow its definition of sedition under the Smith Act: mere advocacy of the violent overthrow of the Government, it held, was totally unrelated to advocacy of action to accomplish that overthrow and hence was not illegal. Five defendants were ordered set free because the only offenses charged against them were membership or office within the Party, both of which together did not constitute a criminal offense.

The Communist Party's position that it advocated no more than a waiting game characterised by the teaching of revolutionary theory and the postponement of incitement to the indefinite future, the Circuit Court of Appeals held, barred Government interference as a First Amendment violation. This, of course, made no difference to the Government, which carried its harassment to persons who had been guilty of no more than surviving the deaths of their Communist relatives: it stopped Social Security payments to the widows and children as well as to Communists themselves. The ACLU's denunciation of such vindictive breach of contract went unheeded. At the same time the Government treated the Party, illegal though it had been declared, as an American business organisation that owed payroll and other taxes, and, without notice and in the absence of any sign that the assets might be dispersed or concealed, the Treasury raided the Party headquarters and *The Worker's* offices to satisfy claims for $389,000 taxes owed by the Party and $46,000 owed by the paper. The Union's protest resulted in the return of some of the piddling assets seized.

The state loyalty oaths were under constant but rarely successful ACLU attack. In New York State all applicants for admission to the bar were required to say whether they belonged to organisations seeking directly or indirectly to change "the form of government provided by the Constitution." Current Communists were barred by statute from jury duty, regardless whether membership was innocent or deliberate, and unscrupulous judges allowed questions as well on past membership though it was not a bar: under pressure from the New York Civil Liberties Union some retreats were made by individual judges. The Union won Governor Harriman's veto of a bill to require public housing tenants to swear that they were not and had never been members of organisations blacklisted by the State Board of Regents. Arkansas' oath bill was vetoed as a danger to innocent persons—vetoed by the same Governor Orval Faubus who was defying the Supreme Court's order to integrate schools. The Illinois Supreme Court upheld the state's Broyles Law, requiring loyalty oaths of all persons paid wholly or partly with state funds. The ACLU found itself in bed with the Wisconsin Department of the American Legion in successfully opposing a bill to bar *subversives* from meeting or speaking in tax-supported buildings; and California, inconsistent as always, defeated a bill that would have denied tax exemption to any non-profit organisation allowing its buildings to be used by blacklisted groups or their members.

But injustice had reached such proportions by the second half of the 1950's that the Senate felt constrained to set up a commission to investigate and recommend remedies. Its Loyd Wright Commission lacked the courage or the wisdom to produce more than suggestions for a centralised general loyalty program; the Union countered that what was needed was a basic revision of the civil-service law to provide full due process and appeals on loyalty questions not only, for those already employed but also for applicants. At the same time the Union challenged, without success, the legality of basing determinations on the Attorney General's list. The Justice Department had never been overly assiduous in respecting the statutory provisions by which an organisation could achieve its removal from this index: it took the Independent Socialist League, its youth affiliate, the Socialist Youth League, and the long extinct Workers' Party that had died in spawning them ten years of fighting to be dropped. But the National Lawyers' Guild was immediately removed when it sued the department. The fact that the Justice Department was not after all impervious to the claims of justice may have influenced the AEC to allow its suspects to have counsel at the informal proceedings that preceded their hearings and to provide that they should be notified directly and privately, instead of through third persons, that Big Brother wanted to see them. Big Brother in uniform continued penalising soldier members of the organisations removed from the blacklist, and Army Secretary Brucker brusquely refused the Union's request that his service conform: all aspects of any suspect's political life would continue to be checked. Despite the absence of any such provision in the Communications Act, the FCC began to demand loyalty oaths as conditions of broadcasting licenses; again the ACLU was ignored. But the Union had better luck with Pennsylvania, which it persuaded to eliminate political questions from its employment applications, and with the National Municipal League, which agreed to expunge loyalty references from its model civil-service law for the states. New York State split a bargain, in effect, with the Union: more honorable than Washington, Albany found that unemployment pay could not be withheld from a former employee of the CP when the state had accepted tax payments from it; but, under the 1954 state Communist Control Act, the state could refuse to accept such payments of taxes.

Somehow the beginning of the current decade seemed to bring with it a beginning of decency here and there. The Supreme Court overthrew a Florida loyalty oath because of its extraordinary ambiguity: "I have not and will not lend my aid, support, advice, counsel or influence to the Communist Party." Alone among federal agencies, the AEC allowed accused employes and applicants to confront their accusers, unless these were Government intelligence agents whose identities could not be disclosed—not an unmixed gain in its obvious invitation to evasion; but in such case, or if the accuser had died, consideration would be given to the lack of opportunity for cross-examination. This was followed by the defeat, with the assistance of the Union, of a HUAC-sponsored bill that would have enabled the Secretary of Defense to eliminate the right of five million workers on war contracts to confront and cross-examine. (The HUAC over-reached itself and may well have contributed to its own defeat by antagonising the House through the parliamentary maneuvers of its friends on the Rules Committee, who got the bill to the floor under a forty-minute debate limit and with a prohibition of amendments.) The Union's affiliates in Massachusetts and Michigan defeated bills that would have required high schools to teach indoctrinational anti-Communism courses. ACLU opposition played a strong *rôle* in the million-vote margin by which Californians rejected a constitutional amendment that would have authorised any judge, attorney general, grand jury or "duly constituted federal body or officer" to declare any person or organisation subversive without redress: the victim would be barred from the ballot, forbidden to function as a political party, ruled ineligible for state or local office and disqualified from claiming tax exemptions.

As the decade advanced, common decency encroached farther in spite of the counter-attack of the simultaneously growing native Fascists. One of the most significant gains was made in the Defense Department, which, after conferences with the Civil Liberties Union, considerably revised its procedures. Ordering its investigators and boards to respect "lawful civil and private rights," the Department specifically forbade questioning employes and applicants on their religious and racial views, their "non-subversive" political beliefs and associations, their opinions on legal policies, their union memberships. "Questions regarding personal and domestic affairs, financial matters and the status of physical health," the directive stated, "fall in this category unless evidence clearly indicates a reasonable basis for believing there may be illegal or subversive activities, personal or moral irresponsibility [an undefined term leaving far too much latitude to self-constituted censors], or mental or emotional instability involved . . . questions about conduct which have no security implications are unwarranted." Even the Coast Guard yielded somewhat to the long-standing attacks by the Union and made some improvements in its procedure for clearing merchant seamen. It would no longer ask them whether they had ever been subject to or under the direct or indirect influence of foreign governments (a question that would have automatically barred any seaman whose parents had not had the wisdom to get him born here), whether they had any relatives in Communist countries (a fact that, totally irrelevant as it is, might still be unknown to an individual), or whether they subscribed to or distributed the publications of any of the 300 organisations on the Attorney General's list (the Attorney General then being Robert F. Kennedy, to whom civil liberties are something one talks about but does not act on). But the ACLU objected to the retention of queries as to past and present memberships and the writing of articles for publications of any of the 300 outlaws. Suit was instituted on behalf of a Florida Negro denied clearance because he had once joined the CP in the hope that it might really be concerned with equal rights and for no other reason, and who had left it immediately on learning better.

Mr. Kennedy did not reply to the Union's request that he drop all pending McCarran Act prosecutions in the light of two Supreme Court rulings. One affirmed a Circuit Court decision that the CP could not be forced to register as an action organisation under the act because the registration could be accomplished only by the surrender of the self-incrimination privilege of the individuals who would have to sign the documents; the other, discussed in the next chapter, was the Supreme Court's assent to review the ACLU's defeat on the registration of front organisations. The Supreme Court also took under review Louisiana's anti-subversive laws, which, the Union's brief *amicus* contended, were merely a cloak for the harassment of civil-rights workers. Not only were these laws invoked to ground raids on the offices of the Southern Educational Conference Fund; its attorneys' homes were also ransacked, the data seized by the state were subpoenaed by Senator Eastland's federal scavengers, and the organisers were ordered out of the state at midnight—all on the ground that the civil-rights organisation was a Communist front. On the score of subversion, the ACLU argued, the state law had been superseded by the various federal statutes; in addition, its prohibitions of free speech and association violated, *prima facie*, the First and Fourteenth Amendments, and due process was further violated by the state court's refusal of evidence attacking its constitutionality.

A similar Indiana law, though by no means limited to Negroes and their friends in its application, overcame ACLU attack in the courts of that state, which has always been exceptionally hostile to the Union and has defied even its own Governor by consistently refusing to allow the Union to meet in a public building in Indianapolis, national capital of the American Legion. The Indiana law provided that, "whenever two or more persons assemble for the purpose of advocating or teaching the doctrine that the Government of the United States or of the state of Indiana should be overthrown by force, violence or any unlawful means, such an assembly is unlawful, and every person voluntarily participating therein by his presence, aid or instigation shall be guilty of a felony." In this case three were assembled: Ralph Levitt, James Bingham and Thomas Morgan, students at the University of Indiana, were officers of the Young Socialist Alliance, at a meeting of which a member of the Socialist Workers' Party declared that, if necessary, Negroes would (not *should*) achieve equality by force. They were promptly indicted and convicted of advocating the overthrow of the government.

In Arizona's Supreme Court the Union was defeated in its challenge of the state's loyalty oath for its employes on behalf of a Quaker teacher in Tucson who contested it as a matter of conscience and contended that it not only is vague but operates as a bill of attainder denying due process and freedom of speech and association. The Union's brief *amicus* relied on the 1964 Supreme Court decision that invalidated a similar Washington State oath, saying: "The state may not require one to choose between sub-scribing to an unduly vague and broad oath, thereby incurring the likelihood of prosecution, and conscientiously refusing to take the oath with the consequent loss of employment, and perhaps profession, particularly where 'the free dissemination of ideas may be the loser.' "

Whether the Supreme Court's writ extends to Arizona re-mains to be seen. Regardless of the outcome, one may be con-fident—and immeasurably grateful—that the American Civil Lib-erties Union exists to fight for the thesis of its brief in this case: "When dealing with free speech in an age when government continually seeks more control over the individual, all doubt should be resolved in favor of the individual."

12

Off With Their Heads!

The purge—by dismissal, by exclusion, by detention within the borders, by imprisonment—did not begin to approach its apogee as an instrument of policy in the modern world until the twentieth century was attaining its majority. In the forty-five years of the American Civil Liberties Union's life the purge as an approved weapon of government has become almost commonplace. Only two things differentiate the American version from those of the fully developed totalitarianisms—Fascism and Communism: the American Government has never legalised violence, and the American public has never wholly accepted the right to purge, though it has at times, notably in the First World War and after the Second, come frighteningly close to acquiescence in this ultimate consolidation of government.

In September, 1917, the Government bagged hundreds of members of the Industrial Workers of the World in a nationwide round-up; within three weeks the IWW's president, William D. Haywood, and 165 others were indicted in Chicago for conspiracy to obstruct the war effort—despite the fact that, of the 521 strikes between April and October of that year, exactly three were the IWW's. But the IWW had for twenty years preached the elimination of capitalism, the classless society and the brotherhood of man. Most of its members were migratory workers—in agriculture, in lumber, in mining, in unskilled factory labor—whose annual earnings averaged $600 at a time when experts saw $800 as the bare minimum for a decent standard of living. Like every other union and most of the employers they fought, the Wobblies were often guilty of sabotage. Certainly they were the victims of violence— by the law, by industry and by the mob—more than any other group of their period: lynchings, beatings, kidnapings, mass deportations over city and state lines. Equally certainly, they did not oppose the war as agents of Kaiser Wilhelm II: their one enemy was the capitalist system.

Three months after the Chicago indictments, the Governor's Mansion in Sacramento, California, was bombed. It was immediately assumed that the bombers were Wobblies and the Sacramento *Bee* cried editorially: "It would be a waste of time to have [them] arrested and tried. The best thing to do is to shoot them, and not wait for sunrise, either. The sooner the better, even if there is not time to permit them counsel or benefit of clergy." The police, instead, rounded up forty-six Wobblies, including a woman, found that they had nothing to do with the bombing and therefore had them indicted for violating the Espionage Act. At the same time thirty-five IWW men were arrested in Kansas for conspiracy to sabotage oil production. The first two indictments, eight months apart, were quashed because they accused the men of committing their acts on dates when they were in jail; two years after their arrest—all of which time they spent in jail— they went to trial on a third indictment. But both the Kansas and the California trials were overshadowed by that in Chicago, though the filth, vermin, rats and excrement storage imposed on the Kansas prisoners quite distressed some people. Besides, virtually all the Kansas defendants were freed by a successful appeal after spending hardly three years in these expense-free quarters.

Immediately after the Chicago arrests the Justice Department embarked on a long campaign of arrests and property seizures against the IWW everywhere, confiscating everything that it did not smash, and thus crippling the efforts of the IWW's General Defense Committee to raise funds, supply evidence and retain counsel. Roger Baldwin committed the infant and impecunious National Civil Liberties Bureau to do all it could. He and George T. Vanderveer, the IWW's chief attorney, appealed to President Wilson to drop the Chicago case; and, on the ground of preserving labor harmony in wartime, they were strongly backed by Secretary of War Baker, Secretary of Labor William Wilson, Supreme Court Justice Brandeis, Colonel House, George Creel, the director of war propaganda, and James Tumulty, the President's personal secretary. But President Wilson refused to see Baldwin and Vanderveer, though he did listen to Clarence Darrow; in the end, however, the great humanitarian Democrat who made war to make the world safe for democracy (and Fascism and Communism) fell back on his own belief that the IWW was "certainly . . . worthy of being suppressed." The trial began in April, 1918, and ended in August.

During these months the Post Office held up the General Defense Committee's mail and withheld some of its checks; the Government ordered the American Express Company to refuse all the Committee's shipments, in or out; publications carrying its advertisements were threatened with the loss of second-class mailing privileges. Baldwin's pamphlet, *The Truth About the IWW*, contended that the organisation had been always and only a legitimate labor group whose objectives were economic, not political, and that it had never advocated violence, disloyalty, treason or pro-Germanism: therefore the Government suppressed the pamphlet. The trial itself, according to *The Nation*, which was hardly pro-Government, was scrupulously fair. The Government could prove that individual Wobblies and one branch—but not the organisation—had opposed the war and advised conscientious objection to the draft. Witnesses testified to sabotage of private industrial property by Wobblies. Vanderveer countered by proving that the IWW as an organisation had actively supported the war effort and that its members had registered for induction, served in the army and bought Liberty Bonds: as for the destruction of property, it was intended to coerce employers and had nothing to do with the war. In one hour of deliberation, overwhelmed by wartime prejudices, the jury convicted ninety-six of the 113 who had gone on trial.

Haywood, who had found that Judge Kenesaw Mountain Landis, later the commissioner of the baseball industry, had been "fair to us, absolutely square throughout the whole trial," was stunned by Landis' sentences. Haywood was sentenced to serve twenty years and pay a $30,000 fine; the sentences of the others ranged from one to fifteen years. Most of them, like most of the Sacramento defendants, whose sentences ranged from a $100 fine to ten years, were sent to Leavenworth. The National Civil Liberties Bureau immediately began an unending campaign, inherited by the American Civil Liberties Union, for their release, which was ultimately conditioned on individual clemency petitions that would amount to admissions of guilt of crimes that they had not committed. In August, 1922, after Baldwin went to Leavenworth to confer with the IWW men there, the General Defense Committee published an *Open Letter to President Harding* from fifty-two of the Leavenworth prisoners who explained that principle prevented their individual applications; in addition, having been convicted as a group, they were, in their own admirable words, convicted "of a 'conspiracy' of which we were all equally innocent or all equally guilty." Citing their unsuccessful appeals, the *Open Letter* pointed out that the higher courts had thrown out every accusation of sabotage, property destruction and other "industrial" offenses, leaving of the indictment only this crux of their crime, in the indictment's own words: "the offense of unlawfully, feloniously and willfully causing and attempting to cause insubordination, disloyalty and refusal of duty in the military and naval forces of the United States when the United States was at war; and this through and by means of personal solicitation, of public speeches, of articles printed in certain newspapers called *Solidarity, Industrial Worker . . . Il Proletaro, Industrial Unionist . . .*" Pointing out that they were in prison "for the expression of opinion and nothing else," the letter added that no overt act of hindering the war had been either charged or proved: " . . . we are charged with conspiring to hinder the war by means of spoken and printed words. This is the charge, but truth is that we are in prison for recognising the irrefutable fact of the class struggle and for advocating the solidarity of labor."

Their conviction, the signers of the letter said, had been the springboard for an open-shop drive, a wage-cutting campaign and other anti-labor acts by both business and government. Then they quoted the appeal made to President Wilson by Captain Alexander Sydney Lanier of the Military Intelligence Corps after a painstaking review of the evidence: "I am of the opinion," the President was told by this career military officer who could be accused of no emotional or intellectual sympathy with proletarian revolution, "that these men were convicted contrary to the law and the evidence, solely because they were the leaders in a revolutionary organisation against which public sentiment was incensed and the verdict rendered was in obedience to public hysteria and popular demand, due to [sic] the hysteria of the time."

To bolster their argument that they were the targets of a purge the men offered further facts: Two of them had had their sentences increased from a year and a day to twenty years because Landis objected to their comments on the verdict. Attorney General Daugherty had admitted publicly that, had anyone but Eugene V. Debs, the Socialist leader, told a crowd of men that "you deserve something better than to be cannon fodder," the sentence would have been nothing like Debs' ten years. A man convicted of selling American arms to Germans in Mexico after our entry into the war had been released. Eight wealthy men convicted under the Espionage Act had been pardoned without ever seeing the inside of a cell. Six German agents caught red-handed had been given ludicrously petty sentences. Jacobsen, the notorious spy who had plotted to blow up the Welland Canal, dynamited other installations and poisoned several people, was running a prosperous business in Chicago, having had his sentence commuted after serving sixty-four days.

"We believe in and uphold civil liberties because we are convinced that only through open and free discussion can the right idea prevail," the letter said. "Ideals are matters which cannot be altered by force." But that is a proposition that the mass of mankind everywhere will never be able to comprehend: that is why men purge other men, pathetically hoping to purge their ideas as well.

In the 1920's there was not too much other official use of the purge—its advocates were discouraged by such deterrents as the Supreme Court's invalidation of a wartime Iowa law forbidding teaching in all foreign languages. Unofficial purgatives flourished, however, and such cleansers as the Daughters of the American Revolution, the Klan, the Knights of Columbus, the American Legion, the National Association of Manufacturers and unchartered mobs did enough damage to warrant their being separately considered later. Mayor Curley of Boston was impartially bigoted: over ACLU protests, he banned both the Klan and the Socialist Defense Day rally. But, as it became obvious that Nicola Sacco and Bartolomeo Vanzetti were going to be murdered by the state of Massachusetts for being anarchists (it is almost universally conceded today that there was far from sufficient evidence to prove them guilty of the common hold-up murder of which they were accused), protest meetings in all parts of the country sprang up and were suppressed—when possible, before they could be held. In general, the state of public opinion, and hence of judicial temper, was such that the Union was as unsuccessful on behalf of the protestants as it was in its aid to the two innocent men. In New York, as in many other cities, the Board of Education maintained a blacklist of "radical" or "controversial" organisations to which it would not allow the use of its buildings—the existence of the New York blacklist, which, being illegal, was supposed to be secret, was revealed when the ACLU was barred from school property.

The depression of 1929-33, like every major economic crisis, was a boon to certain industries, among which was the purge. Ominously foreshadowing Martin Dies and Joseph McCarthy, Representative Hamilton Fish Jr. of New York set up and headed a House committee in April, 1930, to investigate what was already becoming known as the Red Menace. Fish was largely influenced by New York City Police Commissioner Grover Whalen, who published the anti-Soviet forgeries of Ralph M. Easley, patriot by trade; under whose aegis the police were ordered to use whatever force they liked against "radicals," and who was responsible for the years of false arrests of innocent women on framed charges of prostitution. "Down With Whalen's Police Brutality", a sign on the Communists' headquarters said, whereupon thirty dangerous radicals were arrested. Fish thought this sort of thing was great, as did his numerous vocal friends among the White Russian colony in New York: they and Whalen were his major champions. But this was not enough to keep his witch hunt going and after a year it collapsed in a shambles of recommendations and recantation. Fish called for the deportation of all alien Communists, the outlawry of the Party from the ballot and of its publications from the mails, and the creation of an alien spy squad in the Justice Department. In 1930 this sort of thing evoked even more ridicule then excoriation—no one could foresee the infinite gullibility of the American press, public and government—and the laughter was uncontrollable when Fish finally admitted that the "half-million" Communists he was investigating came to exactly 12,000 in a head-count (he included the few thousand members of the ACLU in the tally).

The first few years of the New Deal were relatively free of similar idiocies from official sources—it was special interests, such sterling journalists as Hearst, professional patriots and the mob that did most of the purging. Army and Navy pressure for sedition bills and military propaganda against pacifism and "radicalism"—both of which would, if successful, have forced the military to work for a livelihood—were summarily halted by Roosevelt after he received a spate of protests. Similar protests forced the War Department to withdraw an over-honest how-to pamphlet on the violent repression of strikes and demonstrations. There were exceptions to the Government's *laisser-faire,* of course, such as the rudimentary loyalty oath imposed on teachers in the District of Columbia at Hearst's insistence: on each payday they could not collect until they had sworn that in the preceding pay period they had neither taught nor even explained Communism to the tender minds of their young charges. And the states, of course, were as eager to please the demagogues and the populace. After the bloody May Day repressions of 1932 and 1933 in Philadelphia and other cities, there were years of calm on that date. But, from 1936 on, the purge business picked up considerably in New York City under LaGuardia, who ordered Police Commissioner Valentine to suppress jobless rallies and who strengthened the blacklist restricting the use of city buildings. California, not to

be outdone, bowed to the American Legion and discharged a pub-
lic-health nurse for consorting with radicals and a teacher for accepting "Soviet gold"—interest on Soviet Government bonds. A
notably refreshing exception was the action of the county commissioners in Washington State who offered their offices for an
ACLU meeting when the police had bullied every hall owner in
the area into refusing to rent. The outbreak of the Spanish Civil
War brought not only the foreseeable attempts to gag the friends
of the Loyalists but also the first important attempt to limit travel
by Americans, when the State Department barred all voyages to
Spain. The Union was prepared to challenge the ban in court but
refrained when the department began almost immediately to make
hundreds of exceptions. But this, though neither the ACLU nor,
probably, the Government recognised the fact, was the second
ominous indication of the purge weapon to be made of the passport after the Second World War.

It was at about this time that the Congress of the United States
threw itself whole-heartedly into the business of purging the nation of its heretics by setting up, on a temporary basis, the House
un-American Activities Committee to look for evidence of possible domestic manifestations of the Fascist, Nazi and Communist
ideologies spawned abroad. Headed for years by Representative
Martin Dies of Texas—a Roosevelt Democrat, there being no other
kind at the time—it proved at once its partisanship by concentrating
virtually all its efforts on Communism alone. It was not primarily for
this reason that the ACLU immediately denounced its establishment and for almost thirty years has consistently demanded its
dissolution: the major argument against the HUAC was and remains the simple fact that it was created as a weapon to silence
opinion, criticism and dissent—the Union is as vigorous today in
its opposition to similar projected HUAC probes of the Klan and
of other native Fascisms. These projects are a highly belated phenomenon that is open to the grave suspicion of being no more
than a grandstand gesture intended to make the HUAC seem impartial and to clear it of the stigma of bias earned not only by its
own history but by the enthusiastic support it has always had from
every individual and organisation identified with professional
militant know-nothing-ism, from Hearst and the McCormick-

Patterson press through the American Legion, the John Birch Society, the various Catholic lay groups and the Reverend Gerald L. K. Smith's Christian Nationalists.

For several years Dies' special committee remained on a temporary basis, but in 1945 Representative John Rankin of Mississippi, one of the narrowest minds in the national history, offered a resolution to make it a permanent independent standing committee, primarily to "investigate the extent, character and objectives of un-American propaganda activities in the United States," with independent unsupervised powers of subpoena and the privilege of functioning regardless whether Congress was in session. A year later legislation was enacted to establish the HUAC as the only standing committee in the history of the House with the permanent power to investigate non-governmental activities. In 1965 the American Civil Liberties Union redoubled its efforts to mobilise sentiment to influence Congress to dissolve the committee, on four principal grounds:

—The committee's mandate is unconstitutional in that it violates the freedoms guaranteed by the First Amendment.

—The committee's contribution to legislation—the putative purpose of every Congressional committee—has been virtually nil.

—The Committee's methods abrogate many of the elements of due process guaranteed by the Constitution and embodied in the democratic concept of justice and fair play.

—The committee is largely responsible for the tacit institutionalisation of "un-American" inquisitions and loyalty oaths in many aspects of the national life. Its collection of *dossiers* on the past and present political activities of, and mere suspicions against, thousands of people and its random public exploitation have created an atmosphere of fear, suspicion, betrayal and gag rule. Despite its disclaimers of any such intent, it has materially impeded the free discussion of pressing social issues and thus delayed their solutions.

In its entire career, which several million dollars of public funds have been spent to maintain, the HUAC has been responsible for exactly two laws, both under attack as unconstitutional, and an amendment to one of them. Its first legislative achievement, in 1950, was the Subversive Activities Control Act, requiring the registration of the Communist Party and other specified "Communist action" groups. This has never been enforceable, if only because, as has been shown, Supreme Court decisions have prevented its enforcement despite the court's acceptance of the principle of registration. In 1962 the HUAC obtained Congressional passage of an amendment repealing the original act's requirement that the Defense Department list each strategic war facility at which Communists might be employed: the Justice Department had complained that the HUAC had in effect supplied a "guidebook" for saboteurs and for military enemies looking for targets. The HUAC's other accomplishment is a 1964 law (fought by the ACLU) that empowers the Secretary of Defense to dismiss summarily any employe of the National Security Agency without charges, a hearing, knowledge of the information against him, the right to cross-examine or the right to appeal. Even Representative Francis E. Walter, once a HUAC chairman, admitted as late as 1960 that the HUAC should be a sub-committee of the House Judiciary Committee. The HUAC counters that, as a sentinel of the nation's soul, it has indirectly "inspired" other Congressional committees to sponsor legislation of the first importance to the salvation of us all, such as extending from three to ten years the statute of limitations in espionage cases. (Frankly, one felt no more and no less safe under the three-year rule.) How the HUAC has snatched us from destruction is instructive; the story is further enhanced by the heroic feats of the various state HUACs created in emulation of the original. The guiding philosophy was summed up by Representative Harold Velde, the 1964 HUAC chairman: "It is better to wrongly accuse one person of being a Communist than to allow many to get away with Communist acts"—in contrast to one who is reputed to have said, in the course of founding the faith to which Representative Velde adheres, or professes to adhere: "There is more joy in heaven over one sinner that repenteth than over ninety and nine righteous men." But Jesus never had to campaign for the votes of the rabble and had no private property to worry about.

Dies early allowed his committee to be used as a soundingboard for anti-democratic propaganda, most of which, ostensibly, was aimed at the Communists and some of which, overtly, was aimed at the Jews. He impugned his own integrity by appointing as his chief investigator J. B. Matthews, a former Socialist and fellow-traveler renowned chiefly for his virulence against those he had renounced and, later, for his absurd contentions that the Protestant clergy, of which he had once been a member, was riddled with Communists. No opportunity, from the first, was given to any person or organisation accused by the HUAC to refute the charges; the ACLU helped to place itself among the accused by its opposition to the HUAC and its demand that Matthews, as a self-styled expert on the subversive left, be balanced by an at least equal expert on the subversive right— a demand that was never met. It took Dies a long time to have to admit that the Union was not Communist, Communist-dominated or Communist-duped. Smaller local HUACs took even longer to expunge the ACLU from their blacklists. Their mentor lost no time in appealing to the xenophobia never far below the surface in this country of former foreigners. HUAC admirers across the country besought it to investigate their various local Communists, but often the ACLU was able to stalemate such heresy chases. The early years of the war materially strengthened the HUAC's hand: were not the Communists the allies of the Nazis and did not birds of a feather flock ever together? In such an atmosphere hardly a voice was raised with that of the ACLU to protest the HUAC's totally illegal seizures and publication of the membership lists of the organisations that it convicted by accusation. Roosevelt himself condemned this practice, but no step was taken to stop it. The transmutation of the hated Reds into glorious participants in the Grand Alliance of the Four Freedoms did little to slow the HUAC or its imitators.

Largely inspired by the HUAC's "disclosures," legislation in the states multiplied. One of the favorite purge laws was the type that either crippled minority parties or forced them off the ballot altogether under the color of ostensible legality—by stipulating previous polling figures as a condition of listing—as well as frank outlawry because of their doctrines. The 1940 election set a record in this kind of activity. Though the Communist Party was the major victim, its intra-left opponents suffered equally:

the Socialists, the Socialist Laborites and the fanatically anti-Stalinist Socialist Workers. So did such perils to the health and welfare as the Prohibition Party. The Union battled for all of them and won only a few of the combats. Its call for uniform state laws to establish a national standard for eligibility to the ballot was barely heard—it dared not demand a national law, as both logic and justice required then and still require. Not only state but federal prosecutions became purge instruments, as in the case of Earl Browder, head of the Communist Party, who was unquestionably guilty of passport fraud but whose sentence of four years was double what would have been imposed on a non-Communist (it was later commuted by Roosevelt). The military had its own purgative method, which was to deny promotion to Communists and to veterans of the fighting in Spain—a discrimination always denied by the War Department and rather often successfully overcome by ACLU intervention.

In 1943 Dies broadcast a list of thirty-nine "subversives" whom his committee had declared unfit for federal employment: the list included a number of persons long distinguished for their opposition to Communism—and, of course, should never have been published at all. But it was not enough to suit Representative John Kerr of North Carolina, who reviewed it and incorporated it into a fantasy of his own that included dozens of organisations that he disliked and that were therefore Communist. Among their members were Dr. Goodwin Watson and William E. Dodd Jr. of the FCC and Professor Robert Morss Lovett, on leave from the University of Chicago as Government Secretary of the Virgin Islands. The House promptly tacked on to a money bill a rider that would have compelled their dismissal, but the Senate—temporarily—frustrated the saviors in the chamber. These were not cast down, however, and in no time they had appointed a Select Committee to investigate the FCC, later the subject of an ACLU memorial to the House in support of the Commission.

The gravamen of the charges was buried under a mass of allegations of domination by Chairman James Lawrence Fly (later a director of the Union), unlawful exercise of FCC powers in furtherance of political aims, terrorisation of the radio industry, attempts to control all communications and cut off free speech, usurpation of Congressional function by determining legislative policy, imperiling the national security, setting up a Gestapo, taking reprisals against its enemies, seeking publicity (Freud used to speak of auto-characterisation) and, finally, the seeming crux: "the adoption of the reputed Communistic technique of cessation and gradualism [whatever that might mean]." The chairman of the Select Committee was Eugene E. Cox of Georgia; it was, of course, pure coincidence that he called for the creation of the committee after the FCC had begun to investigate his recent purchase of a radio station whose application for the renewal or sale of its license was before the FCC. It was investigating because Cox had bought the station with money that the broadcaster had paid to him. Chairman Cox, denying any bias, heard a host of hostile witnesses but, as the record showed, would not allow the FCC to reply: such favorable testimony as was offered was suppressed in Cox' publicity and any neutral testimony was distorted. Whatever Cox had really sought to do—essentially, to get clear in his own questionable transaction and to try to undermine government regulation in general—remained unachieved.

If the HUAC had really been looking for activities inimical to freedom, it could well have been kept busy in its own back yard. But freedom and democracy were not its concerns, as it demonstrated immediately on achieving permanent status: the United States, the HUAC insisted, neither was nor was intended to be a democracy but "only a republic." The Union, consistent with its principles, demanded that the newly permanent committee be given a chance to prove its good faith: this it proceeded to do by demanding the scripts of radio commentators, issuing subpoenas for a New York City election candidate and his sponsor, and citing and threatening to cite for contempt, because they would not give the HUAC the lists of their contributors, the Joint Anti-Fascist Refugee Committee, the Council for Soviet-American Friendship and the National Committee for Constitutional Liberties. The ACLU then called again for the abolition of the HUAC, whose "methods proved to be as irresponsible as its concepts of un-Americanism." The HUAC thereupon demanded that the Union produce all its records; the ACLU refused on the ground that no presumption of its un-Americanism could be sustained, and the HUAC said nothing—for then.

Dies was no more; the HUAC was now headed by Representative J. Parnell Thomas of New Jersey, a vociferous advocate of all that was right and American until he went to prison for his loyalty to an old Roman maxim: *pecunia non olet*. In 1947, coincidentally with the issuance of its pamphlet on *Post-War Hysteria*, which demanded ordinary due-process protection for all accused individuals and organisations, including the right of being heard, the Union filed briefs *amicus* in two unsuccessful suits challenging the HUAC's mandate—a move opposed by a strong minority within the Union on two equally untenable grounds: that the cause was lost in advance and that the Union's public position (the *image* had not yet been discovered by publicists) would be weakened. The minority within the ACLU made so much noise that a referendum had to be held before the briefs could be authorised; the result was a resounding defeat for the opportunistic faction whose dedication to civil liberties was subordinate to its concern with *What will people say?* Of course, as events soon enough proved, the Supreme Court as it and public opinion then stood was not going to upset contempt convictions for defiance of HUAC subpoenas; and equally of course the trembling *bourgeoisie* (which in this country is a psychological rather than an economic class, cutting across the entire social spectrum) would not think better of the ACLU for its courage. Nonetheless it continued to battle—by foredoomed litigation, by publicity, by generally fruitless lobbying and negotiation—every new enormity of all the purgers. To catalogue all would require the volumes of an encyclopedia. Some of the more revolting are listed in the ACLU's 1964 pamphlet, *The Case Against the House Un-American Activities Committee*:

—Wide newspaper, radio and television publicity on all persons—both witnesses and those they mention—whose names in any way come before the HUAC, without opportunity to rebut.

—Frequent dismissals from employment for such persons and often for relatives unconnected with them except by blood or marriage.

—Increases in the circulation of "hate" literature and harassing annonymous telephone calls. At the last meeting of 1964, Norman Thomas told the directors of the ACLU that in his recent tour of the country he had encountered a flood of complaints of such telephone calls, poison-pen letters and other harassments, such as the sending of hearses to homes, that was exceeded only by the persecutions of the Palmer period.

—HUAC counsel Richard Arens addressed witnesses as *Comrade* and referred to absent persons by the same title; he forbade witnesses' counsel to be heard, even to object to his methods: their only right, he said, was "to advise their clients." This was denounced by the Board of Governors of the California Bar Association.

—The names of 110 teachers summoned by the HUAC were given at once to the press, in advance of their hearings—which were never held. Copies of HUAC files on the teachers were sent to their employers.

—HUAC files consist of testimony, letters, clippings, memoranda and other raw data subject to no investigation and are offered by the HUAC as proof, with the implication that such proof has been established in adversary proceedings. A separate file is maintained on each individual and organisation whose name is ever brought to the HUAC's attention, regardless whether there was ever an appearance either under subpoena or voluntarily. A major source of data is the paid stool-pigeon, usually a former member of a "subversive" group, who finds perjury or betrayal more lucrative than working. One of these scum, Manning Johnson, has said publicly that he would commit perjury "a thousand times over " for the FBI (at what rate per perjury was not specified).

—A Seattle molder was called a Communist by a HUAC witness but was never invited to testify; daily telephone calls to his employer followed and cost him his job.

—A Rhode Island housewife who refused to testify was socially ostracised with her entire family and barred from the PTA (a dubious loss for any civilised lady), and her child was hounded by schoolmates.

—A Miami building contractor who constitutionally invoked the Fifth Amendment before the HUAC lost his home and his business through the resultant boycott.

—A girl lost her job washing pots because her husband and her father similarly invoked their privilege against self-incrimination.

—A fire-department captain who denied current CP membership but refused to discuss his past was fired when he was within two months of retirement benefits.

—Hundreds of persons were cited for contempt because, although they talked freely of themselves, they rightly refused to incriminate others, and as a result of their contempt citations they lost their jobs.

—A San Francisco news broadcaster was suspended as soon as he received a HUAC subpoena.

—HUAC files are made available to private persons and others seeking to use them to discredit third persons; conversely, the HUAC accepts and acts on the allegations of irresponsible individuals such as the Reverend Billy Hargis and organisations such as the White Citizens' Councils: hence the HUAC attempts to label Communist the Reverend Martin Luther King, most of the leaders of the NAACP, dozens of Protestant and Jewish (not Catholic) clergymen and other prominent or obscure inividuals often totally apolitical.

—Accusation and subpoena by mistaken identity, without investigation of mere similarities of name.

—Countless instances of loss of income, employment and profession because of premature and mistaken identification of an individual as a HUAC suspect, despite subsequent clearance from the HUAC.

—Efforts to censor the choice of books by libraries, schools and universities.

—Intimidation of the Secretary of the Air Force and compelling the latter's agreement not to issue or recommend publications without the prior approval of the HUAC.

—Persecution of pacifist and civil-rights movements and their leaders, through trumped-up charges and specious "evidence" of Communist infiltration or domination.

"To the un-American Activities Committee," an editorial in *The Washington Post* said in 1962, "protest is synonymous with subversion." Nor is such pairing limited to the HUAC or its imitators, as we have already noted and shall have too much occasion to observe again. Even the New Jersey police became politically conscious and exerted pressure on owners of halls to bar rentals not only to the Communists but also to the American Veterans' Committee and Henry Wallace's pathetic Progressive Party. Frightened by Ernie Adamson's wistful reminder, when he was HUAC counsel, of how well the Nazis had handled the Jewish problem, the Motion Picture Association, awaiting the granting of its plea for laws to bar "subversives" from its industry, instituted its own purge of suspect writers, producers, actors and directors, taking its targets from the "files" of big and little HUACs, American Legion denunciations and, later, the defamatory publications of AWARE, which served its country by selling the names of "subversives" at so much a head, the scale being a sliding one based on the buyer's ability to pay and on the prominence of the name. The MPA, like the broadcasting industry, was also served by AWARE's go-getting competitor, *Counterattack,* an anti-Communist magazine that published an annual *Index expurgatorius* called *Red Channels.* Until John Henry Faulk had the courage to fight back at AWARE, denunciation on a piecework basis was a profitable undertaking in the United States. AWARE, the trial of Faulk's libel suit revealed, regularly swapped lies with the HUAC and the New York City Police Department, and each enjoyed the use of the others' files. But no court would entertain damage actions against big HUAC or its spawn, even by the most innocent victims. Among the most celebrated, innocent or otherwise but still victims, were the so-called Hollywood Ten, leading film writers who refused to answer Thomas' questions as to their membership in the CP or the Screen Writers' Guild on the ground that these were personal matters beyond the power of a Congressional committee to examine. They paid for this intransigence with their livelihoods, though the Union upheld their stand. Incomprehensibly, however, the Union conceded that the questions might have been proper if the HUAC had first established that Communist influence in film production was a fact. But why should the Communist Party have any lesser or greater right to such influence than the Catholic Church or Reform Judaism or the Government?

One damage action, against California's own HUAC, the Tenney Committee, did reach the Supreme Court, where Frankfurter rejected it. One Brandhove had been subpoenaed by Tenney solely because of having petitioned the Legislature to abolish the inquisition. Tenney read into the record a recital purporting to be Brandhove's criminal career and had him convicted of contempt for refusing to testify, whereupon Brandhove sued for damages under the old post-Civil War Civil Rights Act, alleging a deprivation of Constitutional rights by a state officer acting under color of law. Frankfurter found the legislator's immunity impervious to the statute, even if his purpose was questionable; of Tenney's reliance on his immunity Frankfurter could not forbear remarking: "One must not expect uncommon courage even in legislators."

In the lull between the Second World War and Korea, American hostility to any economic concept other than the so-called free-enterprise system rapidly became obsessive. Suppression of its critics and opponents increased not only in the United States but in the foreign territories under occupation by American troops and military government, which could not understand that to advocate the nationalisation of industries was not tantamount to preaching Communism. Even had it been, what right had Americans then—or now, or tomorrow—to tell other countries how to run themselves? What would have been laughable, if its results had not been so tragic for so many people, was the purgers' utter ignorance of the manifold doctrines, organisations and individuals they pursued. The case of Jacob Kutcher is a classic example: a legless combat veteran fired from a job in the Veterans' Administration on the ground of aiding the Soviet enemy through his membership in the fanatically anti-Soviet Socialist Workers' Party.

Kutcher was discharged in 1948 and began a campaign that, assisted by the ACLU, took years and that was complicated by the Gwinn Amendment, which barred his strongly conservative father from living in federally aided housing because the younger Kutcher was convicted, without a hearing, of "giving support to the enemy." By *enemy* was meant Soviet Communism, in antagonism to which even the United States Government had to take second place to Kutcher's Trotskyite party. While Kutcher was battling in the courts, he was deprived of his disability pension on the ground that he had said that the Government was composed of "cheaters, crooks and oppressors of the workers," and that he had urged friends to get key jobs and then strike. No one cared that Kutcher had given up both his legs in defense of that Government; nor did anyone care that Kutcher denied having uttered either the criticisms or the exhortations. Eight years after he had been dismissed, when the Circuit Court of Appeals found that the VA had violated Kutcher's rights to due process of law, that Trotskyite allegiance was not ground for dismissal and that the other charges were irrelevant, the VA announced it had no proof of any of the matters of which it had accused him, and Kutcher was reinstated with full seniority rights. There was still the question of earnings lost during his eight years in the wilderness: the Comptroller General of the United States said he could not pay out money to anyone who believed in the violent overthrow of the Government; so Kutcher was back in court again. A full decade after his dismissal, Kutcher, on a direct appeal to President Eisenhower, was finally able to collect the monumental sum of $17,000 for his eight years of unemployment.

The wild rampage of McCarthy and the wide support he gathered among the savages combined with the HUAC havoc to intimidate the State Department, never notable for its courage in any case, and the department found a way to implement the national lust for suppression by the refusal and revocation of passports, briefly used to the same end in 1929 and only rarely since. McCarthy had a loyal supporter in the head of the Passport Division, Scott McLeod, who, disregarding the rulings of lower Federal Courts that he could not withhold a passport without a statement of his reasons and a hearing for the applicant or holder, made it his business to see that no one legally got out of the United States who might be anathema to McCarthy, the HUAC or their disciples and collaborators. From the first the ACLU contended that, except in time of war, the right to travel abroad was absolute except when substantial evidence showed that the citizen sought a passport in order to evade prosecution or sentence on a criminal charge or to work against his country, and hence that the denial of freedom of movement was a violation of the Constitution, compounded when it was based on *ex parte* action naked of due process. Later the State Department was to go even farther and to forbid the travel of Americans to specific countries of which it disapproved, under penalty of loss of passport and criminal prosecution. Both forms of purge by immobilisation are still under challenge, by the Union and others, in 1965.

In its efforts to circumvent the Union's challenges, the department, in September, 1952, issued passport regulations barring Communists and their sympathisers, with provision for appeals and final decision by the Secretary. These were at once attacked by the Union because of their vagueness, their lack of definition of Communists and sympathisers, their omission of any criteria for refusals of passports on other grounds and the opportunity created for canceling the right of travel on the ground of utterances abroad that, however unpalatable to McLeod or McCarthy, might still be legal. But the Subversive Activities Control Act made it a crime *per se* for a Communist even to apply for a passport or use an existing one. It took ten years to win invalidation of this ban by the Supreme Court.

But such action was hardly surprising in a State Department that, again yielding to the know-nothings, had banned several hundred books by forty authors from United States Information Service libraries abroad under an order eliminating all the works of authors found to be "controversial persons, Communists, fellow-travelers" and so on. Malin protested to Dulles on both practical and philosophical grounds: aside from avowed Communists, the other categories of taboo authors could never be feasibly established or applied; and every book should be judged by its intrinsic merits, not by its authorship. But in July, 1953, the department (without alluding to the derision it had endured abroad and, at home, from the more enlightened) revised its library policy so that in large measure it met the position of the Union. On travel, however, it has remained adamant, and the ACLU has had to devote considerable energy and resources to the defense of the Constitutional rights not only of travel but of due process violated in the process of limiting travel.

Without explanation, for instance, the State Department refused a passport to Albert Einstein's executor for travel in connection with the liquidation of Einstein's estate: the ACLU entered the litigation and the department was ordered to list its reasons. The decision prescribed the kind of hearing to be held; instead, the department issued the passport at once. Similarly, the Union forced the issuance of a passport to Max Schachtman, head of the Independent Socialist League: it had been denied because the League was on the Attorney General's list, despite the fact that for six and a half years it had been petitioning to be removed. But court decisions meant little to McLeod or his colleague, Mrs. Ruth Shipley: when litigation went against them, they evaded court orders by issuing passports but, when there was no court challenge, they continued to rely on the wicked principle that they had absolute discretion and that a passport was not a matter of right. While the Union was petitioning the department to revise its policy to conform with the law, and at the same time lobbying for a better statute, it was backing the appeal of William Worthy Jr., a Negro journalist, for a new passport to replace the one withdrawn because he had gone to Communist China, and it was fighting the denial of a passport to Eleanor Roosevelt for travel to the same infernal realm. In addition, the State Department refused to allow A. L. Wirin, Southern California CLU counsel and attorney for Mr. and Mrs. John B. Powell, on trial for sedition for their publications outside the United States critical of the Korean conflict, to go to China to collect necessary evidence—and China countered by refusing to admit him if he did get the passport! A federal court refused to entertain the prosecution unless the passport was granted: the State Department bowed to the need to punish the heretic and China withdrew its ban on the lawyer's entry. In the end the Government had to drop the Powell case as unfounded. Passport applications by Corliss Lamont, a former Union director; Rockwell Kent, whose art was branded pure Red, and Dr. Walter Briehl, a physician, were refused because none of the three would say whether he held a CP card (actually, none was a member) and the Union lost in the lower courts, which relied on the "international Communist conspiracy" (of which none of the men was proved a part), the Government's authority in foreign affairs and the existing "emergency"—which was not identified but which, presumably, was that proclaimed by Truman when fighting started in Korea and never officially ended (the Korean "emergency" flourishes still in 1965).

In 1958 the Supreme Court declared without qualification that Congress had never authorised the denial of a passport on the basis of political beliefs or associations, laying the groundwork for its 1963 invalidation of the SACA's unconstitutional prohibition of passports to Communists and their sympathisers. The 1958 decision, a clear victory for the Union, which had handled the appeal, forced the issuance of passports to the three silent applicants, whereupon Eisenhower and Dulles immediately demanded a law—which the Union helped to kill—that would have undone the court's ruling and extended the authority of passport refusal to include anyone who might "seriously impair the conduct of foreign relations." That the defeat of the bill was in no way to hinder the execution of its intentions soon became evident. Under the 1958 decision the Union renewed the Worthy battle and, simultaneously, revised its own policy: it called now for the unrestricted issuance of passports valid for travel to any country with which the United States was not at war, regardless whether the applicant might engage abroad in "subversive" activity. While the Worthy case went through another round of court defeats, the Union won its fight against the Administration's effort to legislate the 1958 decision into limbo but lost its battle for a new and liberalised passport law. And, in spite of the decision, the State Department refused to issue a passport to Waldo Frank, a leftwing author invited to lecture in China; it did, however, allow journalists of paler tint to go there. The Supreme Court refused to review a Circuit Court ruling against the Union and Worthy on the ground that "a blustering inquisitor could throw the whole international neighborhood into turmoil," rejecting the ACLU's argument that information on China might assist American foreign policy (it is obviously so much better to suppress the truth about an antagonist against whom one seeks to inflame a nation).

As Malin poined out, this left untouched the authority of the Secretary of State to curb travel to countries that he considered harmful to the national interest; it also upheld the Secretary's power to shackle the movement of any person whose presence abroad he might consider a peril to the security of 193,000,000 Americans at home. Thus Kennedy's man, Dean Rusk, added Cuba to the list and rejected the Union's argument that a citizen should be permitted to waive the Government's protection if he wishes to visit troubled areas. Students who defied the Cuba ban were subjected to investigation (and did their cause no good by behaving as boorishly as their persecutors) and Immigration inspectors instituted a policy of regularly asking all returning travelers whether they had visited Cuba after the attempted 1961 invasion sponsored by the Central Intelligence Agency: those who answered affirmatively or refused to answer at all, standing on the visa stamps in their passports, lost the documents and faced criminal prosecution. This harassment sharpened after the 1962 Cuban "crisis," when the United States, whose rockets on the Russian-Turkish border were permanently at the ready to fire into Russia, threatened again to invade Cuba because Castro had admitted Russian weapons and troops—a manufactured crisis in which Khrushchev subordinated his country's right to make compacts with Cuba, analogous to ours with Turkey, to the threat to world peace posed by Kennedy's intransigent disregard for intellectual integrity, international law and the treaty of the Organisation of American States. James Peck, a noted pacifist writer who had never gone to Cuba, was subjected to protracted harassment, as well as the insolence of the immigration agents, because, on his return from abroad, he refused to answer the clearly unwarranted question whether he had visited the realm of the Crown Prince of Darkness in the Antilles. The Union had to battle to have his name removed from the blacklist maintained by Dean Rusk, but Rusk ignored the Union's demand that he abolish his index of "persons suspected of traveling or known to have traveled in Cuba." The State Department circulates the list to immigration agents at all ports of entry. The Union, appealing to the Supreme Court the department's refusal to endorse a passport for travel to Cuba, lost; it relied on the 1958 decision and on the 1963 ruling in its defeat of the SACA passport prohibition.

Relying on the SACA prohibition to get round the Supreme Court ban on the denial of passports for political reasons, the State Department refused to allow Elizabeth Gurley Flynn and

Herbert Aptheker of the CP to leave the country. The Union sprang at once to their defense, despite its ouster of Miss Flynn from its own directorate in 1940 because of her CP allegiance, and won another Supreme Court victory for the Constitutional right of movement: the court held the SACA's ban a violation of the First Amendment and ordered the passports issued. But the loyalty oath on passport applications, though ruled illegal in 1958, was still in being: the State Department pleaded that it had not been erased because of the cost of junking these forms and replacing them with legal ones. Corollarily, the State Department, opposed by the ACLU, used its entry-visa power to bar two highly undesirable individuals whose politics, however repugnant and for whatever reasons (the Union certainly did not share the Government's reasons), should not have been allowed to keep them out: Mme. Ngo Dinh Nu of Viet Nam and Premier Moïse Tchombé of Katanga. The pretext was the belief that they might "engage in activities prejudicial to the national interest," and it can certainly be convincingly argued that the purpose of each—to win American involvement in his own struggle for power and in his country's domestic affairs—was, to say the least, distasteful. Nonetheless, as the Union rightly contended, they had the right to enter without subjection either to prior censorship or to conviction by anxiety. One would go farther and defend their right not only to enter but also to propagandise for their shoddy aims, if the Constitution means what it says.

Naturalisation too was a purge weapon. In a letter to the raw Attorney General, Robert Kennedy, the Union asked that citizenship applicants be no longer required to state whether they had ever violated a law without being arrested and whether they had ever knowingly joined the CP or anything remotely connected with it, given it anything of value or advocated or believed in Communism. Affirmative answers, the Union pointed out, would at least technically bar any applicant who had ever bought a copy of *The Worker* or belonged to any group that the Party might also have favored. As far as one has been able to discover, Kennedy gave no satisfaction.

Besides their own HUACs, the states found a most effective instrument of the purge in the license to practice a profession or ply a trade. As early as 1925 Elmer Smith, attorney for eight IWWs in Centralia, Washington, sent to prison for twenty-five years for defending their office against a mob, was disbarred on the ground of association with his clients and participation in their beliefs, and it took Smith and the ACLU five years to reinstate him in the practice of his profession. The licensing power was early invoked against teachers, both in public and in private institutions, and is more fully covered in the chapter on academic freedom. It was not available to the Federal Government (except in the District of Columbia) but the military adapted it to their own needs by refusing Medical Corps commissions to doctors of questionable ideology. Some state Supreme Courts, like Florida's, refused to countenance the disbarment of a lawyer refusing to answer questions as to his affiliations, but upheld the disbarment of those who were "subversives"; the United States Supreme Court even upheld, under the anomalous states'-rights theory, the disbarment of a Texas lawyer because, though not political, he shared office premises with a colleague believed to be a Communist. The same court approved New York's withdrawal of a doctor's license to practice medicine because he refused to give the HUAC the records of the Joint Anti-Fascist Refugee Committee, but in this case Black, Douglas and Frankfurter refused to concur. Black dissented on three grounds: Dr. E. A. Barsky had the right to contest the HUAC's constitutional powers, there was no issue of his professional or personal character, and the invocation of the Attorney General's list (the Refugee group was on it) operated as a bill of attainder. Douglas attacked the destruction of Barsky's right to work. Frankfurter insisted that a state should not be permitted to destroy a man's professional career for reasons irrelevant to his fitness to pursue his profession.

The Union was particularly concerned with the purge of lawyers, whose oath pledges them to defend the Bill of Rights, not only because of the manifest contradiction inherent in such action and of the injustice to the individuals barred, but also because of the havoc such purges would inflict on the public seeking legal counsel in the protection of its rights. The ACLU was appalled when the New York State Bar Association called for the disbarment of all attorneys who maintained their membership in organisations on the Attorney General's list, as well as the suspension of lawyers who invoked the Fifth Amendment for any reason. The California Bar Association, however, joined the ACLU in defeating a bill to penalise such lawyers and their colleagues or any who were "disrespectful" toward inquisitors, but it split from the Union to approve the disbarment of those who advocated the overthrow of the Government. The ACLU won Supreme Court rulings that past CP membership was no evidence of bad moral character that would justify the refusal of admission to the bar.

Impartially the Union also defended the rights of former Spanish Falangists and German Nazis to practice professions. It defeated a California bill to revoke the professional or business license of anyone—from lawyer to plumber or barber—who took the Fifth Amendment on any subject. But Indiana imposed a loyalty oath on professional boxers and wrestlers. Employers like the United Press Associations, which fired reporters and editors for refusing to incriminate themselves, were also excoriated: the Union devastated the UP's argument that its people were cloaked with a "public trust" that was polluted by their refusal to put themselves or others in a pillory. McCarthy's mass victims at Monmouth, New Jersey—civilian workers fired by the army on the basis of charges loosely made against them by McCarthy and his shoddy repertory company of witnesses, aided by the egregious Roy Cohn and David Shine—were finally vindicated in court, years after their ouster, when the army was found to have violated its own regulations in not informing them why they were held to be security risks.

But the Union could never win Supreme Court support for its challenge to the HUAC. In the case of Lloyd Barenblatt, a Vassar College psychology instructor, the Union relied on a 1957 case in which that court had overturned a conviction for contempt of Congress—the contempt consisting of refusing to answer a committee's questions—because the witness had not been told in advance of the pertinency of the questions to the committee's purpose. Barenblatt and the Union contended that HUAC questions as to his political beliefs and acts were not pertinent because the HUAC's mandate, even if valid—and this too was challenged—did not extend to education and the HUAC's sole *raison d'être* was publicity and exposure. But the court held that a legislative committee's investigation of Communism was proper because the national interest involved in defense against the menace overrode the individual's interest in not revealing his associations: in such case, the court held, the public interest is paramount to the rights granted under the First Amendment, on the basis of which Barenblatt had remained silent, rejecting the self-incrimination privilege. The court found it had no authority to probe the HUAC's motives and called Barenblatt's attribution of them unwarranted by the record—which is astounding (there is no other word) ; while the mandate to the HUAC may have been vague, the court added, the House had given it "pervasive authority" to investigate the Communist "menace" as part of its concern with national security. Admitting that the content of education is not open to Congressional investigation, the court insisted that the question of a teacher's Communist membership was a legitimate subject for inquiry. The questions asked of Barenblatt and their relation to the subject of the inquiry—the influence of Communism in the teaching profession—were clearly stated. A minority of the court refused to join in this piece of unskillful casuistry: "Exposure and punishment is [*sic*] the aim of this committee and the reason for its existence," the minority emphasised. The dissent added that a mandate for the investigation of beliefs and ideas, rather than of actions and conduct, amounted to an unconstitutional abridgement of free expression because of the inquiry's hostility to views "peacefully expressed in a place where the speaker had the right to be."

The Uphaus case in New Hampshire was analogous, in its substance and in the defeat of the Union's position. Dr. Willard Uphaus was the director of the World Fellowship Center, an adult camp investigated by the state Attorney General. Uphaus—not because he was a subversive (as indeed he was not) but because of the fundamental principle of civil liberties and Constitutional rights at stake—refused to turn over his membership lists and was convicted of contempt. But, as in the Barenblatt case, the Supreme Court upheld the New Hampshire courts' decision that a state had the right to combat "subversion" of which it was the target; and, as in the Barenblatt case, the minority of the court correctly dissented on the ground that the investigation had no object but exposure for its own sake.

Some signs of light did begin to appear as the 1950 decade was ending. The Supreme Court threw out some dismissals in which the security suspect had not been allowed to confront and cross-examine his accusers, and the Union, which had been instrumental in effecting these gains, was able to exploit them in similar pending cases. The cumulative effect of educational propaganda by the Union and the many other bodies and individuals outraged by loyalty oaths in the United States—most Americans opposed the loyalty oath only when Communist countries demanded it of their own so-called subversives—brought the repeal of some state loyalty-oath laws; in Washington State a four-year ACLU battle on behalf of Professors Howard L. Nostrand and Max Savelle against the oath and the use of the United States Attorney General's list as a loyalty criterion resulted in the retention of the oath but the elimination of the list.

After the HUAC hearings in San Francisco that brought about sixty-eight false arrests of protesting witnesses and spectators —and one commitment for trial, which resulted in an acquittal— the HUAC put together a clever bit of fraud called *Operation Abolition*. This was a film consisting of newsreel clippings of the disturbance, re-arranged out of sequence to convey the impression of a riot and accompanied by a propaganda commentary by HUAC members. This was widely shown round the country—thirty prints were ordered by the military and displayed to recruits long after the forgery of the film had been exposed— though in some areas the ACLU succeeded in having it shown only in conjunction with counter-propaganda of its own or, more rarely, with *Operation Correction*, a firm made by the ACLU of Northern California with the same clips, in their proper sequence and accompanied by a straightforward factual narration and an explanation of the making of *Operation Abolition*. A massive educational drive by the ACLU, to win support for the abolition of the HUAC, was launched through magazine articles, reprints of newspaper statements by public figures opposed to the witch-hunt, testimony of persons victimised, television and radio tapes and public debates: all these emphasised not only the Constitutional issues and the principles of justice but, for the cost-conscious millions, the waste of public moneys. The HUAC has survived, like so many entrenched institutions whose strength has nothing to do with their morality and much to do with panic and propaganda. It could not be discredited even by its own idiocies— one member, Representative Donald Jackson of California, expected the nation to believe his statement that the National Council of Churches was promoting obscene books written by Communist sympathisers, and Richard Arens, HUAC counsel, questioned President Eisenhower's patriotism in introducing his grandchildren to Khrushchev.

The Smith Act also survives, in the face of all reason and justice, with the Subversive Activities Control Act. Despite the ACLU's Supreme Court victory outlawing the conviction of Steve Nelson of the Communist Party under a Pennsylvania imitation of the Smith Act, on the ground that the federal law had pre-empted the state statute, Nelson was convicted under the federal act; this was followed by the conviction of Claude Lightfoot and Junius Scales under the same statute, though the sole evidence against them related to their reading and disseminating what Government witnesses understood to be Communist literature. In this case Marxist-Leninist theory was equated "by necessity" with the advocacy of force and violence. The irony of Scales' case lay in the fact that he had long since ceased to be a Party member and that his six-year sentence was one of the longest imposed in such trials—it resulted in a long, under-cover fight for commutation, carried to success by more than a hundred nationally prominent persons of all political complexions. It took two trials to purge Scales: the first conviction was reversed because of the unreliability of the Government's witnesses and, after the second, the Supreme Court called for a re-examination of the Constitutional issues. The Union contended there could be no clear and present danger in an affiliation that was unaccompanied by acts, but the court found the mere membership constitutionally sufficient for conviction if Scales knew—as he had known—what he was joining and what its aims were.

Gestures toward purgation of Fascist and proto-Fascist persons and organisations have been infrequent, but the Union has denounced every such effort. The Union has fought Philadelphia's effort to eliminate policemen who belong to the John Birch Society as it has fought for New York policemen who used to be Communists: in both instances, the ACLU says   properly, the sole criterion for hiring or firing is how a man does his job, not what he believes. Only if it could be proved that a policeman's politics (or religion, or hobbies, or sex life) actually interfered with the performance of his duties would it be a proper factor to be considered.

The official purge reached into broadcasting in 1962 when the Senate Internal Security Subcommittee launched an investigation of the politics of the Pacifica Broadcasting Foundation and its personnel and guest broadcasters—a move that naturally inspired the FCC to hold up action on the foundation's periodic renewal application. Pacifica, which is supported by its listeners, has been notable on both coasts for the courageous freedom of policy under which it presents adherents of every possible viewpoint—a courage fully matched, unfortunately, by the prevailing incapacity of its speakers to keep one awake (this in itself should have demonstrated how preposterously little danger of revolution exists when it is advocated by bores). After a delay as interminable as the average Pacifica talk on the air, the foundation and all concerned were cleared and the license was renewed.

One further type of purge deserves to be noted—the official purge based on sexual dissent. McCarthy's and others' efforts to make *homosexual* a synonym for *subversive* were on the whole lamentably successful in the State Department, in the armed services and in "defense" industries; the backwash has reached even into the White House in the case of the unfortunate Walter Jenkins, victim of a multitude of injustices by his colleagues and superiors: victim of police spying, victim of a monstrous prejudice skillfully inflamed in the unlettered populace, victim of a nationwide publicity for which there was no ground, victim of a superior devoid of loyalty and common decency. For him, unfortunately, the ACLU could do nothing. But for those homosexuals of the District of Columbia who have been fortunate enough to be unentrapped, unspied on and undenounced, the Union won a worth-while victory: the defeat of a Congressional bill to prevent fund-raising by the Mattachine Society, which attempts to educate the public mind to a semblance of a civilised attitude toward the homosexual. The bill would have forbidden fund-raising in the District by any but organisations "beneficial to health, welfare and morals." As long as a culture judges homosexuality by "moral" standards, its health and welfare must lack the benefit implicit in the success of the Mattachine Society's work.

Not even the most legitimate and laudable efforts to combat poverty and juvenile delinguency are immune to the purgers. The New York Civil Liberties Union has been deeply committed to the preservation of the city's Mobilisation for Youth program against the combined attacks of Red-baiters. Deputy Mayor Paul Screvane (Mayor Wagner, son of the Senator responsible for the National Labor Relations Act, has been heard to utter nothing but sterile platitudes in this controversy) fell over his own feet in his haste to curry favor with the mass-circulation rabble-rousing *Daily News*, a tabloid that fabricated a series of articles "exposing" the corruption of Mobilisation for Youth by a massive Communist complot, the evidence of which was seen chiefly in the organisation's support of tenants who withheld rent from landlords unwilling to bring their premises into compliance with the city's health, sanitation and housing laws. Screvane called on the always ready FBI, which interrogated MFY's 300 employes and otherwise "investigated" them by its customary unpublicised methods. It found two CP members and three members of non-Communist left-wing groups; in addition there were thirty-two persons alleged to have had past ties with the Party or fronts. Some of these ties consisted of mere signatures to petitions sponsored by organisations on the Attorney General's list—signatures protected by the First Amendment. One menace to the municipal tranquility was discovered to have visited Cuba. As a result, the city held up MFY's budget until it purged itself or was purged. Both the NYCLU and the ACLU, of course, have called on the silent Mayor to take the only position legally open to him: that the sole basis for judging MFY and its personnel is the administration of its program of combatting poverty and delinquency, training young people for employment and finding jobs for them.

By far the finest, the most irrefutable argument against any kind of purge was stated in 1961 by Justice Black:

"I once more deny, as I have found it repeatedly necessary to do in other cases, that this nation's ability to preserve itself depends upon suppression of the freedoms of religion, speech, press, assembly and petition. But I do believe that the noble-sounding slogan of 'self-preservation' rests upon a premise that can itself destroy any democratic nation by a slow process of eating away at the liberties that are indispensable to its healthy growth. The very foundation of a true democracy and the foundation upon which this nation was built is the fact that government is responsive to the views of its citizens, and no nation can continue to exist on such a foundation unless its citizens are wholly free to speak out fearlessly for or against their officials or their laws. When it begins to send its dissenters . . . to jail, the liberties indispensable to its existence must be fast disappearing. If self-preservation is to be the issue that decides these cases, I firmly believe they must be decided the other way. Only by a dedicated preservation of freedoms of the First Amendment can we hope to preserve our nation and its traditional way of life."

13

Let Every Voice Be Heard

The many rapid changes, social and political, that followed the end of the Second World War confronted the American Civil Liberties Union with a host of new problems of freedom. Not a few of these had already begun to manifest themselves before the war—some in the Union's earliest years. Freedom and the threats to its exercise were suddenly far more vast and complex than the relatively narrow scope that had occupied the attention of the ACLU in its first twenty years, when it was concerned first of all with the political-economic struggle, the emergence of labor and the pacifist and the conscientious objector. For a long time, as a later chapter will disclose, the Union either fought shy of or approached with the utmost reluctance all questions of "moral" censorship; it has always regarded academic liberty and the church-state conflict as special, almost autonomous departments of freedom, and for that reason, as well as the convenience of the author, they are so dealt with here. In the Union's early years it had relatively rarely to cope with such encroachments on freedom as the misuse of the laws of libel, the suppression of news as a matter of Government policy, the need for diversity in broadcasting and the prevention of private censorship, the invasion of privacy by the press, and the protection of the rights of franchise and representation against abridgment not only for racial but for other reasons.

In its proper concern for holding to the minimum the restraints on freedom of opinion and utterance—which includes the expression of opinion through the vote—the Union has sometimes seemed to defeat what Justice Brandeis called the greatest civil liberty of all: "the right to be let alone," the right of privacy; it has sometimes seemed to lose sight of the difference between rights that are inherently universal and rights that are by their nature limited. Hence it has allowed itself to be seduced by an absolute idealised goal of universal suffrage, which Flaubert so justly denounced as one of the three great fallacies of western civilisation—the others being papal infallibility and the divine right of kings. Thus the Union has found itself contesting a judicial ban on press coverage of certain aspects of a trial for reasons as invalid as those for which the ban was imposed and hence, in effect, impeding a fair trial and exposing persons to obloquy, just as it has put itself in the position of upholding the voting rights of persons manifestly unable to comprehend the issues before them and thus strengthening that tyranny of the ignorant and the prejudiced that is most dangerous to the Union's own goal of maximum civil liberties, as expressed in its 1946 pamphlet, *The Case Against Legal Restraints on Racial Libels and Anonymous Publications.*

This document appeared when the clamor for legal prohibitions against utterances derogatory of racial, religious and other groups was at a peak engendered by the tides of such propaganda that had preceded and accompanied the war and by the Negro's new awareness of his own strength and his own rights. Efforts to induce Congress to legislate such a ban on propaganda derogatory of Negroes, Catholics, Jews, Orientals and others had largely failed, at least in part because of the educational and lobbying efforts of the Union and of some of the minority-group organisations—the more forward-looking and honest saw at once the dangers to themselves in laws of this kind, to say nothing of the fundamental violation of principle involved. But similar bills had been enacted in some states (Rhode Island's was vetoed by its governor but in the 1952 Beauharnais case the Supreme Court ruled against the

Union and upheld the Illinois law) often from perfectly acceptable motives—to cut down prejudice against a given minority group. All such statutes had quickly proved themselves unworkable and readily susceptible of perversion to unworthy aims—New Jersey's law designed to silence American Nazi anti-Semitism was soon distorted to muzzle the criticisms of Catholicism made by Jehovah's Witnesses. The position taken by the Union on this subject is worth recapitulating because in sum it represents the essence of the Union's basic and totally unchallengeable stand on all freedom of utterance:

—Any penalty on speech or publication endangers all free discussion of the excluded subjects, and its constitutionality is dubious.

—No general agreement on a definition of what constitutes racial or religious prejudice is possible, and any such law can easily be turned against those whom it seeks to protect.

—Even if prosecutions under such laws could achieve their laudable objectives, they would serve only to advertise further what the law sought to silence.

—Successful prosecutions would simply drive the merchants of prejudice underground, promote clandestinity and make it more difficult to overcome bias.

—Anonymity, in some parts of the country, is a preventative of a very real danger—e.g., the reprisals that would be visited on Negroes in the south if they were identified as the authors of integrationist propaganda. Anonymity itself tends to discredit what it cloaks. If disclosure is to be compelled, then it should be demanded of all publications, not merely those dealing with race and religion. (In California in 1962 the ACLU went to court on behalf of an anonymous pamphlet whose sole thesis was a call for the suppression of the ACLU.)

—Libels against individuals have an existing remedy in the courts; any group-libel law is too grave a threat to free expression. When such libel threatens the public order with a clear and present danger, the existing criminal statutes can be invoked.

—*All mere utterances are entitled to the same protection even if the acts that they advocate are themselves punishable* (italics mine).

It is the final statement that is the most important and the least acceptable to all those driven by their interests or their terrors to trumpet incessantly the *credo* of Dr. Pangloss. And it is the soothing self-delusion of Dr. Pangloss, quite as much as the hypersensibility of the judicial arm, that has always sought to invoke the law of criminal libel or the citation for contempt of court against those who have legitimately or otherwise castigated Justice for the functioning of its machinery or government for the mysterious ways in which it moves, its wonders to perform. In the first twenty years of its life the Union had occasion to come, with varying success, to the aid of orators and editors whose comments on official personalities brought them into court on charges of criminal libel, like the editor who characterised Roosevelt as "a charlatan, a mountebank and a hypocrite" in his Presidential capacity. Similar prosecutions had been mounted against other editors who had shown a comparable lack of charity toward Roosevelt's Republican predecessors. The ACLU—a generation ahead of the courts, generally—took the right and reasonable view that a man in public office or public life has no right to expect immunity from criticism or attack for his performances (the Union was too polite—or too *naïve*—to note that, when every fool has a vote, no man can achieve any elective office above that of dog-catcher without consistently being those things imputed to Roosevelt and his precursors). In subsequent years the courts recognised the fundamental right of every citizen to criticise and even to denounce, within the common law of actionable libel, those whom he pays to be his nominal betters.

But the learned judges resisted longer and harder when the ACLU lent its assistance to those who claimed the right to question the bandaged wisdom of the bench: that was contempt, *ipso facto*, whether the criticism dealt with the conduct of a trial or with the judgment of the bench. Again the ACLU was well in advance of the courts in its appraisal of the Constitutional protection of such freedom of comment, but the Supreme Court caught up in 1946 when it upheld the right of a newspapr to criticise the conduct of a trial. But as early as 1941 the court had held that condemnation of a judicial decision could not constitutionally be punished as a contempt. It overthrew the prosecution of Harry Bridges for a telegram to Secretary of Labor Perkins calling a state court ruling "outrageous" while an application for rehearing was pending; the telegram also implied that the enforcement of the decision might bring on a strike. Unanimously, too, the court upheld the right of *The Times* of Los Angeles to criticise jury verdicts when the trial judge was still considering aspects of the cases; in another *Times* case a one-judge majority upheld the right to comment on a pending sentence. But the Union, while heartily endorsing these reinforcements of free expression, supported bans on "coercive" picketing of courts, although one must confess one finds it impossible to arrive at a reasonable definition of this.

The issue produced a curious split in which the national ACLU and its Maryland affiliate became, temporarily, adversaries. A Maryland judge forbade radio comment on pending court cases, and this was challenged by the Union, the American Newspaper Publishers' Association (which was to find itself more and more lining up with the ACLU) and the National Association of Broadcasters. But the Maryland affiliate supported the judge's ban on the ground that the rights of defendants to fair trials might very well be jeopardised by prejudicial comment and publicity while their cases were pending. The Maryland Court of Appeals quashed the trial judge's order, but, to one who believes that the right of the individual to privacy and a fair trial is greater than the right of the public to be inflamed or titillated, the Maryland affiliate's wisdom in 1949 was superior to that of the national Union. In 1952, the New York City judge presiding over the trial of a Social Register pimp excluded the press on a day when testimony was about to be given concerning a specific "unnatural" (!) sexual technique, on the ground that the publication of the testimony would jeopardise the community's morals. The Union at once appealed the ruling, and, except for the defendant's right to a public trial, for reasons as bad as the court's: the Union emphasised the right of the public to know what went on in the courts. But this right is not absolute: the society exists for the individual, the individual is not—or should not be—the plaything of the society. Justice Francis Valente's ban was proper, not because it would protect the community from learning what could be found in any "exotic" or how-to book advertised in the *Book Review* of *The New York Times* but because it would protect the witness from public obloquy and the defendant from possible prejudice. The Union was absolutely correct in attacking Valente's pseudo-reasoning but utterly wrong in the premise on which it based its attack. The Union erred similarly a few years later when it upheld the right of the publisher of a "true-crime" magazine to splatter a family tragedy over his pulp pages in order to titillate the vicariously-living mass and thus line his pockets, regardless of the damage to the sensibilities and the reputations of the survivors of the tragedy. Amazingly, too, the Union upheld the right to publish, in the guise of aiding public morality, the details of a private *liaison*.

This much misunderstood right of the public to know and to be informed is hardly unqualified. In challenging and seeking to end the Government's deliberate distortion, falsification and suppression of information the Union has been on unchallengeable ground: news of Government is by definition affected with a public interest and Government has no right to tamper with it despite its contention that, since information is a weapon, the Government has a right to use it as it chooses. The Union has sought time and again to enforce the right of free access to public records and documents, not too often succeeding; it has battled the ridiculous imposition of secrecy on material that any foreign agent can get from the newspaper, and the categorisation as "classified" that has literally barred the author of a technical document from rereading it because, though he did all the research and wrote the paper, he has never obtained a security clearance for subsequent access to his own work.

But the public has no right to know or to be informed of the private lives of individuals, whatever their positions or prominence, and the Union is doing a grave disservice to civil liberty when it professes the existence of such a right on the theory that there is no privacy in a court proceeding. Divorces, suicides (unless clearly political), licit or illicit *liaison*s, illegitimate births are the business only of those directly involved; and it should not be beyond the talents of legislative draftsmen to frame a statute that, without in any way infringing the legitimate freedoms of expression and knowledge, would protect the individual against the prurient curiosity of his fellows and the exploitation of that prurience by panders. Correctly, the Union has successfully opposed laws, such as that in New York State, that sought to bar publications "dealing principally in bloodshed, lust or crime," for the law's vagueness is a lively threat to press freedom (and, had it been sustained and enforced to the letter, one wonders what would have happened to Hearst's mealy-mouthed New York publications moralising every juicy bit of every juicy scandal, or to the *Daily News* with its "family-newspaper" tracking down of unwed cohabitators and its minutely detailed lip-licking divorce and fornication inventories). Those who need to read about bloodshed, lust and crime have every right to it—but only as long as the rights of the victim, the perpetrators and their friends and relatives are not trampled on by publishers who gain their incomes by catering to the lowest level of frustrates and *voyeurs*. What is sadly disappointing in the American Civil Liberties Union is its dereliction in concerning itself so little with the greatest civil liberty of all. Privacy cannot be wholly protected by the law of libel, for not every invasion of it, even the most offensive, need necessarily be libelous.

Only in the purely criminal areas of the conflicting claims of the individual and the so-called public right to know has the Union begun in the past few years to be active. Rightly concerned with the growing infringements in criminal practice on the right to a fair trial, the Union has sought to enlist the bar and the communications media in a joint effort to formulate a code of behavior that, while in no way infringing the legitimate freedom of the press or the right of the public to information, will not allow these to be perverted into the denial of fair trials and due process; but in general it is only the bar that has shown itself at all concerned. Press, radio and television have resisted every effort to hamper their exploitation of the alleged criminal for gain, without regard for his possible innocence or for the prejudice that may be stirred against him to the detriment of a fair trial. The hippodrome atmosphere of the arrest of Lee Harvey Oswald and the eager cooperation of the egocentric Dallas police and their superiors in the suppression of the rights of the probable trigger-man in the assassination of President Kennedy are only the latest and most spectacular instance of an injustice that even the tendentious Report of the Warren Commission could not blink away.

Not only the press but public officials have fought the efforts of the Union and the bar to preserve the rights of defendants, the most notable of the *revanchistes* being the Mayor of Philadelphia, James Tate, and New York City's Police Commissioner, Michael Murphy, who has often proclaimed his opposition to due process for arrested persons on the ground that, "if we let them know their rights, it makes our job harder." The new Attorney General of the United States, however, stands out in contrast to such primitives and to his predecessor, now removed to the Senate. In February, 1965, Nicholas de B. Katzenbach, who as Acting Attorney General had already pointed up these contrasts by proving his belief that law is meant to be enforced, not merely talked about in pious platitudes designed to win the votes of every faction at once, prepared an order to all federal attorneys that would sharply curtail, along the admirable British model, pre-trial information on arrests. Such announcements to the press would be limited to a copy or summary of the charge; the defendant's name, age, residence and marital and employment status; the place and time of the arrest and the name of the arresting agency. This order would be a particular blow to J. Edgar Hoover, who has always thrived on fulsome publicity designed to show that his FBI has saved the nation from unimaginable perils.

The New Jersey Supreme Court has also forbidden prejudicial statements by police, prosecutors and defense attorneys; but bills to this effect in various legislatures wither on the vine. Their attrition is assisted by the "gentlemen" of the press who fear the inhibition of their lust for notoriety (and their employers' lust for sales) entailed in the elimination of publicity fantasies such as those elaborated by New York's Murphy whenever his police make a possibly political arrest or murder a fifteen-year-old boy out of a racial ghetto. Courts, however, have tended increasingly to declare mistrials when the inflammatory panderings of the irresponsible reporters and editors have prejudiced the public, or to release prisoners unjustly convicted because of the press-created lynch atmosphere that brought about their convictions. Justice will be defeated, however, until our courts, like the British, can punish pre-trial gossips.

Even before the advent of television, the growth of broadcasting had begun to pose new civil-liberties issues, particularly as the major networks—American, Columbia and National Broadcasting—began to assume some characteristics of monopoly and the development of frequency-modulation opened a number of new broadcasting channels. In 1946 the Union declared that a new emphasis must be added to its concept of civil liberties: the desirability of optimum diversity of ownership and operation of the means of communication in order to further the expression of more kinds of opinion and reduce the threat of domination by powerful forces. Constantly aware of the potential of censorship inherent in the Communications Act and its administration by the FCC, the Union recognised too the unpleasant truth that freedom must be protected not only against restraints by law and regulation but equally against infringement by the absence of positive statute and prescription. For any philosophical anarchist this is an almost indigestible dose; but for freedom's sake it has to be swallowed. When the FCC, at the end of the war, released its standards for the issuance and renewal of broadcasting licenses and its philosophy of the licensees' responsibilities, the industry screamed: the only freedom it recognised was the freedom to make profits, and this could be exercised only by pleasing the sponsors who bought time and by not antagonising the potential clients who might buy it. The FCC, with the full approval of the ACLU, had made a station give equal time to atheists when it had broadcast attacks on them; but neither the FCC nor the ACLU, despite their concern in the matter, had been able to find any way to protect those commentators who were legally bought off the air by nervous-Nellie sponsors and stations.

In a widely distributed 1946 pamphlet, *Radio Programs in the Public Interest,* the Union backed the FCC's new standards, sought to answer the industry's objections and called on the public to assure the FCC of its support by letters. Not all the FCC's rules were specifically objected to by the industry, which could not deny out of existence the mass of complaints to the FCC and Congress from angry listeners, giving the lie to the broadcasters' contention that everything was fine as matters stood. Nor could they pretend that they had not promised, in order to avoid legislative restrictions, to clean the Augean stable and that they had not yet even ordered the shovels. In essence, the FCC's new rules were these:

—Controversial questions should be fairly dealt with from all sides and adequate time should be provided for the presentation of important public issues.

—Local issues and local talent should be adequately represented on network stations.

—Every station should run a reasonable number of sustaining programs at desirable listening times.

—Advertising excesses (purely quantitatively considered, in terms of the proportion of total broadcasting time given to commercials) should be minimised.

—Broadcasters should not editorialise.

The NAB, of course, howled *Censorship!* But the Union countered that, unlike the press or the film, radio does not have unlimited avenues of distribution: there are just so many channels, which are in the public domain. In franchising their use, the FCC had the same rights and duties as those of the Post Office in awarding second-class mailing privileges: like the Post Office, it could prescribe a ratio of advertising to text, and the *Esquire* case (see Chapter 16) had proved that the Post Office could not control the content of what were in effect its licensees. The argument that the FCC had no legal authority for setting any standards was countered by quoting the law empowering it to license on the basis of the "public interest, convenience and necessity," and expressly excluding any right of censorship.

The most specious of the NAB's arguments was the contention that the FCC was abridging freedom of speech, whereas it was patent that the rules were encouraging it, except for the ban on editorials. The Union supported this ban (which later it was to attack) on two grounds. Radio, being Government-licensed, unlike the press, was therefore obligated to be open to all sides on equal terms; and, by its power to select and reject material, it already had sufficient editorial power. The second argument, of course, was and is equally applicable to the press; both were ultimately to be abandoned by the ACLU. While the industry claimed the right to editorialise, it had always been too fearful to exercise it and, in the one instance of a radio editorial in 1938, the majority of the broadcasters had supported the FCC's punitive action. When in recent years the FCC modified the rule, few stations took advantage of the right to present their managements' views: business would be better if one said nothing that might offend someone. This was the same sort of moral courage that made broadcasters withdraw Easter programs lest they offend Jews and, after the advent of television, suppress the film of *Martin Luther* in Catholic areas—both of which acts of faith were roundly—and soundly—criticised by the Union.

On one point the broadcasters had some pragmatic right on their side: "the false assumption that sustaining programs would necessarily be in the public interest" as that interest was conceived by the FCC and the ACLU. It was true, as both charged, that most commercial programming was gaited to the sponsors' interest; but the sponsors' sole interest was catering to the public taste, however depraved, in order to sell their merchandise and services. To assume that sustaining programs would be on any higher level was at best *naïf*: no station was going to chase away the morons whom it needed for the sponsored program that followed the *cultural* sustaining period.

Finally, the NAB argued despairingly that FM would open up so many new channels that the argument of radio's physical limitations had to fail. On the contrary, the Union pointed out, there would still be a finite number of channels in each geographical area. It was this finiteness that led to the formation of the Union's Radio-Television Committee, composed of broadcasters, lawyers, writers and laymen. This committee is pioneering the new thinking in the Union that recognises, despite the fundamental opposition to government action based on the concept that it is necessarily an anti-libertarian force to be feared and checked, the unwelcome but inescapable parallel concept that the force of government can and must be used not only to protect but to further liberty. Subsequently the NAB, which had for a brief period become the National Association of Radio and Television Broadcasters before reverting to the more convenient name, produced a self-regulation code strongly attacked by the Union because the code, inordinately fearful of audience caprices and Congressional restraints, called for an internal censorship that largely blocked any free trade in ideas. A House committee was already, in 1952, engaged on one of those endless investigations of immorality, crime, bloodshed and corruption of the young on television that have never really ceased and that have all missed the fundamental point that communication should be as free as the right not to listen or watch and to inculcate taste in one's children. Then as now, the Union opposed any form of censorship.

It also opposed proposals to broadcast judicial proceedings, but, under stated safeguards, it offered to acquiesce in the transmission of sessions of Congress and its committees. The safeguards included the omission of defamations privileged by Congressional office, full due-process protections in hearings, frequent identification of hearings as such and as non-judicial proceedings, distinctions between voluntary and involuntary witnesses, adequate post-hearing exposures for involuntary witnesses, as well as for persons unfavorably mentioned, and fair treatment in camera techniques. The FCC refused to hear the Union on these points, but the House investigators listened and approved. Nothing, of course, ensued. The Union endorsed the FCC's new rule for equal time for all political candidates on equal bases, despite the costs it imposed on the broadcasters. A further problem was that of possible defamation on the air, which in later litigation was to be left essentially unsolved: when KING-TV in Seattle canceled a contract with Senator McCarthy lest he slander Senator Cain, the Union went at once to McCarthy's defense, contending that the station could have asked him for an agreement to indemnify it for any losses arising out of a libel action. Subsequently the courts have endorsed this theory in holding stations primarily liable; but other decisions have ruled that stations have no such liability and only the person actually uttering the defamation may be sued. The Easter and *Martin Luther* suppressions particularly troubled the Union because it was as eager to protect majority views as minority ones, but the networks and stations were far too frightened to even consider anything remotely "controversial."

(This McCarthy incident was atypical. McCarthy was one of forty-four Senators who signed a manifesto in 1951 criticising Truman's drastic orders for Government news secrecy as "violation of press freedom"; but, when *Time* criticised McCarthy, he publicly threatened the magazine with reprisals. The Union bade him withdraw the threat and, if he thought the criticism libelous, sue; instead he repeated his menace, but he never acted on it.)

In general, neither the Union nor the FCC has much modified its basic stand, nor, aside from the questions of broadcast editorials and equal time for political broadcasts, has either had much occasion to change. The equal-time rule (which in essence became Section 315 of the Communications Act) proved to have too many flaws. Enforced to the letter, it would have put a prohibitively costly burden on all broadcasters; consequently, in practice, it became equal time for the two major parties and virtually none for any others. In the 1960 Presidential campaign, the FCC suspended the rule in order to allow the grand show of the Kennedy-Nixon "debates." In that campaign, a survey of sixty stations showed, Kennedy had nineteen hours on the air, Nixon had eighteen and the Socialist Workers' party enjoyed a total of one-quarter-hour on a six-station network. Therefore the Union called for a revision of the rule to provide "equitable time" for all, rather than mathematically equal exposure, and thus to allow more opportunity to minority parties and candidates to present their positions. At the same time the Union saw no civil-liberties reason why every attack made by the President should demand necessarily an appropriate provision of rebuttal time, but this viewpoint, it emphasised, did not relieve stations of their basic duty to present a full discussion of all sides of controversial issues.

When the question of subscription-television first arose, the Union postponed any determination of policy on the matter until there had been ample opportunity for study; it now approves subscription-television in principle, provided it does not become a monopoly and provided further that it conforms in general to FCC standards for free television. In 1964 the voters of California adopted a proposition forbidding subscription-television in the state and the Union's committee condemned the vote as an in-

valid limitation of free speech and a deprivation of property
without due   process. The committee has also recommended
that the Union call on the FCC to open all ultra-high-frequency
channels and stiffen its standards for set manufacturers to assure adequate reception. The FCC's *fairness doctrine* has won
the endorsement of the full ACLU in principle though the Union
remains alert to the dangers arising when government even ap-
proaches the area of content of publications or broadcasts. The
endorsement is based on the FCC's determination to preserve
freedom to differ and its concern with the good faith in which its
licensees conduct their business. The doctrine contains three
major tenets designed to protect the right of persons (whether
candidates for office or private citizens), organisations or causes
attacked on the air to have "comparable" time for reply.

One of the most complex aspects of freedom of expression
that the Union has sought to advance is the vote. Its stated policy position, which would be unassailable in Utopia, or even in a
world in which there was some genuine foundation for the idealistic eighteenth-century belief in the infinite perfectibility of man,
declares that every citizen of voting age should be permitted to
vote. The best argument against such preposterous *naïveté* is
the caliber of the candidates embraced throughout history by a
deliberately uninformed, demonstrably uneducable and militantly inert mass electorate. As the ACLU should long since have
learned, not only from all recorded history but above all from
its own considerable experience with the tyrannies of the majority, no government can pose so great a danger to freedom as can
and does *Massenmensch*, eternally susceptible to the manipu-
lations of demagogues only slightly more cunning.

"That man is intellectually of the mass," Ortega says, "who,
in face of any problem, is satisfied with thinking the first thing
that comes into his head. On the contrary, the excellent man is
he who condemns what he finds in his mind without previous effort, and only accepts as worthy of him what is still far above him
and what requires a further effort in order to be reached." The
mass, Ortega makes it plain, is a thing not so much of multitude
as of inertia, and the mass-man pervades every class (if indeed,
culturally, there is anything but a universal middle class today).

Every great advance in freedom, as history demonstrates with tiresome abundance, has had to be imposed by a fluid, open, democratic *élite* of Ortega's "excellent men," activist minorities without which true democracy and freedom are not possible, against the inevitable resistance of precisely that inert conglomerate mass that is to be the beneficiary. Such an *élite*, by its nature forever recruiting new members and encouraging dissent, is a very different thing from the rigid, closed, autocratic *élite* that plays so large a *rôle* in both Communist and Fascist philosophies—both "typical movements of mass-men," to quote Ortega again, "directed, as all such are, by men who are mediocrities, improvised, devoid of a long memory and a 'historic conscience' "—or that enforced by soldiers or priests.

The two great revolutions of modern history—the American and the French—were originated by no inert masses: they were the creations of tiny but wide-open and democratic *élites* that were compelled, by the ironic essence of human nature and society, to use every tool of dictatorship to further their idealistic end: that liberal democracy, based on technical knowledge, that Ortega rightly calls the highest type of public life yet known. "The health of democracies," Ortega warns, "of whatever type and range, depends on a wretched technical detail—electoral procedure. . .Without the support of a genuine suffrage, democratic institutions are in the air." But, if this genuine suffrage is perverted, because of the "deadly hatred of the mass for all that is not itself," its "unwillingness to share life with those who are not of it," as in the modern Dark Age in which we live, the truly classless inert majority does its best to abort democratic *élites* and to bar their access to leadership or even to influence. That is one of the highest prices of the big society. It is also one of the highest barriers to freedom, which in the United States owes so much to what, however the creditor strives to deny his character, is almost the paradigm of a democratic *élite*: the American Civil Liberties Union, which pursues a noble goal with singleness of purpose and integrity of action, and welcomes every "excellent man" to its ranks.

The problem of the freedom of suffrage to which the Union addresses itself has always been complicated—quite aside from the fallacy from which the Union proceeds—by the calculated perversion of the views just sketched: a perversion designed to deny the vote to those persons and groups that might otherwise be able to dilute the power of the mass-minded ruling class, if not to unseat it utterly. Hence the purge of parties from the ballot; hence the cynically dishonest application of the comprehension test—which, fairly administered, would be unexceptionable—to Negroes carefully excluded from schools while white trash too inert to learn is exhorted to make its faltering X on the ballot or have its finger guided to the "right" lever on the voting machine. The ACLU's demand for the right of the Negro, the Indian, the Puerto Rican, the Communist, the Prohibitionist, the Trotskyite to vote would be far better founded if coupled with the demand that no citizen, of whatever color of skin or politics, be allowed to vote unless he could demonstrate, in an examination justly composed and universally administered in complete color-blindness (and this is not beyond practicability, given a modicum of good faith and an illimitable courage in the Federal Government —or is one falling into ingenuousness?), a reasonable comprehension of what modern society is all about.

But there is still another aspect of the freedom of the vote, on which the Union is on far sounder ground. This is the denial of representation in defiance of Constitutional and statutory provisions proportioning the number of legislators to population and stipulating periodic reapportionments, on the basis of census figures, to maintain the proportion. The arbitrary delineation of voting districts to maintain a given imbalance of power or to exclude from representation a specific element of the population— gerrymandering—is a political practice as old as politics, but in the first two-thirds of the Union's life there were many more pressing issues confronting it. Primarily it was the relatively recent militance of the Negro's claim for the rights so long and so viciously denied him that brought the Union to grips with this problem (its contribution to the arduous and limited victory against the primarily anti-Negro poll tax is dealt with in the chapter on the civil-liberties aspects of racialism). In 1958 the Union urged House Judiciary Committee approval of a bill to establish numerically equal districts that were continuous—in one piece—

and compact, within a state (opposed, of course, by political machines whose control might thus be jeopardised, as well as by the rednecks of the Confederacy). To dilute the effectiveness of citizens' votes, the Union declared in a policy statement, is as serious an act of discrimination as to deny them the right to vote. While the legislation was pending, a Federal Court in Minnesota, before which the Union had appeared *amicus*, compelled that state so to act. In other states local courts refused to act on similar suits, contending the issue was a purely "political" one, even when there had been no reapportionment for as long as a half-century.

Successful in its Supreme Court attack on the Tuskegee gerrymandering, in which a voting district was carefully redrawn to eliminate its overwhelming Negro majority, the Union pressed its fight also against Georgia's infamous county-unit system, under which candidates were elected not by the total of their popular vote but by the majority of counties that they carried, and this too was eventually overthrown. In Indiana, which one always regards as a kind of Midwestern enclave of the Sullied South, state officials simply spat on court orders for reapportionment; in Tennessee, one legislator might represent only 2300 constituents while a colleague was the sole voice for 78,000. Finally, in a Union appeal in 1962, the Supreme Court ruled that the lower Federal Courts had not only the power but the duty to review the fairness of the distribution of seats in state legislatures and that an unfair apportionment violated the Fourteenth Amendment's guaranty against any state's denial of equal protection of the laws. A year later the Supreme Court threw out Georgia's county units because the concept of political equality, Justice Douglas said, could mean only: "One person, one vote." Under the voided system, he pointed out, a resident of the state's smallest county had ninety-nine times the political power and influence of an Atlantan.

Corollarily, the Union, assisted by the American Jewish Congress (whose devotion to civil liberties has not always been absolute) and the NAACP's Legal Defense and Educational Fund, attacked apportionments in six states that threw a disproportionate share of political power into the hands of rural areas by discriminating against urban voters. Because minority groups tend to congregate in cities, the three organisations contended, discrimination of this kind operates not only against the urban voter but also against the minority groups, and hence the equal protection of the laws is denied, unfair per-capita tax benefits ensue and underrepresented cities, deprived of state funds, must seek federal aid. The briefs called on the court to reaffirm the equal-population principle, and in essence it did so in the 1963-4 term. Immediately Congress sought to nullify the decision by means of a rider on a foreign-aid bill (this kind of chicanery is its own commentary), which was fought so hard by the Union, the national bar and other groups that it was substantially modified.

Some dozen years earlier the Union had tried to remedy the evils of the Congressional filibuster and cloture. Concerned as it was with the protection of minorities against what Tocqueville has so aptly called *the tyranny of the majority*, the Union was equally alert to the paralysis of a democratic majority by obstructionist minority tactics. In October, 1951, Malin testified before the Senate Committee on Rules and Administration, contending—rather unarguably—that a filibuster, regardless whether it was employed to promote or to destroy a worth-while objective, was analogous to dictatorship. But the Olympians could not, of course, accept this thesis, and the evil, like so many others, has remained irremediable.

The atmosphere at that period of Korea and mccarthyism was hardly favorable. Truman, approaching the end of his tenure, tried hard to justify his seizure of the steel industry to terminate a strike and, characteristically, made a bad matter worse by adding gratuitously that, in a sufficient emergency, the Government could constitutionally take over the press and the radio. Malin protested at once, citing the difference between the dissemination of information and other forms of enterprise and resting on the First Amendment, and asked Truman to clarify. The President knew enough to recognise (a) that he had been wrong and (b) that he had long since learned not to debate with his intellectual betters, of whom, like the common people, God had made so many, and so he did not reply. But the example of his intem-

perance and of his restraints on Government information inspired a number of happily defeated state efforts to probe and curb
the press.

In the two decades since the end of the Second World War the
Union has had to fight again and again the battles that it won
in the two decades before the war. Cities and states have enacted the same kind of bans on meetings and handbills that the
Supreme Court had outlawed, and again the Union has had to go
into court, often meeting defeat in state tribunals that either did
not read Supreme Court decisions or did not care about them (a
state of mutiny that intensified as the John Birch Society and
Senator Eastland denounced the "Warren court" as the shock
brigade of the Kremlin). Vagrancy statutes were invoked to arrest political soapbox speakers as "lewd and dissolute persons"
—and the arrests were thrown out. Self-appointed vigilantes,
without permission, published private letters from friends who
criticised the American or friendly Governments and one Fulbright scholar who had written such a letter lost her stipend despite the Union's protest. Postcards critical of Eisenhower were
banned from the mails as "filthy and indecent" because the
writer invited all his fellow-voters for the President to kick his
buttocks in public—in spite of which he was elected lieutenant
governor of Oklahoma.

Most astonishingly, the Union upheld the New York police in
arresting protestants who refused to participate in so-called
civil-defense tests: it argued that the right to petition does not
mean the right to do so indiscriminately regardless of circumstances, time and places. The theory may be valid; its application is indefensible in this case. The anomaly of the Union's
action was emphasised by its attempt to compel newspapers to
accept paid advertisements seeking funds for the defense of
persons indicted under the Smith Act. The question of the publisher's right to refuse advertisements he disapproves, however,
has never been definitively resolved within the Union: among
its free-speech committee there is strong sentiment for the view
that integrity cannot be compelled and that even a monopoly publisher cannot rightfully be compelled to lean over backward if
he prefers not to do so. The same committee is more unevenly

divided on the right of public figures to privacy. Many years ago it defended the author of an unauthorised biography of Serge Koussevitzky; at present it has a forceful minority defending the objections of a professional athlete to a biography that specu-lates on his personal life (he gave the author no assistance or interviews). What was still in early 1965 a committee minority contends, with utter justice, that only the exchange of ideas is en-titled to the protection of the First Amendment and that this guar-anty neither does nor should extend to the exploitation of third persons' private lives for gain. That there could be even doubt on this score is incredible.

Despite even the protests of Hearst's renegade-Communist house philosopher, George Sokolsky, and former HUAC Chair-man Francis Walter, the Post Office continued to occupy the Union's attention by its rule—later reinforced by a statute enact-ed by Congress over the opposition of President Kennedy, Attor-ney General Kennedy, Secretary of State Rusk and Postmaster General Day—restricting the receipt of foreign "propaganda" to registered foreign agents and, later, to persons signifying their willingness to receive it (and, by implication, to be thus enrolled on a blacklist of questionable individuals). Under what is known as the "rotten apple" doctrine, the Post Office claimed the right to hold up and destroy a whole shipment of books or magazines if one piece of forbidden fruit was found in it. The Union opposed, as clearly unconstitutional censorship, not only the restriction but the doctrine under which it was enforced: an extension of guilt by association without a hearing. For ten years the rule and the later statute were contested and, as noted in Chapter 1, both have at last been thrown out by the Supreme Court. Corollarily, Gov-ernment agencies have taken it on themselves to bar suspect publications—such as *Saturday Review* or *The Nation*—from newsstands operated as private concessions on Government property, and state and municipal administrations have emu-lated them. In almost all cases, the index of heresy has been compiled without hearing or investigation on the basis of lists supplied by such self-styled patriots as the various veterans' organisations. Similar political censorship has been imposed on reading matter in prisons. The Union's unremitting fight on all such suppression has an almost evenly balanced record of victories and defeats. The Union was less successful against USIA cancelation of art exhibits abroad because of the artists' politics and the State Department's ban on a tour by the Symphony of the Air because the egregious Representative John J. Rooney (of Brooklyn) declared that some of the musicians were "Communists." Malin failed to overcome the refusal of the city of Providence, Rhode Island, to accept a statue of Tom Paine, one of the men who inspired the American Revolution, because he "was and remains a controversial figure"—one wonders about George Washington and Abraham Lincoln.

Freedom of speech for the military has been a difficult question for the framing of Union policy, predisposed as it rightly is toward minimal limitations. The problem is of course confused by the quasi-official status of any military officer above the two lowest ranks and by the fact that his position of command can in itself intimidate those of his men who might otherwise dissent from his views. The political and philosophical powers of the military mind are at best to be regarded with the utmost caution when it departs from the *Manual of Arms* and the *Articles of War*; yet a dedication to civil liberties imposes on its adherents the obligation of suffering, however ungladly, not only fools but fanatics. Yet, when an admiral or a general expresses a political view, there is an almost irrebuttable presumption that he speaks for Government, however explosive, domestically or internationally, his profound elucidations. After much internal conflict within the Union and a handful of apparently contradictory public positions in individual cases, it evolved a purely pragmatic position: in effect, enlisted men, non-commissioned officers and the lower ranks of commissioned officers should not be subject to the restrictive Presidential directives that had followed a war-cry by Admiral Arleigh Burke, since it is impossible to confuse them with voices of policy and since they would have to sacrifice their careers without compensation in order to speak freely; but the high-level officer should properly be curbed not only because what he says can reasonably be misconstrued as authoritative but also because he is in a position, if he objects to conforming to discipline, to retire on pension and fulminate like a veritable General Walker. Roger Baldwin, in a discussion on this subject, has raised the analogy of the corporation and its employes and its right to forbid those rightly considered its policy representatives to express views that might be taken to commit it to viewpoints that it does not hold.

Enforcement of the right of assembly continues to devil the Union because of the constant effort of politicians—some to please the right, some to please the Negroes, some to please the Jews, some to please everyone—to circumvent the law and the prophets and the Supreme Court. Over and over again the Union has had to fight for the right to meet without a permit, the right to utter offensive doctrines (its defense of George Lincoln Rockwell, commander of the American Nazi Party; Gerald Smith, the Klan and the White Citizens' Councils has cost it Jewish, Negro and Catholic members), the right to picket for political purposes, the right to seek petition signatures in public places. Virtually every harassment has been overcome, but no victory has prevented the next attempt. Licensing laws were invoked to prevent the sales of literature and merchandise from Communist countries—fees of $1000 to $5000 a year were set, and even merchants displaying their licenses were summarily closed by local police. The first act of the new Georgia affiliate of the ACLU was to assert and enforce the right of the Klan to meet in a public park and to withhold its membership lists from the authorities (similar rights for the NAACP had to be fought for in Florida, whose legislators sought to prove the organisation Communist-dominated).

In a throwback to all its old libel litigations, the ACLU, with the ANPA, won Supreme Court vindication of *The New York Times'* right to run an advertisement, signed by Negro leaders, criticising the violations of law committed by the public authorities of Birmingham and Alabama, and the reversal of a $500,000 verdict against *The Times* and the signers of the advertisement. The New York Civil Liberties Union, in 1963, was put into the remarkable position of being on both sides of the same controversy. *The Brooklyn Daily* bitterly attacked the NYCLU for its successful brief on behalf of a cabaret license for the Playboy Club, a night-club catering to sexually arrested adolescents of all ages and adequate finances; the paper also denounced the judge who rendered the decision, and it was promptly indicted for criminal libel. Thereupon the NYCLU went back into court on behalf of its attacker and won a dismissal of the indictment.

"No civil-liberties victory," as Baldwin truly remarked in December of 1964, "ever stays won."

14

"Did He Who Made the Lamb Make Thee?"

In the earliest years of the ACLU it was little concerned with the racial aspects of civil liberties. No intelligent person, black or white, saw any possibility of substantial amelioration in the foreseeable future, and the NAACP enjoyed a virtual monopoly of Negro problems that it guarded with a certain mistrust of white offers of assistance. A kind of unofficial *entente* between the ACLU and the NAACP left the monopoly undisturbed, even in cases of lynching: by agreement, the ACLU concerned itself only with those fatal to whites. In North and South alike, the Negro generally "knew his place" and there seemed no likelihood that he would ever have another. Since he was so well represented by the NAACP and it was not always receptive to cooperation, especially from an organisation that had opposed its efforts to prevent the showing of *The Birth of a Nation*, the only racial minority to engage the ACLU's attention was the American Indian, despite the presence of James Weldon Johnson, secretary of the NAACP, on the ACLU's board of directors.

The Indian had a full catalogue of injustices. It was only in 1924 that Congress granted him full citizenship; but this was hedged with so many restrictions that the ACLU formed a Committee on Indian Civil Rights under Nathan Margold, a New York lawyer, to seek first-class citizenship for the descendants of those from whom the country had been virtually stolen as Israel was to be seized from the Arabs. Thousands of Indians were segregated on reservations and deprived of control of their lands and funds, denied their tribal governments and treated as wards of the United States who were somewhere between the Negro and the human being on the prevailing evolutionary scale. Their schools were as segregated as those of the Southern Negro; special colleges existed for them here and there; the spectacle of the many off-reservation Indians who functioned in daily life just like white folks was regarded with somewhat the same attitude as that of Dr. Johnson toward a dog that could walk on its hind legs alone.

Though the first major reforms were initiated by President Hoover, who appointed two Philadelphia Quaker business men, Henry Scattergood and Charles Rhoades, to a special commission that really worked to aid the Indians, neither the aborigines nor the Union's efforts on their behalf received much of a hearing until the beginning of the New Deal, when their lands and tribal governments were restored to them. Somehow the Indians of Oklahoma were omitted from the Indian Reorganisation Act of 1934 and in 1935 the Union backed a bill to extend the new situation to them. This was bitterly but vainly fought by the American Indian Federation, which accused the ACLU of wanting to hand the Redskins over to Red Moscow. At the same time the Union called on the Commissioner of Indian Affairs to remove the gag on criticism of his Bureau by its employes. The injustices at which the 1934 Act was directed were not wholly corrected by it—again, "states' rights" to do wrong. In part the law had resulted from the ACLU's *Indian Primer* of 1932, according to which there were 350,000 Indians in 200 tribes. Two-thirds of them were wards of the Government on reservations; those in New York State were its wards as well.

Congress had granted (!) American citizenship to all the Indians in 1924 as a reward for their service in the First World War, but it had not ended federal guardianship. As a result, some states refused to let them vote. Without the consent of the Bureau of Indian Affairs, no Indian could make a contract or a will, borrow money, retain counsel or get control of his own money, which the Bureau held and administered in trust for him. His only tribunals were the Reservation Courts and appeals were virtually impossible. The Indians' schools were as bad as the Negroes' and, like the Negroes, they were turned out of school with no training for either work or further education. They were restricted to their reservations by an old espionage law, which deprived them of normal civil rights and restricted their contacts with "outsiders," a law that the Union sought to have repealed. It asked in addition the establishment of tribal councils authorised to exercise the rights of property, contract, seeking legal aid and so on; the recall of any Indian agent declared unwelcome in a tribal referendum, the imposition of penalties for the abduction of Indian children into Government boarding schools (a not uncommon practice) and the incorporation of the Klamath tribe to act as an ordinary business corporation with minimal supervision. This would have been a laboratory test for further liberation of all Indians.

In 1936 Senator Burton K. Wheeler of Montana, an on-and-off New Dealer with occasional spasms of civil-libertarianism until he joined America First, tried to repeal the Reorganisation Act, but then everyone forgot about the Indians again—everyone except the ACLU, which could not refresh the others' recollections until after the Second World War. In 1946 Congress set up the Indian Claims Commission to settle long-neglected financial matters arising under the ancient treaties with the various tribes but did nothing else. The Union, however, began its struggle against the denial of the vote to Indians by Arizona and New Mexico; in the first case they were disfranchised because they were "wards of the state," in the second because the state constitution excluded "Indians not taxed" from eligibility, though, of course, all Indians paid excise and other taxes. Both states were clearly violating the Fourteenth and Fifteenth Amendments. The New Mexico ban was then voided by state courts; Arizona reversed itself by finding that the Indians were not after all "under guardianship." But new litigation was necessary to compel both states to admit the original Americans to the benefits of the social-security laws.

Congress' reawakened interest in its Indian constituents consisted chiefly of efforts to invoke new discriminations against them, but ACLU action prevented the inclusion of an anti-indigene clause in the bill for Alaskan statehood in 1950 and defeated the bill sponsored by that disgrace to the Senate, Pat McCarran, to confiscate the Piutes' lands in Nevada. These negative gains were offset by the appointment of a new Commissioner of Indian Affairs, Dillon Myers, who, having been in charge of the Japanese "relocation" camps, sought to liquidate the Indian reservations as he had eliminated the camps, terminating the Government's guardianship of the reservation Indians and thus stripping them of their lands for the inevitable benefit of land-greedy whites. This proposal was immediately and successfully opposed by the ACLU. It was followed by attractively titled "emancipation bills" that would have unilaterally abrogated the Government's treaties with the various tribes, deprived them of protection that was still needed and, as the politically motivated Emancipation Proclamation of 1863 had done to the Negroes, thrown the hapless Indians to the wolves of our "competitive free-enterprise system" without the slightest preparation for self-preservation in its jungle. These bills would have deprived any Indian ruled "competent" of his rights to Indian schools and hospitals, bad as these were; what rights each Indian had would be based on the Government's determination of the percentage of Indian blood in his body (how Hitler must have snickered in Walhalla in that enlightened year of 1953!) and the bills would have dissolved the tribes. Abetted by the Union, the noble savages proved they were people and citizens and the legislation was killed. But positive legislation was needed in Congress to reverse the administrative trend that was tending toward the result sought by the defeated bills; Utah was persuaded to repeal its law denying the vote to reservation dwellers in 1956.

Two years later the Senecas of New York were joined by the Union, which had originally seen no civil-liberties issues in the matter, in their battle to prevent the expropriation of their lands for a dam and reservoir. This had been authorised under a general appropriations law that did not mention either the Senecas or the 1794 treaty with them, signed by President Washington, that guaranteed the peaceful possession of their lands in perpetuity. The Union contended that the legislation deprived the Senecas of their tribal existence, their religious and cultural customs and their property without due process: Eisenhower vetoed the bill but his veto was overridden. A year later a Navajo religious group sued to void a Tribal Council ordinance forbidding the use of peyote, a hallucinatory drug that had long been part of the group's rites: the Circuit Court of Appeals in Denver ruled that tribal governments were beyond the writ of the Bill of Rights. The Union contended, quite properly, that the Bill of Rights applied wherever the Government's sovereignty extended, but the Supreme Court would not listen.

In 1965 the Union is still actively fighting for the right of the American Indian to treatment as a human being. A three-year Senate Judiciary Subcommittee study of the status of Indians, completed late in 1964, confirmed every charge the Union had ever made against federal Indian policy and the various states with large Indian populations: frustration of Indian efforts at effective self-government, denial not only of all due-process safeguards but also of health and welfare services; police brutality and rape; and, above all, the indifference of state and federal officials. After all, why should the elected officials of a democracy of 193,000,000 people worry over the status of some 300,-000 widely scattered individuals who had no pressure tactics and could not carry even a single precinct? To lessen this disability, the National Congress of American Indians and similar groups have been formed on the Negroes' models.

The United States Circuit Court of Appeals in San Francisco, however, showed somewhat more concern with justice than do the elected representatives. It threw out the conviction of Madeline Colliflower of the Gros Ventre tribe because the tribal court that convicted her of trespass acted without a shred of evidence of the offense alleged—"no evidence was introduced at the trial," the Union's brief pointed out, and "no witnesses were examined or cross-examined." The brief added that Miss Colliflower was the victim of a tri-une combination of prosecutor, "witness" and judge in the same person. The Circuit Court made it clear that, even though the tribal courts imposed on reservation Indians by the Government must be considered sovereign and their jurisdiction is largely exclusive, they, like any other tribunals, are bound by the Constitution to respect the fundamental right of the defendant to due process of law. Most remarkably, the Union's position was supported by an unusual brief *amicus* from the Department of Justice.

The Union has also been constantly alert to protect the rights of Orientals and Mexican-Americans. It fought for the right of entry and citizenship for Orientals through the repeal of the unbelievable Oriental Exclusion Act, which resulted from the *yellow peril* hysteria sustained on the West Coast by labor unions and the unscrupulous Hearst and echoed elsewhere by those two rabble-rousing jingoes, Colonel Robert R. McCormick of *The Chicago Tribune* and his cousin, Captain Joseph Medill Patterson of *The News* in New York. On behalf of Mexican-Americans, in the western and southwestern states where they are numerous, the Union has had to contend (for the most part successfully) with the identical segregation techniques employed everywhere against the Negro. Because of its understanding with the NAACP, the Union did not undertake any substantial activity on behalf of the Negro until 1930, when various southern states invoked and broadened old post-Reconstruction anti-Negro laws as a weapon against those blacks who dared to form unions or seek entry into white ones. At that time segregation was legally required in seventeen states; thirty barred any and all kinds of racial intermarriage. Mississippi, forever in the forefront of bigotry, enacted a law making it a crime to advocate the social equality of the races. A year later Communists were prosecuted in Atlanta for holding racially mixed meetings. In the twenty-seven lynchings of the preceding five years, only two Caucasians had been butchered.

In 1931 the Union issued its first publication on racialism, a pamphlet entitled *Black Justice*. This was a survey of denials of Negroes' rights in both northern and southern states, and it revealed nothing that is not still, even if quantitatively diminished, part of the "American way": gross deprivations of the vote, racial slums and ghettos, exclusions of Negroes from juries, lack of police, fire and sanitation protections, job discrimination, massive segregation in every phase of public and private life and, in the South, where "we love our Nigras," such an abundance of love that special laws deterred their emigration, whether voluntary or through labor recruiting. Greater love hath no man than his love for a cheap labor force on which, too, he can draw at random for victims to brutalise and women to degrade. *Segregation by day, integration by night* was still the centuries-old rule imposed by the *Herrenvolk*. *Black Justice* and the Union's growing determination to whiten it cost the ACLU a newly recruited National Committee member, former Senator Thomas Hardwick of Georgia, who had only two years earlier undertaken to defend the Gastonia strikers for the Union. The general reaction to the pamphlet outside the south was the customary indifference; when in 1932 a federal judge in Boston refused to extradite a Negro to Virginia to face a murder trial because Virginia excluded Negroes from its juries, it was a phenomenon. What was much more in accord with the way everything happened for the best in this best of all possible countries was the vagrancy conviction of those Denver Negroes who had protested their exclusion from a public swimming-pool, which was almost simultaneous with the gunshot murder of a Negro by six Memphis policemen who had arrested him on a rape charge. The whole disturbing problem of the white southerner's sexual jealousy of the Negro is excellently explored by John Dollard in *Caste and Class in a Southern Town,* a study as valid thirty years after publication as it was in 1935.

Nor did the early New Deal do much for the second-class citizens. In its 1933-4 report the Union noted the impunity with which much of the AFL barred Negroes, and the NRA's southern wage differential, "obviously based on keeping Negro workers 'in their place.' " And, in the first year of the New Deal, twenty-four Negroes were lynched, as well as four of the master race. In the second year, a southerner sitting on the federal bench in the Virgin Islands tried, convicted and sentenced a Negro for theft despite the fact that the prosecutor had dropped the charge because no criminal act had been committed. In contrast, Governor Hill McAlister of Tennessee used troops to prevent the lynching of a Negro awaiting trial—whereupon the disappointed rednecks burned down the courthouse. Then the Supreme Court began to discover that Negroes had rights—but not many. It over-threw the conviction in the first trial of the Scottsboro boys—nine Negroes accused of raping two white whores while all eleven were stealing a ride in a freight car—because the Alabama grand jury that indicted them had been pure white, so for the first time Alabama put a lone Negro on a new grand jury that, need-less to say, re-indicted. The case was to come before the Supreme Court again and again, fought through by the ILD, the NAACP, the ACLU and many other organisations. The court also over-threw the Mississippi murder conviction of a Negro because he had been subjected to the third degree. But the court was not prepared to accept the proposition that a Negro could vote in a southern Democratic primary.

The Democratic Party of Texas had resolved itself into lily-whiteness—among the Texas Democrats was John Nance Garner, elected Vice President of the United States with the liberal Pres-ident Roosevelt. Consequently the New Dealers of Texas refus-ed to let Negroes vote in their primary, and one Negro who did not know his place brought suit under the Fifteenth Amendment, which forbids the states to refuse voting rights on grounds of race, color or religion. The plaintiff lost in every court, including the Supreme Court. In Grovey v. Townsend, in 1935, it tortured logic, fact and morality into the doctrine that a party primary is not a state function even though required by state law, but a purely private affair of a political party, which is a voluntary association of free citizens and, under Texas law at that time, paid for the primary expenses. Any such voluntary private asso-ciation, the court held, has absolute power to determine eligibil-ity for membership and voting in it; only a general election is protected by the Fifteenth Amendment.

By this time the Union was beginning to act on behalf of the Negro's civil liberties. Its first target was the segregation prac-ticed in the theaters of New Jersey and, courageously, it also at-tacked the same practice in the American Library Association convention in Richmond, Virginia. In 1936 the first significant cooperation between the Union and the NAACP, today working so closely together, was brought about by the kind of cynical in-justice that still occupies both: the denial of votes to Negroes in

an Oklahoma county in which they were the majority and where
the local courts struck down every effort to enforce the Constitution until the Supreme Court backed them down. *Black Justice*
was brought up to date and re-issued, augmented by the record
of the Congressional filibuster that killed the anti-lynching bill,
the refusal of the Supreme Court to review the case of one of
the Scottsboro boys, the release of four and the continued detention of four others on the same evidence that had been called
worthless in the case of the four set free. Though the anti-lynching bill was defeated, the ACLU noted, the mere threat of it had
been salutary: successful lynchings dropped to eight (all black)
in 1937, and officials had actually prevented some twenty others.

In 1938 Charles H. Houston, attorney for the NAACP, joined
the Union's directorate, which has never since lacked NAACP
representation. Both organisations at the same time saw a ray of
encouragement in a new Supreme Court decision that indicated
that the old case of Plessy v. Ferguson was not quite so sacrosanct as Holy Writ. That was the case that set up the rule that
states barring Negroes from public schools must give them "separate but equal" facilities: for fifty years there had been no question of the separateness and no shred of equality. If the state
could not provide truly equal facilities, the court now ruled, then
it must admit Negroes to the formerly segregated schools. Under
this decision the University of Missouri was compelled to admit
its law school's first Negro: an order obeyed with a grace that
was rarely to be emulated. Then the court reversed Texas and
Florida convictions of Negroes subjected to the third degree; in
1940—twenty-five years later, however, the decision is still flouted—it outlawed racial segregation in interstate travel. But, when
the draft law was enacted and conscription quotas were set up
on a segregated basis, the court refused to act. Negroes found
the armed forces as segregated as the worst of the south, and
much of industry as well. After three hundred years of oppression they had begun to have enough, and they could see little
justice in being compelled to risk death for a country that made
them do so where they would not bleed on whites and that thus
far had done nothing to inspire their allegiance. To them American participation in a war against bigotry was an exceptionally bad

joke, especially when they were called on to play it. Perhaps because they had endured only three hundred years of oppression, perhaps because so few of them had been able to struggle up out of the muck into which they were thrust, they were far more militant than the Jews whom Hitler found it so easy to destroy after thousands of years of discrimination offset by so many instances of individual acceptance. In any case, the Negroes threatened to march on Washington to demand that the President and Congress, if they were going to make black men manufacture weapons and be shot at for democracy, treat them with a modicum of democratic justice. To forestall the demonstration, which would have been most injurious both at home and abroad to the Government's war effort, Roosevelt hastily set up the first Fair Employment Practices Commission, armed largely with good intentions and political pieties.

It was obvious that this would not be enough in itself unless the new political body was constantly hounded to do its job. Negroes trying to move into a Detroit housing project found themselves the victims of a riot, the leaders of which were indicted by the Government; others in St. Louis were refused employment on a project being built for their own race despite the *numerus clausus* for their employment in the construction contract. Civil suit was instituted by the Justice Department, the Union and the NAACP, and the Union adopted a policy of thenceforth working only in cooperation with the NAACP on Negro civil-liberty matters. The Union at the same time set up its own committee on racial discrimination, headed by Pearl Buck, the novelist. The Justice Department suddenly discovered that, despite the defeat of the anti-lynching bill (an annual ritual), it could prosecute lynch mobs under the old 1866 Civil Rights Law, and actually did so. The War Labor Board insisted on equal pay for equal work regardless of race. The nation needed Negro bodies so badly that it would even listen now and then to Negro voices, if properly modulated. Arthur Garfield Hays and the Union, however, failed to defeat segregation in the draft; but the Union was instrumental in preventing the extraditions of several Negroes to southern states. (Almost overlooked, an old ACLU goal was achieved when Congress, eager for Chinese help in the war, repealed the Chinese Exclusion Act, setting up a quota and making it possible for men with yellow skins to become citizens.)

The Harlem and Detroit race riots of 1943 that cost thirty-eight lives and emphasized the scope of the racial problem were inevitable and there was a certain *naïveté* in the shock they evoked in men of good will, always reluctant to believe the truth about the human animal. The need for an enemy who can be hated, brutalised and exploited is ineradicable: it is immeasurably exacerbated when the victim turns against the torturer and dares to pretend to have rights. To ascribe it solely to economics, in the manner of the fanatic Marxist or of the idealistic "liberal," is to oversimplify and to deny the savagery that will never be extinct in even the most refined of us. Certainly the trash resents the competition of the Negro; but the Negro's economic emergence is as often merely the pretext, the good reason for actions whose real reason is the joy of killing, whether literally or symbolically. In October of 1943 the Union published a pamphlet by the secretary of its discrimination committee, Winifred Raushenbush, under the optimistic title, *How to Prevent a Race Riot in Your Home Town*. Seven cities had already, after the Harlem and Detroit riots, set up committees to prevent recurrences, which were found to be most threatened in overcrowded warplant areas, near army camps, in southern cities where northern Negro soldiers resented Jim Crow laws, in cities where Negro influxes antagonised immigrant populations (the Italian minorities, for obvious reasons, have always been the most anti-Negro), areas where Negroes' living standards are kept down or where racist organisations are busy, and cities inundated by white trash attracted to war industry from the south. The pamphlet called for preventative measures to be taken by local officials, volunteer committees, clerics and the police, including better employment and recreation facilities, the refutation of rumors, integrated policing and educational publicity.

Isolated instances of prejudice were more easily dealt with. Three of the five Scottsboro boys still in prison were paroled through the efforts of Dr. Allan Knight Chalmers of the ACLU's board, which helped to form the Scottsboro Defense Committee. The Union defeated the Army Medical Corps' attempt to reject a qualified Negro doctor barred from the navy. In New York City the Union found and battled racial segregation in the publicly aided Stuyvesant Town project of the Metropolitan Life Insurance Company, which refused to rent to Negroes. The general anti-Negro prejudice, aggravated by that against Orientals, was still operating to exclude Filipinos (though their country was a United States colony) and East Indians from immigration and the Union also sought and gained the end of that racial bar. The navy reluctantly allowed Negroes into some of its less menial services, but issued dishonorable discharges to fourteen in the Seabees who had protested Jim Crow conditions at their base; on appeal to the Navy Appeal Board they received honorable discharges. The Union prepared and distributed a model civil-rights law for state legislatures.

In 1945 the Supreme Court discovered that a Democratic primary was not a private club's social function after all but an integral part of the election machinery, indifferent to color, and it reversed its ten-year-old approval of the barring of Negroes. Very soon afterward lower federal courts forbade racial discrimination in hiring library employes and the segregation of Mexican-Americans in schools. State courts upheld laws banning anti-Negro clauses in union contracts and housing leases. Florida allowed Negroes to vote in the Democratic primary. But other courts upheld racially restrictive housing covenants, acquitted a gang of twenty-eight admitted lynchers and freed a policeman who blinded a Negro veteran. The army misguidedly set up a *numerus clausus* in the draft, proportioning its Negro conscripts to the ratio of Negroes to the general population. Some southern cities hired Negro policemen and public officials, Negroes broke the big-league baseball barrier and more Scottsboro boys were paroled. Again there were contrasts: Governor Dewey of New York whitewashed the police murder of two arrested Negroes, and a federal grand jury whitewashed the Tennessee indictment of thirty-one Negroes for conspiring to defend themselves against a *pogrom* on a Negro quarter—yet only one of the Negroes was convicted, for assault with intent to murder. South Carolina, in a last-ditch effort to bar Negroes from primaries, repealed all its laws on the subject but a federal court invoked the new Texas primary decision and ruled that the primary was a public matter from which Negroes could not be barred—whereupon President Truman's Fair Deal Democrats appealed to reinstate the ban on the Negroes.

The civil rights of black Americans were now a major national issue, constantly clouded by fallacious reasoning that sometimes led to valid conclusions: the preoccupation with what *they* would say abroad about our own brand of Naziism and *Apartheid*. Foreshadowing the inevitable break-through, the Supreme Court voided all restrictive housing covenants and fined the Brotherhood of Locomotive Firemen and Engineers for refusing to admit Negroes. New York and other states enacted legislation banning racial and religious discrimination—a kind of continuing serial that, into the 1950's, consisted of sequential implementation by extending the ban from schools to jobs, public accommodations and all other applicable areas and by gradually adding enforcement procedures and penalties to the laws. But, though it reiterated its positon that Negroes must have educational facilities equal to those of whites, the Supreme Court balked at repeating against the University of Oklahoma, despite identical circumstances, the order that had opened the University of Missouri Law School to Negroes; and Congress went on rejecting legislation to ban lynching, eliminate the poll tax and set up a permanent FEPC.

The Union's pamphlet on *Race Bias in Housing*, issued jointly with the NAACP and the American Council on Race Relations, was a thorough examination of the subject by Charles Abrams, former counsel to the New York City Housing Authority. It pointed up the truism that segregation of one group quickly expands to include others but it warned that "there is today hardly a private community in the whole of America where the atmosphere for a *rapprochement* between the races exists." Abrams traced the use of zoning ordinances to implement segregation and emphasised the insufficiency of legislation to effect gains unless it was backed by education and active official support. "A civil right," he warned, "may be nullified by indifference as by decree." In spite of the prevailing indifference and hostility to racially mixed housing and neighborhoods, he was able to cite not only the peaceful experimental integration of some New York

City projects but the anomaly of similar successes in some southern areas; but there, he admitted, a psychic dominance pattern helped to prevent friction. The restrictive covenant, he said, could logically be extended to include sales of food, clothing or anything else if society did not reject the immoral philosophy behind it. But he added another *caveat* in his appeal for full integration: the quota system must be avoided lest it become rigid and in its turn an instrument of injustice.

The gains were slow and painful. A few states repealed their bans against miscegenation as the decade of the 1950's began; the Georgia Supreme Court ordered the inclusion of Negroes on jury lists in counties with large Negro populations; but the Georgia Legislature enacted a voter test, aimed at Negroes, that was based on the applicant's knowledge of the Federal Constitution and included questions beyond the capacity of the bill's own sponsor. The Supreme Court upheld the overthrow of an Alabama statute calling for the exegesis of the Constitution by the would-be voters. The Commissioners of the District of Columbia unearthed a hundred-year-old law banning discrimination in restaurants and the management of the National Airport in the District thumbed its nose at the Commissioners' compliance order. The Union helped a Pittsburgh Negro avoid extradition to Georgia eleven years after having escaped from a chain gang; though this particular medieval barbarity had been abolished in Georgia, the Circuit Court of Appeals denounced it as an unconstitutional "cruel and unusual punishment." The University of Oklahoma finally admitted its Negro but was upheld by a Federal District Court in confining him to segregated classrooms. Governor Byrnes of South Carolina, a former Truman Cabinet officer, threatened to close the public schools if the Federal Government tried to integrate them—a threat that was to be carried out a few years later by several Virginia counties; but little by little, during the Korean conflict, southern public schools began to accept Negroes without incident.

Under pressure from the Union, the NAACP, progressive political organisations and a host of religious groups, private associations also began to desegregate; the CIO warned its southern locals to admit Negroes and treat them like white

folks; colleges rejected racially restrictive donations and be-
quests. In New York City the Union persuaded the State Commission Against Discrimination to act against the separate black
and white hiring halls of the AFL Seafarers' International Union;
but in the same city no politician dared move against the owner
of the Stork Club when he flagrantly discriminated against Jose-
phine Baker, the great Negro entertainer who became a French
citizen rather than submit to the degradations visited on her race
in the Land of the Free. Airlines were made to drop their secret
code designations for Negroes in the allocation of seats; but it
was much more difficult to persuade cemetery owners that bury-
ing blacks next to whites would not corrupt the upper race in the
next world. Swimming-pool owners feared their water would turn
black. Rape, in the south, continued to be a capital offense only
for blacks; in North Carolina a Negro was convicted of assaulting
a white woman by "leering at her" but the state Supreme Court
could not stomach this.

On May 17, 1954, the "Warren court" delivered the historic ruling that, as the Union contended, segregation in the public
schools was an unconstitutional deprivation of the equal protection of the laws guaranteed by the Fourteenth Amendment. The
disgraceful reaction of a tremendous part of the country, both
north and south, is too recent and too appalling to require re-
capitulation. Related subsequent cases resulted in orders to make
a prompt and reasonable start on school integration, to proceed
with "all deliberate speed" and to prove any affirmative defense
of the need for more time or of the good faith of unsatisfactory
compliance. To Gerald L. K. Smith and his competitors, the
Jewish-Communist-nigger conquest of the Government was now
consolidated.

Further proof was furnished by the relative rapidity with which
states and cities enacted anti-discrimination bills, revised administrative procedures to attain the same end and penalised violators. Big firms like International Harvester did a notable job of
fully integrating their southern plants and, when redneck members of the United Automobile Workers struck in protest at having to work with Negroes, the union president, Walter Reuther,
properly refused them the use of union strike machinery. State

poll taxes began to dwindle: only Alabama, Arkansas, Mississippi, Texas and Virginia retained them, and five years later the Twenty-Fourth Amendment limited them to state elections. The lynchings that might have been anticipated from the school decision did not materialise; but in 1954 there were 195 bombings and arsons, all but a few directed against integrationists of both colors. Rebel southern states, however, began preparing to set up "private" schools with state funds to circumvent Negro contamination of the lynch mobs of tomorrow; and the Union called on the Department of Health, Education and Welfare to withhold federal funds from segregated schools.

Vice President Nixon (who had the grace to oppose the prosecution of a caricaturist calling him *Dick McSmear*) supervised the generally successful Presidential commission charged with preventing job discrimination in federal contracts. Identification of candidates on ballots and voters on registration lists by color or race was increasingly abandoned. The American Legion, true to character, refused to end discrimination in its 40&8 group and, when the Union criticised this typical Legion action, called on Congress to probe the Union. The Pennsylvania Railroad was persuaded by the ACLU, despite its closed-shop contract, to continue employing a Negro who refused to join a Jim Crow union. But in the Ol' Souf, suh, they found means to love their Nigras as before: by cutting off all sales to black merchants and consumers, suspending credit, foreclosing mortgages and, in Mississippi, abduction and murder. In 1955 a minister and a voter were murdered there for being black, as was fourteen-year-old Emmett Till, who may or may not have invited death by whistling at a white girl: in any case, the murderers of these three Negroes were acquitted without delay.

When what finally became the Civil Rights Act of 1957 was introduced with Eisenhower's strong backing—it took almost two years to win enactment, largely because of the cynical obstruction by the Senate Judiciary Committee headed by Eastland of Mississippi—it was endorsed at once by the Union. The bill called for a bi-partisan Civil Rights commission to investigate the whole civil-rights question; a new Civil Rights Division in the Department of Justice to prosecute violators, whether public officials or private persons intimidating voters in a federal election; civil actions (chiefly injunctive) by the Attorney General on behalf of persons deprived of their rights, and the elimination of the old rule that all administrative and state-court remedies must be exhausted before the Federal Courts would entertain an action. While fighting for this bill, the Union had also to fight against legislation in various states designed to penalise and outlaw the NAACP and its members, and, in Mississippi, a law creating a new misdemeanor: urging non-compliance with established customs. The Union called for federal investigation of interference with southern negro voters and for the end of the discrimination practiced by the Federal Housing Administration. It had to battle anti-Negro school gerrymandering in Englewood, New Jersey, and other covert school segregation in New York and other northern cities. Negro residents of Chicago's Trumbull Park housing project, the victims of rioting in 1953, were still in need of daily police protection three years later.

When the Civil Rights Act of 1957 finally passed, it permitted trials for contempt in the violation of injunctions to be held with or without juries in the court's discretion, but added safeguards limiting the penal power in cases heard without juries— the Union opposed a Senate effort to make jury trials mandatory in all cases, on the ground that in the south a jury of White Citizens' Council members, which could so easily be arranged, would impede rather than further justice. But the Act was limited to the protection of only one civil right: the vote. Various public-opinion polls at this period purported to show some improvement in popular attitudes on the race question, but too often the truth was closer to the monotonously identical statements of New York City women opposing school integration in 1964: "I don't hate Negroes *but...*" For all the better popular climate alleged to exist, the Negro found it as difficult as ever to join most unions; an American Newspaper Guild survey (not a poll but a head-count) showed that of 7500 editorial employes of white newspapers exactly thirty-eight were Negroes. Taking a realistic view, the Union sent Malin to visit fifty cities in nine southern states in order to enlist volunteer attorneys—he got none—and a considerable share of the Union's budget was allocated to civil-rights work. In New York City this includes the rights of Puerto Ricans, whose complaints to the SCAD had risen in three years from four in the first year to 155 in the third, or 42 per cent of the total complaint volume.

Strange rulings came out of courts in the next few years. The success of the Montgomery, Alabama, bus boycott and of the Reverend Martin Luther King Jr.'s campaign of non-violent action encouraged Negroes and their few white friends elsewhere to begin "sit-ins": that is, to enter a shop or restaurant, request service and, if it was refused, simply remain until either served or ousted by force, which was not resisted. Hundreds were arrested, but some courts ruled that they had committed no offense; others fell back on disorderly conduct, breach of the peace, vagrancy and the other customary catch-alls of small minds. California found that a barber shop was a place of accommodation but a dentist's office was not. Florida farms set up separate toilets for Puerto Ricans in addition to those marked *white* and *colored*. Various New York beaches suddenly became "private clubs" in order to bar Negroes and Puerto Ricans. Florida, forbidden by the United States Supreme Court to bar a Negro from a state law school, claimed the right to do so under the police power giving it the right to prevent the riots that, the state hopefully contended, would inevitably result from his admission. The Union filed a brief *amicus* in the NAACP's successful appeal from a fine of $100,000 for refusing to comply with the Alabama law for the registration of out-of-state organisations, enacted solely to get rid of the NAACP. The NAACP had similar problems in Florida, where it was accused of Communist domination and its membership lists were subpoenaed. The Civil Rights Act was of little help because of Congress' deliberate delays in confirming Eisenhower's appointments under it. Georgia, Louisiana and Florida enacted laws ordering blood banks to label their stocks according to the donors' racial backgrounds; *hybridisation* was forbidden in transfusions.

One of the two outstanding outrages was of course Governor Faubus' defiance of the school integration decision in 1957, requiring the use of troops to enforce United States law in Arkansas; the other was the eight-year dereliction of duty by Attorneys General Brownell, Rogers and Kennedy and FBI chief J. Edgar Hoover in confining the action of this so-called *élite* police to mere token attention to civil-rights violations. Hoover deserves special condemnation for his frequent public libels on the civil-rights movement and its participants as instruments of that "Communist conspiracy" that at all other times he boasts of having destroyed and that counts, among its 8000 card carriers, probably 4000 special agents and hired stool-pigeons of his own FBI. The rationale for the dereliction has always been dual: first, the argument that the FBI's function is only investigation, nothing more—an argument overthrown every week by its constant arrests for every other kind of violation of law; second, the factitious plea of states' rights that cannot be invaded by the Federal Government.

Advocates of this specious shibboleth always conveniently forget that it was born of expedience, when the "Founding Fathers" were at their wits' end to unite thirteen provincial principalities irrationally jealous each of its own untenable sovereignty. "States' rights" was a makeshift, a questionable means to a legitimate and even essential end. If, as a certain school of constitutionalists forever argues, we must always, in interpreting, take into account (when we can descry or plausibly confect it to suit our own purposes) the "intent of the founders," the facts in themselves suffice, by these men's own standards, to annihilate the basis of the concept. Obviously the founders never intended to re-create the kind of congeries of pseudo-nations that existed in so much of Europe until Bismarck and that survives today in the Balkans (and is rapidly being imitated in Asia and Africa). To argue otherwise is to subvert that *one nation indivisible* to which our uncomprehending children daily pledge allegiance, and to replace a national government *with liberty and justice for all* by half a hundred local tyrannies of bigotry, caprice and greed, in which the civil liberties of the individual enunciated in the Constitution become a gallows-joke. To the extent that Government is a necessary evil, big government is a bigger evil: but can the biggest single government approximate the cumulative evil of fifty competing sovereignties not one of which is capable (if, incautiously, one should ascribe to it so much generosity) of envisaging the well-being of the whole? If any state is to have the right to decide for itself which of the Federal laws and Constitutional articles and amendments it will accept, as well abolish the Federal Government and recognise an equal "right" in each individual to choose which state law he will honor. It is inconceivable that the framers *intended* to empower the states to destroy those rights that were declared to be the natural rights of man and hence sacrosanct even to the national sovereign. In leaving to the states the power and even the duty to legislate for local needs, the framers of the Constitution never contemplated authorising the states to negate the Constitution and the federal laws enacted pursuant to it. To argue the contrary is to be guilty of the most flagrantly dishonest subversion of Constitutional interpretation, to make right and morality a matter of geography and to leave the individual to the mercy of caprice and anachronism, of power-mania and greed. The American Civil Liberties Union has always stood for the complete federalisation of all civil liberties regardless of state jurisdictions, and the extension of this principle by the United States Supreme Court has been one of the great achievements of the law and of the Union, guaranteeing the same liberties to more people than ever before.

Each state, however, seemed in the late 1950's (as so many still seem) to have devised its own circumventions of law and justice. The ACLU compelled California to grant a probation-officer post to a white woman who had been rejected solely because her husband was a Negro. It persuaded Pennsylvania to eliminate racial questions from license applications in some twenty trades and professions. It fought the Jewish mass builder, William J. Levitt, who refused to sell houses in his unesthetic developments to Negroes. It fought too the tendency to make metropolitan public housing all-Negro and to clear Negro slums for new buildings restricted to whites. It fought in the United States Supreme Court for the overthrow of Virginia decisions finding the NAACP guilty of barratry in paying the legal costs of Negroes persecuted by the commonwealth. In its battle for school integration in the south the Union had an unexpected ally in the Catholic Church, whose courageous position for free-

dom on this issue was in such anomalous variance with its repressive stand on almost all other questions of freedom for non-
Catholic entities and individuals. In employment, particularly in
the south, the NAACP reported, the Presidential orders against
discrimination in Government contracts and the commissions set
up to enforce them were blatantly flouted, particularly by the
large oil, aircraft and chemical companies—as late as 1961, Lock-
heed Aircraft's plant in Marietta, Georgia, had separate *white*
and *colored* time-clocks!

Despite all the defiance, and the chicanery by which it was
sought to be accomplished, the Supreme Court was steadily extending its recognition of the Negro's status as a human being.
Segregation in publicly supported recreation facilities was outlawed; the decisions ordering integration in interstate travel were reiterated and strengthened—and in practice torn to shreds by the
vicious mob attacks on the Freedom Riders and their persecution
by local officials under unconstitutional laws, against which the
Kennedy brothers mouthed platitudes. Nor did they move to re-
inforce the weak Civil Rights Act of 1960 that they had pledged
to replace with a real civil-rights law: instead, they rebuked Congressional sponsors of a bill that would have really protected rights
and liberties, and they promised executive orders that were never
issued lest the Democrats of the south be antagonised. The 1960
Act did little more than set up a complex system of voting refer-
ees; it was a considerable disappointment to the Union, which had
been lobbying for something respectable. As a matter of protection for Negroes, the Union endorsed its provisions for filing anonymous complaints with the Civil Rights Commission provided that
accused voting registrars were ultimately allowed to confront and
cross-examine their accusers; this was upheld by the Supreme
Court, on the ground that complaints to the Commission were
not adversary proceedings, in which alone the right of confrontation and cross-examination obtains, but merely investigative. But
both the Union and later, in some instances, the court had insisted
on this right in loyalty-security hearings and in Congressional
committee investigations, and one is inclined to believe that it is
the latter position that is the only just one. Concurrently, the
Commission was investigating the practice of the Louisiana Legis-

lature encouraging voting registrars to reject new Negro regis-
trants and purge the rolls of those already registered.

The growth of the sit-ins at store restaurants raised a legalistic
problem for both the Union and the courts. Government authority to enforce integration in traditional places of public accommodation—transport, hotels, restaurants—had been upheld; but the
question of the local privately owned store was new. The Union
relied for its defense of the sit-ins not only on the First Amendment but on the further argument that "there is a firm legal basis
for the position that, once a person has been invited into a place
of business—as Negroes are in the South—the store owner cannot
pick and choose what wares he will sell to customers; his place of
business becomes at the very least a quasi-public facility and he
must sell to all people who want to buy." In essence the courts
have supported this view and, properly, carried it even farther:
for it is patent that the mere opening of a place of business is an
implied invitation to all to be customers, regardless of color, and
the state cannot constitutionally enforce the owner's bigotries.
Barbers pleaded they lacked the special skill allegedly required
to cut Negroes' hair, and lost; reducing *salon*s were compelled
to accept Negro customers. State laws extended the ban on housing discrimination to private construction. But bigots found underground means of perpetuating and spreading their hatreds, particularly in the housing field; the major weapon was block-bust-
ing, which converted whole neighborhoods into ghettos—at a substantial profit—by playing on the biases of the residents. Housing
segregation in cities, of course, led naturally to *de facto* school segregation, both of which the Union fought, backing the policy of
allowing children to attend schools outside their residential districts.

The Union's victories in the civil-rights field, like those of all
the other combatants, are largely paper in the face of the colos-
sal prejudice and oppression by the white majority. Courts have
ordered the end of discriminatory voting tests, voided some state
laws against miscegenation, forbidden legislative and police harassment of civil-rights organisations—but no court has been able
to halt the abuses it has condemned. President Kennedy's administrative orders did achieve some amelioration of job discrimination

by large federal contractors such as RCA and General Electric, and his marshals did save a church besieged by frustrated mobs that had run out of Freedom Riders to maim; but only in conspicuous cases of national challenge has there ever been law enforcement in any real sense on behalf of victimised minorities. The 1963 Birmingham church massacre and the murder of Medgar Evers of the NAACP in the same year, for which no one has ever been convicted; the uninterrupted series of convictions of southern Negroes by all-white juries on questionable evidence; the murder of three civil-rights workers in Mississippi in 1964 still unpunished because of deliberate frustration of law enforcement by those supposed to be charged with it; the immunity of New York City policemen for killing Negroes and the commitment of a CORE official to a psychopathic ward for attempting to exercise a legal right; the sly segregation all across the country in every aspect of normal life; the 1965 beatings and murders of Negroes who seek to register for the vote and the calculated disfranchisement of thousands of others; the beatings, burnings and false arrests that beset every effort to assist the southern Negro, the closings of Negro universities in reprisal for student civil-rights activities, the brutal repression of Negro demonstrations everywhere—none of these has been touched by the enactment of the Civil Rights Act of 1964. The Union has endorsed every bill of this nature; it has committed funds and talent and energy to almost every case; it has called on the executive arm to enforce the legislation, by statute and decision, that is already available and adequate if the United States ever gets a government that puts right above re-election—but what can be done by the Union, the NAACP, CORE and all their allies in an anomaly that allows the voters by referendum to legislate a ban on the very anti-discrimination laws that the Federal Government enacts for its own irrationally circumscribed jurisdiction? In 1964 California voted overwhelmingly to outlaw all legislation preventing discrimination in housing. The ACLU has before the courts two test cases challenging the power arrogated by states to forbid marriage between persons of different races—the Supreme Court has already vindicated interracial cohabitation. Of what value will favorable decisions be, of what value are the federal laws against segregated housing or any other injustice unless these decisions, these laws are made to apply everywhere? The whole future of civil rights and civil liberties—not only for the Negro or the Catholic or the Jehovah's Witness or the Jew or the unbeliever—rests on the answer to one question: whether the United States will ever have a national government of laws, not of ostensible men, that will be both the sword and the shield of freedom.

15

The Volunteer Attilas

We must not "rest our hopes too much upon constitutions, upon laws and upon courts," the late Judge Learned Hand of the Circuit Court of Appeals warned a few years ago, for "liberty lies in the hearts of men and women; when it dies there, no constitution, no law, no court can save it; no constitution, no law, no court can even do much to help it."

Taught empirically in the earliest days of the National Civil Liberties Bureau, this fundamental lesson was perhaps the most valuable asset of the NCLB's legacy to the American Civil Liberties Union. In *War-Time Prosecutions and Mob Violence*, a two-year record published in pamphlet form by the NCLB in 1919, some of the reported instances of mob violence attendant on the First World War were listed under three headings—for voicing pacifist sentiments or refusing to salute the flag, buy Liberty Bonds or contribute to the Red Cross; for participation in labor disputes; and for political causes. The inventory was separate from the hundreds of mob assaults on parades, meetings and radical and pacifist offices. All figures came from the records of the public authorities, who did little more about the outrages than note them with satisfaction.

276

For preaching pacifism and refusing to aid the war effort:
four persons were painted various colors (preferably yellow)
    from scalp to sole;
twenty-two were forced to kiss The Flag;
two were fatally hanged;
thirty-one were tarred and feathered;
twenty-four were kidnapped and whipped;
nine were physically deported from the towns in which they lived.
    For participation in labor disputes:
one person was fatally hanged;
one was hanged for a while and then cut down;
twenty-seven were tarred and feathered;
twenty-five were kidnapped and whipped;
one thousand eighty were physically thrown out of the towns in
    which they lived.
    For political heresies:
one person was painted;
six were tarred and feathered;
six were kidnapped and whipped;
twenty were physically deported from the towns in which they
    lived.
    To recapitulate the grand totals by category of action:

Forced to kiss the flag	22
Fatally hanged	3
Partly hanged	1
Painted	5
Tarred and feathered	64
Kidnapped and whipped	55
Physically deported	1109

The number of vigilantes involved against these 1259 victims
is not recorded: but in at least that number of hearts liberty had
died. In the hearts of those untallied millions who, abjuring violence for whatever reason, destroyed the heretic with ostracism
and economic boycott, liberty was just as dead. The knout is not the
only scourge; it is not even the most effective or the most vicious.
But in the early years of the ACLU it had mostly to contend with
the less sophisticated kind of volunteer Attilas who knew nothing

better than the knout. Frighteningly often the sworn upholders
of law and order looked the other way when the knout was wielded; quite as often they were in full attendance in order to assist
the mob and cut off the escape of its victims; almost equally often
the law-enforcement authorities, without even the intellectual
divertissements of a Pontius Pilate, herded the victims into the a-
rena and turned loose the mob; hardly less frequently they relied
on the mob to provide them with game. In 1921, for instance,
Harold O. Mulks, a Chicago lawyer, went to Shreveport, Louisiana, to defend IWW cases and was savagely beaten and thrown
out of town; in the same year the hired mobs of the Pennsylvania coal operators beat up Arthur Garfield Hays in the midst
of a speech and turned him over to the police, who threw him
into jail.

There were sixty-one lynchings in 1922; violence against the
Klan virtually matched the number of assaults launched by it.
Brutal beatings of labor organisers, radicals and pickets on public streets were a commonplace in the southern states, the southwest, California, Illinois and Pennsylvania. "Citizens' committees"
were publicly praised by officials whenever they accomplished a
new atrocity. California's Better America Federation, Inc., and the
patriots inspired by it specialised in assaults on IWW people and
property until the late 1920's, when they traded in the IWW for
the still-new Communists. Armed American Legionnaires formed
ranks with police in Wilkes-Barre, Pennsylvania, to break up a
Lenin memorial meeting and force 400 persons, mostly aliens, into the wintry streets, where they were solemnly compelled at gun
point to kiss The Flag. Legion posts across the country began to
discover their political power and dragooned officials into forbidding labor, radical and ACLU meetings—those held in defiance
of the bans were broken up by violence, in which mobs were allowed, when not invited, to join. As the decade advanced, left-
wing union members clubbed, stabbed and shot right-wing union
members in some areas; in others, right-wing unionists clubbed,
shot and stabbed the leftists. The Workers' Party, before and after becoming the Communist Party, broke up meetings of other
left-wing parties as a matter of policy.

Against so much primitive savagery the rational arguments of the ACLU were almost totally ineffective. Its protests—by letter, by conference, by pamphlet—were ignored by the Communists as persistently as by the Legion and by most public officials; but here and there a braver man protected a heretical meeting despite the threats of the voters. The Union denounced the violence against the Klan, which soon surpassed its own lawlessness, as much as the Klan's persecutions; neither was reduced. Mobs trampled labor lawyers and ACLU speakers; lynchings, though they declined, were never wholly renounced. In enlightened New York City, the police were usually pre-occupied by sudden emergencies elsewhere whenever pickets or distributors of handbills for birth control or pacifism or free thought were savaged on the sidewalks and streets. Meetings, indoors or outdoors, to protest the interminable Sacco and Vanzetti frame-up and the ultimate murder by the Commonwealth of Massachusetts were mobbed with particular joy; so were rallies of the unemployed and organisational union meetings—usually by crowds who had the most to gain by the success of the labor movement. In the Wild West, the tar-and-feather mobs were sporadically active; even when there was overwhelming evidence against them, grand juries refused to hear it.

Rather touchingly, the ACLU believed it might be able to reason at least with the saviors of the proletariat whom it had so often defended. A special Union committee under Professor William L. Nunn entered into negotiations with the Communist Party—the only left-wing political organisation practicing disruptive tactics against its competitors: the Trotskyites, the Lovestoneites, the Musteites, the Socialists and all the other right and left-wing *deviationists* and *wreckers* and *lackeys* scrupulously abstained even from heckling rival meetings—and, after much parleying, the CP agreed to desist from flagrant disruption but maintained it saw no violation of civil liberties in heckling. This debatable point was made in the same negotiations in which, by letter as well as conversation, the Communists blandly insisted that civil liberties should never be universal but should apply only on behalf of the elect of Lenin. The pledge they gave in 1932, however, proved worthless within two years, when Communist leaders and street-fighters made havoc of a Socialist Party rally in Madison Square Garden protesting Austrian Fascism—a violation of treaty that led to a major internal crisis in the Union, whose inner circle held representatives of both the aggressors and the aggressed.

When mob violence was clearly a matter of good guys and bad guys, however, the good guys rarely saw the inside of a police station, let alone a court. A Kentucky jail warden who allowed a mob to lynch one of his prisoners was absolved by the Governor despite ACLU efforts to have him brought to book; four unemployed men beaten up by Legionnaires and police in Gary, Indiana, were convicted of rioting; union men who defended their offices and their persons against mobs were jailed for assault, often for assault with intent to murder. It was not uncommon for union members to be beaten on the streets and then indicted and convicted for inciting to riot. For years the Union publicly offered a reward of $1000 for every instance of the presentation of evidence leading to a conviction for vigilante violence but in all its history, as has been noted, it has had only one claimant—a man who witnessed a 1946 attack on Japanese-Americans and whose testimony led to the conviction of the assailants and the payment of the reward.

No cash offer had any power against what was probably the most outrageous lynching in American history. In 1934 two white men accused of kidnapping were arrested in San José, California. and lodged in jail. Mobs formed almost at once, proclaiming their determination to lynch the prisoners: Governor James Rolph Jr. announced equally publicly that he would make no effort to protect the suspects. The resultant lynching was a gala affair, crowned by Rolph's congratulation of the butchers, his assurance that they would not be punished and his exhortation to Americans at large to emulate his brave fellow-Californians. He was hailed not only by the entire state but by that eminent social thinker, Westbrook Pegler, in a syndicated newspaper column that slavered with delight. *Pro forma,* an investigation of the lynching was set up and full absolution was quickly granted. The Governor of Maryland, on the contrary, ordered out the militia to arrest the leaders of a lynch mob identified by the state police; but they were exonerated by a jury of their peers. Both barbarities were still fresh when a San Francisco mob led by professional patriots destroyed the headquarters of the striking longshoremen's union,

rounded up hundreds of strikers and turned them over to the police, who gladly accepted them. No one in the New Deal Government turned a hair: Secretary of Labor Perkins' department
promptly moved in to deport any aliens among the captives. The
ACLU sued the city and county authorities for damages, on behalf of the victims, contending that neither the city nor the county
had provided the police protection to which it was obligated, and,
surprisingly, recovered judgments.

Farm strikes were erupting at this time and the Socialists, led
by Norman Thomas, formed a Southern Tenant Farmers' Union,
which immediately became the target of innumerable mob attacks.
In Hardin County, Ohio, where the prevailing wage was fifteen
cents an hour, the union leaders were kidnapped and taken out
of the state: one of them, who identified sixty-seven members of
the mob, was found guilty on a weapons charge because he resisted abduction, but the sixty-seven kidnappers were never prosecuted by the state. Roosevelt's Attorney General, Homer Cum-
mings, refused to move under the new Lindbergh Law making interstate abduction a federal offense: he argued that the law applied only to kidnappings for ransom although by its terms it covered abductions of every kind and for every purpose.

Besides the unorganised mob, the private army was beginning
to appear in the United States at this time, largely unchecked and
in at least one instance aided by an Act of Congress, which turned over 75,000 "obsolete" rifles to the American Legion: these
were used by many Legion posts for the drilling of the Legion's
own phalanx to combat "subversives." Then as now, the Union
coupled its defense of the right to preach Fascism with absolute
opposition to the levying and training of private armies like this
of the Legion, the later troop raised by Victor McLaglen, the
Hollywood actor, and the newest underground, that of the Min-
ute Men who are convinced that Chinese Communist shock
troops in force are billeted in western Canada and Mexico. The
Legion was actively abetting the anti-radical campaign of the
Hearst press across the nation and, in New York City, a Legion
post tried City Councilman Paul Crosbie, a member, for "conduct
unbecoming a Legionnaire" in joining the Communist Party.
He was exonerated but the state department of the Legion order-

ed all posts to expel Communist members. Some posts simply refused; isolated Legionnaires round the country, many of them
members of the ACLU as well, actively combatted the bigotry of
their fellow-veterans of the war to make the world safe for democracy but were prevented from enforcing democracy in their
own organisation. Like Captain Edward P. Coll of Centralia,
Washington, who had abandoned his business in order to work
without compensation for the Union in its ultimately successful
parole appeals for the Centralia IWW members who were serving
twenty-five to forty years for defending their headquarters a-
gainst an armed assault by Legionnaires on Armistice Day, 1919,
such men paid a high price for their courage.

In a few instances the ACLU obtained some redress for outrages, such as the attack on a meeting of the Modern Democrats
by the police of Tampa, Florida, who gave three of their victims
to the local Klan for tarring and feathering. For *lagniappe*, the
Klansmen also beat them so savagely that one Modern Democrat
died ten days later as a result of his injuries. Seven men went to
trial for this modified lynching and, despite much Red-baiting
during the trial, five were convicted of abduction and assault.
Secretary of the Interior Harold Ickes, a member of the Union,
was moved to address its annual meeting with an excoriation of
A Nation in Nightshirts.

During the New Deal the most vicious oppressors were mobs
and private groups, most of them beyond the reach of federal
prosecution even had the Government wished to act. What was
more criminal than the vigilantism itself was the collaboration of
local police and sheriffs and the general refusal of local and state
authorities either to prevent or to prosecute; in the rare instances
when grand juries did act, either they found no true bills or, as
in the case of the prolonged mob attacks on farm strikers, in the
Imperial Valley of California in the mid-1930's, the courts simply dismissed the charges against the mobs and excoriated the
victims. But violence was not all: other forms of pressure had rapidly grown, wielded chiefly by the Legion and the Daughters of
the American Revolution, which used to be taken quite seriously.
Often aided by Catholic clerics and lay organisations, these and
other professional patriots occupied themselves with stirring up

the press, lobbying in legislatures and making demands on public officials, all concentrated on further restricting the utterances and activities of pacifists, labor organisers, radicals, "pornographers," atheists and agnostics and any other dissenters from the norm. Such "respectable" organisations as the National Association of Manufacturers and, to a much greater extent, the United States Chamber of Commerce too often lent to the various forms of censorship the immeasurable influence exercised by business in a society that worshipped what it called success, backing and at times financing campaigns of repression. Their further influence as advertisers was exploited to swing newspapers into line whenever possible; hardly any effort was necessary to dissuade the timorous broadcasters from either protesting or even allowing the other side a hearing.

The Government itself, until the overthrow of the National Industrial Recovery Act and Administration by the Supreme Court, did not hesitate to mobilise a subtle economic and psychological vigilantism against those *entrepreneurs* who, for whatever reasons, rebelled at the "voluntary compliance" that the New Deal sought to enforce on them, and the ACLU here was completely derelict in its duty to its own principles. Unquestionably the dereliction was motivated in large part by the commitment of the majority of the Union's governors to a drastic revision of the social and economic order and by a doctrinaire astigmatism that enabled them utterly to overlook injustices committed in pursuit of a goal that they held laudable, as we shall see when we consider the Union's utter indifference to violations of Constitutional protections in the enforcement of the Prohibition law. As long as the NRA survived, Government skillfully harried the sheep into boycotts of all enterprises that did not display General Johnson's Blue Eagle. The Union's unbroken silence on this governmental exploitation and encouragement of economic vigilantism, Baldwin admitted thirty years later, was one of the relatively few instances in its career when it lapsed.

On the other hand, the New Deal's consistent espousal of unions, the legislation it enacted to protect them and the growth of their membership tended together to reduce actual violence against labor even if it aggravated other forms of pressure. Now and then—in the south, of course—organisers would be kidnapped, tarred and feathered (old regional sports take a long time to die); and at a Pan American Exhibition in Dallas, significantly, three Californians were savagely beaten by an impromptu mob because their cars bore CIO stickers; but in this case the Governor sent in the Rangers, after the event, and it was not repeated. In Hoboken, New Jersey, however, next door to Mayor Hague's preserve, the police refused to protect a Workers' Defense League speaker from a mob. And in cities with large Jewish populations the various pro-Nazi groups were increasingly mobbed as persecution in Germany mounted and war became more obviously inevitable.

The imminence of war was largely responsible for the 345 mob attacks on Jehovah's Witnesses in forty-four states in the single year of 1940. Public resentment of the Witnesses was aggravated, too, by the sect's singular intolerance of competing faiths and its outspoken denunciations of their dogmas and practices. Most of the attacks took place in small communities where the authorities either closed their eyes or lent active assistance to the aggressors. *The Persecution of Jehovah's Witnesses,* a 1941 Union pamphlet signed by a dozen Protestant and Jewish clergymen, is studded with the affidavits of victims and witnesses testifying to the connivance of police and elected officials. Nor can any record afford to gloss over the indisputable fact that many of these mobs were egged on and physically led by Catholic priests and lay leaders enraged by the Witnesses' frankness about the other *one true faith*—a lively demonstration of the fact that the major link between the Irish-dominated Church in the United States and the Catholic Church in more civilised countries is the hallowed tradition of teaching the heretic and the infidel to love their neighbors through such pedagogical instruments as the stake and the rack and such educational examples as St. Bartholomew's Night. In Jackson, Mississippi, the *Daily News* editorially congratulated the mobs; in Maine, French Catholics united with the Salvation Army to storm a hall where the Witnesses were meeting; when the gun barrage of the mob was returned by the defenders, the Witnesses alone were arrested, tried and convicted.

Despite the Witnesses' compliance with the draft law, their enemies often invoked the pretext that the sect was a Nazi agent—

whereas thousands of its members were in German concentration camps because of its refusal of Nazi doctrine. Under an Indiana law originally directed against the Klan and covering "three or more persons who unite to do an unlawful act in the night time," two female Witnesses, aged fifty and seventy, were tried for riotous conspiracy in refusing to salute the flag and were sentenced to two to ten years. Interstate abductions of Witnesses were frequent and unpunished; arrests without warrants were common practice; mobs were turned loose against their lawyers. Not only were Union reward offers futile against the *pogroms*: virtually no newspaper condemned them and, though both Attorney General Jackson and Solicitor General Biddle deplored the violence, the only federal action occurred, with remarkable irony, in Harlan County, Kentucky, where a federal court forbade the state to invoke its sedition law against the sect. In West Jefferson, Ohio, where, as has been noted, the police exempted themselves from the Constitution, the town's fire-alarm siren was used to call a mob to the assault. Pressure by the Legion and labor unions was employed for economic persecution. The Union's pamphlet called for protests to be made to local, state and federal authorities and for complaints to be lodged as well with the Civil Liberties Unit of the Justice Department; but none of these did much good.

The war diverted energy, men and materials from lynching, and even, to a great extent, from vigilantism against unions and radicals, except where it had always been endemic, in Kentucky and California; Japanese-Americans acceded to the title of scapegoat-in-chief. Once they had been largely disposed of for the duration, the shortage of gasoline and the siphoning of large numbers of strong, restless brawlers and potential brawlers into the armed forces militated also against great outbreaks of mob movement. In the subtler areas of non-physical pressure, the traditional harassment of the different through economic channels and the refusal of platforms went on as usual, with the usual targets, though labor enjoyed somewhat of a respite and Nazis and Fascists had to share the martyr's crown with Communists, real or imagined. But then the war ended, and so did the shortages; millions of men trained for years to kill the enemy came home to their old dull lives of mediocre frustration; millions of others, trained to hate although they had never left home, had for the moment no one to blame for their equally mediocre frustrations; office-holders and -seekers had no demons with which to frighten the electorate—for the briefest of whiles. But, as soon as all of them had caught their breath, they rediscovered, larger and more menacing than ever, the Communists (with whom many of them bracketed the Jews automatically) and, much more realistically, the dark-skinned tenth of the population that was no longer satisfied to be the sometimes patronised, generally exploited hewers of wood and drawers of water for the fair-skinned nine-tenths. If they demanded rights—worse still, if they made overt moves to enforce rights, they too must be part of the Communist encirclement and infiltration. To simplify matters, everyone else who in any way departed from the pattern—the atheist, the alien, the pacifist, the writer and publisher of "smut," the chemist who advocated fluoridation—was thrown into the same pot, and a large part of the surplus national energy was converted into fuel to boil the contents. As always, the fire department could not see or smell the flame or the smoke and it was left to random volunteer firemen here and there to try at least to contain, if not to quench, the more or less spontaneous conflagrations constantly fed by the official distributors of hell-fire and their periodic selections of sacrificial victims. J. Edgar Hoover, who in 1940 had written a pious platitude against vigilantism for a Sunday supplement, called on all his fellow-patriots to let his stokers know wherever there might be more for burning.

Thus blessed, one of the first and most dramatic flash fires after the war was the twinned 1949 riots in Peekskill, New York. While the Klan was once more riding and burning crosses and beating heretics in the south—where Atlanta and Alabama banned the wearing of masks in public—and while Jewish groups, rightly opposed by the Union, were suing to keep *Oliver Twist* and *The Merchant of Venice* out of school libraries and forcing the withdrawal of the filmed *Oliver Twist* by boycott threats, the heroic war veterans of New York State were preserving the nation from other Jews, Negroes and Communists. The Civil Rights Congress, a left-wing organisation, had leased private property in

Cortlandt Township for an outdoor concert to be given August 27 by Paul Robeson, a distinguished Negro singer who was also a Communist. The area, long resistant to industrialisation and steeped in a tradition of political violence, was largely pro-Klan and anti-Catholic; it lived principally on its summer colonists, most of whom were Jews ranging from artists and professional people to "radicals" and who were hated for every one of their attributes except the money they spent. Well in advance of August 27 the Peekskill newspaper began inflaming public sentiment against the concert and proposing that the good Americans turn out *en bloc* and disperse the rebels: the admirable citizenry responded with such fervor that performers and audience were driven away, and so the concert was rescheduled for September 4. "The time for tolerant silence that signifies approval is running out," the Peekskill paper proclaimed. It filled its editorial page with letters from the local American Legion commander and other model citizens inciting fresh violence for September; the propaganda was leavened with a few letters *contra,* the writers of which were kept busy being threatened by telephone. Protests were made to Governor Thomas E. Dewey, who had almost become President, but the little man on the wedding cake, as Alice Roosevelt Longworth (a Republican Roosevelt) once called him, did not climb down from his sugary Olympus.

"We're going to get those goddamn Jews," Legionnaires posted along the roads to the concert site told every passer-by on September 4. The *white Jews* wearing Jewish War Veterans' regalia who assisted the Legion and the Veterans of Foreign Wars were exempt, however, and they were allowed to lend a hand (though some of those who lost their identifying caps were clubbed by allies who could not tell a *white Jew* without his hat). Before the concert began, ninety-one witnesses of all skin and political colors told an investigation (conducted by the ACLU, Americans for Democratic Action, the American Veterans' Committee, the NAACP and the Council Against Intolerance), the various brands of veterans barricaded the roads leading to the site and started fires on the perimeter, in order to prevent the escape of the quarry. As soon as the concert began, one of the patriots cut off the lights of the amphitheater and joined his fellow-veterans in a wild charge that was later alleged to have followed—though in fact it preceded and brought about—the stabbing of one of the uniformed heroes. By flashlight the crusaders distinguished between white Christians, who were ignored, and Jews and black Christians, who were clubbed and stoned with complete impartiality as to age and sex. The heroic veterans had announced that they would prevent the concert by whatever means might be required, and had failed to win a federal injunction against the recital because Judge John W. Clancy assumed, he said rather surprisingly, that everyone intended to obey the law and that the veterans wanted only to protect their own rights (what rights of theirs were threatened was not made clear).

During both riots the local sheriff was an absorbed spectator; both the county and the state had ignored requests for protection. Dewey had sent 1000 police to the second concert; but many of the 3000 spectators from New York City, having learned just how reliable policemen are in such matters, had brought their own baseball bats for protection. Amid the usual martial outcries against the "niggers" and the "kikes," the veterans fell to. Robeson did not sing; the routed audience began to drive home. They had to run a two-mile gantlet of stone-throwing rabble, not once interfered with by the county police, fraternising with the *canaille* along the route; some of the state police attempted to restore order but they were brushed aside. In towns between Peekskill and New York, every car that came through with broken windows was stoned again for good measure. The same district attorney who had refused to take preventative action was named by Dewey to head an investigation by a special grand jury, which found that the veterans had acted justly out of resentment of Communism and of the "armed guard" in the audience. Nothing comparable was to occur again until the Supreme Court's 1954 school-desegregation decision was seized on by the trash for a new series of mob violence in the south that has mounted steadily in the ensuing decade and that neither the state officials nor the Great Society of President Johnson seems seriously inclined to curb despite the most dolorous lamentations out of Washington.

Almost concurrently with the Legion's blow for democracy

in Peekskill the nation began to feel the real strength of private pressure groups. The Legion and the DAR, with rather less help from the Sons, had long been successful in minor purges of campuses, libraries and public auditoriums by public officials who shared all their bigotries and in addition feared their votes; now the private pressure group began to make new inroads. One Ted Kilpatrick, formerly a henchman of J. Edgar Hoover, had founded a magazine called *Counterattack,* which he circulated (for a price) among the terrified to frighten them still more. As a further public service, he published (also at a price) *Red Channels,* a directory of actors, writers, directors, producers and others in the entertainment business whom he and his equally competent and objective collaborators had determined to be Communists or Communist instruments (this venture was to lose its monopoly very soon when a rival public-service organisation called AWARE went into the same line of character assassination for profit). Kilpatrick's selfless exposures caused the trembling readers to protest the employment of those he listed, and tiny insecure organisations like General Electric began to break contracts with listed entertainers hired for broadcasts. The Superintendent of Schools of Newark, New Jersey, ordered *Red Channels* distributed to all teachers. Only American Broadcasting among the networks defied Kilpatrick and the American Legion of Illinois, which had called on ABC to drop Gypsy Rose Lee because Kilpatrick had put the brand on her. NBC became so confused with panic that, although it swore by *Red Channels* and canceled Eleanor Roosevelt's appearance with Robeson, it tried to break its commitment to put Kilpatrick on the air: the ACLU, which denounced the blacklist, offered him its help to enforce his right to be heard. At the same time, an ACLU director, Merle Miller, the novelist, began its investigation of blacklisting in the entertainment industry that was published a few years later by Doubleday as *The Judges And The Judged.*

Miller found, not surprisingly, that blacklisting was regularly practiced by pro- as well as anti-Communists, though the pro-Communists, lacking the funds and the prestige of the anti's, had to work very secretly and not too effectively. The anti-Communists' blacklists were largely based on the fear of losing customers by employing suspect individuals, and Kilpatrick freely admitted he sought to wreak economic havoc among those he listed and the organisations with which they were linked. Only Government security agencies, Miller countered in defiance of fact, could really protect the nation against subversion by song and dance (as if the suppression of every unproved subversive by the witch-hunters, licensed or unfranchised, would not merely drive the dreaded foe underground and thus heighten his lure). The loyalty oaths demanded of every employe and contractor by the networks were unworkable, Miller found, because real Communists would not mind committing perjury and many non-Communists were either disgusted or frightened into abstaining from signing. He concluded that the broadcasters, the advertising agencies and the sponsors so concerned with truckling to "public opinion" to protect their economic interests could do so just as effectively by rejecting instead of embracing the tactics of the Communist enemy: by confuting them in democratic argument rather than by suppressing them. Miller's book was virulently attacked in the right-wing Socialist *New Leader* by a member of the ACLU board, Merlyn S. Pitzele; but a board committee composed of Angell, Seymour and William L. White of *The Reader's Digest*, hardly a Stalinist apologist, vindicated Miller's book and the Union promptly complained formally to the FCC against blacklisting by the major networks and some individual stations, asking a general investigation and the denial of license renewals until the charges had been disposed of. The FCC said it would make all renewals temporary pending such disposition; ten days later, under frantic attack by Kilpatrick and Fulton Lewis Jr., the phonograph of the extreme right, it reversed itself.

Not only corporations and other associations set themselves up to purge the nation; there was no lack of presumptuous "personalities" like Ed Sullivan, proprietor of a television *vaudeville* and of a gossip-mongering column that can be used as a nation-wide club because it appears in and is widely syndicated by *The News* of New York. Sullivan learned that 300 seats had been purchased by *The National Guardian*, a left-wing periodical, for a benefit performance of *Wonderful Town*, a Broadway musical. Sullivan raised a hue and cry so loud and so prolonged that the producer canceled the performance for which the tickets had been bought, refunded the money and refused to sell the *subversives* tickets for any other performance. The American Civil Liberties Union was moved to inquire publicly whether the United States was about to institute loyalty tests for theater-goers.

The Legion and other groups made a gladiatorial shambles with *Red Channels,* using it to bully elected officials and theater owners alike into canceling personal appearances by people named in it. Two hundred motion-picture people and 250 broadcasting workers were put under interdict; the American Federation of Radio Artists began to purge its membership, ignoring ACLU condemnation; *Collier's Magazine* fired Bucklin Moon, an editor involved in the fight for racial equality, on the unproved charges of a gang of professional anti-Communists in California and refused the Union's demand that it explain what the publisher called "a private matter." Moon got other jobs, but John Henry Faulk, the victim of Kilpatrick's major business rival, Vincent Hartnett of AWARE, spent seven years starving in the wilderness because of Hartnett's irresponsible charges against him. Faulk's case, reported in full in his own book, *Fear on Trial,* is a horrifying case history of the power of the private pressure group.

Faulk first attracted Hartnett's notice by seeking office in the broadcasting artists' union, of which, as a highly paid commentator for CBS, Faulk was a member. Someone—it has never been explained who—told Hartnett that Faulk had appeared, as an entertainer performing for a fee, before various groups that Hartnett considered subversive; Faulk denied the charges and they were never proved, but what matters most is that, true or false, they should have been totally irrelevant to Faulk's eligibility to practice his profession or hold union office. But the union was thoroughly dominated by AWARE. Hartnett immediately denounced Faulk not only to his employer and to each of the many companies sponsoring Faulk's programs, but also to the HUAC. Hartnett, in the subsequent trial, admitted acting as a HUAC agent and obtaining information by trading lies with the New York police and by wearing a hidden microphone and recorder when he attended private and public dinners. All Faulk's sponsors fell away; so did his employer and most of his friends, though Edward R. Murrow offered to underwrite all Faulk's living and legal expenses when he decided to sue AWARE, Hartnett and Lawrence Johnson, a prosperous grocer who threatened every Faulk sponsor with a boycott on his shelves, for libel.

Just after Faulk filed his action, AWARE gave a cocktail party in New York for the entire HUAC and prevailed on it to subpoena Faulk—an effort that proved vain, since he had nothing to hide. He sued for $5,000,000 and recovered $3,500,000, later reduced to $550,000, in a trial in which a parade of responsible witnesses from the broadcasting and advertising industries cited an endless series of case histories exactly like Faulk's: entertainers denounced and destroyed for fighting AWARE, criticising the HUAC, refusing to incriminate their colleagues and acquaintances, and of a few broken men and women allowed to catch crumbs again when they recanted and said the things that AWARE wanted of them. Hartnett, fittingly, was destroyed in his turn, with his blackmail business, and will probably spend the rest of his life paying the judgment in installments, Johnson having died insolvent before the end of the trial.

Not only individuals but publications and films have more and more been prime targets of the vigilantes. In smaller communities it is common for the patriots to be able to bully libraries and newsstands into refusing to handle such publications as *The Nation, The New Republic, Saturday Review* and even *Consumer Reports* on the ground that they are subversive of "the American way"—and, if this is the American way, the sooner its subversion is accomplished, the better. Similar tactics are employed against theaters and television stations by these and other groups determined to suppress films that offend them politically, whether the union propaganda picture, *Salt of the Earth,* or *Martin Luther,* which Catholics kept off a Chicago television station. But the strongest vigilante efforts at suppression—more virulent even than the attempts to gag *subversives*—are aroused by what everyone from the DAR and MUD (Mothers United for Decency) to the NODL (the National Organisation for Decent Literature) and the Catholic Legion of Decency resoundingly brands "filth." Filth includes birth-control literature, magazines picturing nude ladies, magazines picturing nude gentlemen, portions of the Sacred Scriptures and virtually every accepted author from

Homer on, as well as the kind of out-and-out slop that one hates to see one's children reading but that one knows one has neither the right nor the power to suppress. The MUDs, the NODL-heads and the rest periodically descend on newsstands and bookstores to demand the right to purge their shelves; they bully police chiefs and district attorneys into making pseudo-legal raids based on their own omniscient catalogues of objectionable publications; they threaten merchants and theater owners with boycotts and sometimes with violence. The position of the Union on all such vigilantism is clear, simple and unchallengeable: a MUD who prefers not to read obscenity (however defined) has every right to abstain and no right to try to bully other citizens or public officials into enforcing her standards on others, and, wherever possible, the Union seeks by negotiation, by persuasion and, if necessary, by litigation to prevent such private censorship. Its position is, in effect, that of the New Orleans District Attorney who refused to prosecute James Baldwin's *Another Country* for ostensible obscenity (New Orleans is in the South and Baldwin has had the temerity to say in public: "I'm not a nigger: I'm a man") : "If anyone thinks the book is obscene, he doesn't have to read it."

Once more one is compelled to identify the principal offenders—monotonous as the repetition may seem, the facts of the whole civil-liberties struggle compel it—as the American Legion and the Catholic Church and almost all its subsidiaries. The Legion, for instance, forced innumerable bans on *Limelight* not because of anything in the film but because the Legion disapproves of the life and views of Charles Chaplin. Francis Cardinal Spellman, forced to apologise for calling Eleanor Roosevelt anti-Catholic because, like the more enlightened of the Eminence's own constituents, she opposed taxpayer aid to private schools, called on the faithful throughout the land to boycott *The Moon Is Blue*. One Connecticut VFW post that tried to improve on the Legion by appealing for stool-pigeons to supply it with the names of forbiddable texts in the schools retreated when Malin and the Union denounced it (and one lone Indiana resident demanded a ban on Robin Hood in the schools until the Sheriff of Nottingham solemnly cleared the late Hood of Communist domination; whereupon the same red-blooded American demanded the excision of all reference to Quakers from the textbooks in the state's schools).

Contemporaneously (to list, without a break for variety, the catalogue of intellectual idiocies is too discouraging) the less cultivated vigilantes carried on their suppressions under the benevolent disregard of the authorities in the south, where Catholics and Jews as well as Negroes were chiefly favored with attention. Adlai Stevenson, when he was Governor of Illinois, called out the National Guard at the Union's urgent request when the police of Cicero set to to assist a mob beating and pillaging new Negro residents of a "white" area; North Carolina convicted sixty-nine Klansmen who savaged not only Negroes but also Aryans of whose morals the Klan did not approve. On the other hand, a myopic outfit assembled to call for the end of the Marshall Plan was raided and dispersed by a gang of "enlightened" rowdies, if only to prove that the right has no monopoly of the wrong.

For more than a dozen years the American Civil Liberties Union has been unable to meet in the state-owned and -operated Indiana World War Memorial in Indianapolis because the Legion will not permit it. In 1953 no one in the city would rent space to the Union; ultimately a Catholic priest, Father Victor L. Goosens, offered the use of his parish hall. In 1954 the Legion again banned the Union's use of the memorial, repeating its charge that the Union is "controversial" and standing firm despite the condemnation of the local press (which at the same time reiterated its dislike for the Union), the diocesan publication and even the VFW and the Order of the Purple Heart. As recently as 1964, not even the Governor's appeal to the Legion, coupled with his acceptance of an invitation to address the ACLU, could alter the patriots' ban.

Father Goosens' defiance of the bigots among whom he had to live affords a violent contrast to the Catholic attacks on Jehovah's Witnesses and the efforts of the Church in America to enforce its tenets on the populace through such arms as the NODL and the Legion of Decency. The Pauline Puritanism of this Irish-dominated section of Catholicism is in fact grossly misrepresentative of the humanity that the Church in civilised countries has begun to achieve, at least with respect to private behavior. The *Index,* it is true, emanates from the Vatican, and at more or less regular intervals popes inveigh, if only for the record, against carnal pleasure (unless, of course, it is to swell the wombs and the ranks of the more or less faithful). But, whether guided by a basic human respect for privacy or by the worldly wisdom and accommodation in which Holy Mother Church has no rival (very often Mother does indeed know best, in her practice if not in her preaching), the Church in Europe, having said what tradition requires it to say, goes on about its other, more important business, well aware that souls, if they exist, are to be neither saved nor damned through bodies.

But the Church's American Bishops, according to a 1956 ACLU statement signed by Angell and Malin, have themselves created the very worst of all the private censorship organisations in the country: the NODL. It receives its instructions from the priests and other functionaries of the Church, but it seeks to impose their views on the whole nation, in part by trying to enlist the cooperation of non-Catholics. The NODL's right to propagate its views in all directions is unchallengeable, the Union agreed; what it condemned was the NODL's attempts to coerce merchants into observing its own unofficial purge list by threatening boycotts, issuing "certificates of compliance" to those who truckle to it, publishing periodic lists of merchants who conform and of those who defy it, inciting vigilante check-ups and bullying local district attorneys, police chiefs and military commanders into enforcing its proscriptions. One hundred fifty authors, editors, publishers and other lay and clerical leaders signed another Union pamphlet documenting these practices, as a result of which the NODL, for example, had prevailed on a Michigan district attorney to prosecute sellers of a book on sex for teen-agers that had been approved by various Protestant churches, a number of parent-teacher groups and *Parents' Magazine*—but the fertile brood mares who make up the NODL had been told not to like it by their virginal spiritual guides. In considerable amazement, the Union paralleled its criticisms of the NODL with the incredible fact that a film of the opera, *Manon,* had been withdrawn from television exposure under pressure from the Legion of Decency.

It was inevitable that these two busy Catholic crusades would sooner or later evoke Protestant emulation. In 1957 a group of evangelicals, distinctly not supported by the National Council of Churches, formed a Churchmen's Commission for Decent Literature that showed a certain subtlety. It planned to set up local review boards to classify publications, on the basis of which a checklist would be issued to guide the flocks, and to press for legislation to dam the flood of filth, in the rhetoric of the trade. It has since been followed by innumerable unaffiliated "neighborhood" groups that decide what is fit for the public to read and, each in its own jurisdiction, patrol the vendors with soft words and then with threats, not infrequently taking along a policeman for the look of the thing.

A more sophisticated form of private censorship—censorship of people, not of utterances—was scuttled by ACLU exposure. This was the secret machinery of the real-estate industry in Grosse Pointe, Michigan, which black-balled any broker who did not play the game. Every candidate for the purchase of a house in this expensive suburb of Detroit was to be judged on his fitness for admission by the nationality of his ancestors, his accent, his standard of living, his mode of dress and the extent to which he was "typically American." Perhaps it was the sabotage of such characteristic free-enterprise know-how that caused the Indiana American Legion to protest the formation of a student ACLU at the state university and that inspired Paul J. Bitz of the same state's Senate to declaim, without a shred of documentary or other evidence, that "the ACLU is considered a subversive organisation by the Attorney General and J. Edgar Hoover"—but then Bitz had said the same thing of the League of Women Voters. It is quite possible that he was telling the hidden truth, particularly about Hoover, but all the evidence went the other way.

In 1962 the Committee for the Elimination of Salacious Literature of the Committee of Religious Leaders of the City of New York (so it styles itself, leaving some doubt as to whose salacious literature is its concern) was put together by a coven of local clergymen of all big and little faiths—one of the few occasions when the rabbis have stooped quite so far—to outdo the MUDs, the NODL-heads and the Churchmen's Committee, not by altering but by intensifying their techniques. The CESLCRL-NY's first act was, of course, to issue a list of proscriptions. The producer or exhibitor of one "filthy" film or play, the publisher or seller of one "smutty" book or magazine, was to be totally boycotted no matter what praiseworthy products he might also offer. The Union roundly condemned this as a violation of the spirit of the First Amendment's guaranties of free expression; but the phraseology of the Union's statement leaves an uncomfortable impression that it has yielded on what it calls "a primary boycott aimed at one book or play," for it does not make it clear whether it is accepting such a primary boycott as permissible when the sponsors seek to win the adherence of the community to it. Nonetheless the ACLU has continued to fight private as well as public censorship, winning the support even of *The Catholic Messenger* and gaining the assurance of the National Junior Chamber of Commerce that it would not attempt to compile guides of acceptable and inacceptable literature or issue seals of approval.

The force that is built from the prejudices of various majorities, however, whether it calls itself Mothers United for Decency, the Ku Klux Klan, the Black Muslims, the White Citizens' Councils, the toiling masses, the Chamber of Commerce, or "just old-fashioned Americans," remains the greatest threat to civil liberties because it is the least amenable to control. It has no intelligence and less principle; it is the willing tool and the ruthless tyrant of every rabble-rouser; it is in the end the maker and unmaker of governments and societies. That is why Huey Long, who more than any other American was in a position to know how to use the rabble, was so wholly correct in 1931 when he said: "When Fascism comes to America, it will call itself democracy." The crowd will always want Fascism as much as it will always hate democracy, because the average man will always dread the burden of responsibility for his own life and fear the demands made by true freedom on his infinite blind egotism.

16

Unclean! Unclean!

"The case against censorship," Emile Capouya, novelist and critic, wrote in *The Nation* in December, 1963, under the title, *The Varieties of Love,* "is always that the best books are the most controversial and therefore the first to be suppressed." Though he has stated only part of the case against the censor, it is apposite to quote further from Mr. Capouya before enlarging the indictment and proceeding from the general to the particular:

The Western tradition appears to regard sexual energy as a scarce resource, to be managed according to the prescriptions of that characteristic Western science: economics. Frugality, abstinence, careful husbanding of one's means, cautious investment of the same—that is what is wanted . . .

An economic good is well on the way to being a commodity and, sure enough, under certain conditions, love comes on the market. The material, physical kind is bought and sold, and so is the abstract, literary variety . . . Everything being equal, commercial love, physical or literary, is likely to be of inferior quality. Love is peculiarly a field for the gifted amateur. The artist does better work than the hack because he has love on his mind rather than cash.

298

Generally speaking, publishers and law courts cannot tell the difference. Or rather, generally speaking, publishers favor the article of commerce, and in a commercial society the law smiles on it too. Most of the books that an intelligent and cultivated person would find offensive in their treatment of love will never run afoul of the law. Falseness, sentimentality, displaced emotion of the filmy *négligée* school—none of that is thought likely to impair the morals of a minor. But, if evil communications do, in fact, corrupt good manners, the young have far more to fear from the books that are freely available to them than from those the postmaster has been impounding since Mrs. Grundy first took the job. Nevertheless, in an industrial society that depends for its life upon a strict and galling discipline, the felt danger is that the tastes and manners of the young may *not* be corrupted to the point where they will accept what that society can best provide; against that danger the law and public opinion are vigilant.

For, unfortunately, real love, like real art, is subversive. The one is, and the other hints at, an ideal state that swears at the imperfections of our working arrangements, conventions, codes of conduct. Art and love are revolutionary in their essence, and must be tamed or suppressed.

That is exactly what has been sought for centuries by the Anglo-American-Pauline code with its ineradicable hatred of women and its unshakable fixation on excretion—a code that, offensive as it is to any individual of sensibility, must yet enjoy the same right of freedom that it seeks to deny. The rights of due process, of equal protection of the laws, of freedom of expression and expression and association and belief, inhere as much to the "foul" as to the "fair;" if they are stolen from the foul, the tool has been forged to rob the fair as well. Hence the long battle of the ACLU to hamstring the censor, whatever his target—a battle in which, despite the reluctance with which it came late to the struggle, the ACLU is to be faulted only for having too long been stopped short by the shibboleth of *clear and present danger*. The question is not whether *fuck* is a word of art in a Grove Press book and a dirty word on a wall. The "sexy" comic books, so-called, are no more and no less objectionable than the pitiful exhibitionism and fecal play of a Norman Mailer or a Joseph Heller or a Calder Willingham or a John Rechy—the "comics" are in fact less unhealthy because they are primarily meretricious: honest pandering that does not pretend to *soi-disant* intellectuality. The inadequate and hence woman-hating little boys who have taken over American fiction since the war cannot themselves be sure how much of their inartistic exhibitionism results from the desire for money and how much they simply cannot help: but no one has to read them. The "comics" and the *graffiti* novelists alike are the creatures of the same society: if it is ashamed of what it has wrought, let it look away, not murder its young.

For too long the American Civil Liberties Union too looked away from the society's infanticide. Its early leaders were almost obsessively preoccupied with the political-economic function of civil liberties; aside from Baldwin and a few others, most of them tended toward Emerson's perverted ideal of plain living and high thinking, and a good many were men of God. It was really not until Morris L. Ernst joined the National Commtitee and became general counsel that the Union learned the facts of life: they fascinated Ernst and he hated nothing so much as censorship. It seems reasonably safe to say that, had not Ernst and Elmer Rice in a sense taken the Union's modest maidenhead, the ACLU would never have made its tremendous inroads on the Establishment of Prurience, and the American cultural scene, for all its televised titillation and mother-hungry breast cult and tasteless "comics," would still be at the stage of Mrs. Humphrey Ward.

The annual reports for the first few years of the Union's work mention no activity against the censor. His occasional suppression of a work on birth-control or anthropology is cited and deplored, but there is no sign of any disposition to broaden the civil-liberties fight in his direction, beyond opposing, generally unsuccessfully, local bans on birth-control meetings. Obscenity prosecutions did not really interest the Union very much until 1927, when David Gordon, an eighteen-year-old scholarship student at the University of Wisconsin, published a poem called *America* in the *Daily Worker,* likening the nation to a brothel. He was convicted of obscenity, rather obviously for political reasons despite the allegation that his poem roused lascivious longings (an interesting piece of involuntary self-revelation by the prosecutor), and was sentenced to three years. The paper was also indicted and threatened with federal prosecution: the ACLU admittedly entered the case only for political reasons, and had Gordon out in a month; the harassment of the *Worker* was abandoned. One does not know whether the poem was worth all the trouble. Sex apparently was not, for the Union did nothing about the refusal of Glenn Frank, president of Gordon's university, to allow the bisexual Liberal Club to hear a discourse on the subject by Earl Russell's current Countess. But in 1928 the Post Office barred a six-year-old YWCA pamphlet, *The Sex Side of Life*, and its author, Mary Ware Dennett, was convicted of obscenity. The Union organised a committee for her appeal and began to think of legislation to bar the growth of film and other censorship. Heartened by its eventual overthrow of Mrs. Dennett's $300-or-300-days for her little book, which had been used for years by social workers and teachers, the Union rejoiced when Massachusetts amended its law so that a book could no longer be banned for an "obscene" word or passage but must be considered as a whole.

Then Ernst went to work. The year was 1929; the "dirty books" were Dreiser's *An American Tragedy*, Lawrence's *Lady Chatterley's Lover*, Voltaire's *Candide*, Hall's *Well of Loneliness*, Schnitzler's *Reigen*, Remarque's *All Quiet on the Western Front*; the cleansers were the New York and Boston police, the Post Office and the Customs. Ernst made the Union fight for all the books, but only *Candide* was cleared—probably because of its age. In Florida two men seeking to bar "psycho-analytical" books from schools were indicted for "obscene" mailings because they sent excerpts from the volumes through the mail, but the Post Office lost this case in short order. Two years later the Customs lost its battle to send Marie Stopes' excruciatingly dull handbook, *Married Love*, back where it came from (England). By now the Union had a National Council for Freedom From Censorship, headed by Professor Hatcher Hughes of Columbia and including Fannie Hurst, a popular novelist, and Elmer Rice, lawyer and playwright then considered radical (but the *tempora* and the *mores* have revolved considerably since). Aligning the Union with

New York's playwrights and actors, they defeated a drive to censor the city's theaters and persuaded the Legislature to exempt stage-hands and actors from any obscenity prosecutions: producers alone would be answerable. But Clarence Darrow's film about human development, *The Mystery of Life*, was cut to ribbons by the state censors, the Board of Regents.

By 1932 the Union had formulated its position on censorship of alleged "obscenity." As in the case of political utterances, the Union opposed all prior censorship and all suppression except when matter was found obscene by a jury in a criminal trial with all due-process protections; in such cases the Union would aid the defense whenever it was satisfied that the accused matter was not obscene. It was a primitive position, poorly reasoned and, probably, expediently motivated, at least in part: the Union did not wish to jeopardise its political civil-liberties work by antagonising the Puritans among its allies. The reasoning was poor in that it conceded to the enemy a right to suppress obscenity in any circumstances and that it appeared to admit that obscenity could be objectively defined and might be harmful. (As the Union became more sophisticated, fortunately, it abandoned these early errors.) In 1934 the ACLU published a pamphlet containing all the cuts that had been made in films by the New York Regents, who promptly ceased supplying the Union with this information. A vicious postal censorship bill prepared by Roosevelt's Postmaster General and political creditor, James A. Farley, would have rendered not only senders but recipients of obscene matter liable to prosecution—an obvious move to make proceedings possible in the *Hinterland*, far more interested than the city slickers in buying "pornography" and hence, inevitably, far less likely to acquit: the sinner caught has no enemy so ferocious as the sinner undetected.

The iniquitous Customs censorship of imports, which early in 1933 had held up reproductions of Raphael's frescoes on the ceiling of the Sistine Chapel in the Vatican because of their obscenity, was almost mortally breached before the end of the year by the *Ulysses* case. Random House had contracted with James Joyce for an American edition of the novel, the importation of which had long been forbidden, and had sent to Paris for a copy of an authorised edition, which of course the Customs men (who certainly could not have understood any part of it except perhaps Molly Bloom's soliloquy that begins on page 723), immediately sequestered. Ernst and his firm went into Federal Court for the defense in United States of America versus One Book Called *Ulysses* and won a historic decision by Judge John M. Woolsey after both the Government and Random House waived a jury trial (however unwise the Government's waiver, that of Random House was imperative if obscenity was to be judged by any standard above that of lavatory-wall decorators and tabloid readers).

Woolsey's opinion, widely disseminated by the Union, went back to the definition of *obscene* arrived at by his learned brothers: "tending to stir the sex impulses or to lead to sexually impure and lustful thoughts." Woolsey then, accepting the definition (which is repugnant to all reason and logic, since it means that men and women are *obscene* when they stir the sexual impulses of people of their own or the other sex), attempted to find a method of applying it that would not limit all art to landscapes. "Whether a particular book would tend to excite such impulses and thoughts," he ruled, "must be tested by the court's opinion as to its effect on a person with average sex instincts— what the French would call *l'homme moyen sensuel*—who plays, in this branch of legal inquiry, the same *rôle* of hypothetical reagent as does the 'reasonable man' in the law of torts and 'the man learned in the art' in questions of invention in patent law·" Woolsey recognised the danger that arbiters might inherently tend, in his words, to make the reagent too subservient to their own idiosyncrasies; he dared not take the only possible farther step demanded by the whole problem: the recognition that the effect of anything on a man's emotions and thoughts, like those reactions themselves, is no business of government and that hence obscenity cannot be a crime.

What constituted "obscenity" or "pornography" (D.H. Lawrence's magnificent 1929 polemic, *Pornography and Obscenity,* has come as close as anyone can to an actual definition, but his would be as unacceptable to the verbal exhibitionists as to the Bible Belt) was a matter of caprice. An earnest film, *The Birth of a Baby*, was banned far and wide in 1937 because it show-

ed how we had all got here, and the issues of *Life* that contained
stills from the film were also barred in many places besides Boston, which pre-censored all publications intended for newsstand
sale. In the next year the illustrations in Professor Maurice Parme-
lee's *Nudism in Modern Life* barred it from the mails for months.
In Chicago, where police censorship of films had not yet been
supplanted by a board composed of four housewives and a man,
The Fight for Life, a film made by the United States Public
Health Service, was forbidden because the police found any portrayal of pregnancy or birth "obscene and corrupting." Obscenity was made a pretext for political censorship of the novels of
John Steinbeck, whose characters sometimes "talked dirty" and
whose books were unpleasantly truthful. Even the entry of the
United States into what was everywhere touted as a war for survival left time and energy free for the protection of morals, not
only by the ubiquitous Post Office at the instigation of the Catholic Bishop of Fort Wayne, Indiana, but also by Fiorello LaGuardia of New York. The Bishop's own regiment of the NODL prepared a list of sixty "dirty" magazines for the Postmaster General to bar; in addition to these he also refused to allow his mails
to be stained by Professor Paul Popenoe's *Preparing for Marriage* because this handbook was, like Mrs. Dennett's a decade
earlier, "too explicit." Mayor LaGuardia, though like the Union
he resisted pressure from the Powerhouse behind St. Patrick's
Cathedral to close Richard Wright's play, *Native Son*, decided
that burlesque shows were a menace to the nation's largest city
and ordered the burlesque theaters' licenses revoked. Some producers revised their sorry spectacles in an effort to stay in business and were convicted of obscenity by juries that never saw
their shows but rendered their verdicts on the basis of hearsay
evidence. The Union appealed the convictions on precisely this
ground but it found it necessary, in its annual report, to take
great pains to explain to its members that it was doing so because
of the principle involved and not because the American Civil
Liberties Union enjoyed bad men's-room jokes and the pathetic
gyrations of aging strippers.

The more intense the war against the Fascist demons in foreign climes, the more virulent the crusade to protect the souls

of those who stayed behind on the home front, and the ACLU became, according to one's viewpoint, St. George or the dragon. The Reverend Ilsley Boone of Mays Landing, New Jersey, secretary of a nudist organisation, was held for a federal grand jury because a truck delivered to him a copy of his own magazine, *Sunshine and Health*, which contained pictures of nudists in their working undress (it is difficult to conceive anything less conducive to lust than universal nudity). Two years later the Union persuaded the Justice Department to dismiss charges. *Truth*, a Mormon publication, was prosecuted for the obscenity of advocating polygamy but the trial judge threw out the case because there was no trace of obscenity in either the theory or the arguments advanced. Then came, in September, 1943, what was to be the first major defeat of the postal Grundys. The Post Office barred *Esquire* from the mails, first alleging obscenity and then dropping that charge in order to adopt a much more bizarre one: the magazine was "not of a public character contributing to the arts, literature and the sciences." The statement is at least as true today as it was then—insofar as any such judgment can be valid for anyone besides him who makes it—and certainly as irrelevant. If this were to become the criterion for print and films, we should have virtually nothing available but engineering treatises and (some) doctoral dissertations.

The *Esquire* case was a grave mistake for the Post Office. Not only the Union came to its defense, sending Hays and Seymour to argue the appeals; the Curtis Publishing Co., which has never printed an off-color hint; *The Reader's Digest*, the American Newspaper Publishers' Association and the Authors' League joined in briefs *amicus*, and thousands of persons who would not be found dead with *Esquire* supported its unqualified right to amuse the perpetual adolescents, even if it did nothing to advance their culture. How the Post Office had arrived at its decision to harry this slick-paper publication was explained in the Union's 1944 pamphlet, *What's Obscene?* The Post Office had the power to bar without a hearing any matter that its legal department found obscene; only when the second-class-mailing privilege was involved was the Post Office obliged to grant a hearing, and court review was forbidden except on the narrow ground of abuse of the Post Office's limitless discretion. Hence the "pin-up" pictures on which *Esquire* largely relied to garner the half-dollars of the celibate were susceptible of being declared obscene, like such other perils to salvation as *how-to* books for the married, nudist magazines and preachments for polygamy. Readers of the Union's pamphlet were urged to write to Congress and, ingenuously, the Postmaster General, demanding legislation that would put the Post Office under the regulations imposed earlier on the Customs, largely under ACLU pressure: if an importer protested a seizure, the matter was immediately referred to the local United States Attorney and was sent before a judge and jury for determination. The defendant was no individual or corporation but the thing seized. The Post Office, of course, fought tooth and nail against this invasion of its tyranny; it was even angrier when, having lost in the Circuit Court of Appeals on both *Esquire* and Popenoe's book, it was told by the Supreme Court that the content of publications was no basis for the revocation of second-class mailing privileges.

The Postmaster General, Judge Thurman Arnold of the Circuit Court said in his opinion, had revoked *Esquire's* privilege "because he thought its dominant purpose was to publish writings and pictures described in his order as being 'in that obscure and treacherous borderland zone where the average person hesitates to find them technically obscene but still may see ample proof that they are morally improper and not for the public welfare and the public good...A publication, to enjoy these *unique mailing privileges* [emphasis added] . . . is bound to do more than refrain from disseminating material which is obscene or bordering on the obscene. It is under a positive duty to contribute to the public good and the public welfare.' " Judge Arnold, unfortunately, chose to accept the Postmaster General's concept of a publisher's duty to make such a contribution, which it is indeed hard to conceive; and his acceptance of the concept leaves the danger undiminished by his *addendum*: "But it does not follow that an administrative official may be delegated the power first to determine what is good for the public to read and then to force compliance with his ideas by putting editors who do not follow them at a competitive disadvantage." Next, however, Arnold destroys his own endorsement of the ridiculous "duty" concept by quoting with approval Holmes' dissent in Abrams v. United States that free trade in ideas must be protected—and Holmes did not limit the kinds of ideas by quality, content, morality or intellectuality.

Arnold disposed of the Government's jesuitical argument that there was no censorship because *Esquire* could still, at an annual increase of a half-million dollars, mail its magazines first-class: the second-class privilege, Arnold said, was not an award for merit. Even if there were a right to censor, which he denies, Arnold ruled that no court might review "the issue of dominant vulgarity on its merits"; if the right to censor existed, Arnold further ruled, "in practical effect it amounts to a power in the Postmaster General to impose the standards of any reputable minority on the whole nation. In addition, the record suggests that the power claimed here would be used by sincere and conscientious officials to bind modern periodical literature to the standards of a former generation."

A parallel victory was scored in Boston, where a municipal judge not only cleared Erskine Caldwell's novel, *Tragic Ground,* of obscenity but denounced the practice of making censors of policemen. Once again LaGuardia set himself up as a guardian of public morals as solicitous as John Sumner and his Society for the Suppression of Vice: LaGuardia, currying favor with a group of Protestant clerics and being the incarnation of what Mencken called a *wowser,* tried to destroy the license of a theater presenting *Trio,* a play about Lesbians, unless the play was withdrawn. In exhausting negotiations with the Union, he finally backed down and agreed to limit the power of censorship to the courts—whereas, of course, it should simply have been abolished. Instead, LaGuardia's License Commissioner revoked the license of a film house that had ignored censors' cuts, and this time the Union could not wilt the Little Flower. Elsewhere the whole censorship problem remained as muddied and sick in peace as in war. Serious novels like Lillian Smith's *Strange Fruit* were obscene; in further proof of Mr. Capouya's thesis, slop to masturbate by, like *Forever Amber,* was given absolution. Edmund Wilson's *Memoirs of Hecate County* was banned widely although it was somewhat less salacious and more soporific than a gynecological paper in the *Journal* of the American Medical Association. A film called *The Outlaw* was banned because, though impeccable under the titillating standards of the Hollywood code, it was advertised "obscenely"; a French film, *Amok*, which included a fatal abortion, was just downright "immoral". The post-war years present a monotonous honor roll of books, films and plays attacked by know-nothings on all levels, including the *Kulturkampf* of police forces in cities from Philadelphia to San Francisco and Los Angeles who raided bookshops and publishers' warehouses with and without warrants to confiscate everything in sight under the same "rotten apple" doctrine unsuccessfully employed for political censorship. Judge Curtis Bok of Philadelphia ruled, utterly incomprehensibly, that literature was not *obscene* unless it was *pornographic!* He added that even then it could not be prosecuted unless there was a reasonable likelihood that its dissemination would result in crime—comprehensible but no more intelligent. Unfortunately this kind of thinking became a basis for the evolution of a new Union policy on obscenity prosecutions: that they were unconstitutional unless it could be shown that someone reading or seeing the dirty stuff would proceed, as the psychoanalysts say, to *act out* as a direct result of the stimulus to his *libido*. But the censors, some of whom were overruled, would not take this risk with such dangerous material as:

The Respectful Prostitute (Sartre), *Stromboli* (because it was made by Roberto Rossellini and starred Ingrid Bergman, and they were living in sin and Italy), *The Bicycle Thief* (de Sica), *Tropic of Capricorn* and *Tropic of Cancer* (Miller—Henry), *La Ronde, Native Son, The Moon is Blue* (Cardinal Spellman's *bête bleue*, but not that of the Maryland courts), *Tobacco Road* (an atavism), *The Game of Love, Lysistrata* (written 3000 years earlier but only now brought to the attention of the Post Office), *City Lights* (by the unspeakable Chaplin), *Diamond Lil* (everyone but the Atlanta censor had forgot this), *M* (thirty years old, but banned in Ohio because "it is not of a moral, educational or amusingly harmless nature"), *Il Decamerone* (Boccaccio), *Tom Jones* (Fielding's 200-year-old novel), the works of Rabelais, *The Naked and the Dead* (Mailer), *From Here to Eternity* (Jones), *Pilgrim's Progress* (Bunyan), *20,000 Leagues Under the Sea*

(Verne), *Moby Dick* (Melville), *The Canterbury Tales* (Chaucer), *Mom and Dad* (a film that showed a Caesarean section), *I Am a Camera,* reproductions of *David* (Michelangelo), *Notre-Dame des Fleurs* (Genêt), *The Rabbits' Wedding* (a juvenile banned in Atlanta because one rabbit was white but the other was black), *Lolita* (Nabokov), *The Defiant Ones* (more integration, this time of people), *Peyton Place* (Metalious), *The Lovers* ("Somebody," the Mayor of Milwaukee explained, denying censorship, "has to scrutinise films before they are shown to the public"), *Don Juan* (a film of Mozart's *Don Giovanni*), *Memoirs of a Woman of Pleasure* (Cleland—also known as *Fanny Hill,* slavered over throughout my adolescence by other boys who, like me, had never seen a copy and ultimately found for themselves just how dull a piece of writing a "dirty book" can be, and how psychologically inaccurate)—the list is endless and could be lengthened to encyclopedic proportions if it included the various magazines and "comic books" that fell under one or more bans.

A remarkable obscenity prosecution was knocked down by the United States Supreme Court in 1950. Not only was it remarkable in its facts; it raised disturbing questions over the freedom and privacy that Americans boast they have to a greater degree than all lesser breeds without the law. A man wrote an indiscreetly passionate letter to his wife and somehow the Post Office got hold of it, whereupon he was duly indicted, tried and convicted for sending obscene matter through the mails (first-class). The conviction was of course thrown out when his appeal reached the highest court (though the same court, as will presently appear, was willing to tolerate the invasion of marital privacy by electronic eavesdropping). Corollarily, the Post Office sought to cut off all mail addressed to publishers or distributors of matter that it thought obscene, but it was frustrated by the courts, which held that, under the law, only mail dealing directly with the so-called obscenity could be stopped and sent back, even though legally the Post Office lacked the right to open the letters in order to ascertain their contents: the Post Office had no right to put a company out of business, a result that would inevitably ensue if its mail were cut off.

Censorship, the Union concluded in the mid-1950's, could be defeated only when it could be made the subject of litigation. But by far most censorship was that of prior suppression, rendering court tests difficult and costly. The biggest problem was the pressures of the mob and its various segments and the influence it wielded on officials who were afraid to offend it—surrenders condemned by the New Jersey Supreme Court. Lobbying against censorship legislation was not often effective, though the Union did prevail on Dewey to veto a New York bill that would have banned all comic books; the Union also helped to defeat a Minnesota bill that was equally vague and indefinite in its attempts to set standards. Both bills—like any attempt to legislate censorship—were so inherently inclusive that virtually any publication could have been held to come within their prohibitions. In Congress the Union helped to defeat a bill that would have upset the *Esquire* case by authorising the Post Office to bar publications from second-class mail for their contents. New York enacted a law branding immoral anything whose "dominant purpose or effect is erotic or pornographic; or which portrays acts of sexual immorality, lust, vulgarity or lewdness; or which expressly or impliedly presents such acts as desirable, acceptable or proper patterns of behavior" —all of which, the NYCLU pointed out, would proscribe the portrayal of Salome's dance in a Biblical film, to say nothing of the westerns in which crime is incited by those good citizens who throw out the bad sheriffs. The Mayor of Baltimore, in his capacity as "conservator of the peace," banned a painting, approved by an art jury, lest it "corrupt youth"—an argument, the ACLU vainly pointed out, that had been in bad odor since the death of Socrates—but a Midwestern judge refused to forbid books against which the same charge was made, calling it irelevant.

By 1957 the Union had refined its policy stand on "obscenity," declaring that there was no special category of obscenity or pornography to which one could constitutionally apply tests different from those by which all other expression was to be judged. To be Constitutional, an obscenity statute must at least meet the requirement of definiteness, the Union said, and it must further require that, before any adverse finding is possible, the material must be shown beyond a reasonable doubt to create a clear and present danger that it would in normal circumstances induce behavior that had validly been made criminal by statute. This was a decided advance. In practice, if adhered to, such a viewpoint would effectively prevent any prosecutions for obscenity; but in principle it remained defective by even theoretically allowing the *clear and present danger* doctrine to determine the legality of the expression. That doctrine is as pernicious in the field of obscenity as it is in that of political censorship: freedom of speech comprehends the integrity and the courage to risk its transmutation into action and, if speech succeeds and makes lawful what has previously been unlawful, that is part of the calculated risk entailed in being alive rather than committing suicide to escape change.

But the Supreme Court did not share the ACLU's view. In the Roth case of 1957, which set a rule for years to come, the court held that the Consitutional protection of free trade in ideas was not intended to include obscenity; and the court evolved a highly dangerous definition of the term. *Obscenity*, it declared, is material that "deals with sex in a manner appealing to prurient interest" and found so to appeal "by the average man applying contemporary community standards to the dominant theme of the material taken as a whole." This definition was no definition: it merely raised the need for handful of new ones. What is *prurient interest?* what is *the average man?* what community's standards are to be applied? Justices Black, Douglas and Harlan dissented, declaring that the opinion of a judge or a jury that material has an undesirable impact is not enough unless unlawful action flowing from it can be proved; and all three challenged the influence of obscenity on deviations from "community standards." In essence, though they used more legal language, they repeated what Al Smith said when he vetoed a New York censorship bill: "I never knew of a girl who lost her virginity by reading a book." Frankfurter endorsed the aphorism when he reversed a ban based on the potential effect of the taboo material on the young: this unconstitutionally invaded the rights of the adult. But even so narrow a view as the Roth rule was too radical for New York, whose courts upheld a statute permitting ban by injunction—prior restraint—on matter declared obscene.

No matter what the courts decided, the Post Office paid as little attention as the Ohio cops who relaxed by brutalising Jehovah's Witnesses. The postal men publicly burned a hundred sacks of "trash and nudism" in Chicago and seized cases of "pornography" sent to Dr. Kinsey's Institute for Sex Research and to psycho-analysts, anthropologists and other scholars. All protests by the Union and by various professional and scholarly organisations were ignored; in some instances court action gained the release of some of the material. In western cities two or three policemen would raid a bookshop or warehouse, leaf through the seized matter unadvised and, without further study or consultation, decide which—generally, all—of the publications were to be banned without further legal process. In the south *Island in the Sun* was banned because love between the races was judicially determined to constitute obscenity: under the rule of the Roth case, the determination was valid because it dovetailed with the local bigotry and might hence be applied everywhere. But the New York Appellate Division found reasonable disagreement possible over the meanings of "immorality," "the dominant purpose or effect" and "acts of sexual immorality, perversion or lewdness."

Thirty years after its publication, the Union helped to win postal passage for *Lady Chatterley's Lover,* barred by Eisenhower's Postmaster General, Arthur Summerfield, because to him it was obscene: the court held that he could bar only materials properly found illegal and he had no discretion. Summerfield's peers in Congress sought to give him the power to open all mail in his righteous quest for filth, but the Union's opposition helped to kill the bill in the Senate, where the level of culture is slightly higher than that of the House. But the Representatives' thinking must have been representative, because the Union's fight for an *avant-garde* literary magazine, *Big Table*, was defeated by a Chicago postal examiner who said that, though the magazine "would not arouse the interest of the average reader in sex, it goes beyond the customary limits of candor in literature." He was overruled later. In the light of "thinking" of this kind, one cannot legitimately be surprised that the Post Office tried to bar postcards promoting the film, *Naked Maja*, by reproducing Goya's portrait with some text: the Post Office admitted that neither the picture nor the text was obscene but insisted that, put together, they spelled *filth*. The Justice Department, however, appealed to by the NYCLU, refused to do the needful for the mailmen.

The Customs, despite statute and decision, had its own way of violating the law. Daniel Bell, an ACLU director, returned from Europe with Genêt's *Notre-Dame des Fleurs* and it was taken away from him by a Customs inspector because it had been published in Paris by Olympia Press and all Olympia books were presumed obscene by the Customs. Malin wrote a protest to the Treasury Department, which said the inspector was in error; but the Treasury refused to answer Malin's question whether it maintained a blacklist of banned books. Bell got his book back because, the Treasury said, the inspector should have advised him of his right to protest the seizure on the ground of literary merit.

Even under the Roth rule, too many frightening books and films, as well as "comic books" and "sexy" magazines, were being allowed to circulate, in the view of the patriots, the MUDs and the rest of the "decent element," all of whom raised such outcry that Pennsylvania legislated the rule into statute. At the same time Massachusetts set up a commission to recommend prosecution by the state Attorney General whenever smut was put "on sale or was about to be placed on sale." The Union vainly fought both these bills, as well as one in New Mexico defining pornography as "material designed in its entirety to stimulate human senses in a manner and to a degree offensive and corrupting to public morals"—the legislators not having yet learned the distinction between senses and sense. There is no record of their reaction to the United States Supreme Court's clearance of the filmed *Lady Chatterley* with the statement that "the Constitution protects the advocacy of the opinion that adultery may sometimes be proper, no less than the advocacy of Socialism or the single tax." A Chicago court overthrew classifications based on age groups, amplifying the earlier Frankfurter decisions: "A film either is or is not obscene," the decision pointed out; "the criteria cannot change with the age of the beholder." But the Union failed to overthrow a Pennsylvania law setting up a pre-censorship board that could bar obscenity in advance, as well as any film deemed unsuitable for children because it showed as acceptable conduct "the commission of any crime or manifesting of contempt of law." This, the Union pointed out, would make it illegal to show *Tom Sawyer* or *Huckleberry Finn.*

In 1959 the Supreme Court handed down a decision that was to undo a host of obscenity prosecutions, voiding a Los Angeles ordinance that held booksellers criminally liable for the possession of obscene literature even if they did not know its contents or its obscenity. Because there is a physical limitation on the number of books that one can read and because such a law would induce booksellers to offer only those books that they had read, the court said, "the state will have imposed restrictions on the distribution of constitutionally protected as well as obscene literature...The door barring federal and state intrusions into the fundamental freedoms of speech and press cannot be left ajar. It must be kept closed, and opened only the slightest crack necessary to prevent encroachment upon more important interests." Decisions such as this eminently sound one, coupled with the ostensible crusade for the protection of youthful innocence, brought on demands for Constitutional amendments that would allow each state to decide questions of "decency" and "morality" on the basis of its own public policy, bar any abridgment of the right of states to legislate on these subjects and suspend the guaranties of speech and press freedom for any materials found to fall within the Roth rule. That Eastland of Mississippi was one of the sponsors should surprise no one; that Estes Kefauver, the LaGuardia in a coonskin cap, was another should surprise very few. Malin testified for the Union against both proposals, which never got far.

The Union backed a proposal, which failed, for a House investigation to see whether obscenity played a causal part in juvenile delinquency; but it opposed the creation of a Senate Committee on Noxious and Obscene Matters, predicated on the existence of such a cause. Investigations in Massachusetts and elsewhere had uniformly found no evidence of even a contributory *rôle.* Some states had followed Pennsylvania in enacting the Roth rule into statute, but obviously they had no Hearst papers or tabloids, which such a law would have closed. Oregon's statute barred any publication that "tends to incite to lustful thoughts," without stipulating whom it might incite. The Postmaster of San

Francisco cleaned off the newsstand in the federal building there on a simple criterion: "As far as I'm personally concerned, the test to [sic] what is good literature is whether or not [sic] I would want my teen-age daughter to read it." No doubt such a man really believes he prevents his teen-age daughter—or son—from reading what he forbids.

The six widows of ward-heeling politicians who composed the Chicago censorship board banned a French film, *The Lovers*, and were emulated in, among other cities, Cleveland, where the exhibitor was convicted of two felonies—possessing the film and showing it—by three judges who found the film covered by the Roth rule. Since this conviction jeopardised his application for naturalisation, the exhibitor appealed, with the help of the Union, which, pending the progress of this case to the Supreme Court, was also occupied with the refusal of the Times Film Corporation to submit *Don Juan* to the widow-ladies in Chicago and the consequent interdict of the film there, sight unseen. The Supreme Court seemed to throw all its previous decisions into oblivion when it upheld the ban. "Liberty of speech is not absolute," the court said, and Chicago had a legal right "to protect its people against the dangers of obscenity in the public exhibition of motion pictures. It is not for this court to limit the state in its selection of the remedy it deems most effective to cope with such a problem, absent, of course, a showing of unreasonable stricture on individual liberty." But this majority decision was attacked by Chief Justice Warren and Douglas.

"I know of no Constitutional principle," Warren protested, "which permits us to hold that the communication of ideas through one medium may be censored while other media are immune." And Douglas hit harder: "Under the censor's *régime* the weights are cast against freedom ... whether the pressures are for a conformist moral code or for a conformist political ideology, no such *régime* is permitted under the First Amendment." But these were dissents, unheeded by such states as Rhode Island, which set up a State Commission to Encourage Morality in Youth through the blacklisting of sellers of smut, the threat of police action and prosecution by the state Attorney General. This problem too was to come before the Supreme Court after the reversal of the ACLU's 1960 victory against the Commission, whose activities were found unconstitutional by a state judge.

While the Cleveland and Rhode Island cases were taking their interminable way to the Supreme Court—Nick Jacobellis, the Cleveland exhibitor, had to make two trips—the Union was nearing the end of three years of re-examination of its own position on the whole censorship problem. On April 16, 1962, the board of directors arrived at a new policy declaration that rejected not only the Roth rule but the later criterion imposed by the Supreme Court: the necessity that, to escape prosecution for obscenity, the accused material must be shown to possess "redeeming social importance"—a requirement as absurd and as unsusceptible of objective determination as every other, including the definition of obscenity itself. "Limitations of expression on the ground of obscenity are unconstitutional," the Union finally enunciated with an unequivocal boldness that was about thirty years late; but the Union sought a practical compromise with the fact of life that obscenity statutes were still being invoked (whereas it would have done much better to confine itself to the challenge of their constitutionality). In applying them, the Union urged, the courts should require proof beyond a reasonable doubt that the expression under attack would directly cause, in a normal adult, behavior that "has validly been made criminal by statute;" if the expression is directed to a youthful audience, there should be proof beyond a reasonable doubt that it would directly cause criminal behavior in a juvenile. In all prosecutions the Union called for the scrupulous observance of all due-process protections: the clear statutory definition of the offense, the right to counsel, the right to a prompt, fair, public trial by jury (though the prospect of putting one's fate in the hands of twelve good men and stupid is far more frightening than the dubious mercy of a single judge) and the right to appeal. No action, the Union said, should be possible against persons who lacked knowledge of the contents of the material and substantial responsibility for its creation and distribution. This, indeed, was merely another—but a vitally needed—way of calling the courts' attention to a fundamental principle of criminal law that they so often tended to forget: the fact that criminal intent is an essential element of crime. Before any individual or corporation is prosecuted, the Union added, the actionability of the material should be determined in an *in rem* proceeding. If the courts could be made to live up to such a proper code, the Union would of course achieve its end of eliminating all censorship for obscenity because one cannot prove what cannot happen—the commission of a crime caused by reading a book or seeing a film—but it would do so by a subterfuge that would never establish the principle that the Union had properly enunciated.

The Supreme Court had some trouble with its own Roth rule, however, even without considering this new statement by the Union. The Post Office had banned three homosexual magazines showing nude and semi-nude men. Rightly, the court wanted to overthrow the ban; wrongly, it fell back on its own fallacious rule and wrenched it to fit the facts, finding that the magazines were neither "patently offensive" nor an "affront to current community standards of decency." But at the same time the court refused to reverse the Baltimore conviction of a distributor of what are quaintly called *girlie* magazines. It is respectfully submitted that both the naked ladies and the naked gents are entitled to the protection of the Constitution no matter whom they offend or what standards they affront. This was the view taken by the Union in its opposition to Chicago's creation of a "blue-ribbon" censorship board to hear appeals from the vetoes of the widow-ladies: censorship, the ACLU contended, is censorship whether practiced by learned men of good will or cultural illiterates of ill will.

Before its second hearing of Jacobellis' convictions for possessing and showing *The Lovers*, the Supreme Court found Rhode Island's Commission to Encourage Morality in Youth had exceeded the Constitutional boundaries by forcing a wholesaler, without judicial process, to stop handling those books and magazines to which it objected. The commission's operations, the court found, were "a form of effective state regulation superimposed upon the state's criminal regulation of obscenity and making such regulation largely unnecessary. In thus obviating the need to employ criminal sanctions, the state has at the same time eliminated the safeguards of the criminal process." Corollarily the court noted that the Commission, though created to protect the young, was also *protecting* their elders, and that it allowed no appeals from its ukases. The court abstained from declaring the Commission illegal, but a year later it dissolved itself with no heirs except a similar *Kulturbund* in Georgia.

When at last the court resolved the Jacobellis case it largely ignored the points made in the Union's brief *amicus*, no doubt for reasons of convenience and "public relations." The brief contended that all expression should be protected in the absence of a clear and present danger of its producing a substantive evil, adding that there was grossly insufficient evidence to show that obscenity produced any evil at all. The Ohio law under which Jacobellis was convicted, it argued, violated not only the First but the Fourteenth Amendment in that it required no knowledge by the exhibitor that his wares were obscene; and he was put into double jeopardy by the lodging of two charges—possessing and showing—based on a single act. Jacobellis was fined $500 for possession and $2000 for exhibition: the context of the law, the ACLU said, showed that the offenses were "inextricably intertwined, and the indictment, the bill of particulars, the evidence and common sense demonstrate that it was all a single transaction." Finally, the Union insisted unchallengeably, the whole question of what arouses "prurient interest" or "lustful thoughts" is a vast guessing game; and the Roth rule of contemporary community standards violates due process by providing no ascertainable standards of guilt and because the use of the "average person" as a guide is equally perilous since it is indefinable and includes millions who will never be exposed to any obscenity.

The court avoided all these broad considerations of principle and achieved a desirable result by rather less laudable means. It merely enlarged the Roth rule to mean the community standards of "the whole nation" or "society at large," rather than some local community, insisting on the need for one national standard rather than varying local and state standards for a freedom protected by the federal Constitution. Unfortunately this highly logical and practical as well as moral conclusion has yet to be imposed by the court on the practitioners of all the other abuses—racial discrimination, voting eligibility, wiretapping and all the other sabotages of civil and economic liberties—so jealously guarded under the wholly specious doctrine of "states' rights": the right, that is, to negate the national Constitution and laws and to perpetuate injustice for emotional or economic gains. But, almost immediately after this ruling had been handed down, the Ohio Supreme Court took heed and voided a law penalising the exhibition of an "indecent" or "immoral" film by one who knew its alleged character.

(In 1965 the United States Supreme Court achieved another of its desirable ends through undesirable means, striking down New York and Maryland film-censorship laws not on the proper ground that such censorship is unconstitutional, as the ACLU had urged in both cases, but because—as the Union's briefs had also pointed out—the statutes put the burden of proof on the accused. The decisions reaffirmed the Union's contention that the burden of proof lay with the censor, but they evaded the central issue raised by the Union.)

The broadened rule employed by the court in Jacobellis' case was applied by it a year later to clear Miller's *Tropic of Cancer* and a bit of trash called *Pleasure Was My Business*. The Union's brief to the Supreme Court on behalf of *Tropic of Cancer* relied on an argument that in private the Union itself had long since transcended and that, if it had been taken seriously, would have compounded the whole evil and, for example, brought an adverse decision against the ostensible autobiography of a madam that was cleared with Miller's cumbersome work. "The issue," the brief urged, "cannot turn on *who* may find a work important, or *where* it may be so found, but simply on *whether* anyone anywhere finds it to have worth. No city or state may hold its residents down to a lesser freedom of expression, a smaller right to read, than any other city or state, or the nation." A much wiser and at the same time more courageous and honorable view was taken by Justice J. Irwin Shapiro of the New York Supreme Court, who held, quite properly, that merit is irrelevant and who dismissed obscenity indictments. "There are those," he pointed out, "who, because of lack of education, the meanness of their social existence or mental insufficiency, cannot cope with anything better. Slick-paper confessions, pulp adventures and 'comic-book' types of magazines provide them with an escape from reality . . .

Coarse these books are, but so is much of our civilisation."

What Justice Shapiro said applies equally to the merchandise of Ralph Ginzburg, for whom the Union has a brief pending in the United States Supreme Court. In complete defiance of that court's latest rulings, the Third Circuit Court of Appeals upheld Ginzburg's conviction, based on a shoddily pretentious "art" magazine, *Eros*; Liaison Newsletters and the *Housewives' Handbook on Selective Promiscuity*. *Dreck* these talismans of the mental masturbator certainly are, as the Circuit Court found. "What confronts us," the opinion reported quite accurately, "is an operation on the part of experts in the shoddy business of pandering to, and exploiting for money, one of the great weaknesses of human beings." But the assessment of the facts, however valid, shows no evidence of violation of any but unconstitutional law. It is not illegal to pander to human weaknesses—states themselves sell liquor and run race tracks; and the churches flourish—or even to make money thereby, though it may be distasteful to some to participate: they have the freedom to abstain. Some birds eat fruit and others thrive on dung: each has an equal right to the sustenance he needs, and it is to be hoped that the Union can persuade the Supreme Court that a sentence of five years and a fine of $28,000 for constitutionally protected utterance represents a miscarriage of justice.

In the Government itself the Union has had still to battle official illegality—the General Services Administration's criteria of "popularity and good taste" for publications that it allows to be sold on newsstands in federal buildings—and legislative imbecility. The Union's opposition helped to defeat in the Senate a bill passed by the House that would have empowered the Postmaster General to punish for contempt persons or firms who sent mail to addressees who had indicated that they found it morally offensive. The Union pointed out that this might very soon put CORE or the White Citizens' Councils or the United Jewish Appeal out of business, for the punishment the Post Office demanded was the power to completely cut off the mailing privileges of all offenders! But perhaps the acme—or nadir—of governmental wowserism comes from that other California, Florida. There the Legislature's Johns Committee, which is making a life career of pursuing subversion under the sun, issued a lengthy report on homosexuality as a threat to the state—and the Attorney General of Florida at once banned the report as obscenity! Noting this flagrant violation of due process, the Florida Civil Liberties Union felt obliged to condemn the action "even though the FCLU has regarded each and every report of the Johns Committee as being richer in fiction than in fact."

17

You Can't Teach That!

The American Civil Liberties Union's concern with the freedom
of teachers, scholars and students arose initially out of its preoccupation with the rights of anti-militarists, labor and radicals. The
Union's enthusiasm for academic freedom mounted and broadened
more rapidly than its concern with non-political censorship or with
the rights of criminal defendants and victims of privacy invasions,
simply because its original entrance into the field of the rights of
the academic brought it almost at once to confrontation with so
many and various injustices interwoven with those that were its
earliest concern. During the First World War, for example, some
states forbade the teaching of German in the schools; some went
even farther and prohibited the teaching of any language but
English (the descendants of these ostriches turned up again during
the next World War and some survived into the so-called cold war
to try to ban the teaching of Russian).

Many of the early cases were based on the intrusion of religion and so-called patriotism into the schools, the Klan and
the Fundamentalists taking a leading part in both. One Louisiana
case cost the Union's national committee the only prominent
Catholic cleric ever to hold a major ACLU post. Monsignor John

322

A. Ryan of Washington left the committee when the Union was criticised by a Louisiana bishop for supporting a Louisiana State University professor dismissed for his novel, *Cane Juice,* which was charged with reflecting unfavorably on the "morality" of Creole youth. The professor won a judgment for damages but could not regain his job.

In the first years of the ACLU one of the worst exemplars of the shackling of education was New York, though it did not match those western states that limited language teaching or, like Oregon, attempted by law to compel all children to attend only public schools. New York's Lusk Laws of 1919 provided that all private schools except those of religious and fraternal orders must be licensed by the state but no license would issue "where it shall appear that the instruction proposed to be given includes the teaching of the doctrine that organised government shall be overthrown by force, violence or unlawful means, or where it appears that such school, institute, class or course is to be conducted in a fraudulent manner." As soon as the Lusk Laws took effect an investigation of teachers in New York City and State was launched and a special assault was mounted against the left-wing Rand School of Social Science, which refused to seek a license. At the same time the New York City Board of Education initiated the practice of pre-censorship of the speakers and subjects scheduled for meetings to be held on school property. Morris Hillquit, a distinguished old-line Socialist lawyer who often ran for the mayoralty, challenged the laws on behalf of the Rand School, citing their unconstitutional denials of free speech, due process and equal protection of the laws, and was rebuffed by a decision that they represented a lawful exercise of legal state power denying no rights. But in 1923 the Lusk Laws were erased by the Legislature under the leadership of Governor Al Smith.

Such legislation was one aspect of the academic freedom for which the Union fought. Another was the administrative actions of school and college officials who restricted the persons and subjects that might be discussed on their campuses. In 1921 the president of Clark University forbade a lecture by Scott Nearing, an economist then a Union member, on the ground that Nearing's views of capitalism were such that students should not be allowed to know them. The Union's protest failed; but the incident, coupled with the dismissals of teachers under the Lusk Laws and the refusal to reinstate them after the repeal of the statutes, moved the Union to form its first Committee on Academic Freedom in 1923 under Professor Clarence R. Skinner of Tufts College, offering its services to any and all victims of academic repression. Its first client was Benjamin Glassberg, a 1919 sacrifice to the Lusk Laws and the American Legion, which had protested his comments on Russia in his classroom; the Union's appeal to the State Education Commissioner failed. Its committee, meanwhile, distributed gratis a handbook on free speech for school and college debaters, with free material for relevant debates. The committee scored its first success with the United States Bureau of Education, which had allowed the Legion to dictate an intolerant militarist program for the Bureau's American Education Week set for November, 1923. Already perturbed by the angry withdrawal of the YWCA from participation because of the Legion's *Diktat*, the Bureau eliminated everything demanded by the heroes. Further encouragement was found by the Union in the Supreme Court's invalidation of the Iowa law banning the teaching of foreign languages and of Oregon's bar, inspired by the Klan, on attendance at private and parochial schools.

But in 1925 the climate turned suddenly frigid. School boards all over the country, even without the pretext of some law under which to act, began dismissing teachers for "unpatriotic" utterances. Missouri legislated a ban on the "unpatriots," and laws requiring Bible-reading in the schools erupted everywhere despite the protests of Catholics, Unitarians, Lutherans, and Jews, none of whom accepts the King James Version universally stipulated in the statutes. Congress enacted a law for the District of Columbia that authorised the dismissal of anyone teaching "disrespect of the Holy Bible." And Tennessee forbade the teaching of evolution and of any other theory denying the Biblical legend of the Creation.

The Union leaped at the bait, offering to defend any teacher dismissed and indicted for the misdemeanor of defying the law, and its open advertisements for shock troops brought a prompt response when John Thomas Scopes of Dayton High School volunteered and was accordingly indicted. His whole defense was financed by the Union, which could never have anticipated the circus that the trial would become, through an appeal to the American Association for the Advancement of Science. Naturally it made Tennessee and, by extension, the United States the butt of the civilised world. The passions it roused among the Fundamentalists were such that a pamphlet describing the trial and challenging the law, written by Robert S. Keebler of the Memphis bar, was ordered expunged from its archives by the president of the local bar association.

Detemined to win, the state and the Fundamentalists retained former Secretary of State William Jennings Bryan to assist the regular prosecutor. Bryan had multiple assets: he had almost become President, he was a mellifluous orator of the school so dear to southerners, and he was as frightened of Darwin and of hell-fire as were those who retained him. The Union assisted Scopes' counsel of record, John R. Neal, with Hays; Clarence Darrow, the great criminal lawyer; Dudley Field Malone, a suave and expert New York courtroom practitioner, and Bainbridge Colby, once Secretary of State. All served without fee. For weeks Bryan thundered like an inferior Old Testament rhetorician and Darrow and Malone made a fool of him. The defense relied on the First and Fourteenth Amendments as well as on a worldwide galaxy of scholars and scientists on the subject of evolution. Ultimately, of course, Scopes was found guilty and the law was upheld. Scopes was fined $100 and appealed to the state Supreme Court, which also upheld the law; but it reversed his conviction, preventing the case from going to the United States Supreme Court.

Tennessee's law became a model for scourges in other states, notably those that, now as then, have fought doggedly to remain in the Stone Age: Louisiana, Mississippi, Texas, Arkansas. Bigger and better in bigotry as in everything else, Texas set its Text Book Commission in 1927 to the laborious task of excising every reference to evolution from every text used in the state. Louisiana's Legislature killed an anti-evolution bill, so the State Superintendent of Schools banned the teaching of it. In Tennessee a Fundamentalist high-school principal who hated Darwin as the Devil was forced to resign because, on a student's request, he defined the word *evolution*. As late as 1930 the electorate of Arkansas voted solemnly in referendum to banish Darwinism from the schools.

Elsewhere teachers and students alike were feeling a variety of lashes, which became more numerous as the sacrosanct Prosperity of the 1920's was martyred by the depression. Three New York City teachers were refused promotion because of "radical" views. Olivet College, in Michigan, proved the thesis of Dr. John E. Fitzpatrick's book, *The American College and its Rulers*—that academic freedom was being infringed—by sacking him for publishing it. Outraged by criticisms of its operations in the student magazine of the University of Illinois, the zinc industry persuaded the University to expel the authors. Five students of Kansas City Junior College in Missouri criticised the college officials in their magazine and it was suppressed: when they started a new publication they were suspended. Four who apologised sufficiently abjectly were reinstated; one who refused to crawl was expelled. A Lynn, Massachusetts, teacher discharged for her refusal to lead a flag salute and suing with Union aid was elected to the School Board that had fired her. Only public outcry prevented Woodbury, New Jersey, from trying a teacher for being an active pacifist. The Legionnaires of West Chester, Pennsylvania, procured the ouster of two teachers in the State Normal School there who had formed a Liberal Club and criticised the United States Marines' occupation of Nicaragua—but one "buddy" stood up before an ACLU meeting in Philadelphia to denounce his fellows' gag rule. The University of West Virginia, however, barred the gate to any speakers not approved by the Legion or the beldames of the DAR. City College in New York suspended two anti-ROTC students for "disrespect for the authorities"; the University of Minnesota threw out thirty-six.

Wesley Maurer, assistant professor of journalism at Ohio State University, was ousted for commenting favorably on the United Mine Workers: one trustee of the university was a large coal operator. Three men were dismissed and one was suspended from the University of Missouri for circulating a sex questionnaire for the sociology and psychology departments. The University of Pittsburgh, a frequent offender as time passed, discharged an instructor for being secretary of the local ACLU committee, broke up the campus Liberal Club and ousted two students—all because of a program devoted to the frame-up of Tom Mooney and Warren Billings in California. The Union sued for a writ of *mandamus* against the Los Angeles school board, which refused high-school diplomas to students with "Communist" views. Milwaukee disciplined a boy for organising a Communist club in high school. New York City forbade Baldwin to address students in a school building because it was "improper" for them to hear an advocate of civil liberties as defined by the ACLU. The University of Pittsburgh extended its jurisdiction beyond the campus and expelled students who met in the town to hear Professor Harry Elmer Barnes of Smith College. In some of these cases the American Association of University Professors, as well as the Union, sought redress; it was seldom gained. Nor could either organisation abort the growth of teacher loyalty oaths that began in 1930. Monroe, New York, lacking a loyalty oath, refused to hire a teacher because she was a Catholic: here the Union was able to have her hired, and the anti-Catholic principal fired, by an appeal to the State Education Commissioner. But in New York City a history text was banned because one clergyman called it "too liberal."

The disgraceful record swelled in the 1930's. Columbus, Ohio, discharged a teacher because the DAR called him a pacifist. One balky New York boy was responsible for the revelation that since 1919 it had been impossible to get a high-school diploma in the city without a loyalty oath, which the Union immediately set out to overthrow. City College furnished considerable work for the Union as student organisations, publications and protest meetings fought the censorship imposed on them by the Board of Education. The same board was under attack by the Union because of its continuing dismissals, suspensions and transfers of teachers with the wrong views on public questions; the Union was also contesting similar action in California, South Dakota and Colorado. One encouraging fact was its perfect score in defeating nine teach-

er-oath bills demanded by the DAR; but the University of Pittsburgh needed no law to impose its own loyalty oath as a condition
of student admission. Syracuse University in New York required
every student to pledge his acceptance of dismissal without charges
or hearings. Brown University student editors in Providence were
threatened with prosecution for publishing the Oxford Oath. A
Los Angeles law teacher was dismissed for having done legal
work for the Union and the ILD on his own time. Here and
there a flicker of sanity appeared, but only a flicker. When the
University of Pittsburgh had three students arrested for protesting its choice of General Douglas MacArthur, the conqueror of
the Bonus March (see chapter 18), as a Commencement speaker,
a judge freed the students and excoriated the University for having lodged charges. A Maryland judge ordered the reinstatement
of a student ousted by the state university for refusing to join
the ROTC, but this order was quickly reversed. But many cases,
the Union believed in 1934, afforded no basis for court action
because the institutions were private and no contracts were violated: the only recourse was publicity, the Union's directors
thought, and this was used to the full. In addition, the ACLU
committee under Professor William Heard Kilpatrick of Teachers' College circulated to all teachers and administrators the
first of its pamphlets on *Principles of Academic Freedom*, which
combined the philosophical approach with demands for ordinary due-process protections. In later years, however, the Union was able to establish a sound basis for action against private as well as public institutions practicing gag rule.

Much of the repression, of course, was inspired by pressure
groups whose voting strength—or whose claims to voting strength—
always terrorised the tribunes of the people. These were joined
during the New Deal's early years by the then powerful Hearst
newspaper chain as well as the militantly know-nothing Mc-
Cormick-Patterson papers (later to try to rally the nation to a
holy war on what they called *doubledomes* and *eggheads*—i.e.,
people who could read, write, reason and be more or less objective: Reuben Maury of *The News* in New York was to write
of Professor Arthur Schlesinger Jr. that "the intellectual is always a figure of fun"). Such later heroes of the forward march

as Herbert Lehman, then Governor of New York, were always sensitive to these voices: Lehman signed a teacher-oath bill on Hearst's urging. In Academe as elsewhere in the society this was the worst period of repression since the First World War, and further instances multiplied, especially in Mayor LaGuardia's New York City. Elsewhere the plea of economic retrenchment was naturally invoked to cover the dismissals of the unorthodox. The New Jersey State College for Women dropped an anti-Nazi professor whose department head heiled Hitler. A Chicago school fostered a student flying squad to conduct political inquisitions, with physical torture, of fellow-students, but public exposure brought this to a reluctant end.

In New York City the Riot Squad was used to silence speakers urging new schools at an open meeting of the Board of Education. The Superintendent of Schools called for the ouster of radical and subversive teachers, ignoring the protests of the Reverend Reinhold Niebuhr, new head of the Union's Committee on Academic Freedom. Suspensions and dismissals of teachers and students multiplied; the ACLU protested that even parents and taxpayers were gagged by the Board of Education. In two cases Osmond K. Fraenkel, representing the Union, made the Board retreat: he won an order for a high-school diploma refused to a boy for having criticised his school lunch-room, and a salary increase for a teacher from whom it had been withheld because of an accusation that had never been brought to trial. But he could do nothing, despite considerable efforts, for twenty-one anti-Fascist CCNY students who traveled to Yankee Stadium to protest the city's welcome of Mussolini's athletes, though even the dean of CCNY urged the Board of Higher Education not to invoke sanctions. Somehow a bill became law that opened a slight door for the teachers under persecution: they might seek redress in court, which had hitherto been forbidden. The city's schools were the target for a legislative investigation of radicalism, but it died quickly.

Violations of academic freedom were by no means limited to public institutions or unknown in the higher learning. Harvard tried to discharge two economics instructors who had organised a teachers' union, but they were cleared by a presidentially ap-

pointed committee of nine professors after 130 faculty members
had signed a petition of protest. Three years later Harvard was
to bar a campus speech by Earl Browder because of his conviction of passport fraud: so eminent a precedent was eagerly followed elsewhere. Other schools got rid of faculty men who favored the Spanish Loyalists, spoke well of labor unions and "unduly stressed" sex in courses on family life. Hays sued to compel
Columbia to reinstate a student ousted for leading a demonstration at the home of the univesity's president, Nicholas Murray
Butler, to protest Butler's acceptance of a Nazi Government invitation to the University of Heidelberg. And, in 1940, LaGuardia once more demonstrated the worth of his liberalism by giving
all the aid and comfort at his command to the successful effort
to prevent Earl Russell from filling an appointment to teach at
City College.

Russell's views on sexual freedom were almost outmoded by
the time City College thought it safe to have him teach philosophy—his principal field of knowledge and interest and one in which
there would be little or no opportunity, even if the aging noble
lord were so minded, to press the sheltered students of CCNY
into lives of sin. The appointment was denounced by reverend
clergy of all shades, as well as by such staunch family newspapers
as *The Journal, The Mirror* and *The News,* all of which lived
—handsomely—by purveying juicy vicarious sexual experience to
the city's *Analphabeten* in equal parts with fulsome coverage of
Holy Mother Church. A taxpayer's suit was filed against the Board
of Higher Education—Lord Russell was nowhere represented,
though the Union protested that he should have been made a
party to the action and Fraenkel volunteered to represent him.
Fraenkel's diaries reveal that whatever defense the Board might
have wished to make was hobbled by directives from LaGuardia,
whose own inordinate Puritanism was far stronger than any interest he might ever have had in civil liberties or intellectual freedom. Russell was not made a party, the taxpayer won his action
in a judicial *rodomontade* on Russell's moral unfitness to enter
the stainless City of New York, and an appeal to the state's highest court failed on the shabbiest technicalities, such as the lack of
a verification of the defense's answer to the complaint and the

fact that one step had been taken a day later than the statutory time.

Not long before the United States' entrance into the Second World War the New York Board of Education adopted a resolution forbidding the teaching of Communism, Naziism or Fascism "for the purpose of indoctrinating students." What the Union objected to here was what it had fought seven years earlier when a similar rule was legislated for the District of Columbia: that in New York as in Washington Hearst or one of his ilk might persuade the Board that even the explanation of a philosophy was indoctrination. In the ensuing years, even explanation was expressly forbidden in the statutes of a number of states, some of which stipulated that Communism might be explained provided the instructor explained also that "Americanism" was of course infinitely superior. There was always the risk that some students might hear about Communism even if it was not in the curriculum: the University of Michigan forbade its charges to join the American Student Union, which later became American Youth for Democracy. Though New York City never explicitly went so far, the continuance of LaGuardia's extra-legal methods in dealing with problems of the schools, as well as with those of public employes and criminal defendants, made it necessary for the Union to censure him publicly.

On the whole, the period of the Second World War was a relatively calm interlude on the campuses. Even the bluenoses were too preoccupied with other dangers to the body politic to give much attention to what went on among the long-hairs, and the nation went back to viewing the teacher with the same more or less tolerant condescension in which it had held him until the First World War. But even before the beginning of the cold war the hot pursuit was renewed. American Youth for Democracy was outlawed on several campuses and the Union protested that any group—Communist, Fascist or whatever—should have full freedom on any campus, on the ground of visibility as well as that of principle, unless it was deceptive as to its real character. In Newark and New York the Catholic domination produced another incursion on the liberty of the schools: the Boards of Education of both cities discontinued their subscriptions to *The Nation* because of

Paul Blanshard's articles exposing that domination. Not long afterward, at the instigation of the barely remembered Sons of the American Revolution (presumably the brothers of the matriarchal daughters), the HUAC called on a hundred colleges to submit their social-science texts for inspection as to the degree of their Americanism, and only some colleges refused. An effort in Illinois to repeal the tax exemptions of the University of Chicago and Roosevelt College because of their alleged un-American activities was defeated, but it was a sign and a portent. So was the Michigan Supreme Court's approval of the expulsion of a student, without a hearing, because of his off-campus political activities.

In Febuary, 1949, the Union's Committee on Academic Freedom, now headed by Professor Eduard C. Lindeman of the New York School of Social Work, published a twelve-page pamphlet called *Civil Liberties of Teachers and Students.* It included a statement of policy by the Union's directors, who made three points:

—The Union opposed any prohibition of employment as a teacher to anyone on the sole basis of his political views or associations.

—The Union would not defend teachers discharged after proof that they had misused their positions to indoctrinate their students.

—The Union might intervene in appropriate cases of college teachers whose discharges were not based on the judgment of their colleagues, as distinguished from the judgment of trustees or administrative officials, and in contested cases of public-school teachers where the principles of tenure were not observed.

Indicating some willingness to entertain modified standards for purely religious institutions, the pamphlet defined *academic freedom* as the liberty to investigate, to present and to discuss facts and ideas concerning the phenomena of human society and of the physical world in all branches and fields of learning, with no limitations other than those imposed by the generally accepted standards of conscientious scholarship. It includes the right of both teachers and students to be free, both within and without the institutions of learning, from any special limitations regarding the investigation of facts and the expression and discussion of ideas. The community, the pamphlet emphasised justly, "has neither the right nor indeed any social justification to demand that deviations from accepted principles be excluded from teaching. It may properly insist that such deviations be clearly labeled as such and that students will not be led to believe that they in fact meet general acceptance." While the community might reasonably expect of a teacher the same standards of personal conduct expected of any responsible professional (a concession that is not a loop-hole but a tunnel) and a standard of professional conduct consonant with his position, "the teacher must not be deemed to have sacrificed any of his rights as a private citizen."

The pamphlet was precise in its stipulation of the right to free research and publication (without prejudice to professional duties), to free classroom discussion of relevant matters and to encouragement of discussion of controversial matter. A positive stand on a public issue, the Union said, does not impair the critical state of mind required for research and teaching; nor does adherence to a professional organisation for the protection of group interests. Students should be encouraged to engage in extra-curricular activity providing "a working model of democracy" without pre-censorship of any form of expression and with the right, when a student organisation must have a faculty adviser, to participate in his selection.

The document itself is characteristically academic. There is little to which one can take exception except its omissions: the most important was the right of the student to a private life in which his lawful participation in community issues, on or off campus, was not subject to inhibition by the school. Nothing was said in this roseate leaflet about procedures for the protection of teachers who might be accused of behavior frowned on by their employers: a child-like confidence in the good faith of their fellow-educators seems to have unduly mellowed the authors and distracted them from such realities as the denial of due process. Subsequent pamphlets and policy revisions, however, were to remedy the lacks and to ground a constantly more virile program of practical aid to the basic concept of academic freedom. Very soon the library as well as the school was to be embraced in the Union's concept, for the need was already being made manifest by the Bartlesville, Oklahoma, vigilante committee that made the local library throw out *The Nation, The New Republic, Soviet Russia Today,*

Negro Digest, Consumer Reports and the librarian, Ruth Brown, who had held the job for twenty-five years but had made the tactical error of participating in a YWCA interracial program.

A thousand local McCarthys pursued the academicians. The University of California dismissed eighteen and had to drop the forty-eight courses they taught because of refusal to sign a loyalty oath, later invalidated, and a disavowal of subversion. The Union went into court for eight New York City teachers dismissed for insubordination and "unbecoming conduct" because they refused to say whether they had ever subverted; and Queens College disciplined a student group that invited one of the eight to speak. The school board of Levittown, New York, ordered the destruction of phonograph records made by a company some of whose personnel had "questionable" connections. The American Legion in Fairlawn, New Jersey, compelled a nursery school to drop other records made by blacklisted performers and containing a story of a city's foundation that omitted all reference to private business. The United States Supreme Court upheld New York's Feinberg Law, which barred *subversive* teachers from the public schools, and this precipitated a fresh outbreak of persecution because of the refusal of the decent element in the teaching profession to play stool-pigeon. In contrast to "liberal" New York, San Antonio and its conservative element helped the Union to overthrow an effort to label every book in the city's libraries that the blacklisters considered either "Communist" or merely "subversive." The store operated by the University of California refused to handle *The National Guardian* because some students called it Communist (it was merely fellow-traveling), explaining that as a matter of policy the store would not handle any publication complained of by more than three students. A Niagara of complaints against Hearst's *San Francisco Examiner, The Reader's Digest, Time, Life* and the *Saturday Evening Post* swept away the "policy." But, at the height of mccarthyism, an Alabama court voided the state's law requiring all textbooks to contain warranties that their authors and the authors of any works cited by them were politically clean.

Queens College warned Harold Lenz that it would relieve him of his deanship if he continued "political activities offensive to his community," and it carried out the threat, against which the Union was powerless. The Union condemned the University of Colorado for using private detectives to investigate its faculty's past and present politics and for refusing to protect its teachers against irresponsible attacks. In Iowa a Catholic public-school teacher was fired for sending his own child to a parochial school. A number of colleges suspended publications, organisations and meetings under rules modeled on the McCarran Act, alleging but never defining "subversion of the college"—again the Union could win no modification. In Pawtucket, Rhode Island, all study of the United Nations' Educational, Scientific and Cultural Organisation was forbidden because the UNESCO was under "atheist domination." Sapulpa, Oklahoma, school officials burned all books condemned by a local women's group for obscenity, subversion or "improper language in the treatment of ideas." But the Union aborted the efforts of the patriots of Englewood, New Jersey, to dictate the choice of teaching materials.

A House committee under Representative Carroll Reece of Tennessee launched an exhaustive investigation of tax-free education foundations for what it called leftism, statism and internationalism. One recalcitrant committeeman, Representative Wayne L. Hays, read aloud several documents circulated by various foundations and denounced by the committee's expert as closely comparable to Communist ideals: Hays then identified the material as excerpts from encyclicals of those dangerous radicals, Popes Leo XIII and Pius XI. The crusade of one section of American academics against colleagues who adopted Lysenko's biological theories and thereby became Communists was thrown into confusion in July, 1954, when the Soviet Union, which is so like the United States in so many respects, forbade further teaching of Lysenko theory as subversive of Communism. Senator Jenner of Indiana demanded federal supervision of loyalty in all colleges, private and public; McCarthy sought to end tax exemption for those that, in his view and cliché, were "soft on Communism." Some school districts withdrew trucking contracts from any company that also carried UNESCO literature; teachers who had already answered every possible question were dismissed when on this ground they refused to answer again, and, amazingly, the Lincoln, Nebraska, post of the American Legion demanded that they be let alone. A Brooklyn College professor's Fulbright Scholarship was revoked because his wife refused to testify about her own politics.

The Union revised its pamphlets on academic freedom to insist first of all that in the selection of teaching materials the teacher alone should judge their fitness. In addition, the Union came out of the grove and into the arena, demanding for accused teachers the customary presumption of innocence and the right of confrontation and cross-examination of accusers. Summary dismissal, the Union said, should be limited to those instances in which serious violations of law or of "morality" had been admitted or proved before competent courts—a position flawed by its concession to the herd on private conduct. Special awards were made by the Union in 1954 to those pitifully few who stood firm against the know-nothings and made a reality of academic freedom: the voters, newspaper and school board of Scarsdale, New York: Professors Frank Richardson and Walter Van Tilburg Clark of the University of Nevada, President John A. Mackay of the Princeton Theological Seminary, President Robert M. Hutchins of the University of Chicago and the Ford Foundation. Against this honor roll was a series of episodes in Philadelphia that characterised the behavior of the overwhelming majority of school boards and administrators throughout the nation. The following instances are summarised from a 1954 pamphlet of the Greater Philadelphia Branch of the Union, *Academic Freedom*: *Some Recent Philadelphia Episodes*.

On February 27, 1953, Dr. Barrows Dunham, chairman of the philosophy department at Temple University, took the Fifth Amendment before the HUAC. The Supreme Court had long since ruled—reiterating the traditional common law—that no one was warranted in drawing any inference against any witness or defendant who relied on his privilege against self-incrimination. But Temple suspended Dunham pending a "loyalty" investigation of its own: in this inquiry he answered all questions freely insofar as they concerned only himself and he was found to be unquestionably "loyal." This having been accomplished, he was discharged without hearing or explanation. When the Union protested, the university replied that, if the matter were made public, further charges would be made against Dunham in retaliation. Dunham refused to be blackmailed and, despite the widest publicity on his case, the university took no reprisal. At no time did it allege against Dunham any incompetence, moral delinquency or conviction of crime. There was no faculty participation. Though he was heard on a loyalty charge, he was dismissed on that of taking the Fifth Amendment, on which he had no hearing.

Later in the year Jefferson Medical College questioned a number of its teachers on their political associations. Each spoke freely of himself and was found not only "loyal" but also "not subversive"; but none of them would discuss third persons. Thereupon they were discharged without any explanation either to them or to the public. At no time had there been any participation by the faculty in the investigation; and in mid-course, without warning to the accused, the rules of procedure had been changed and the college insisted that it was under no obligation to the accused to let them know that they were now being tried under a new code.

The city's Board of Education was simultaneously combing out the menaces from the public schools. Twenty-six teachers who had satisfactorily answered all the Board's questions and taken the state oath required by Pennsylvania's Pechan Act were summarily dismissed when they refused to perform for a HUAC roadshow appearance in Philadelphia—where the HUAC's counsel turned out to be the man appointed by the state Attorney General to find violations of the Pechan Act and where the HUAC spectacle had been well prepared by a flood of propaganda exploiting the Smith Act trials and the "Red menace" at the shores and borders of the Home of the Brave.

The principles and procedures in these cases were further refined elsewhere. The California Supreme Court in effect nullified the rights of teachers to invoke the Fifth Amendment by ruling that teachers as a class must answer certain questions when an affirmative reply meant automatic dismissal. The Massachusetts Supreme Judicial Court approved the dismissal of a non-tenure teacher who refused to say whether he had ever lured innocent children into the Party's lair: his refusal to answer, the court held, was conduct unbecoming a teacher because, even if in truth he had never lured a single child, his silence destroyed public confidence in him and thus rendered him ineffective as a teacher. But the real test of a teacher's *sincerity* was not his willingness to strip himself naked for the crowd: it was whether he would e- qually degrade others. Compulsory stool-pigeon activities were most insisted on in New York—Harvard refused to act against fa- culty members who insisted on respecting the right of others to privacy, but Cornell threw them out. The Union took up the out- standing New York case, that of Professor Harry Slochower, who had been dismissed from Brooklyn College solely for his refusal to submit. The New York City Board of Education ordered all teachers questioned about their colleagues to answer in detail, but this ukase, protested by the Union, was overruled by the State Ed- ucation Commissioner, James Allen, not only because it was out- rageous but also because the Board already had the power under the iniquitous Feinberg Law to conduct an inquisition of any teacher it chose. It was not a teacher's duty, Allen and the Union held, to be a stalking horse for his nominal superiors.

The Supreme Court refused to allow New York to get rid of Slochower solely for refusing to answer the impertinences of a Senate committee. In court after court the Board of Education sought to overrule Allen's reversal of the stool-pigeon order un- der which it hoped to confirm Slochower's ouster, but, after con- sistent defeats in the state courts—where not only the Union but also the Teachers' Guild, the American Jewish Congress and the Public Education Association joined to back Allen—it was at last constrained to yield.

In 1955 the chairmanship of the Union's committee passed to Louis M. Hacker, a professor of economics and a dean at Colum- bia, and an aggressive, practical civil-libertarian whose first work for the Union, twenty years earlier, had been a pamphlet, *The Struggle for Civil Liberty on the Land*, which set forth the right of farm owners, tenants, laborers and sharecroppers to organ- ise and picket. Hacker, who justly prides himself on his executive and administrative ability, included both non-New Yorkers and non-academics on the committee, set up sub-committees for in- dividual knotty problems and soon built the committee into an unofficial mediator in disputes as well as an investigator of complaints and a remarkably successful friendly intervenor.

There were some early defeats under Hacker's chairmanship, when southern states were banning textbooks that "did not accord with the southern way of life" and teachers who advocated "planned economy, collectivism, one-world government and other anti-American doctrines," and when the University of Texas tried to force out a student editor who, like President Eisenhower (fortunately beyond the university's reach), opposed a Congressional bill to protect an industrial monopoly of natural-gas resources. Nor could one committee contest at the same time each of the hundreds of dismissals for lectures, refusals to blacken colleagues and invocations of the privilege not to incriminate oneself. And the committee's work was surcharged by a new pretext for denying academic freedom: integration. The advocacy of integration and activity to further it were to be the cause of penalties not only for teachers but for students in many parts of the country besides the Slough of Despond below the Mason-Dixon Line. The right of teacher and student to be citizens, as well as the right of student organisations to keep their membership lists to themselves, were to be zealously furthered by the Union, which began also to concern itself with the growing problem of the disclosure of school and college records of students. The growth of the Union's activity for academic freedom was, in at least one recorded case, to mean the loss of an academic job on the sole ground of the applicant's membership in the ACLU.

In Illinois the Union failed to overthrow the state's Broyles Law requiring loyalty oaths of teachers, on the ground that the law's intent was found to be "not to probe minds with the intention to punish for unorthodox beliefs . . . but rather to ascertain a primary quality for the instruction of youth . . . the state must protect the integrity of its schools against their perversion to subversive ends." But the Chief Justice of the United States sided with the Union on behalf of academic freedom by striking down the contempt conviction of Professor Paul M. Sweezy, who, having lectured on Marxism at the University of New Hampshire, refused the state Attorney General's demand for a transcript. But it took nine years for the Supreme Court to undo the Washington law that had purged two professors from a university because of their refusal to sign an oath—a case that came before the Supreme Court several times as, on remand to state courts, the law and the Constitution were ignored and the Union had to file new appeals for Professors Nostrand and Savelle. Ultimately, avoiding the issues of the First Amendment and the law's provision for dismissal without hearing, the Supreme Court found unconstitutional for vagueness the two oaths required of teachers: a pledge to promote respect for government institutions and an affirmation that the teacher was not a "subversive person."

To an organisation dedicated to protecting and furthering the whole philosophy of civil liberties, with particular emphasis on those of students, a survey of 560 freshmen at Northwestern University in 1957 must have been singularly disheartening. The overwhelming majority of these neophytes of the higher learning rejected out of hand the right of an accused to confront his accuser, the Constitutional reservations of rights to the people and the protection against double jeopardy; a bare majority approved the principle of public trials, the right of public assembly and the privilege against self-incrimination. A series of such surveys over the 1951-61 decade was to prove even more discouraging as high school and college students everywhere indicated massive repugnance to freedoms of speech and religion, to due-process protections for criminal defendants and to rights of conscience. In highly ironic contrast, parallel student surveys in Japan disclosed an overpowering preoccupation with the protection and expansion of civil liberties in accordance with all the basic principles of the Bill of Rights that so revolted the young of the nation for which it was framed.

Meanwhile, despite the battlements erected by red-blooded American youth to keep out ideas and keep down whatever intellect it might possess, the Union widened its few breaches in the fortifications of bigotry and opened a few new ones. Further discouragement was met—and overcome—in the teaching profession: the National Education Association generally pussyfooted on all real issues of academic freedom, and even the American Association of University Professors revealed a high content of foot-clay when the furor in the south over professors who backed integration led the AAUP to find that its profession was exposed to grave harm by any teacher's "ill-advised public acts or utterances" on this or any other general issue. The best way to correct abuses, the Union had to point out to the pusillanimous pedagogues, is to expose and combat them. In 1957 the Union's Committee on Academic Freedom issued a carefully reasoned critique of the 1953 statement of the Association of American Universities on *The Rights and Responsibilities of Universities and Their Faculties.*

The AAU's document was intended to curb the heretic-hunts but the Union found, constrained by the internal evidence, that if anything the AAU would further them if its members felt bound by the statement (its constitution left them at least theoretical autonomy). Though the AAU professed to endorse full freedom of research and teaching, it inveighed against the teacher's exercising his rights as a citizen in unpopular causes; worse, it called on the profession to be "united in loyalty...to the moral code, to the country and to its form of government" and to be "diligent and loyal in citizenship." The Union rightly objected to the use of a word so peculiarly susceptible to misconstruction and perversion as *loyalty*: what of the teacher who lied about his residence in order to obtain a divorce, the Union asked; or who criticises specific government policies; or who prefers the British system of government? The AAU condemned Soviet "thought control—the dictation of doctrines which [the academics had not read Fowler] must be accepted and taught by all parties." The Union was at least as opposed as the AAU to *thought control*—but what, it asked, was the AAU's recommendation of professorial silence on many matters touched by what the AAU called "the prevailing anxieties"? The Union's retort was sharp: "The presidents of our universities are on dubious ground in endorsing an orthodoxy of fear." Similarly the Union rightly denounced the AAU's condemnation of defiance of abusive inquisitions and its analogy between ideas considered abhorrent or dangerous and the menace of deadly disease or military invasion.

Such cowardice as that of teachers and students alike, of course, made it even easier than it might otherwise have been for the passage of the 1958 National Defense Education Act, which endangered experiment and diversity and retained the old provision, long challenged by the Union, and later by President Kennedy, that every student seeking federal financial assistance must sign a loyalty oath and disavow subversive memberships,. Similar procedures governed awards by the Board of Foreign Scholarships appointed by Eisenhower. Many colleges refused federal funds; the student ACLU chapter at the University of Indiana was denounced in the Legislature as a "Red front"; a University of Nebraska law professor was formally accused of belonging to the Union. Though none of this sort of thing eased the Union's work, its intervention helped now and then to restore the jobs of teachers unjustly ousted on political grounds; the imminent danger of litigation and its attendant publicity must also have influenced some administrators. Others, like those of the University of California at Berkeley, ignored the ACLU. As long ago as 1958 it had vainly challenged the order of that institution forbidding recognised student organisations to take any positions on off-campus issues (at UCLA, at the same time, the faculty anticipated a Union policy declaration by several years, refusing to disclose private and political information about students to prospective employers). The Berkeley tyranny has been the target of persistent student and Union attack ever since, particularly because of its invocation to curb student support of civil rights.

The growth of restrictions on students was paced by a resurgence of attacks on textbooks and libraries toward the end of the 1950 decade. In the south, of course, integration was the principal victim, but its leadership was closely contested by publications furthering "Communism" and internationalism: Texas and southern California in particular have been more frightened than any other state by the United Nations and the UNESCO— the UNESCO's offense is "preaching world citizenship." Elsewhere the most general tests for reading matter were what the patriots termed "common-sense economics," *subversion* in general, *fads* and *frills*: what was called for was a hard-headed return to "the three R's." Its advocates relied for their judgments on the DAR, the FBI, the United States Chamber of Commerce, *The National Review* and America's Future, Inc., which set up an evaluation board. In Florida a legislator attacked one book because, he said, it praised the ACLU for its dedication to the overthrow of the Government. Tennessee and Texas, in 1965, are still screening textbooks for references to evolution. But Torrington, Connecticut, resisted the NAACP's demand to suppress any book containing the word *nigger* (one wonders whether the NAACP would have excepted the writings of Dick Gregory on behalf of civil rights). In Florida, Orwell's *1984* and Huxley's *Brave New World* were outlawed under the *aegis* of an Education Commissioner who, when questioned on the blacklist, admitted that he had never heard of either book or its author! As late as 1962 the Union fought—and beat—the dismissal of four Maryland professors who assigned *Lolita, Lady Chatterley's Lover* and *Tropic of Cancer* to their classes. Texans for America opposed giving both sides of controversies because to do so would only confuse the young.

Even the Special Preparedness Subcommittee of the Senate Armed Services Committee had got its bellyful by 1962, when it issued its report, quoted by the Union two years later in a pamphlet called *Combatting Undemocratic Pressures on Schools and Libraries,* on *The Military Cold War and Speech Review Policies,* which said: "We concur with Rear Admiral William O. Moot, Judge Advocate General of the Navy, in his statement that amateur anti-Communists 'are about as useful as amateur brain surgeons' and that we have no need for 'space-age witch-hunters.' " The Union's pamphlet restated the basic position on freedom of utterance, summarising some of the more outrageous attempts to purge schools and libraries—even Plato was subversive in many communities, and the DAR denounced all books referring to the United States as a *democracy* rather than a *republic*. Intended as a guide for local communities threatened by academic and library censorship, the pamphlet instructed the reader, whenever the fire was lighted, to form citizens' committees and agitate for resistance, enlist press help and turn to local colleges, various educational and library associations and the Union itself.

Meanwhile the Union's activities on behalf of individual teachers began to show increasing success—except in the south, where teacher attitudes on integration were the major source of invasions of academic freedom and where the Union could not hope to play Canute against the sea of bigotry. Four Philadelphia teachers who had invoked the First and Fifth Amendments before various Torquemadas were assisted to reinstatement when the Pennsylvania Supreme Court held that their discharges were reprisals for their use of their Constitutional privileges and that the exercise of such privilege was irrelevant to any judgment of professional competence. The Union went to the defense of Professor Edward V. Sittler of Long Island University, dismissed solely because of the malicious disclosure that during the war he had renounced American citizenship in order to propagandise on the radio for the Nazis: his professional competence was unquestioned, as was his classroom conduct. The Union backed the appeal of a California teacher discharged for writing letters to newspapers that criticised the public-school administration and the bureaucracy of the state teachers' association. The Union battled the dismissal of Leo Koch by the University of Illinois for having advocated pre-marital sexual experience—advocacy contained not in class lectures but in the college newspaper's symposium on sexual ethics.

The Union's battle against the oath of loyalty and the disclaimer of subversion required under the National Defense Education Act made no practical headway though it gained distinguished and sometimes unexpected allies. Harvard, Yale and Princeton led twenty-two universities in withdrawing from the program set up by the Act, solely to protest its repressions, which eighty-three other institutions had publicly disapproved. Catholics formed a new civil-liberties group, the Catholic Council on Civil Liberties, which denounced all forms of oaths and disclaimers, and the American Legion for advocating them. A study made by the Union showed that federal financing was supporting two-thirds of the nation's research in schools and posing the gravest threat of federal control through these subsidies, the "clearances" imposed on faculty and students, the furtherance of so-called *team* research and the deterrence of individual exploration (a characteristic of the century, not only of the nation or of capitalism, and especially dangerous to an ostensibly anti-collectivist society—though no society is really anti-collectivist), and the neglect of the humanities and of social studies (inaccurately called social *sciences*). Ultimately Congress retained the oath, without the disclaimer, in the Defense Education Act, adding authority, denounced by the Union, to withhold government aid when such action is found to be "in the best interests of the United States" or when the applicant is a knowing member of any organisation that may be found to be subversive.

Both Government and private employers regularly sought from colleges not only information on the scholastic and professional competence of job applicants but unwarranted information on their private and political lives. Many corporations, like General Electric, advised executive aspirants that they should have no record of or interest in action on controversial matters; many Government agencies, like many employers, relied on the most absurd and irrelevant evaluations of character and personality to guide their selections of personnel—and thus, often, to eliminate those who could contribute most—and not only the charlatans of the testing business but the applicants' former teachers were asked to supply information. Though it was primarily concerned with political discrimination, the Union called on teachers to resist such violations of the right of privacy from whatever source. In a 1961 pamphlet called *Teacher Disclosures of Information About Students to Prospective Employers*, the Union reminded the school men that the teacher-student relation creates a privity and privacy analogous to those of doctor and patient, lawyer and client, priest and penitent. Recognising the fact that every job should be filled by the man best fitted for it and the further fact that some highly sensitive Government work required assurance of loyalty, the Union insisted, with complete justice, that the teacher should answer no outsider's question relating to a student's loyalty and patriotism, political, religious, moral or social beliefs and attitudes, general outlook or private life.

In the current decade the problems have not altered for either teachers or students; the offenders have become not more numerous but more surprising: Brandeis University was castigated by the Union when it reprimanded a professor for criticising Kennedy's indefensible provocation of Cuba and Russia in 1962. The Union backed the University of Illinois when it announced its support for Professor Revilo P. Oliver, whom the "liberals" wanted discharged because of his manic Fascist attacks on Kennedy; the ACLU had to attack the University of Minnesota, however, because it refused to permit meetings of Barry Goldwater's acolytes, Young Americans for Freedom. Probably the most indefensible act of recent years, which the Union is still contesting, is the fingerprinting of all teachers in Maryland. Prophylactically, the Union hopes to minimise future invasions of academic freedom

by its issuance of pamphlets for, and its initiation of direct negotiations with, the vast number of new colleges springing up everywhere without any concept of the meaning of academic freedom.

18

Set a Thief to Catch a Thief

I think it a less evil that some criminals should escape than that
the Government should play an ignoble part.

—Justice Holmes

"I know that we missed coming to grips with the settled police
malpractice all over the country," Roger Baldwin said in 1954.
"But the police everywhere are petty tyrants and no effort short
of a change in the whole American concept of the relation between police and public, say along the lines of the British, who
respect civil rights, would have got rid of the tyranny. But it is
an immense task beyond our resources." The American Civil
Liberties Union is nevertheless, despite its early indifference
to the problem, the only organisation in the country that has devoted a quarter-century and more to an implacable war against
the tyranny, often with no allies at all. Though it is still true, as
Baldwin said in 1964, that the policeman's beat and the minor
courts are where injustice begins and where civil liberties are
most flouted, the Union has scored such significant triumphs in
its battle for the basic rights of man guaranteed by the Constitution that in some jurisdictions even the indigent defendant now has

a practical chance of justice and in other jurisdictions he may not even be punched or kicked. Perhaps the best measure of the Union's very real accomplishments in making a reality of due process is the number and *timbre* of the howls of those who are the enemies that any man of taste would choose.

In a non-moral sense, the fact of any criminality by police, whether brutality or blackmail or perjury, should shock no honest mind. Police work, in any society and under any form of government, can by its nature attract only the less admirable elements of the population. Minority groups afford virtually the only valid exception, since to their members police work often appears —fallaciously, as they learn—the only egress from the unwalled ghetto maintained by the majority. This exception aside, almost every policeman everywhere is a potential Fascist: if he were not, he could never contemplate being a policeman. *It takes one to catch one*, the old folk belief about police, is not unfounded: where but in the police can one gratify with impunity one's need to extort and tyrannise and to vent sadistic drives, whether physical or psychic? Coming as he does from the crowd, the policeman can hardly be expected to rise above its fears, its envies and their consequent hatreds.

Arrests and convictions, furthermore, are his only ladder to advancement. If there are not more false arrests and unjust convictions, it is only because the fabrication of charges and evidence is limited by the policeman's knowledge of what the traffic will bear and by his appraisal of the probabilities of success. Policemen (and prosecutors, their twins), like politicians, are an unfortunate necessity of society, but both are armed servants who must be kept under constant restraint lest they enslave their creators.

In the preoccupation with loftier matters that characterised its first decade, the ACLU hardly noticed the daily violations of civil liberties and law by which Prohibition was enforced. It has been suggested that in part this blind spot might well have arisen out of the fact that so many of the Union's early leaders were social workers, clergymen and reformers to whom, at least in the abstract, Prohibition seemed genuinely desirable because of the manifold evils of drink. It had appealed, too, to the architects

of the proletariat's paradise, who had viewed liquor as a tool of
capitalist enslavement and who believed that in a workers' state
no one would even want alcohol; but they had reluctantly given
in to the reality of that human appetite, if no other. But the ACLU
was too concerned elsewhere even to think about it or to take
cognisance of the greater evils uniformly practiced in the holy
war against the brewer, the vintner and the distiller. The same
or analogous evils, however, rapidly became familiar to the Union in its defense of the non-criminal. To every policeman and
prosecutor—and to far too many courts, even after almost a
half-century of ACLU struggle in which even the bar associations
have often been enlisted on the side of the angels—every Constitutional guaranty is merely an obstacle to his work that is to
be avoided or overcome by whatever means. In those courts
susceptible to either the passions of the mob or the fear of its power, these guaranties meant no more than they did in the back
room of the police station or in the office of an ambitious prosecutor. Arrest of persons and seizure of property without warrants;
the issuance of warrants with full knowledge of their insufficiency
or defectiveness; brutality in arrests and interrogations; coercion
of confessions; perjured testimony; denial of the right of counsel;
unreasonable detention *incommunicado*; denial of the right to
confront and cross-examine; unreasonable postponements of
trial; excessive bail; cruel and unusual punishment; commitment to asylums without examination—these were the common-
places that a complacent citizenry refused to acknowledge or
even condoned in the pursuit of some *noble* goal, as it connived
at the frequent rejection of the common-law presumption of innocence.

Neither the police nor the magistrates were necessarily hamp-
ered by what the statute books said. In 1921 the New York City
police broke up a ball given by a magazine called *The Liberator*,
alleging as the sole ground for allegations of disorderly conduct
the fact that "Negroes were dancing with white women." In
Old Forge, Pennsylvania, in 1923, town officials kidnapped and
deported two Socialist speakers, then arrested them for returning to town. The Mayor of Johnstown, in the same state, ordered
all Negroes and Mexicans of less than seven years' residence to

leave, but Union protests forced him to withdraw the order (he was defeated in the next election). Baldwin and eight other members of the American Organising Committee of the Russian Industrial Colony Kuzbas, a high-minded experiment intended to further pure collectivism in Russia with American help, were indicted for grand larceny on the basis of charges made by the infamous Bureau of Investigation and its political division headed by J. Edgar Hoover, as well as New York City's Bomb (!) Squad. Arthur Garfield Hays procured a court order for the inspection of the grand jury's minutes, which were so shockingly barren of evidence that a judge dismissed the indictment at once.

The outstanding instances of unconstitutional prosecution and conviction in the decade after the First World War were, of course, those of Sacco and Vanzetti in Boston and of Mooney and Billings in California. Through a special committee headed by former Mayor Henry T. Hunt of Cincinnati, the Union was active in both (until Mooney, despite his gratitude for the Union's efforts, asked it to withdraw and leave his case entirely in the hands of an *ad hoc* labor defense committee), but Sacco and Vanzetti were executed despite the insistence of eminent lawyers and jurists here and abroad that they had never had a fair trial and that in all probability they were innocent; and Mooney and Billings, who could not escape conviction, had to fall back on pardon proceedings, which were ultimately successful. In the Sacco-Vanzetti case, the Justice Department withheld from the defense (though it was a state prosecution) evidence that it knew would have helped the accused, and the Union's disclosure of the fact was shrugged off. Tom Mooney and Warren K. Billings, union organisers arrested in 1916 on false charges of having planned and executed a Preparedness Day bombing in San Francisco, were promptly convicted and sentenced to life imprisonment on the basis of evidence that the Governor of California later denounced as having been bought and paid for—and faked. Even the trial judge and jury, a dozen years later, were convinced that they had convicted and sentenced innocent men, but the state allowed itself to be bullied by propaganda by public-utility companies frightened of the "revolutionaries"—though Mooney was a single-

minded union man who had rejected all political philosophies
and Billings had never known or cared about ideologies of any
kind. For years the Union was instrumental in aiding their fight
for pardons, until in 1933 Mooney asked it to withdraw. Twice
John F. Finerty of the Union's board went to the Supreme Court
on *habeas* writs but California ignored the court's orders to re-
open the case. The pardons followed a few years later.

In contrast, mob leaders and "peace officers"—police, sheriffs,
militia men, private police—who wantonly beat, shot and killed
labor organisers, radicals and ordinary pickets and strikers
were regularly acquitted, if indeed they were brought to trial.
In few instances could the Union compel the authorities to act
against these licensed savages; nor was it often successful when
bail for radicals and unionists was denied and, in contravention
of the Constitution, judges refused writs of *habeas corpus*. In New
York City, Police Commissioner Grover Whalen ordered a policy
of brutality against labor meetings, radicals and rallies of the unemployed. Not only the Union but so many other organisations,
many of them impeccably respectable, denounced his practices,
whose victims included, with a fine impartiality, common misdemeanants as well as political perils, that he resigned under
their fire, though both the Mayor and the Governor refused all
requests to remove him. Even after the famous Seabury investigations of the brutalities and frame-ups condoned and approved by
Whalen—hundreds of innocent women were arrested and convicted for prostitution on trumped-up charges made by Vice Squad
policemen trying to become detectives—nothing was done. His
successor was almost as bad; knowing the futility, the Union
nonetheless formally protested each incident of brutality for the
record. It was equally unsuccessful in its protest of the orders
given by the Governor of Illinois to the National Guard: in labor
disturbances, "shoot to kill." Southern police were of course doing this regularly against Negroes as well as *agitators*, and their
aim was always accurate. Invariably, public opinion sided with
the "peace officers", North and South. It was no less enthusiastic
in its support of President Herbert Hoover and General Douglas
MacArthur in the summer of 1932, when in the dead of night, under
Hoover's orders, MacArthur turned loose troops and tear gas a-

gainst the men, women and children camped outside Washington
in the march of the Bonus Expeditionary Force demanding payment of the soldiers' bonuses promised during the war almost
fifteen years earlier. Though forty-one prominent Americans
signed the Union's angry protest, Hoover's secretary refused delivery of that "tissue of misrepresentation of facts."

The public at large had equally refused delivery of the Report
of the Commission on Law Enforcement appointed by Hoover and
headed by Wickersham. Its report dealt not only with the immigration abuses already described but, specifically, with prosecutions, police, criminal procedure and what Wickersham himself
called "lawlessness in law enforcement." The report had helped
to awaken the Union to the neglected rights of the non-political
American unlucky enough to run into trouble with the law, and
already the Union had helped to defeat a bill that would have
legalised wiretapping, a practice only about five years younger
than the telephone. Throughout Prohibition the Government had
resorted to wiretapping to gather evidence, and in 1928 the issue
was first presented to the Supreme Court in Olmstead v. United
States. Chief Justice and former President William Howard Taft,
looking as narrowly as possible at the issue, rejected the argument
that wiretapping amounted to search and seizure without a warrant, prohibited by the Fourth Amendment: that amendment, he
held, applied only to things that could be physically seized. He
also rejected the argument that the privilege against self-incrimination was violated, since no one was compelled either to
use the telephone or, using it, to make damaging admissions.
Further, he declared, under common law the admissibility of evidence was not tainted by any illegality in its procurement—a ruling that in effect made mincemeat out of any prohibition against
methods of obtaining evidence. Both federal law and that of the
state where the case arose prohibited wiretapping.

The Olmstead case was notable not only for the injustice that
it consecrated but for the dissents that upheld the Constitution
and the rights of the individual and that have only piecemeal become, to a limited extent, the law today, when the "democratic"
sovereign still seeks to hold itself above its own law. Most notable
was that of Holmes, who was a philosopher as well as a judge,

and old-fashioned enough to believe in *noblesse oblige* as well as the *clean-hands* rule of equity. "Apart from the Constitution," he said, "the Government ought not to use evidence obtained, and only obtainable, by a criminal act...It is desirable that criminals should be detected, and to that end all available evidence should be used. *It is also desirable that the Government should not itself foster and pay for other crimes when they are the means by which the evidence is to be obtained* [italics added] . . . I think it a less evil that some criminals should escape than that the Government should play an ignoble part...The Constitution seems to me logically to lead to excluding evidence obtained by a crime of the officers of the law." That attitude was then, as it remains today, far too honorable for the crowd and its self-styled leaders: in my lifetime there has not been a President of the United States who has forbidden or even condemned entrapment by Government or its procurement of illegality in order to obtain convictions. Nor can any man of my generation name a single elected executive anywhere in the country who has imposed such a minimal standard of decency on his hired watchdogs. It is not a matter for wonder that crime grows in all levels of a society that condones and applauds lawless acts by its governors.

Brandeis also dissented, as did the arch-conservative Pierce Butler, who, however, did not concern himself with ethics: he was a property buff. "The communications belong to the parties between whom they pass," he said. "During their transmission the exclusive use of the wire belongs to the person served by it." But Butler went farther, rejecting Taft's fundamentalist literalism and so laying a foundation for many other broader interpretations: "This court has always construed the Constitution in the light of the principles on which it was founded. The direct operation or literal meaning of the words used do [*sic*] not measure the purpose or scope of its provisions. Under the principles established and applied by this court, the Fourth Amendment safeguards against all evils that are like and equivalent to those embraced within the ordinary meaning of its words."

With the latter part of his colleague's dissent Brandeis agreed; but he amplified its principle, and in addition he pointed out that it had already been agreed that the privacy of the mails fell within the protection of the Fourth Amendment (which perhaps should be recalled to the Johnson Administration and its admitted postal surveillance, as well as the FBI). Brandeis saw in wiretapping "the invasion of [the] indefeasible right of personal security, personal liberty and private property, where that right has never been forfeited by conviction of some public offense," and hence a forbidden "forcible and compulsory extortion of a man's own testimony or of his private papers to be used as evidence of a crime or to forfeit his goods." In this respect, Brandeis said, the Fourth and Fifth Amendments merged. "The mail," he said, "is a public service furnished by the Government. The telephone is a public service furnished by its authority. There is in essence no difference between the sealed letter and the private telephone message . . . The makers of our Constitution . . . sought to protect Americans in their beliefs, their thoughts, their emotions and their sensations. They conferred, as against the Government, the right to be let alone—the most comprehensive of rights and the right most valued by civilised men. To protect that right, every unjustifiable intrusion by the Government upon the privacy of the individual, whatever the means employed, must be deemed a violation of the Fourth Amendment. And the use as evidence, in a criminal proceeding, of facts ascertained by such intrusion must be deemed a violation of the Fifth . . . Experience should teach us to be most on our guard to protect liberty when the Government's purposes are beneficent." Defying the whole degrading trend of this century and as if warning what was to happen—and did happen—in a few years, Brandeis continued: "Decency, security and liberty alike demand that Government officials shall be subjected to the same rules of conduct that are commands to the citizens. In a government of laws, the existence of the Government will be imperiled if it fails to observe the law scrupulously...If the Government becomes a law-breaker, it breeds contempt for law; it invites every man to become a law unto himself; it invites anarchy. To declare that in the administration of the criminal law the end justifies the means...would bring terrible retribution. Against that pernicious doctrine this court should resolutely set its face."

In the forty years since these dissents were written, the American Civil Liberties Union, whose whole philosophy is summed up here by Brandeis, has spent almost all its energies in turning that court's and every court's reluctant face, in agonising inching progress, against the fatal hypocrisy with which the cynical tribunes of the people have sought not only to subvert justice within the nation's borders but to spread injustice throughout the world by economic sanctions and flagrant invasions of sovereign nations under a banner of selflessness as brazen as Hitler's "counterattacks with pursuit" against fictitious aggressions and Stalin's and Khrushchev's "liberations" of unenslaved peoples. What Brandeis decried and deplored has become, instead, the guiding "principle" of a Government that invades the rights of its subjects and the territories of its most distant and weakest neighbors, a Government whose subversions of honor both foreign and domestic have made its noble pretensions anathema among honest men at home and abroad. But is that to be wondered at in the light of the findings of Wickersham's investigation of lawless law enforcement some thirty years earlier?

For his time and his background Wickersham was, to the police and the prosecutors, a dangerous radical: his most heinous offense was to tell the truth without regard for their delicate sensibilities, and the recommendations that he made were largely embraced by the ACLU, which has in turn helped to win some acceptance of them by bar and bench. Prosecutors, federal and state, the report urged, should be taken out of the political area. Their function should include the protection of the rights of the accused from the moment of arrest; this, Wickersham believed, would minimise the need for public defenders and voluntary systems for the help of indigent defendants. The prosecutor's task, he added, was needlessly complicated by a great volume of unenforceable laws, notably Prohibition and its analogues, and by the prevailing low standards for police departments at all levels, as well as their poor pay and lack of modern communications equipment.

The report called also for revisions of criminal procedure, notably the elimination of arrest in petty offenses and, instead, the issuance of summonses. Jurors' examinations should be conducted by the court rather than by opposing counsel, and persons who wished to do so should be allowed to waive jury trial. The sim-plification of appeals procedures was also urged.

But the most important part of the report dealt with the law-lessness of the law enforcers. Some two hundred pages were de-voted to case histories of third-degree procedures alone, both physical and psychological—this was the subject of a special re-port by Professor Zechariah Chafee Jr. of Harvard Law School, Walter Pollack and Carl S. Stern. There were in addition 150 pages of documentation of other unfair police procedures. Wicker-sham and his assistants found no area where abuses were not widespread, especially the use of the third degree and various types of misconduct by prosecutors and judges, all of which were condemned in the strongest terms. Among the most common abus-es of process were unreasonable delays in trials, unjust choices of venue and the deprivation of counsel. The report concluded with specific concrete recommendations that read as if tailored for the ACLU, except for possibly two: permission for a judge to comment on a defendant's refusal to testify and authority for the court to discuss the weight of the factual evidence. These were the other recommendations:

—Statutes allowing the defense a minimum time for the prepa-ration of its case.

—State statutes on the model of the federal law automatically disqualifying a judge when a defendant files an affidavit of facts sufficient to constitute a real possibility of prejudice.

—The obligation of the prosecution to give a list of its witnes-ses to the defense in ample time before trial.

—The right of counsel in all cases except where the penalty is minimal or the right has been expressly waived.

—The elimination of discrimination in the selection of jurors.

—Clarification of the law covering the admissibility of evidence of crimes other than that charged.

—The abolition of the use of fines and costs to pay judges, pro-secutors and court officials.

—Authority for appellate courts to reduce sentences without new trials.

—Power in the appellate court to grant a new trial if justice re-quires it even when the defense has taken no exceptions in the trial court.

The Wickersham Commission's recommendations—which, surprisingly, dealt little with illegally obtained evidence—and the various opinions in the Olmstead case are essential to an understanding of the chasm between textbook principle and police and judicial practice that the Union set out to fill. Inevitably the battle for Constitutional protections was to spread beyond the courtroom into the hearing-room of the legislative investigating committee and ultimately into the practices of public and private institutions enjoying a punitive power over employes who in the increasing complexity of the economy were rapidly becoming the subjects of a vast interlocking confederation of management. But this is a relatively late development arising in part out of the lessons learned in the protection of the indigent and other criminally accused deprived of their rights *ab initio.*

Let us for the moment, charitably, concede that the corruption of justice by policemen and prosecutors may arise, not from whatever curious inner need drives them to be, as the common law so justly termed the Crown's counsel, the pursuers of their fellow-men; not from the power that their functions vest in them; not even from a Stakhanovite system that makes advancement in grade almost wholly contingent on a high output of arrests and convictions; but from daily contact with the evils with which they must contend. Even if it were valid, so merciful an explanation cannot become an excuse, let alone a justification, for illegality and immorality in the name of law and virtue: it serves only to underline the need for eternal super-vigilance to maintain the dignity of the law and of society: of man. That is why the Union is fighting today for independent civilian boards in all localities to review all complaints of police illegalities and why it has inaugurated a program to organise and collect studies of police practices relating to arrest and treatment in police stations, the results of which have been submitted to the American Bar Association's committee considering the development of national and uniform standards of criminal procedure.

One of the Union's earliest assignments in the area of what may be loosely termed due process was its successful fight to prevent the extradition of Robert Elliott Burns from New Jersey to Georgia, where he had escaped from a chain gang. The Union's arguments for Burns, author of *I Am a Fugitive From a Chain Gang,* were two: that the chain gang was a forbidden cruel and unusual punishment and that Georgia had previously broken its promise to set him free if he returned voluntarily. Hays and former Judge Harry V. Osborne of Newark volunteered their legal services and Governor A. Harry Moore (who later appointed Mayor Hague's young son to the state's highest court "to please his daddy") promptly granted their plea. But the Union's efforts to persuade the Georgia Legislature to look into a penal system without chain gangs got nowhere. In New York City in 1933-34 its protests against LaGuardia's police, who, headed by Major General John J. O'Ryan, were as brutally repressive as ever, resulted in the disciplining of two policemen, an investigation and a request to the Union to prepare a handbook for police control of outdoor meetings. Fraenkel and Dorothy Kenyon, the first woman judge in the city, were particularly active in the field of police lawlessness, and Judge Kenyon later headed a Union committee to study and seek to abolish the third degree.

New York was long to be a major blot on police "honor," as it is today. When his police commissioners seemed to be softening, LaGuardia ordered them to have their men "muss up" what the progressive Mayor called "tinhorn gamblers" and all other alleged criminals: to LaGuardia they were never merely suspects but guilty men even before their arrests. The Socialist Mayor of Bridgeport, Connecticut, Jasper McLevy, repeatedly countenanced the brutal beatings of demonstrators by his police, and in Boston and Cambridge students of Harvard and the Massachusetts Institute of Technology were clubbed down and trampled by police horses for anti-Nazi rallies. In Jersey City the police regularly arrested persons at random for "vagrancy" and held them *incommunicado* for days. One victim was so outraged that, after his release, he constantly wore a large sandwich board bearing his name and address, and he was not picked up again. The Supreme Court, sensitive to the Wickersham Report, reversed the convictions of all the Scottsboro defendants because Negroes had been excluded from the panel from which their jurors had been drawn: a clear statement of law that has been and still is violated every day in the south and on which the Union has scored victory after meaningless victory on appeal.

Through the decade before the Second World War the Union's activity in this area of civil liberties mounted steadily, though for the most part it did not intervene in purely criminal matters. Victor S. Gettner, a lawyer specialising in real-estate practice and dedicated to civil liberties (for years he has been chairman of the NYCLU), defended a group of relief workers accused of disorderly conduct, and fired from their wretched jobs, for having engaged in union activity. But the Union did not hesitate to line up with Hearst on one of the rare occasions when he was a victim: a Senate committee investigating lobbying subpoenaed from the two national telegraph companies their file copies of every message sent to or received by specific corporations and individuals. This, the Union said, was analogous to wiretapping or mail interception: a form of search and seizure without a warrant. The rigid radicals denounced the Union for *taking Hearst's side*—whereas it was taking no one's side—and they had to be reminded that had such procedures been taken against their favorite causes they would have howled even louder than Hearst and the National Association of Manufacturers.

At the same time Judge Kenyon's third-degree committee, working with the Association of the Bar of the City of New York, produced a set of bills, backed by the lawyers, that would have ended the practice. Despite the fact that the United States Supreme Court had just reversed the murder conviction of a Mississippi Negro who had been subjected to police torture, the Albany Legislature rejected the Union's proposals because of the brazen opposition of police lobbies that made no secret of their insistence on preserving the "right" to coerce and extort testimony. The practice was general throughout the nation, and good Christians and Jews who every week repeated *Thou shalt love thy neighbor as thyself* saw nothing wrong in it: after all, the victims must have done something terrible or they would never have been arrested. Nor was the third degree absent from the Bureau of Investigation or its successor, the FBI, whose director had so long headed the political police of the United States—the General Intelligence Division of the BI, covering radicals, aliens and spies— and who had distinguished himself as the leader of the Palmer raids. As Fred J. Cook points out in *The FBI Nobody Knows*, the

FBI has never altered its attitude, for instance, toward what its instructors and agents call *niggers*. Its director, Hoover, is distinguished today, as always, not only by his hallucinatory powers but by his bitter venomous opposition to efforts to curb police lawlessness and enforce Constitutional safeguards.

In the years just before the war the Union was fighting the Senate lobby investigators again, Mayor Hague and the Detroit chief of police, among other violators of due process. The Senators, without even a subpoena, asked the Treasury for—and got—hundreds of personal income-tax returns without any opportunity to the taxpayers involved to resist this invasion of their privacy, which also violated the law making tax returns confidential. Hague trumped up a fraud charge against John R. Longo, a young Catholic circulating a petition for Hague's recall, and had him stored away for nine months. It was at this time that Moore appointed Hague *fils* to an appellate court before which litigations against Hague *père* were pending: Moore ignored the Union's criticisms. Brigadier General Heinrich Pickert, Detroit's chief of police, announced formally: "The police department will continue to arrest people and search homes without warrants whenever, in the personal opinion of the commissioner, such action should be taken." In Chicago the Union could get no action against a policeman who killed his prisoner because Illinois law forbade citizen complaints against policemen: they could be legally accused only by their chief. In another Chicago case a policeman was cleared of brutality charges by his department because both the victim and his witness had arrest—not conviction—records. "It is unthinkable," the police commissioner said, "that police officers would use force to secure [*sic*] a confession, but if they did they would not be so foolish as to allow anyone to witness it."

In California, arrested strikers were subjected to variations of the old Chinese water torture. Los Angeles, notorious for its police lawlessness against the hated radicals, was revealed to have become less biased: its police department maintained a spy network that harassed, by wiretapping and trumped-up charges, any prominent or even obscure citizens who criticised the municipal administration. Three of the guardians of law and order went on trial for murdering a private detective in whose car they had planted a bomb. A breach-of-the-peace suspect who refused to be fingerprinted was brutally beaten—in England no one may be fingerprinted against his will unless he has just been convicted. For the first time the Union began to fight for the rights of the derelict, who in Los Angeles' jails had no rights. One acloholic was beaten until his skull was fractured; another died while strapped to a table with a folded blanket over his face—the common Los Angeles treatment at that time. California law made it a misdemeanor to aid indigents, even close relatives, to enter the state, and the Union fought convictions under the law, which the Supreme Court was to void. Along the roads that led to California from the Dust Bowl, the migrants had already been harassed by police, who drove them away from every stopping place and framed traffic and vagrancy charges against them, as a few years earlier a protest caravan of unemployed had been brutally stormed off a highway near Albany by the New York police. In Cleveland, the Union forced down the police by protests coupled with publicity, as a result of which a murder suspect forbidden all communication was finally allowed to consult counsel.

It was during the 1940 decade, despite the increased burdens put on it by the war, that the Union began to broaden its due-process activity. Professor Edwin M. Borchard of Yale Law School headed a Committee on State Relief for Persons Erroneously Convicted, who enjoyed no statutory rights in most states. The committee drafted and pressed for the passage of a model statute based on the 1937 federal law allowing such persons wrongfully convicted in federal courts to sue for damages without a special enabling act in each case. A number of states ultimately adopted such legislation. The Union, which had contested from the start the fingerprint mania that began before the war—in some areas every school child had to be fingerprinted—opposed the general practice of fingerprinting alleged misdemeanants and of retaining the prints in police records even if the accused were acquitted (much later the Union was to go to the logical stand that *all* arrest records of innocent persons should be destroyed immediately on their acquittal—a charity too Christian for a frightened and basically hostile society). A United States Supreme Court decision in 1945, allowing victims of illegal search and seizure by federal agents to sue for damages in federal courts, was to reduce somewhat the incidence of that particular abuse by the FBI, which, however, continued tapping wires.

The sublime confidence of the policeman in his absolute power to compel anyone to identify himself was rudely assaulted in 1947 when a New Jersey court overthrew the disorderly-conduct conviction imposed on a girl hitch-hiker for refusing to tell the police her name. In Berkeley, California, the Union aborted a random police crusade against venereal disease in which the brass-buttoned experts merely arrested any woman who seemed to warrant the trouble. Four such women, who were held for four days and freed without the slightest evidence of infection, were helped by the Union to sue for damages. State and local police were consoled, however, by a Supreme Court ruling that seemed to exempt them from the national law and Constitution: in an arrest, with warrant, for check forgery, the police also found and seized forged draft cards and lodged a charge accordingly. The Supreme Court held that, if police find evidence of one crime while seeking evidence for another, no specific warrant for the unsought evidence is necessary. Not only did this violate the specific wording of the Fourth Amendment, the ACLU protested: it invited the broadest abuses by the police. In addition, it provided a natural basis for the 1964 New York legislation—now being enviously eyed by what used to be a model of civil liberties, the United Kingdom—permitting arrests and searches without warrants. This legislation is currently under Union attack: the outcome depends on whether the courts follow the Constitution or the vindictiveness of a public adroitly whipped into blind hatred by rabble-rousing "newspapers."

The same "newspapers" now so busy attempting to justify convictions based on forced confessions raged at the Union in 1948 when it entered the case of the so-called Trenton Six and won a new trial for them because they had been found guilty of murder on the basis of extorted admissions; in addition the state had not allowed the defense to examine the murder weapon for prints. Not all the howls arose solely out of the hunger for vicarious vengeance, it must be conceded: the Six were Negroes whom the Communists immediately adopted as victims of racial bigotry, though the Union found no evidence of that. Corollarily to the

Trenton decision, the United States Supreme Court barred the use of a confession by a state prosecutor who obtained it during the illegal detention of the accused. At the same time the court cautiously went somewhat farther in other cases, ordering the reversal of a conviction when a state court committed error prejudicial to a defendant who had no lawyer. In a masterpiece of *pilpul* the court barred from a federal criminal trial all evidence illegally seized by state officers, but only if they had been joined by federal police before the seizure. But soon afterward it validated a state prosecutor's use of evidence obtained in possible violation of federal laws against interstate wiretapping!

The Supreme Court also outlawed the use of the third degree by a private detective working with city police and holding a special policeman's card. This decision was reached under the Reconstruction Civil Rights Acts, but the Constitutional rights were reaffirmed by it. By refusing to review a Circuit Court of Appeals decision, the Supreme Court also established the beginning of a Federal Court rule on evidence obtained by tapping telephones. This was the espionage trial of Judith Coplon, whose conviction was reversed by the Circuit Court, where the Union actively aided Miss Coplon. Despite the vigorous denials by Attorney General J. Howard McGrath that the Justice Department would stoop to such base (and illegal) conduct as wiretapping, the court found that no other evidence against Miss Coplon existed. The Union protested not only the taps but also the Government's deliberate destruction of all its notes relating to them. The Circuit Court agreed, and buttressed its reversal with the further fact that Miss Coplon had been arrested without a warrant or, in its absence, any proof that she was about to flee; hence the papers seized in her premises could not be admitted. In addition, the court upbraided the Government for making it impossible for the defense to determine whether the original "confidential informant" against Miss Coplon was not her own telephone.

Holdings by Federal Courts in various districts that witnesses before Congressional and legislative committees could invoke the Constitutional privilege against self-incrimination infuriated the probers and their supporters and brought on a long battle in

Congress to abridge the privilege. As might be expected, the chief movers were Senator McCarran and Representative Walter; but they got such "respectable" support as that of Keating of New York and Emanuel Celler of Brooklyn. The Union consistently but futilely fought every new effort to curb the Constitutional guaranty but it was ultimately defeated when in 1954 Congress enacted a law, signed by Eisenhower and upheld by the Supreme Court, revoking the privilege of any witness concerning whom two-thirds of an investigating committee approves immunity from prosecution for any revelations made in compelled testimony. Congress, the Union pointed out, could not enforce this fraudulent promise. The law made similar provisions for testimony before a federal grand jury or court on approval of the Attorney General. Both parts of the law specifically barred immunity for perjury, of course, and both specified that this abridgment of the Fifth Amendment applied only in investigations and trials dealing with the national security and defense and also, in grand-jury and court proceedings, with violations of the Atomic Energy and Immigration and Naturalisation Acts. The predators were to find, however, that some spirits were bold enough to brave the new law and others, abandoning the plea of the Fifth Amendment, would invoke the guaranties of the First concerning freedom of belief, utterance and association.

The Supreme Court itself seemed to limit the Fifth Amendment privilege in 1952 when it held that, if the privilege was not invoked at the first of a series of questions, it might not be relied on later, when general queries became specific. In upholding the 1951 law requiring gamblers to register with the Internal Revenue Service and pay a $50 annual license tax on an occupation barred by law, the court apparently not only approved the Government's collection of revenue from what it called *crime* but also demanded that men incriminate themselves without any corresponding immunity. In another curtailment of Constitutional rights, which this time seemed to conflict with its earlier decision overthrowing a Negro's conviction by a state excluding Negroes from jury panels, the court refused to review a Virginia sentence of Negroes to death for rape though Virginia had never executed a white man for the same crime.

The Union could find no violations of civil liberties in any aspect of the arrest, trial, conviction and execution of Ethel and Julius Rosenberg as spies; Communist allegations of anti-Semitic influence were proved to be as ridiculous as they seemed. But the trial of William Remington for perjury before a federal grand jury in denying past CP membership justifiably disturbed the ACLU, for, when Remington's conviction was reversed and a new trial was ordered, the Government instead indicted him for a new perjury, which supposedly consisted of his denial that he had earlier committed perjury. He was convicted. The Union was equally rightly exercised over the contempt proceedings against Harry Sacher and other defense attorneys in the major Smith Act trial, who were given inadequate notice of the citations and who were brought to trial before the same judge, Harold R. Medina, who was their accuser and who was reversed by the Supreme Court.

Despite its fundamental opposition to wiretapping, the Union was prepared to concede its legalisation in cases of treason, sabotage, espionage, abduction or threats of any of these, under a multitude of optimistic safeguards. In thus yielding to the emotional confusions of the time the Union was abandoning its own basic position that any invasion of civil liberties for a "good" cause becomes the precedent for further invasions for causes of possibly less merit; it completely lost sight of Brandeis' dissent in the Olmstead case. Having successfully fought a New York City prosecution of two women accused of prostitution as a result of wiretapping, in the absence of all other evidence, and having helped Judith Coplon to overthrow a political conspiracy conviction similarly grounded, the Union should indeed have known better. It persuaded New York Police Commissioner Monaghan to set up a departmental panel to hear charges of police brutality and a course on citizens' rights for his minions (eleven years later police entrapment of prostitutes and homosexuals, often by procuring the act alleged, or, even more usually, by fabricating evidence against anyone known to have such a record, goes on as merrily as ever, and brutality and killings by armed off-duty policemen are whitewashed with the utmost consistency). Evidence in New York has been obtained by pseudo-psychiatric therapy—and thrown out in court—and in other jurisdictions by the compulsion of drunkometer and lie-detector tests and by the forced use of a stomach-pump on a man alleged to have swallowed the evidence against him.

In 1952 the Supreme Court upheld the denial of cross-examination by federal agencies in the case of a conscientious objector whose claim to exemption was denied by a draft board on the basis of secret evidence; Chief Justice Vinson, learned in the law, held that an administrative hearing is not a formal procedure governed by the Constitution, to which Black, dissenting, retorted: "If the aim is to protect the underground of informers, the FBI report need not be used. If it is used, then fairness requires that the names of the accusers be disclosed...The prejudices, the credibility, the passions, the perjury of the informer are never known." There was no difference between the character assassination in which Vinson saw no wrong and the physical murder by a Chicago policeman who, in "self-defense," killed two unarmed boys and wounded a third in a parked car. In this case the Union's protests brought on prosecution and conviction. The Illinois ACLU then called on victims and witnesses of police brutality to come forward, and it was backed by the press. One man, shot at and beaten without cause, recovered $50,000 damages in court; another, beaten savagely, held forty hours without a charge, then booked for disorderly conduct and released, suffered actual damages of $4000 and won a verdict for that amount, which the trial judge cut to $40. The Philadelphia ACLU challenged, and eventually defeated, the local police commissioner's orders to arrest a whole docket of "known criminals" on sight. New York Police Commissioner Monaghan's deal with J. Edgar Hoover, under which Monaghan minions guilty of brutality in violation of the Civil Rights Act would not be turned over to the Justice Department, was attacked on the floor of Congress.

Four dramatic ACLU interventions in seven weeks prolonged the life of a condemned man in Utah despite a never executed threat to hold the Union in contempt if it did not desist. Utah ignored a stay of execution issued by Justice Clark of the United States Supreme Court for the presentation of new evidence; the executioner was told to disregard Clark. But the prison warden and the state Attorney General, apprised of the stay by the ACLU, ignored the local judge's order for execution. The defendant's counsel had been so lax that in effect he had been deprived of counsel; the victim's weeping widow, identified to the jury but not to the defense, had been allowed to lament beside the jurybox throughout the trial; the prosecution had knowingly used perjured testimony and had suppressed evidence. Despite the ACLU's proof that otherwise the defendant could not have been convicted, the Supreme Court finally refused to review and the man died.

But a Court of Military Appeals reversed the murder conviction of soldiers who had not been informed of the accusation against them, of their right to be silent and of the fact that anything they said would be used against them. A Circuit Court of Appeals found that a defendant had been deprived of counsel by the fact that a secret agent of the prosecution had joined the defense legal staff and turned over everything he learned to the prosecution. Another Circuit Court outlawed compulsion by a prosecutor who threatened to hand a witness' papers to a Congressional committee but did not tell the witness he was entitled to legal representation and to protection against self-incrimination. In shocking contrast, the United States Supreme Court found no violation of due process in a state prosecution in which hidden microphones had been placed in the defendant's garage, hall, closet and bedroom. The Circuit Court in Denver found no denial of due process, and hence refused to reverse a conviction, in the fact that a defendant had no lawyer when the jury brought in its verdict and the court imposed sentence, and it denied his motion for a new trial, since no prejudice was shown. State courts were no better. Utah permitted adverse inferences against a witness invoking the Fifth Amendment in a civil trial even though they would have been forbidden in a criminal prosecution. North Carolina found no ground for a mistrial in the fact that the jurors were drunk. California allowed evidence that a driver had refused to submit to a drunkenness test. One Circuit Court of Appeals, however, upheld the Union's position that the Fourteenth Amendment forbade the states to deny due process, and it therefore granted *habeas* for the victim.

The prevailing scorn for the Bill of Rights in the early 1950's was attacked by the Union wherever it appeared—in McCarthy's undercover work with the FBI (Hoover was publicly denounced for violating his own rule against public comment on FBI files and activities); in Attorney General Herbert Brownell's irresponsible charges against former President Truman in reference to the alleged spy, Harry Dexter White, which the Union said Brownell should have made only in formal proceedings in which adjudication would have been possible; in the thousands of federal civil service firings for which Malin protested the refusal of Civil Service Commission Chairman Philip Young "to make it explicit that derogatory file information is not tantamount to discharge;" in the Senate Judiciary Committee's publication of unproved and unsupported charges against Chief Justice-designate Warren; in McCarthy's compulsion of the resignation of J.B. Matthews without a hearing (the same Matthews whose earlier appointment by the HUAC the Union had protested and who now was the victim of his own technique of injustice). When Kefauver proposed a code of procedure for Senate investigations, providing for cross-examination, forbidding the publication of testimony without its rebuttal and setting up a board of appeal, the Union enthusiastically supported him; but his proposal died at birth.

19

What Price Justice?

When it was announced that Senator Arthur Watkins would head a special committee to study the question of censure of McCarthy, the American Civil Liberties Union insisted that McCarthy must have every opportunity to confront and cross-examine the witnesses against him, and Watkins acceded. Thus for the first time in his Senate career McCarthy was to be a party to anything like due process, even though he had recently denied it to Judge Kenyon of the ACLU by his slanderous denunciation of her as a Communist. Nonetheless the Union also pursued the Defense Department because it refused clearances to McCarthy's aides without hearings. McCarthy himself deserved censure, the Union believed, for his vicious conduct in hearings and for his solicitation of Government employes to give him confidential information, but the Union opposed censuring him merely for retorting to his attackers. In all this the Union was wholly consistently adhering to a principle and a practice that in the ensuing decade of confusion and conjuration and compromise have become a laughing-stock to the general: *right for the sake of right*. Nothing could be more alien to the sententious opportunism and pious expediency that characterise the mid-century. The Union was as quick to remonstrate with Senator J. William Fulbright when his Banking and Currency Committee handled accusations against Walter Winchell with the same star-chamber methods employed by McCarthy.

Backing both Attorney General Brownell's proposal that state courts set up public-defender systems for needy defendants and the American Bar Association's offer of free counsel for Government workers accused as security risks, the Union obtained concrete results for victims of local police lawlessness. In Philadelphia it won acquittals for two brothers who savaged policemen invading their home without a warrant: the court found that they had been legally resisting a criminal trespass. In Chicago the Union negotiated an end to police road-blocks and searches of cars without warrants. In New York it won Police Commissioner Francis Adams' agreement to eliminate the weekly dragnet round-ups of "undesirables" ordered by Mayor Vincent Impellitteri if decent legislation could be obtained—round-ups denounced by judges who refused to entertain charges and discredited by the random inclusion of a number of perfectly respectable citizens who happened to be out at hours and in places disapproved by roving police squads. Adams was a civilian commissioner whose tenure stands out as the only bright spot in the recent history of the New York City police.

In California the Union assisted a couple beaten by policemen out of uniform who were searching their home without a warrant on suspicion of bookmaking: the suspicion was based on the fact that the unusually affectionate spouses constantly telephoned each other during the working day. The Union also put an end to Los Angeles police round-ups of Negroes after a disgraceful foray in which 400 were packed into police stations during a general assault ostensibly intended to clear the city of prostitutes, alcoholics, drug addicts and narcotics peddlers (black only, since the police apparently assumed white folks did not do such things) : of the 400, only forty-three were held by a magistrate, for "vagrancy," and three for carrying concealed weapons. Nine of the "vagrants," having no legal help, pleaded guilty; all the others were acquitted when the sole prosecution witness, a deputy sheriff, admitted he could identify none of them. In Cleveland the

ACLU forced a court to cut bail from $25,000—fifty times the maximum possible fine—to $1,500 for a Communist held on a charge of fraud in applying for a driver's license. Another Ohio man, sentenced to ten years for a false car registration because the trial judge thought he was a Communist, was paroled after twenty-seven months as a result of ACLU intervention. In Illinois the Union overthrew the life sentence of a Negro convicted of raping a hallucinative white schizophrenic proved by medical examination to be intact physically: the trial judge arbitrarily cut off defense testimony and denied a new trial on the ground that no one had known at the time that the complainant was insane.

Unalterably opposed to the use of the lie-detector by police, government or industry, regardless whether compulsory or "voluntary," the Union prevented the imposition of it on the entire police force of Paterson, New Jersey, when a filing case mysteriously vanished from police headquarters. ACLU intervention helped to bring fines of $100 each for the mayor of Denver and three police officials who for sixty hours prevented a prisoner from seeing his lawyer; in Cleveland the Union battled to end the local rule allowing seventy-two hours of detention *incommunicado*. By *habeas* action the ACLU ended the same city's practice of sentencing alcoholics and vagrants without hearing, on the basis of jail interviews by probation officers. In St. Louis, the Union discovered, it was common practice to hold prisoners as long as seventy days without charges. In California the ACLU won the dismissal of manslaughter charges against three Mexican-Americans because of the local newspapers' feverish manipulation of prejudice. But in New York the Union failed to persuade Governor Averell Harriman to stay the execution of a man convicted on the testimony of an accomplice who gave conflicting evidence to the grand jury and the trial jury and who lied about the "deal" with the prosecution based on his promise to help convict the defendant.

Wrongly, one cannot help thinking, the Union opposed a ban on the press and public at a murder trial in which the defendants had expressly signed the appropriate waiver of a public trial. It would seem that a civil-liberties advocate can hardly deny the right of the individual to protect himself from the prurience of the public and the pillorying of the sensation-mongering press. Much more admirably, Malin and the Union denounced without qualification the planting of microphones in a jury room, with the consent of the court and the adversaries, in order to make a "scientific study" of jury behavior under a grant from some unthinking foundation. Federal law subsequently prohibited such an outrage. In the 1960's the Union was to have to concern itself with similar practices—not only microphones but hidden peep-holes and cameras—by private employers and the Post Office, fearful of employes' misconduct. Other business practices also aroused the Union, such as Socony-Vacuum's manual for job applicants, which advised them: "Personal views can cause a lot of trouble. Remember to keep them conservative. The 'isms' are out." Norman Thomas' angry protest brought about a revision of this threat; but Malin's protest to the Navy against its distribution of the same kind of thing to all its installations round the world was ignored. Other corporations besides Socony-Vacuum continued to issue such warnings to both applicants and current employes.

Civil-liberties invasions by the military had engaged the Union's attention chiefly in wartime, but the 1956 brutalities that killed six recruits at the Marine Corps' Parris Island training camp caused the ACLU to seek the end of such practices and the punishment of those responsible. The Union assisted the mothers of four of the six recruits, killed by an insane night march, in obtaining affidavits from 124 Marine trainees. Daily slapping of recruits by drill instructors was testified to by 81 per cent; beatings with swagger sticks and rifle butts, as well as kicking, were sworn to by 84 per cent of the trainees; 73 per cent told of warnings never to reveal any of the abuses. Others testified to such tortures by the instructors as being forced to smoke while wrapped in blankets and being made to shave dry faces with rusty razor blades. According to the Union's 1957 pamphlet, *The Marine Corps and Observance of Civil Liberties at Parris Island*, the affidavits were obtained after the corps commandant, Major General Randolph Pate, promised a full and fair investigation and then insisted the corps could not take time from the defense of a nation at peace for the collection of the data needed. Pate rejected the Union's request for an investigation based on the affidavits; the Union raised the question of invasions of private security under the Fourth and Fifth Amendments and the violation of laws that make it a crime to assault an individual on a military post. But Pate redeemed himself somewhat by his order for the prompt court-martial of sixteen marines accused of brutality to Japanese prisoners in the brig.

Civilian police brutality and extortion continued to be a Union problem. It sought action—and got none—on a Florida sheriff's pistol-whipping of a white woman accused of sexuality with a Negro airman. The ACLU persuaded the Philadelphia police department to investigate overwhelming evidence of brutality by one of its men, and the resultant whitewash laid the basis for the unremitting drive by the Union for the establishment of civilian review boards—the first of which was ultimately created in Philadelphia and has won the praise of the Union and the department itself, but not that of the cop on the beat who has lost his immunity. The review-board drive was given impetus by another Philadelphia case at the same time: a shopkeeper resisted a police shakedown, protested, and brought about the dismissal of two policemen and the demotion of a third, whereupon the shopkeeper was arrested for disorderly conduct and summarily convicted (the conviction was reversed). In Illinois the Union sponsored a bill for prompt arraignments of all persons arrested, which the Legislature passed and the Governor vetoed because it would encourage crime, he said; he ignored the Union's reminder that Illinois law already made it a felony to imprison for the purpose of obtaining confessions or incriminating evidence. The ACLU partly defeated a California law that would have allowed police to make spot identification checks on mere suspicion and to hold for two hours, without any record, any person who refused to answer questions: the detention provision was deleted but the identity check was not; nor was another section providing that alcoholics be treated as vagrants rather than as patients. The Civil Liberties Committee of the Michigan Bar Association reported that illegal arrests in the state averaged 20,000 a year: it called—in vain—for a law ordering weekly reports by the police on all arrests without warrants and the erasure of so-called police records of persons arrested and released without charges. The NYCLU protested—also vainly—the police seizure of papers from the clothes of Frank Costello, a prominent gambler, without a warrant while he was being hospitalised after an attempt to kill him. The Union's brief *amicus* demanding that dental equipment and notebooks seized without a warrant be returned without being photographed was equally futile

Philadelphia and a number of states enacted, over ACLU opposition, laws requiring all ex-convicts entering the jurisdiction to register with the police, under penalty of fine and imprisonment. In Westchester County, New York, the Union fought the planting of a microphone in a cell where a prisoner consulted his lawyer and as a result a New York City judge, in effect taking judicial notice of police *Schweinerei,* ordered a prisoner released during part of the day in order to consult his lawyer in privacy. Fighting for the rights of juvenile defendants posed the problem of protecting them from abuse while maintaining the due-process protections often eliminated by well intended legislation that left them to the discretion of courts. A Circuit Court of Appeals upheld the Union's contention that juveniles must be told of their right to counsel and that judges must satisfy themselves that, when it is waived, the juvenile or his parents know the significance of the waiver; further, when there was no waiver and the defendant was indigent, the court must appoint counsel. A Philadelphia boy was freed by ACLU efforts after having been held eight weeks for a mugging that he did not commit: the Union pointed out that he had had no proper trial and the court had acted on hearsay evidence not available to the defense. The victory included a new procedure in Philadelphia juvenile arrests: parents were now notified at once and the youths arrested were allowed to use the telephone. This right had to be fought for in the enlightened year of 1957, but it was not until 1963 that the New York City police accepted its existence under NYCLU pressure. Then they posted signs in Spanish and English in police stations notifying defendants of all their rights: the signs were usually placed just below the hooks on which the men of the law hung their coats.

A Union brief *amicus* in Michigan exposed the imposition of a life sentence at 2 A. M. four hours after the suspect's arrest!

He had pleaded guilty without counsel at a closed trial, the court interpreting the plea as a waiver of counsel. Always concerned by the reluctance of the majority of the bar, despite the lawyers' oath, to defend unpopular causes and characters. the Union fought what might well be termed the attempt to foreclose legal defense for the "undesirable" by penalising those lawyers who provided it. The ACLU helped to defeat efforts to bar former Judge John O. Bigelow of New Jersey from the Board of Governors of Rutgers University solely because he had once represented a client who invoked the Fifth Amendment; the Union also battled official questions posed by Los Angeles to all District Attorney candidates as to whether they had ever represented criminals. Reminding the lawyers of their own Canon of Ethics, the Union condemned the new theory of "guilt by client". The ACLU and the bar alike were outraged when Assistant Attorney General William F. Tompkins denounced bar associations providing counsel to Smith Act defendants as "dupes" of the Communist Party.

In May, 1956, the Union found it advisable to edit for national distribution a leaflet, *If You Are Arrested,* originally prepared jointly by the NYCLU and the Association of the Bar of the City of New York, both equally perturbed by the unchecked abuses of police power in the city. New York had now so many rivals in the invasion of private rights that the ACLU made the pamphlet generally available (it has since been locally edited, in conformance with varying state usages, by many of the Union's affiliates). Explaining what constitutes arrest, the leaflet warns even the innocent not to resist but to rely on a false-arrest action, provided the arrest is unlawful. The leaflet explains when an arrest without a warrant may be legal, what a warrant is, the rights of the police and the limitations on their use of force, the rights of the accused in the police station and, particularly, the worthlessness of any policeman's promise of help in return for a confession. Readers were told of their absolute right to telephone and to seek bail, to a speedy hearing, to legal representation (and to a delay of a hearing until it can be obtained), how to apply for the appointment of counsel if one is indigent, the extent of the powers of magistrates and grand juries, and the dangers of asking for hearings before either without the advice of a lawyer. Thousands of copies have since been distributed all over the country; in some cities, indeed, the authorities make it available to prisoners. But the Denver police forbade an ACLU poster based on the leaflet and approved by the Denver Bar Association.

Two Supreme Court decisions at this period affirmed positions long taken by the Union. The conviction of Clinton Jencks for perjury in a Taft-Hartley Act loyalty oath was overthrown because some of the prosecution's testimony was based on FBI files that he was forbidden to see on the pretext of security: i.e., protecting stool-pigeons lest they lose their usefulness. The court ordered the files opened to the defense, even at this frightening risk, on all matters concerning which a witness testifies, or, alternatively, their absolute withdrawal from evidence. (Congress then took over and enacted rules for such disclosure, empowering judges rather than prosecutors to examine the files for relevancy and limiting disclosure to those containing prior statements relevant to the witness' testimony and essentially *verbatim*). The rule was soon extended to hearings by administrative agencies. The other Supreme Court decision reinforcing the Union was that in Mallory v. United States, which held that an arrested person must be promptly arraigned within a reasonable time or else released. "It is not the function of the police," Frankfurter said, "to arrest, as it were, at large and to use an interrogating process at police headquarters in order to determine whom they should charge before a committing magistrate on 'probable cause.' " Congress promptly sought to overrule the court but was thwarted. The Union collaborated in the fight against the bill.

It is not to be inferred that these or any other Supreme Court decisions necessarily ended violations of law even by federal entities, to say nothing of those of the states. The FBI, despite all that had been written in the case reports about the Constitution and the laws, was ready in 1957 to broadcast its secretly compiled list of alleged ringleaders of the mobs of Little Rock bigots that made it necessary for the United States troops to establish national sovereignty in Arkansas, and only a warning by the ACLU prevented this unwarranted conviction by disclosure. But the FBI has always been in the forefront of civil-liberties invasions while, with his free hand, J. Edgar Hoover issues bromides about freedom. When *The New York Post* projected a series of articles on the FBI, Hoover warned a *Post* advertiser that they would be a "smear"; when the Pacifica Broadcasting Foundation ran interviews with Hoover alumni who were harshly critical, it was called before the Senate Internal Security Subcommittee. Hoover himself publicly praised McCarthy and his methods, and emulated both in irresponsible accusation, having long forgot what Attorney General Stone said when he appointed Hoover FBI director in 1924: "The Bureau of Investigation is not concerned with political or other opinions of individuals." Hoover's insistence on the right to eavesdrop, his intimidations of everyone to his left, his espionage in radical movements, his violations of postal laws (one has only to read the Warren Report on Kennedy's assassination) are, furthermore, backed up by the Justice Department and the national anxiety, regardless who is President. Assistant Attorney General J. Walter Yeagley, in charge of the Justice Department's Internal Security Division, implicitly approved all Hoover's violations of law when he was quoted in *The New York Times* of October 25, 1964, as saying of the CP: "Our objectives are to keep the party off balance, to know what they're up to, to keep their membership low through harassment, to expose their leaders." What is lauded in the FBI is the harder to correct among the run-of-the-mill *canaille*. The authenticated lawless acts of police in the past decade would alone make several volumes. What is our concern here is what the ACLU has sought to do about them, what it has achieved and what it has failed in.

Its complaints in Illinois brought about a federal grand jury investigation of the Chicago police in 1958, resulting in the convictions of two men under the Civil Rights Act. A few of the probers' statistics covering a nine-month period:

—20,000 persons illegally detained more than seventeen hours;
—2000 illegally detained two or more days;
—350 to 400 held three days without charges;
—$156,000 in damages assessed against the Chicago police.
These covered the customary assaults, thefts of suspects' personal

property, false arrests, including one of a woman for gambling (which she had not done) when she asked police assistance.

The Union protested the shooting of a woman by a civilian in a Missouri state police car when she ran a road-block. It defended a Puerto Rican arrested for loitering in New York while conferring with an official of the Puerto Rican Labor Department. It protested the action of two Indianapolis policemen who used their positions to collect private debts for friends. It protested the risible Appalachin raid on a gangsters' convention as harassment for publicity purposes alone without probable cause (none of the resultant cases stood up but for years every participant was blackened with the record of the raid). It overthrew the eviction of a family from a housing project because a son who lived elsewhere was a drug addict, thus ending the policy on which evictions of "undesirables" were based. A Union brief *amicus* helped to overthrow a life sentence based on lie-detector evidence in Kentucky. But it could not end Kentucky's practice of putting criminal charges in cold storage for years rather than dropping them when proof was impossible. In Colorado and elsewhere the Union won court orders that transcripts of court records be supplied free to indigent defendants; in many places it succeeded in instituting public-defender programs, and it persuaded the Philadelphia bar to provide free counsel for needy juveniles in confinement.

The Union forced clean-ups of illegalities in commitments and dententions in the Camden County, New Jersey, Children's Home. It vainly protested the Buffalo Police Department's order to "rough up" juveniles. It defeated some but not all state legislation to legalise wiretaps and wireless electronic eavesdropping. It freed, with the help of the Rhode Island Bar Association and the NAACP, two men held eight months as material witnesses to a crime and deprived of mail, and hence of counsel, for half that time. It prodded Illinois into enacting a law for posting defendants' rights in police stations. In California it failed to dissuade the Governor from vetoing the repeal of the old vagrancy law and hence had to go to court to defend those arrested under this statute, including a girl who walked barefoot, a man talking to friends on a street corner, a nurse coming home late—and escorted—from a date, an artist who was told he would be re-arrested weekly until he got a haircut, a shave, a conventional suit and a necktie.

It opposed, without result, various state laws granting immunity from false-arrest actions to merchants who made on-sight or on-suspicion citizens' arrests for shoplifting. It also lost its fight on New York City's law for the fingerprinting of night-club entertainers. It won a new trial for a parolee convicted twenty-two years before for a murder for which a deputy sheriff was convicted a year later: the parolee had pleaded guilty under the deputy's threat to kill his mother and his counsel had suppressed the fact at the trial. It persuaded a Pennsylvania court that the Fourteenth Amendment applies to a state court that refuses the defense permission to challenge jurors related to the victim of a crime and to a key witness for the prosecution. It won the repeal of a Connecticut law requiring five-year sentences for the sickness of drug addiction. A California affiliate condemned capital punishment as cruel and unusual but the national ACLU saw no civil-liberties issue in the death penalty; in 1965, however, the national ACLU adopted the California view. The California affiliate was actuated largely by the failure of the nine-year battle to save Caryl Chessman from execution. From the start the Union's Southern California affiliate had aided Chessman in every legal step, maintaining steadfastly that he had been deprived of his rights through the wrongful denial of his appeal as a result of the inaccuracies and incompleteness of the original trial transcript filed with the appellate court, which never allowed it to be amended.

The Philadelphia ACLU won court acceptance of changes in the law to allow juveniles, who technically are not criminal defendants, full disclosure of the evidence against them, cross-examination of witnesses and the application of the prevailing rules of evidence (which, of course, prohibited hearsay); it failed to upset the denial of access to probation records to the defense. The Union set a shattering precedent when it won a Supreme Court reversal of a Kentucky conviction for loitering and vagrancy, based on the sole fact that one Sam Thompson had retained a lawyer to contest his first such arrest and had thereafter been arrested, convicted and fined with monotonous regularity. Other "vagrants" defended by the Union with mixed success included a paralysed veteran unable to raise his hands on a police command and a white man whose "vagrancy" consisted in buying a drink in a Negro bar in California. In the same state, however, the Union won the invalidation of all local laws requiring ex-convicts to register. In Philadelphia it prevailed on the police to abandon the policy of raiding "beat" coffee-houses and making mass arrests. It provided counsel for three inmates of San Quentin Prison seeking *habeas* writs for unconstitutional and unlawful detention.

In 1964 the Supreme Court, upholding the Union's brief that cited the Fourth Amendment, finally ruled that evidence seized by state officials in violation of the Federal Constitution might not be used in a state prosecution—a ruling that would seem axiomatic to any believer in justice but the specific promulgation of which was made necessary by the continuing dichotomy between state and federal law in the "United" States. It is disappointing that the Union has never taken a position on this blatant obstruction of justice, and more disappointing that the most eminent of its counsel——men like Fraenkel and Ernst and Edward Ennis, whose dedication to civil liberties is exemplary and whose soundness as Constitutional lawyers is unchallengeable——continue to defend the doctrine of states' rights, principally on the ground of an anachronistically doctrinaire abhorrence of centralised government and secondarily on the argument that this independence of the states, while admittedly a godsend to every bigotry and to the perpetuation of injustice, is theoretically favorable to experimentation in legislation and administration. So it may be; but is experimentation worth the perversion of states' so-called rights into the calculated subversion of Constitution, federal law and judicial decision? The Union thought not in 1962, when it joined the American Bar Association, the League of Women Voters and the AFL-CIO in opposing the "states' rights" amendments by which the State Assembly of the Council of State Governments was clandestinely attempting to blow up the basic rights established by the Constitution. These amendments would have made it possible for the Constitution to be amended by state legislatures alone, without Congressional approval. They would also have restricted federal courts' jurisdiction over the apportionment of state legislative seats. Finally, they proposed to create a Court of the Union, composed of the chief justices of the fifty states, to override decisions by the Supreme Court. This was too much experimentation.

A legal precedent was set in Oregon by the District Court's acceptance of the Union's brief to forbid prison officials to prevent the consultation of counsel, purchase of law books and study of law by convicts. But the Union could win no clarification of the right of the indigent to appeal as far as the Supreme Court, which had held in 1958 that "the only statutory requirement for the allowance of an indigent's appeal is the applicant's good faith" but which had not carried through. The Union helped win a new District of Columbia law providing paid counsel for indigent defendants, juveniles and persons facing commitment as incompetents. It made a Maryland judge abandon his practice of persuading those held for drunkenness to plead guilty in order to save the police the bother of going to court, and it won the reversal of a disorderly-conduct conviction by a Pennsylvania judge who had plaintively explained: "I have to charge him with something." But in California, despite its reliance on the First, Fourth, Fifth, Ninth and Fourteenth Amendments, the Union lost its challenge to a judge's order to an unmarried mother to remain celibate thereafter.

In Washington State and California the Union began fighting for jury trials for traffic offenders; it has never tried to obtain them in New York despite the prevailing usage in the city's traffic courts: "Ten dollars if you plead *guilty*, twenty dollars if you plead *not guilty*." Nor has it attempted anywhere to battle the unconstitutional presumption of guilt that prevails in all traffic courts and makes the defendants' testimony worthless despite the fact that he is no more self-serving than the quota-fulfilling policeman. The Union won more battles against police road-blocks, however, and battled an Iowa law suspending a driver's license automatically on arrest for drunken driving, regardless of the court outcome. The NYCLU protested the denial of a driver's license because of the applicant's past criminal record, and New York's Attorney General was struck down by a court when he forbade the issuance of a driver's license to Ben Davis on the novel ground of political unfitness to drive a motor vehicle: Davis had been convicted under the Smith Act. (A year later Davis was to be the subject of another but unsuccessful ACLU protest: the manuscript of his autobiography, written in prison, was confiscated because, Prisons Director James V. Bennett told the Union, convicts might write in their leisure time in the cells but their manuscripts "may not exploit their own criminal career or that [sic] of others." The Union asked Bennett whether this applied to the works of Tom Paine, Oscar Wilde, Captain Alfred Dreyfus, Eugene V. Debs and Socrates, but none of the names seemed familiar to him.

The NYCLU's sponsorship of an Albany bill to forbid grand juries to publicise presentments criticising persons or policies— except in the case of public officials—unless the commission of a crime is charged was part of the still raging battle between the Union and the irresponsibles. Both the greed and the vicarious appetites of the broadcasters lay behind their fights to televise trials, as the same motivations dictated the consistent flagrant invasions of individuals' right of privacy by tabloids and even by some newspapers, regardless of the damage to the person or, in court cases, the prejudice created for or against one of the parties. Despite its mistaken reasoning in the New York procuring case when, for the wrong reasons, it had protested the exclusion of the press, the Union was and is still striving to protect the right of the defendant to a fair trial as well as the right of the individual to privacy. It has consistently agreed with Justice Douglas that "a public trial is for the benefit of the accused, not the press," though it has not always backed the right of the accused to waive this sometimes dubious benefit. But the Union, in its progressing fight to prevail on the press and the courts to adopt rules like Britain's for the reporting of trials, seems to be adhering to the unchallengeable statement made by Judge Louis E. Goodman in the District Court in which John B. Powell and his wife won a mistrial of their sedition prosecution because of flagrant press distortions. Judge Goodman said: "Freedom of the press is not for the benefit of the press but for the benefit of the people"—a truth that was heavily underlined by the outrageous conduct of press and broadcasters after the arrest of Lee Harvey Oswald, whose murder, the Union was to point out correctly, resulted largely from the compliance of the Dallas police with the unreasonable and unjustifiable demands of the "communicators." Similar police connivance with the sensation- and scandal-mongers resulted in a $540,000 damage suit by three University of California students, backed by the Union, who were involved in the anti-HUAC demonstrations in San Francisco and whose "mug shots" were publicly circulated by the police, in defiance of California law, with pamphlets containing excerpts from various sermons by J. E. Hoover.

The Union made representations to Hoover on the disposition of police photographs and fingerprints sent, under routine procedure, to the FBI from every local department. Hoover assured the Union that the pictures and prints of persons who either were not prosecuted or were not convicted were returned to the senders, at their request, for destruction and that the FBI destroyed its own copies of them. But many police departments admitted that they destroyed no records, regardless of the disposition of the cases and irrespective of the offense charged, so that, for example, a divinity student arrested for demonstrating against the United States' invasion of Viet Nam, even if his case was dismissed, remained the possessor of a police record. The Union is intensifying its battle against the retention of arrest records of persons cleared of criminal charges; its position on the records of those convicted of minor offenses based on political belief or conscience is mired in philosophical considerations perhaps complicated by an unconscious desire to lean over backward. Some states already have statutes requiring the return of all records, on request, to individuals exonerated, or their automatic erasure from the files. The Union's Due Process Committee has urged that questions as to arrest records by private and public employers be altered to ask only whether the applicant has ever been the subject of indictment, information or conviction of a felony; but it would seem not only logical but just that only convictions should be permissible subjects of inquiry: indictment or information, after all, may quite possibly be followed by acquittal.

The question is a harsh practical one, aggravated by the periodic epidemics of round-ups that infect police departments, particularly in areas where prejudices are virulent—whether against Negroes, women in slacks or narcotics addicts—as well as those jurisdictions that rely on dubious vagrancy laws that make it generally easier to plead guilty than to assert a very real innocence. The Union fights all such abuses, as it has fought bills to castrate sex offenders (Pennsylvania) and to compel addicts to register like criminals (Connecticut), and as it has combatted police searches of high-school students and their cars, which in 1961 were routine in Norristown, Pennsylvania, and in Colorado. Some of these abuses were reduced by a 1961 Supreme Court decision that allowed the victims to sue individually for damages those who "under color of law" invade their rights, even though the court exempted from liability the municipalities and states under whose authority the acts were committed. As soon as the decision was announced, the Union filed a number of such actions. The offense that led to the decision was a police raid without warrant on a Negro's apartment: everyone present was stripped naked by the police, searched in all bodily orifices and beaten; one man was then taken off to jail without any charge and ultimately released. In Philadelphia the Union won the release of a migrant sentenced to six months after a fifteen-second hearing in which he was forbidden to speak. In California, the Legislature—aided by Union work—took note of what was going on in the Supreme Court and enacted a law limiting detention without arraignment to two days and without bail to three hours; and other states—where also the Union was pressing—began to make similar laws.

But the Union's growing record of achievement in the Supreme Court was set back in 1961 by a decision that, though wiretap evidence might not be used at all in federal courts and was barred from state courts when federal officers participated, it was wholly admissible in a state whose statute authorised it. Casuists may argue that this vindicates the states'-rights doctrine, as indeed it seems to do, but it makes philosophers, social students and even objective lawyers wonder what *justice* is when an act is illegal in one jurisdiction but licit in another where the same basic Constitution theoretically governs. The court as a whole, obviously, preferred to ignore the clear statements of moral right by Holmes and Brandeis in Olmstead v. United States. Instead, the Government and the states were encouraged to commit their own crimes in fighting others. One of the worst of Government crimes, the deliberate procurement of a law violation by an individual through entrapment, has never, unfortunately, been attacked in court by the Union, which ignored the illegalities of Prohibition enforcement agents as it ignores the activities of police departments whose members pay women and homosexuals to commit prostitution and then prosecute them. When the FBI is put on a pedestal for infiltrating Communist meetings and interstate theft rings and taking part in the operations of both in order to obtain evidence, it is difficult to expect censure of a municipal police force whose plain-clothes men sell diluted heroin to some wretched addict and then arrest him for possession of it, or buy it from a "pusher" and then arrest him for selling it. Government never hesitates to play, as Holmes put it, the ignoble part, and the good burghers never cease to applaud its basenesses.

The Union was opposed by the military when it sought to obtain a semblance of justice in military courts during hearings before a Senate Judiciary Subcommittee on Constitutional Rights. All its proposals to eliminate cruel and unusual punishment, such as bread-and-water diets, and discrimination between officers and men in the serving of sentences were rebuffed; it succeeded only in gaining soldiers a choice between trial by court-martial and non-judicial punishment by officers for minor offenses. But in the civilian Supreme Court California's statute making mere narcotics addiction a crime was ruled unconstitutional and under the Eighth Amendment a ninety-day sentence based on needle marks on the arm of a man who denied addiction was thrown out. In two prostitution cases the Union won new trials: in Minnesota because the court allowed irrelevant testimony as to character, in California because the law there allowed trial on suspicion without proof of actual prostitution. The NYCLU supported a successful campaign by the New York *Herald Tribune* against the detention of traffic violators unable to post bail, who were often held overnight. These heinous offenders were moved to an unbarred area, away from the criminal element, and the number of such detentions dropped 99 per cent. Another NYCLU-backed advance grew directly out of this experiment when the Union supported the experiment proposed by the VERA Foundation to replace arrest and detention or bail on minor charges with summonses and the release of suspects in their own recognisance: the magistrates' courts at once found that the proposal was sound and practicable as well as just. The NYCLU's protests also brought a departmental rebuke for policemen who forced two murder suspects to pose against their will for press photographers.

As unfair as the police, the Federal Trade Commission was also attacked by the ACLU. Its proceedings were analogous to those of a grand jury but were held in public, and the FTC forbade defendant firms' and individuals' counsel to do much more than listen: they were not allowed to object to questions for materiality or relevance, to introduce evidence, to cross-examine or even to make statements for the record. John de J. Pemberton, Jr. a highly able Minnesota lawyer and Quaker Republican who had succeeded Malin as executive director of the Union, offered its full help to any FTC defendant who refused to produce documents for the commission until and unless it amended its rules. In the next year the FTC yielded slightly—but on condition that its hearings be closed when defenses were made—and no one has appeared to accept the Union's offer of assistance in the defiance of a tyranny that the ACLU has likened to the HUAC's practice of convicting by subpoena.

The HUAC and the Senate Internal Security Subcommittee are by no means the only Congressional inquisitorial bodies that the Union has attacked. In a preliminary survey of procedures of Congressional investigating committees, the Union's Due Process Committee reviewed recent history and made specific recommendations. In 1954 Ernest Angell, now chairman of the Union's board, told the Senate Rules Subcommittee that the Union fully recognised the importance of Congressional investigations; but it also recognised the limitations placed on them. The Supreme Court had often stated, the report pointed out, that Congress' investigative power is limited to legitimate legislative purposes and may not intrude into private areas of belief and action protected by the First Amendment; nor may a Congressional committee attempt to perform functions belonging to other branches of the Government, especially the judiciary. Its questions must be pertinent to the subject under inquiry. Not only the HUAC and the loyalty probers in the Senate, the report emphasised, but also Kefauver's monopoly investigation, House committees investigating federal administrative agencies and racial discrimination and the Senate investigation of James R. Hoffa, president of the Teamsters' Union, had been guilty of flagrant breaches in probing and publicising matters far beyond the scope of possible legislation, in blackening characters without giving the victims a hearing, in relying on illegally obtained evidence, in violating Congress' own rules, in harassing and intimidating witnesses and in battering them with impertinent queries, as well as trying to arrogate to themselves the power to settle disputes and adjudicate issues. The Union was urged *pro tem* to accept make-shift reforms, such as some minor protection for third persons who might be incriminated or degraded by witnesses and the creation of a body to screen proposed contempt citations, while continuing to press for the essential major reforms that it had always demanded: full due-process protection for both witnesses and those they named, the elimination of committees' power to cite for contempt, the right to avoid public sessions, restrictions on broadcasting of investigations, the right to obtain transcripts and the abolition of one-man subcommittees.

Throughout the paranoia of the post-war years, the Union, while deploring the exploitation of allegations of homosexuality and the frequent denial of due process to those accused of it, had done little to help. It took the view—not yet altered in official policy by the recommendations of its latest biennial conference for endorsement of the American Law Institute's demand for the legalisation of all private sexual behavior between consenting adults—that homosexuality was by statute a felony that could not concern the Union, whose only interest was in protecting the civil liberties of those accused of it. The Union is particularly aroused by the contemptible descent to entrapment. In 1962 the Union prevailed on the Supreme Court to order a rehearing by the Civil Service Commission for an Air Force Academy instructor whom, after sixteen blameless years, it had discharged without a hearing when he was accused of—and denied—homosexuality. The NYCLU went into court in New York to contest disorderly-premises charges against a Greenwich Village coffee house summonsed on the sole ground that homosexuals gathered there. But nothing was said by the Union to indicate that voluntary homosexuality might be just as non-criminal in its nature as voluntary heterosexuality; and even now, in its apparent readiness to adopt the view of the American Law Institute (which is also that of the British Royal Commission responsible for the Wolfenden Report), the Union is still queasy about the homosexual and sharply divided on the civil-liberties aspects of archaic Catholic-imposed and Jewish-supported statutes forbidding abortions to those who wish them.

In matters affecting juveniles the Union has no such conflicts. It prevented police questioning of a fifteen-year-old girl on a murder charge and in 1961 it won the release of a seventeen-year-old boy from an insane asylum to which a Norristown, Pennsylvania, probation officer had committed him after twice fining him $25 for blasphemy in saying *Jesus Christ!* to a housewife who irritated him. (Local law gave the probation officer judicial power subject to no curbs.) Nor has the Union any moral problem of its own in defending the few rights left to those dependent on public relief. It backed the successful effort by the Federal Commissioner of Social Security to bring the Louisiana Legislature to heel when it sought to cut off relief payments to mothers of illegitimate children —a double discrimination, since most of the mothers were Negroes. In Iowa the Union won the overthrow of a law for the deportation of any person resident for less than a year who asked public assistance. In virtually every other state it is still constantly occupied in defending the right of the poor to be fed, even when those poor are children who did not have enough American know-how to be born to properly married couples. In Chester, Pennsylvania, the Union fought a housing project's eviction of every family in which there was an illegitimate birth: this, the Union said, was not only an invasion of privacy but also an indiscriminate punishment of many innocents for the act of one guilty.

"Certainly lawyers and the courts should be particularly sensitive of . . . the demands of due process," Supreme Court Justice Arthur Goldberg said in 1962 when the court ended Nathan Willner's quarter-century battle for admission to the New York bar: in all that time the Committee on Character and Fitness insisted he lacked both but refused to say why. Warren agreed, in an ACLU challenge to a court-martial of a Marine represented by a layman rather than a lawyer: "Our citizens in uniform," he said, "may not be stripped of basic rights simply because they doffed their civilian clothes." Nor simply because they had no money, the Supreme Court ruled in the history-making case of Clarence E. Gideon, one of the most significant of the Union's achievements in helping to protect everyman's right to due process: overruling its own 1942 decision that only federal courts were bound to provide counsel for indigent defendants, the court held that every state is under a positive duty to provide a lawyer on request of every defendant too poor to pay. In sum (the full story of the case is magnificently told in Anthony Lewis' book, *Gideon's Trumpet*), the case involved the Florida conviction of Clarence E. Gideon, to whom a lawyer was refused and who conducted his own defense against a charge of entering a poolroom with the intent to commit a crime: he was sentenced to five years.

From his cell he wrote his own petition to the Supreme Court, which assigned a District of Columbia lawyer to represent him. The ACLU filed a brief *amicus* through a volunteer attorney, J. Lee Rankin, former Solicitor General of the United States; the attorneys general of twenty-two states also filed briefs *amicus* for Gideon. The Supreme Court ordered Florida to try him again with adequate counsel or let him go. Gideon was acquitted. The state then passed a law ordering each of its judicial districts to appoint a public defender; Colorado authorised districts to do so at their option; Oregon created the Office of the Public Defender; Minnesota and North Carolina appropriated funds to pay for counsel for the indigent; local bar associations in Alabama, Mississippi and South Carolina prepared lists of available lawyers; the Nevada and Kansas Supreme Courts acted to assure counsel for indigents' appeals. These were not mere token gestures, for in companion cases to Gideon's the Supreme Court had held that indigent dedendants with incompetent or negligent appointed lawyers in four states had been victims of discrimination. Congress, however, defeated a Kennedy Administration proposal to create a federal public defender. The Union backed not only this bill but an amendment that would have obligated courts to supply counsel for defendants whose unpopular views made it impossible for them to find counsel regardless of fee — a problem that has always existed and that was the subject of an impassioned *Harper's Magazine* article by Daniel H. Pollitt, a professor of law: *Timid Lawyers And Neglected Clients.* Reprinted by the Union, the article castigated, with case histories, the widespread fear of public opinion and of loss of fees among the profession, which Pollitt reminded not only of its oath but of Supreme Court Justice Benjamin Cardozo's observation that "there is more to membership in the bar than a license to sign a brief or intone a prosy argument."

In the same term with Gideon's case, the Supreme Court revolutionised American criminal procedure by throwing out a confession obtained from a suspect whose lawyer, waiting in the police station, had been refused permission to see him. The decision (in the landmark case of Danny Escobedo) laid down the absolute rule—wholeheartedly endorsed by the ACLU—that every defendant must be advised of his right to remain silent and may not be questioned in the absence of counsel: so-called confessions obtained when he is not allowed to have counsel present are, under the Constitution, worthless. As a result, the more enlightened judges of federal and state courts across the nation have refused to accept statements made by defendants who did not have counsel even if they had not yet requested legal representation. Literally thousands of convicts in all fifty states, whose convictions rested principally or wholly on such illegally obtained "confessions," are now in a position to challenge their sentences; and the careerist police and prosecutors who so assiduously racked up conviction records are plunged in despondent dread, bitterly resentful of the fact that the mere rights of criminals can now block the easy road to promotion.

On the level of the police station and the prosecutor's office the rule of Gideon's case, the exhortations of Professor Pollitt and the latest decisions are anathema. "The only rights you have around here are what we give you, and right now you don't have any," a St. Louis policeman told a suspect who requested a lawyer and urgently needed medical care: the latter, he was told, he could have only if he confessed. Yet police departments across the country denounced the Union and other proponents of civilian review boards as Communists, and Edgar Hoover joined the jeremiads against any effort to make police agencies observe the law. Nonetheless the Union won the establishment of the second such board in Rochester, New York, after police excesses, particularly against Negroes, could no longer be either denied or controlled. The mayor of Newark, however, stood firm against such a board even when it was recommended by the executive director of his own Commission on Human Relations.

Mississippi in 1962 and 1963 was a tangle of ACLU problems. The Union asked the Supreme Court to review the state's rape conviction of a Negro arrested without probable cause, unconstitutionally held in detention, subjected to coercion, denied counsel for two months and then given an incompetent lawyer; and from Justice Black the Union won a stay of execution for another Negro accused of rape whose court-appointed white lawyer had refused to take any action. The state court refused to mail the records of the case to Melvin Wulf, ACLU legal director in New York, so Wulf went to Mississippi and found there had been no warrant, an involuntary confession and the exclusion of Negroes from both grand and petty jury. "Lucky you didn't come here ten, fifteen years ago," Wulf was told, regretfully, by an assistant district attorney who refused to shake hands with him: "you'd have been strung up on that lamppost yonder. We used to defend the niggers ourselves on these rape charges— got 'em the chair," the prosecutor concluded complacently. While the Union was fighting for the beneficiaries of this kind of defense, it was also battling for the state's rabid segregationist Governor, Ross Barnett, whom it supported in an appeal to the Supreme Court from a conviction for contempt of court in disobeying a judge's order not to interfere with James Meredith's registration at the University of Mississippi —Barnett's disobedience will be remembered as having instigated a virtual insurrection. The Union protested that he had been convicted without a jury and thus the judge he had offended had been both his accuser and his jury. No such contempt trial, the Union told the Supreme Court, should be held without a jury—a stand that it wisely modified a year later when Joni Rabinowitz, a white New York girl aiding civil-rights forces, was convicted of perjury by a manifestly prejudiced jury in Georgia. At very long last the

Union had to accept the morally as well as pragmatically unexceptionable right of a defendant to elect whether he wished trial with or without a jury of his ostensible peers.

In 1963, too, the Union was compelled to recognise the civil-liberties issues raised by economic problems other than those of the relief recipient, whose right to refuse work beyond his capacities the Union had successfully defended. In New York City it fought for a subway sweeper dismissed for having fathered two illegitimate children; for a pyschiatrist to whom a notary's license was refused unless he promised not to repeat his offense of refusing to participate in a "civil-defense" drill, and for a coffee house required to have a city license to hold poetry readings—an ordinance that the NYCLU called unconstitutional. In Philadelphia, the Union fought a code that would refuse electricians' licenses to suburban residents. In many cities, especially in the south, the Union was joined by the Justice and State Departments in its battles against prohibitorily expensive licenses for the sale of merchandise from Communist countries. Here the Union charged violation of the Fourteenth Amendment's due-process requirements and abridgement of merchants' freedom of speech in that they were required to disclose the origin of the goods. The Union—to no avail —quoted the Supreme Court's endorsement of the inviolability of anonymity for some groups, especially dissidents.

The Union was disturbed too by a clandestine invasion of privacy and due process practiced by the Post Office and the Justice Department and brought to public attention by a bribery prosecution directed against Roy Cohn, who had been McCarthy's counsel: the Post Office was recording the return addresses of every piece of mail addressed to Cohn, his colleagues and some 750 other persons under surveillance for other reasons. The Union asked Attorney General Robert Kennedy to order the practice halted; characteristically, Kennedy lacked the courtesy to reply (he had not yet decided to run for office). Former Counter-Intelligence Corps personnel insist that this practice has been common at least since the Korean conflict and allege that, in addition, the Post Office and other agencies frequently—and adeptly—open, read and reseal such mail without the knowledge of either sender or recipient. Similar practices were revealed in the Warren Report, and as lately as February, 1965, the Post Office admitted that it has a list of 24,000 persons whose mail is under daily surveillance —a practice that a *New York Times* editorial called "as ugly as wiretapping."

This practice, according to *The Wiretapping Problem Today,* an ACLU pamphlet by Herman Schwartz of the New York bar, is condemned by most state attorneys general, whether it is used to trap call girls and bookmakers or to interfere with civil-rights organisations, as in Louisiana. No enemy agent with a grain of sense, Schwartz wrote, would use any telephone in any country for a business talk. In New York, he added, some 2000 public pay-telephones are under constant tap, and what Holmes called "this dirty business" cannot be cleansed by making it dependent on court order; courts are too subservient to demands, almost universally echoed by the unthinking public, and applications for such orders are necessarily *ex parte,* so that injustice is invited. Besides, he points out, taps can be and have been "doctored" by police. Schwartz concludes that all wiretapping should be outlawed everywhere and that regular procedures should be instituted to see that the ban is enforced. Quoting Frankfurter, he adds that the approval of wiretapping not only violates the Fourth Amendment but also "puts a premium on force and fraud" in law enforcement. But Attorney General Kennedy ignored not only Schwartz and decency but Frankfurter, Holmes and Brandeis and demanded wider authority to spy on his fellow-citizens, as the State Department admitted it did on its chief security officer, Otto F. Otepka, when he fought dismissal. Both the Attorney General and the State Department ignored the Union's protests.

The rights of due process were most coolly regarded, particularly by the communications media that had so consistently violated them, in the aftermath of President Kennedy's assassination and the murder of one of his assassins. On December 6, 1963, the Union issued an interim statement on *Civil Liberties Aspects of the Oswald Case, and Developments Arising Out of the Assassination of John F. Kennedy,* the amplification of which is still awaited. The interim report was harshly critical of Oswald's trial by press, radio and television and of the cooperation in this by Dallas officials who publicly repeated many times that all the evidence

against Oswald was incontestable—though it is still subject to searching challenge in view of the unconvincing Warren Report and the
few known facts—and who forced Oswald to submit to unre-
strained press badgering. The Union held the Dallas law-enforcement officials primarily responsible for the breaches, though the
communications media were almost equally at fault: still the officials
were obligated by their functions not to yield to pressure or alter
procedures for the accommodation of reporters: the police are
unqualifiedly responsible for the safety of their prisoners. The
observance of Oswald's right to counsel was most unclear except
for one fact: the right was not satisfied by the mere act of informing him of its existence. Since neither Oswald nor his representatives had requested ACLU aid and the police had told the Union
that he had refused to request counsel (this statement by the police seems at least partly to have been proved false by the Warren
Report), the Union could not force its services on him, though
they were offered and provisionally declined. In contrast to the
Oswald disaster, the Union noted, the handling of his murderer,
Jack Ruby, was much more nearly proper; but the Union called
on all concerned to refrain from furthering the spate of rumors.
An analysis of the Warren Report by the Union is still in preparation, but it is known that it will be largely concerned with the
recommendations for increased surveillance of all kinds of "subversives" and other dissidents and for their sequestration during
Presidential visits, recommendations that go far beyond any requirements of security and invite the FBI and the Secret Service
to abridge still further the civil liberties of those suspected of
heterodoxy. The Union is also concerned by the Report's disclosure that questioning of Oswald by both the Secret Service
and the Dallas police went into his religious associations and his
belief in a deity.

The Dallas police came under further Union attack in 1964
because of its *shotgun squad,* whose murders of suspects were
defended by the department as "deterrents to future crime." The
department also pleaded self-defense, though the victims were
killed while running away from the shotgun squad, whose savagery the Union properly described as "trying, convicting and executing robbery and burglary suspects." The NYCLU protested the

similar killing of a sleeping suspect by five New York City policemen and the murder of a fifteen-year-old Negro boy by an armed
off-duty police lieutenant who contended that he had to ward off
a knife threat, though the existence of the said knife has been
stoutly denied and has never been established. In addition to attacking the law requiring policemen to carry guns when off duty, the
Union pointed out to the uninterested officials, Mayor Robert F.
Wagner Jr. and Police Commissioner Michael Murphy, that a
"six-foot, 200-pound policeman should be able to relieve a fifteen-year-old boy of a pocket knife without killing him or even
resorting to the use of firearms." The murder by the policeman
touched off nights of rioting in Harlem that spread to Rochester,
Philadelphia and other cities and that were marked everywhere by
police brutality, defended by J. E. Hoover. Encouraged by Hoover,
1200 New York City police jammed a City Council hearing to
help defeat the Union's proposal for a civilian review board.

Other police and judicial abuses continue to occupy the Union
today. Not only has it had to defend a New York man arrested
for wearing women's clothes in violation of an ancient vagrancy
statute barring disguises—a law that could theoretically jail every
woman in New York who wears slacks or shorts. It is fighting the
use of lie detectors not only by police but by Government and
private employers, and in this it has the aid of labor: the campaign
is buttressed by expert testimony to a House committee to the effect that all the equipment is notoriously unreliable, that the witness' reactions can be distorted by his emotional and physical condition and that 80 per cent of those who operate polygraphs are
incompetent. For the pragmatists, the Union has to emphasise these
facts even more than the fundamental principle that the apparatus
violates the Constitutional guaranties against self-incrimination and
the invasion of privacy. The Union has continued to fight for and
win the right of counsel for defendants in courts whose judges
flouted the Gideon case. In the Circuit Court of Appeals it has a
brief *amicus* pending on behalf of James Hoffa because he was
convicted through the Government's illegal use of evidence obtained from an informer employed by Attorney General Kennedy's
Justice Department to spy on Hoffa and his lawyers. The Union
had to go to the Supreme Court to compel the FBI to give a Penn-

sylvania man the testimony of witnesses to a traffic accident. In New York City it vainly fought Judge Edward D. Caiazzo's adoption of a typical southern abuse of judicial power in committing Herbert Callender, a Negro civil-rights worker, to Bellevue Hospital's psychopathic ward for observation because Callender had legally tried to make a citizen's arrest of the Mayor—and Bellevue sent Mr. Callender home in four days instead of the customary ten, since it was not he who required psychiatric examination. In the south itself the Union fought incessantly against the harassment of civil-rights workers and their attorneys, both white and black, not only by mobs and illegal police activities but by trumped-up prosecutions. Once more it appealed to Attorney General Kennedy and once more he lacked the courtesy to reply.

The Union was no more successful in seeking legislation to afford adequate redress to victims of police and other official wrongdoing: Congress refused to recognise that hatred, malice or racial prejudice might be a motive for such actions; instead Congress stuck to the old law that specifically made such motives irrelevant. In New York State the Union and the Bar Association failed to prevent either the passage or Governor Nelson Rockefeller's approval of two laws attempting to nullify the Fourth Amendment. One allows police to stop, search and detain indefinitely on suspicion and forbids arraignment, bail or *habeas* during the detention, which is thus immune to challenge. The other authorises police to enter premises by force without warrants and even without notice or identification to the occupants if the officer thinks he can find possible evidence that *may* be destroyed or when, if he does not break in, danger to life and limb *may* result. That politicians in an election year should enact and sign such illegal legislation should shock no adult; but that in 1965 the Government of Great Britain—of all countries in the world—should model legislation on these two police-state measures is incredible. That the New York laws may fall in the Supreme Court was indicated when the ACLU, late in 1964, won its reversal of an Ohio gambling conviction based on an arrest and search without a warrant because of an anonymous stool-pigeon's tip.

Today the Union is backing legislation to extend to the federal courts the reforms of bail and release of suspects in their own recognisance, successfully proved in the VERA Foundation experiment. Lawrence Speiser, director of the Union's Washington office, emphasises that release on recognisance should not be limited to those unable to pay bondsmen: every defendant, he pointed out to Congress, can better organise his defense and keep his family off the public purse if he is free until and unless proved guilty. The Union's fight against lie detectors is spreading into Government, where severe limitations on its use have been ordered, but thousands of businesses continue to impose polygraph tests on employes whose jobs depend on the fortuitous results and interpretations. The NY-CLU is not only demanding the destruction of arrest records when there are no convictions but also calling on employers, through an educational campaign, to cease asking job applicants whether they have ever been arrested. The Union has ended the denial of bail to needy defendants asking for appointed counsel in Philadelphia; in Wisconsin it has virtually stopped police searches of traffic-law violators; in Seattle it is conducting a study of the police department for presentation to the City Council, which, however, refuses to go farther despite pressure by aroused citizens for official action.

Far in advance of the national board of the Union, the National Capital Area affiliate has formally called on the Government to abolish its discriminatory policy that bans from employment any past or present homosexual and even anyone to whom latent homosexuality is imputed by the so-called personality tests devised by commercial "psychologists" and "sociologists" to whom *ambivalence* is a frightening word, human nature is *terra incognita* and folk-myths about the psyche of the active homosexual are gospel. The affiliate affirms the right to sexual freedom in private, discredits the specious argument that the presence of a homosexual destroys the morale (not the morals) of the heterosexuals (whom the Federal Civil Service Commission apparently considers exceptionally vulnerable and unstable) and points out that vulnerability to blackmail and coercion is roughly the same in all three sexes. In addition the affiliate emphasises the inevitable and inexcusable spying and entrapment to which Government resorts in order to preserve intact the heterosexuality of its payrolls.

The key to much of the future hope of official justice in the nation was offered to President Johnson in February of 1965

when the Union called on him to fill vacancies in the federal judiciary with men capable of enforcing the law fairly and "fully
committed to the Constitutional doctrine that all citizens are entitled to equal treatment regardless of race." Signed by Angell,
Pemberton and the Union's two general counsel, Fraenkel and
Ennis, the letter cited the growth of cases involving racial justice
and the "acknowledged hostility" of many federal judges, especially in the south, to the laws that as a result they simply refuse
to enforce despite their oaths of office. Well aware of the obstruction to be encountered in the Senate, the Union most ingenuously
called on the veteran politician in the White House to have the
courage to abolish the Senatorial privilege that can destroy an appointee's career if one Senator declares him "personally obnox-
ious." Charitably, the Union did not remind Johnson that a number of the federal judges included in its indictment had been appointed by the brothers Kennedy with full knowledge of their
emotional commitments to white supremacy.

As effective as an independent judiciary can be in furthering
civil liberties, the root peril to all liberties, whether the right of
due process or any other, is demonstrated by the Warren Report
to lie beyond the reach of the American Civil Liberties Union or
any other human agency. When Lee Oswald was looking for a new
job, his former employer told the prospective new one: "He may be
some kind of a Communist: if I was [sic] you, I wouldn't hire him."
And fellow-employes told the Warren Commission how much they
disliked Oswald because "he was always propagandising and he
was seen reading a foreign newspaper." No man, no organisation
can enforce due process in the crowd mind.

20

The Survival of the Fittest

In 1944 Edwin Codarre, a thirteen-year-old epileptic, was indicted for the rape and first-degree murder of a ten-year-old girl in New York. He pleaded not guilty. In a pre-trial conference that included his attorney, the judge and the prosecutor —but not Codarre—a compromise was evolved under which he might plead guilty to second-degree murder, in order to avoid execution or acquittal for insanity. When Codarre appeared to plead, the prosecution had an electro-encephalogram conclusively proving that Codarre was an epileptic (under New York law, an epileptic is criminally responsible only for acts committed when he is not in seizure), but the district attorney suppressed it. Expert psychiatrists differed as to Codarre's sanity and as to the question whether his act, if he did in fact commit it, was performed during a seizure. In 1964, when Codarre had served twenty years of his life sentence and was eligible for parole, the United States Supreme Court, on motion of the American Civil Liberties Union, agreed to hear in 1965 a petition for review based on the argument of O. John Rogge, appearing for the Union, that the acceptance of a retarded thirteen-year-old's plea of guilt in a murder violated the Fourteenth Amendment's guaranty of due process of law, especially since the trial judge had admitted that, when he accepted the plea, he had no idea whether the boy was guilty or innocent.

The rights of the diseased have vexed the Union for many years. Not infrequently the insane, the alcoholic, the epileptic, the addicted have been deprived of basic rights because society loathed and feared their afflictions; at least as often both the afflicted and those whom someone—frequently spouse or relative—found it profitable to brand afflicted were deprived of rights because the real or alleged affliction itself was made the pretext for incarceration and deprivation of property without legal process. The Union's first experience with the latter invasion was its success in 1921 in obtaining the release of a Colorado Seventh Day Adventist and her two sons who had been committed because of their advocacy of pacifism during the war. Almost a decade later the Union went to court for Benedetto Bruno, a Newark anti-Fascist whose speeches irritated officials powerful enough to engineer his commitment, on his wife's instigation, and he was freed when what was then still called an alienist offered proof of his sanity. But it was not until the Second World War was almost ended that the Union went farther and began to draft model statutes for the commitment of the insane and for enforced medical treatment of physical illnesses. The latter was becoming an increasing issue as more and more sects arose that forbade some or all kinds of medical treatment, including even vaccination, which most states required for all school children. The Union's concern was nicely caught between the freedom of religion and the health of the community; and between the horns of the dilemma lay the gulf of due process. When the public health overrode private religious freedom, the Union believed (and so drafted its legislative models), it was essential that the paramount good be accomplished only by legal and Constitutional methods and that protestants be protected in their rights to be heard, to prove their religious motivations (where there were penalties for non-compliance) and, whenever possible, to find an acceptable substitute.

Twenty years after the first Union draft of a model bill for commitments to mental hospitals, Congress enacted for the District of Columbia a law closely following the Union's proposals. It appointed a Commission on Mental Health, including a lawyer as chairman, and eight physicians expert in mental illness. Hospitals were empowered to accept voluntary commitments if examination showed a need for them; such patients could be released on their own written requests within forty-eight hours. Those committed at the instance of others and without protest were required to sign statements to that effect that described their illnesses in lay language; they were entitled to the same release as the voluntary patients unless court orders to the contrary were pending. Emergency commitments without warrants were hedged with requirements of certification by hospital psychiatrists, notice to families within twenty-four hours, and release within forty-eight unless the hospital filed written petition for court authorisation of detention for observation for not more than seven days. Such petitions must be filed within twenty-four hours of the patient's admission, and a similar period was set for hearing: the results were to be promptly communicated to the patient's family.

Court orders for hospitalisation, which could be applied for by relatives or public officials, required physicians' certificates of mental illness threatening danger to the patient or others and of the patient's refusal to submit to examination. He was to be notified within three days and promptly heard by the Commission in as favorable circumstances as possible: representation by counsel was mandatory and courts were ordered to appoint lawyers when necessary. If the patient was found sane, or not dangerous, his immediate release was required; the contrary finding was to be reported at once to the courts, which must set trial within five days: the patient or his representative could insist on a jury. If the patient was then found sane or safe, he was to be released at once; otherwise he could be committed for an indefinite period to a hospital or such other treatment as the court found to be in his or the public's best interests. Payment was to be conditioned on the patient's and his family's financial condition; indigents were to be paid for by the Government. But no petition or certificate could be filed by a doctor related by blood or marriage to the patient, or financially interested in or employed by a private hospital to which commitment was sought. Within ninety days of commitment, and every six months thereafter, each patient was to be re-examined and, on proper finding, promptly released. Where there was a difference of findings among doctors, court adjudication was provided. Examinations at the patient's or his family's request were limited to semi-annual intervals after the first ninety days. The right of *habeas* was fully protected by the law, which also forbade commitment to penal institutions in these cases. Each patient's outgoing mail was to be sealed and uncensored, but only incoming mail from his lawyer and doctor had this privilege. No personal or civil rights were to be abridged unless the patient was found clearly incompetent to exercise them. Full notice of all rights, privileges and obligations under the law was to be given in writing—and in simple terms—to the family when the patient was admitted.

In general the law satisfied all the Union's requirements for the protection of patients' and their relatives' civil liberties. The Union would have preferred, however, that open-ward patients have unrestricted sealed-mail privileges; recognising the value of the patients' correspondence in much diagnostic and therapeutic work, the Union nevertheless was apprehensive of institutional censorship, particularly of critical letters from patients. The Union's major drive for the District law had been spurred by the case of Ezra Pound, the poet who expatriated himself to Italy and broadcast for Mussolini during the war: captured by American troops, he was sent home, tried and convicted for treason, found insane and therefore committed to St. Elizabeth's Hospital. Malin attacked this instance of the widespread practice of committing people, in effect, for life. A singularly dangerous decision by the Supreme Court at this time held that California could constitutionally vest a prison warden with final and unappealable discretion to determine a prisoner's sanity. Earlier, without result, the Union had urged the Justice Department to review periodically all its cases involving sanity and quash indictments of persons for whom physicians held no hope that they would recover their sanity.

The Union's activity was helpful in various states. Not only did it obtain the release of an illegally committed Maryland man; it won a new trial for an 18-year-old Michigan boy convicted of robbery for attempting to steal forty-five cents, despite the fact that seven years earlier he had been found to be mentally deficient. In Massachusetts the Union defeated a move to commit a child involved in a riot at an institution. But its protests could not block an Indiana law under which any petitioner, regardless of relationship or motive, could procure another's commitment to an institution without a hearing. In Ohio the Union worked for a bill similar to the District of Columbia law, in contrast to the existing Ohio statute under which commitment could be ordered on anonymous affidavits without investigation. Several states, notably New York and California, preserved McNaughten's Rule, an old legal decision under which a plea of insanity could be entered only if the defendant did not know the nature and quality or the wrongfulness of the criminal act alleged.

In New York, though the state administration favored legislation to override the rule, Manhattan District Attorney Frank Hogan fought to retain it and opposed the proposal, backed by the Union and the state, to allow a plea of insanity whenever a defendant lacked "substantial capacity" either to distinguish right from wrong or to make his conduct "conform to the requirements of the law." The Union based its stand on the great body of medical evidence demonstrating that the ability to distinguish between right and wrong frequently co-exists with severe and dangerous mental illness. In California a state commission endorsed the Union's proposal for a finding of "not criminally responsible" for persons unable because of mental disorders to obey the law.

A 1960 Virginia episode was a tragically ludicrous illustration of the abuses inherent in the legal confusion as to insanity and in the lax procedures tolerated by most states. Police attempting to solve a year-old murder hired—for money—a telepathist-clairvoyant (so he described himself) recommended for the task by a psychiatrist employed in (not committed to) a Government hospital. The necromancer awaited a propitious night, then hovered for some time over the grave of the murder victim until what he called her *emanations* (still unimpaired, apparently, despite a year under ground) reached him and told him that a trash collector had done her in. The mage and the police, his employers, proceeded with undeliberate speed to the trash man's home, got him out of bed at midnight and carried him off to a lunacy hearing convoked for 3 A. M. and conducted by the healer who had recommended the sorcerer to the police. Before dawn the trash man had been legally committed to and installed in the nearest insane asylum. Everyone else concerned, somehow, remained at large. The Union compelled the trash man's release; shortly thereafter, in most mundane fashion, the FBI picked up the actual murderer and he was convicted.

The Union was already at work on its drive for the enactment of the District of Columbia law of 1964, which replaced a statute providing for automatic commitment to St. Elizabeth's for any defendant acquitted by reason of insanity—a provision that the Union called unconstitutional in its presumption of continuing insanity: the Union insisted that a new hearing should be held before any such commitment. As the Senate Judiciary Subcommittee on Constitutional Rights continued to debate the Union's bill, the Union urged that minors between 16 and 21 should have the right to be consulted on commitments by their parents and should be allowed to leave the hospital at will. Virtually every other provision in the law as finally enacted was inspired and fought for by the Union. Similar procedures were sought by the Illinois affiliate for Cook County (Chicago), where interpreters for foreigners and records of drug therapy were also demanded and where the authorities had to be battled because of their endeavor to eliminate all due-process protections for persons involuntarily committed.

Before the new District law was enacted, the old rule was badly battered by the Supreme Court in a case supported by the Union. One Frederick C. Lynch attempted to plead guilty to a check-fraud charge in Washington and the trial judge refused to accept the plea because he believed Lynch was insane; the defendant was thereupon automatically committed. But the Supreme Court ordered him released, finding that the law provided automatic commitment only for persons voluntarily pleading insanity and could not be applied to a man who was declared insane over his own objections. The Union's victory, noted in the preceding chapter, over the Calfornia law making a felony out of an illness (drug addiction) had an incredible sequel in the Supreme

Court when the Los Angeles police and prosecutor asked for a rehearing because the original defendant had since died and the case was therefore moot; but the court upheld the Union's contention that the dead man's reputation and good name were entitled to protection against this lust to uphold a cruel law based in the first instance on savagery and hatred.

A parallel injustice, carried out by the Department of Justice, was protested by the Union on behalf of former General Edwin Walker, the fanatical rightist cashiered out of the army, who was a leader in the rioting at the University of Mississippi in October, 1962, when James Meredith was ordered admitted. At a hearing at which neither Walker nor his counsel was present, Robert Kennedy's vicar obtained an order that Walker be held for mental tests on the basis of testimony given by a psychiatrist who had never met the general. Walker's hearing was held in spite of the Union's protests, and he was found to be quite sane.

The state of Minnesota, however, lent every assistance to a Union move to remedy another injustice originally committed by the state: William Reinholm had spent fourteen years in a mental hospital simply because he lacked the money to get out. His commitment had grown out of an arrest on suspicion of statutory rape: he denied the charge, no criminal proceeding was ever initiated against him and he was forbidden both to call his own witnesses and to cross-examine the state's in the perfunctory sanity hearing that sent him away. In 1960, after ten years in confinement, a medical examination showed that he was quite all right; but he lacked the money for a lawyer or even for the railway fare to his own hearing. The Union prevailed on the state attorney general to provide the needed funds and Reinholm was freed early in 1964. The State Claims Commission has approved his claim for compensation for his wrongful detention and the Legislature is evaluating the monetary equivalent of what he has endured.

The prevention of other such tragedies was materially furthered when, in the same year, Illinois adopted a new mental-health code embodying reforms urged by the Union and the Chicago Bar Association; the Illinois affiliate, in fact, was invited to assist in drafting the code. It included full judicial hearings on request, full transcripts of them, the right to counsel and a public defender for the indigent, the distribution of forms describing their rights to all patients, written notice of the allegations against him to each patient within twelve hours of admission to a hospital and provision for informing the illiterate. Early in 1965 the Illinois ACLU consolidated another gain for the mental patient —more properly, for the former mental patient. An artist who had been in a mental hospital was refused when he asked for the paintings he had done during his confinement, and he was further embarrassed when the hospital, after his release, included these works under his name in an exhibit of patients' art. The Union obtained not only the removal of his name and pictures from the exhibit but the return of the canvases to him.

Having made an initial inroad on entrenched ignorance by the overthrow of the California law making narcotics addiction a crime, the Union (however belatedly) has begun a similar campaign against the parallel callousness that treats the alcoholic as the criminal he is not rather than as the sick man he is. Taking up the appeal of DeWitt Easter of Washington from his seventieth intoxication conviction in twenty-seven years, the Union will attempt to bring the law abreast of medicine and justice. Individual judges in considerable number have long recognised that alcoholism is a disease, but they have been hobbled not only by the prevailing lack of facilities for its treatment but particularly by the middle-class stupidity that keeps on the statute books laws that require men of good will on the bench either to violate their oaths by ignoring evidence or to behave, against all their principles, like Puritan witch-hunters.

21

Where Is the Frontier of Freedom?

It was not only his age—sixty-five—and the length of his ten-ure—thirty years—that caused Roger Baldwin to step down as executive director of the American Civil Liberties Union in 1950. Baldwin had long been convinced that civil liberties in any one country were directly influenced by the ideas that emanated from other countries and by the events that occurred in them. Mussolini's successful persuasion of the State Department to si-lence anti-Fascists here (combatted by the Union) opportunely provided evidence to support Baldwin's belief. Even in its earli-est years, the Union under his direction had never put on the blinders of nationalism or even of territorialism.

Now and for the future, Baldwin said late in 1964, the Union's course is and must be increasingly dictated by events among nations. He dated external influence on American civil liberties from the French Revolution, which was the direct inspiration for the 1798 Alien and Sedition Acts. "The degree of liberty en-joyed in the United States," Baldwin said, "has always been somewhat determined by the attitudes and actions of other coun-tries. The Union was born in one world war and came to matu-rity in the world context of the Russian Revolution, the rise of

Fascism and the Second World War, which made and clarified many of our civil-liberties problems, and now the United Nations is doing this to an even greater extent." Baldwin, who resigned to direct the International League for the Rights of Man, with which the Union is affiliated, serves as the ACLU's international work adviser and as such is in constant contact with United Nations officials. The League is accredited by the UN.

He had become increasingly involved in international work as a result of the Union's concern with the UN's human-rights efforts and his chairmanship of the International League, and he had been an adviser on civil liberties to the American occupation commanders in Germany and Japan. His assumption of new tasks in the international field was a natural extension of interests expressed by the Union from its inception. As early as 1922 Baldwin had formed an International Committee for Political Prisoners, inspired by the fate of the hundreds of aliens deported from the United States to countries where they suffered persecution and imprisonment. He had spent a year abroad in 1927, mainly in Europe and Russia, on their behalf. Baldwin's involvement had been deepened by his leading *rôles* in the League Against Imperialism, a united front of the left with colonial peoples, and the American League Against War and Fascism (later the League for Peace and Democracy), as well as his chairmanship of the American Committee supporting the Loyalist Spanish Government. All these united fronts were smashed by shifts in Soviet policy. By 1950, when Baldwin resigned from the executive directorship of the ACLU, he had become what he has remained: an internationalist promoter of civil liberties. But the Union itself, apart from Baldwin's activities, had from its origin been active in those areas of United States responsibility outside the borders: the island colonies, the protection of Americans in foreign courts, the freedom of international communication by American journalists, political asylum and, in recent years, the UN's relation to civil and political liberties.

Of the various colonies and territories of the United States in the period immediately after the First World War, the first to engage the Union's active attention was the Virgin Islands, through the appeal of an island leader, Rothschild Francis, for help in buying a printing press to publish the first native newspaper, *The Emancipator*. The Union raised the funds for the press. The islands themselves were under navy rule, which had suspended the Colonial Council, the local legislature, and the Union was concerned at this undemocratic government of a democracy's possession. It began drafting a model government scheme for the Virgin Islands, but it was to be several years before Washington made much modification in the colony's garrison rule. Meanwhile the United States marines, to the shock of the Union, were to take over the Governments of Haiti and Nicaragua on the flimsiest of pretexts in order to preserve the holdings and income of various American corporations. The cry of *imperialism* was raised against the United States as justly then as, today, it sums up the conduct of the United States in Asia, Latin America and Africa and the behavior of Russia in those continents and Europe. Imperialism is the monopoly of no political or economic system: it is inseparable, apparently, from every aggressive nationalism.

When the naval governor of the Virgins did restore the Colonial Council, the gesture proved meaningless, for, as soon as it opposed his policies, he dissolved it. Supported morally, not financially, by the Union, delegates of the colony went to Washington to press their appeal for civilian government. The abuses of the military rule were epitomised in the conduct of the courts that functioned under it and that never hesitated to impose contempt convictions without more ground than an editor's criticism of a policeman. The Union won a Circuit Court of Appeals reversal for the editor, Mr. Francis, but its attorney, A.A. Berle Jr., later an Assistant Secretary of State, lost his appeal from a second conviction based on Mr. Francis' criticism of Judge George Washington Williams' first decision. Thereupon Mr. Francis accused Judge Williams of acting out of sheer animus and was convicted a third time, in 1926. By now appeal had been made impossible by a new federal statute for the islands.

The Union was brought into the international aspects of civil liberties in 1929 by events originating in Haiti and Nicaragua. The exiled Haitian Patriotic Union, whose headquarters was in New York, asked the Union's help to agitate for the withdrawal of the marines and to combat official suppression of Haitian nationalist propaganda and meetings in the United States, which was of course a violation of the First Amendment. The marines in Nicaragua deported eight Nicaraguans who were active in opposing the American military occupation of their country and who obviously had no place to go: the Union gained permission for them to enter and live in the United States without visas.

Not long afterward Italy presented a further problem: Italian Government oppression of anti-Fascists living here through the United States Government, through Italian consulates and through plain strong-arm methods. But the Union's efforts to make a full-scale investigation of these persecutions were frustrated by the dread of so many Italian-Americans that their co-operation would bring reprisals against their relatives at home.

Ultimately the Union's representations on Haiti to Secretary of State Henry L. Stimson, one of the most upright men ever to head that department, brought about an investigation by a commission appointed by President Hoover. As a result, marine censorship in the "protectorate" was abolished and, in 1931, Stimson began determined efforts to speed the withdrawal of the occupation forces. This, however, was not to be accomplished until well after the accession of Roosevelt to the Presidency.

The advent of the New Deal brought more attention to the Union's campaigns for colonies and fiefs, though no change in the situation of the Virgin Islands, Guam or Samoa, for all of which the Union sought civilian rather than military government. Roosevelt and Secretary of State Cordell Hull, a man almost as irreproachable as Stimson, took the first steps that were to lead to independence for the Philippines. They completed the withdrawal of the marines from Haiti and offered to end American control of the country's fiscal affairs if the Haitian Senate would permit them to be governed by a committee representing the American holders of Haitian Government bonds—as outrageous a condition precedent as any to be set by Hitler in Europe. The basis of the Union's concern with Haiti and Nicaragua was the assumption of authority to control those countries by the United States, as distinguished from the semi-occupation of South Viet Nam, which the Union considers outside its jurisdiction, under the pretext of "collective defense against armed aggression."

This is an abject surrender to what H. L. Mencken, in Woodrow Wilson's time, so aptly branded "Calvinism in international politics." The Union's principles impose on it the clear duty to condemn the United States' flagrant subversions of the freedom of other nations, whether by money, by arms or by the indefensible injection of FBI and CIA agents into foreign jurisdictions. The Union's duty is equally clearly to protest and combat every American imitation (whether in Viet Nam or in the Dominican Republic) of Hitler's "rescue" of the Sudetens and Khrushchev's "rescue" of the Hungarians. Whenever and wherever the self-styled "liberators" exert *de facto* authority, the Union is bound by its own principles to battle for those rights and liberties that it champions when and where American authority is rightfully exercised.

In 1936 Puerto Rico also concerned the Union. In the agitation for independence, led by the Nationalist Party of Dr. Pedro Albizú Campos, a Harvard Law School graduate, two Nationalist youths killed the island police commissioner and were in turn killed in the police station. As a result, eight Nationalist leaders were tried and convicted for seditious conspiracy to overthrow the United States Government. In its unsuccessful appeal to the Circuit Court, the Union's brief *amicus* argued that a sedition charge was without foundation and, if the Nationalist leaders were chargeable with the commissioner's murder, that should be the only ground for their trial. The brief also attacked the composition of the jury, which consisted chiefly of Americans and Government employes.

Later the police in Ponce attacked a peaceful parade after a permit for it had been denied; a policeman and nineteen Nationalists were killed. The Union at once sent Hays to investigate. Assisted by a committee of distinguished Puerto Rican lawyers, he submitted a report exonerating the unarmed Nationalists of violence because the policeman had been killed by the cross-fire of his colleagues. The Union published the report with photographs taken during the killings; the resultant outcry on the island and in Washington enlisted Roosevelt's attention but no action was taken to punish the police. Heartened, however, by Congressional enactment of the Union-backed bill for civilian government and the extension of the Bill of Rights to the Virgin Islands (though similar action for Guam and Samoa was refused),

the Union formed a Fair Play for Puerto Rico Committee under
Oswald Garrison Villard, which was ultimately to be influential
in the island's achievement of commonwealth status after the
Second World War. Under Governor Luis Muñoz Marin, Puerto
Rico has presented almost a model for other emerging nations.
But in the late 1930's the growing likelihood of war was cited by
Roosevelt as his reason for continuing military government of
the island, and he appointed as the new governor one of his many
strange collaborators, Rear Admiral William D. Leahy, later
the apologist for Pétain and Laval.

The last of the governors from the continent was Professor
Rexford G. Tugwell, a New Dealer. Muñoz Marin's new Popular Party was gaining influence and demanding more autonomy,
and Roosevelt bowed by following Tugwell with the first native
governor, Jesús Pinero. The next step was the logical one of allowing the island to elect its own governor. Muñoz Marin was
chosen in November, 1948, and remained in office until 1964. But
the Puerto Rican Legislature incurred the anger of the Union in
1949 when it enacted three bills intended to suppress the Nationalist movement and modeled on American sedition and criminal-
syndicalism laws: the Union offered its help in any court test.

Muñoz moved swiftly for more autonomy. In 1951 Congress
approved a Puerto Rican constitution adopted by referendum,
granted the island commonwealth status and passed a federal
relations act for the new associated free state. The Union took
no active part in these developments or in the later issue of the
island's relations with the United States, on the principle that
its only interest lay in assuring to the Puerto Ricans, as United
States citizens, the right to choose their status freely. Spanish
became an official school language, though English remained
compulsory. As a result of UN debate over Puerto Rico's status
and the extent of its self-government, Muñoz invited Baldwin in
1953 and again in 1955 to visit Puerto Rico—the first time to observe the island's self-government and the second time to set up
a study of civil rights. The survey was prolonged; when it was
a year old, the Puerto Rican legislature repealed the 1949 sedition act and pardoned all who had been convicted under it. The
Legislature voted also to subsidise the island's political parties

in order to avoid pressure on civil-service employes and undue influence by special interests. In 1958 Baldwin's civil-rights survey was completed, furthered by seven lawyers and a $50,000 appropriation, and the Legislature adopted some of its recommendations: the elimination of (official) racial discrimination, the strengthening of municipal governments, the assurance of minority-party representation in city councils, and numerous others.

In 1960 the hostility of the Irish-dominated bishops to the commonwealth government's educational and birth-control policies prompted the formation of a Christian Action Party, which not only nominated candidates but procured the issuance of a pastoral letter threatening the excommunication of those of the faithful who voted for the Government party. The election of a Christian Action senator and two party representatives was promptly challenged for coercion and fraud; for the first time in its history, the Union's New York office was visited by a Catholic bishop in search of its help, which was rendered. Baldwin, again visiting Puerto Rico at the time, presented to a joint legislative investigating commission the Union's position, approved by its board: regrettable though the entry of the church into politics might be, the church had the right to form a party, the bishops were entitled to discipline the flock, and fraud in getting on the ballot—none was charged in voting—was irrelevant because the election authorities had known of it but permitted the candidates to run. One cannot quarrel with the first point; the second is at least highly debatable when ecclesiastical discipline is invoked for political activity.

Far less autonomy has been achieved in the Virgin Islands, which received a native-born governor at the end of the 1940 decade. When Baldwin visited the islands in 1953 at the invitation of the governor and the legislative council, he found so much division of opinion that the Union called for an unofficial constitutional convention. A year later the revision of the organic act covering the islands was coupled with the appointment of a new governor from the mainland and the movement was considerably set back. In the next few years Baldwin made further visits to confer with experts planning changes in the organic act, and the Union drafted plans for town governments, for which Baldwin won considerable backing. He also gained support for a resident commissioner for the Virgins to sit in Congress and for the transfer of the powers of the appointed governor to an elected governor. The Secretary of the Interior finally approved a bill for the popular election of a resident commissioner but it hung fire for years; when a proposal for the election of the governor was offered in 1962, it could not be furthered until the commissioner question had been resolved. These unsuccessful efforts led to the Legislature's establishment of a Home Rule Committee of legislators and citizens, on which Baldwin was invited to serve. Its efforts led to the popular election of a constitutional convention in 1964 to draft, for presentation to the Administration and Congress, a home-rule law providing for the removal of most federal controls and for authority for the islands to elect their own officials. This the Administration found helpful in answering the charges of colonialism made against the United States in the UN. Baldwin was an adviser to the convention, which completed its job early in 1965.

In 1962 Baldwin visited the Panama Canal Zone, the only area besides the Ryukyu Islands still under American military occupation, and found no civil-liberties issues, despite the intense strain over the perpetual treaty governing the zone and the American authorities' refusal to fly the Panamanian flag there. President Kennedy ordered them to hoist it, but a crowd of students tore it down and rioting followed. The Union took no position, but the International Commission of Jurists, at the invitation of the Panamanian Bar Association, investigated charges that the United States had violated the rights of Panamanians. It found the accused guilty of nothing worse than their accustomed lack of judgment and condescension toward "native peoples."

Baldwin's journeys and the Union's concerns were by no means confined to this hemisphere. In 1947 the War Department invited him to serve as one of the many advisers to the occupation authorities in Japan and Korea, in order to organise local citizen agencies for the promotion of civil and political rights. But Baldwin believed that his position with Japanese and Koreans would be stronger if he went as a private citizen, and he requested permission to do so. General Douglas MacArthur responded with an invitation, and Baldwin's trip was financed by the Union, which was repaid with the proceeds of an article in *The Reader's Digest*. The invitation was a surprising one, noted by the press of the nation; even *The News* in New York approved it in an editorial headed *Smart Cookie, MacArthur*. The histrionic general and the austerely simple libertarian understood each other at once and developed a high degree of mutual admiration during their close three-month collaboration. Baldwin found MacArthur's devotion to the principles of civil liberties to be beyond cavil; their personal relations went far beyond the business that had brought them together and they spent long evenings in philosophical discussion. Inevitably Baldwin found much need for reform in occupation policy on censorship, military functions better turned over to Japanese civilian agencies, and labor relations; MacArthur accepted almost all his suggestions.

But the response of the Japanese was even better. With the help of three bar associations, Baldwin created the Japanese Civil Liberties Union, which is today one of the strongest such agencies in the world. Japan's Attorney General set up a Civil Liberties Bureau, with similar agencies in every prefecture and hundreds of unpaid civil-liberties commissioners in every city and town to report violations of rights. On his return to Japan twelve years later Baldwin found the system operating with considerable success; but during the occupation there was a plague of strikes in government-owned industries, which MacArthur banned against his advisers' counsel. Otherwise the general's interference with civil liberties was slight and infrequent, notably censorship of two books critical of him and a ban on a lecture tour by Margaret Sanger. When Baldwin retired from his ACLU post in 1950, MacArthur sent a highly laudatory message, which in the McCarthy period was to provide considerable protection against irresponsible allegations that Baldwin was a Communist. These charges were based on distortions of statements made almost twenty years earlier and long since repudiated; the statements are sometimes still distorted by enemies of the Union to make them appear contemporary. In 1948 Baldwin was invited to repeat his Japanese experience in occupied Europe; on a second trip in 1951, MacArthur's endorsement silenced House inquiry into his political fitness.

The Army had asked the Union in 1948 to send three delegates to make a civil-liberties survey, and Lieutenant General Lucius D. Clay had added his personal invitation to Baldwin, who was accompanied by Hays and Norman Cousins, editor of the *Saturday Review* and a member of the Union's board. The group made substantially the same recommendations for Germany that Baldwin had proposed for Japan. Drastic revision of the inordinate postal, telephone and telegraph censorship in Austria was also urged, with the foreknowledge that nothing could be done about it until the end of the four-power occupation because it had been forced down the throats of the western powers by the Soviet Union. When Hays and Cousins returned to the United States, Baldwin remained in Germany to set up a German civil-liberties organisation, the *Deutscher Bund for Bürgerrechte,* with occupation funds and the help of prominent citizens, chiefly in Frankfurt. But it could then function only in the American zone. It was weakened by the zonal separation and by the German inclination to look to Government to protect rights. Baldwin returned to Germany several times, invited by the State Department and by his German colleagues, to strengthen the organisation, but it has never made much progress in the German culture. Its members must indeed be shocked, however, by the fact that the Government of the country that gave them their model taps their telephones in direct contravention of the German Constitution, which expressly forbids wiretapping.

(Both the Japanese and the German civil-liberties groups sent visiting delegates to the United States and the Union was their host in New York. The State Department expressed the hope that in the United States they would see how democracy works and take back their new knowledge for transplantation at home. The year was 1950—that of McCarran's and McCarthy's ascendancy.)

Much more than Europe, however, Asia and the Pacific were to occupy the Union's attention. Baldwin did not then visit Okinawa, which was to be a special source of problems; but he did go to Korea in 1947 and he set up a Korean Civil Liberties Union, which, with less success than the Japanese because of the greater vicissitudes of Korea, is still functioning. Baldwin found South Korea a military police state—a situation rationalised by the United States on the pretext of the Communist domination of North Korea—and this he considered, rightly, "a paradox in a liberated country," especially in contrast with Japan, a former enemy country under military occupation. But no one in the American forces in Korea had MacArthur's understanding of civil liberties, and Baldwin's recommendations for change were disregarded.

At the same time the Union backed bills for civilian government for Guam and Samoa; on both islands the navy administration was already making concessions in this direction, but civil rule did not come for some years. In 1958, backed by the Union, Guam sought the power to elect a governor and a resident commissioner: it is still seeking. Though the Philippines had become independent in 1946, the United States retained military bases there and the economy remained firmly gripped by that of this country. The Union unsuccessfully battled a Congressional bill impairing the islands' sovereignty; but it did prevail on the American army to stop its practice of playing policeman on Philippine territory outside its bases and of searching Filipinos' homes.

The major civil-liberties problem in the Pacific since the Second World War is still Okinawa. Both the American and the Japanese Civil Liberties Unions have consistently fought for substantial autonomy on the island. In the early years of the occupation, the situation was aggravated by the suppression of local government, the imposition of arbitrary rules and the seizure of farms for military purposes—one of which military purposes was a golf course—without adequate compensation. Acting as intermediary, the ACLU carried the protests to the Defense Department, which attempted to justify its inaction by citing the debatable conflict between military security and local autonomy. The Union continued its representations for several years and in 1959 Baldwin was invited to visit the Ryukyus during a world tour in connection with UN relations with non-governmental agencies.

The Defense Department allowed him full freedom to hold public hearings on every complaint: principally the Okinawans wanted more control of the executive and judicial branches of their government, more contact with Japan and the relaxation of mil-

itary security measures. Opposition to the continuance of the
American military base was high; the desire for quick reunion
with Japan was universal, despite the clear provisions of the peace
treaty. Reunion, the United States contended, was impractical
for the greatest military base in the Pacific, but it pledged revers-
ion to Japan when the military necessity should end—a pledge
far too indefinite and remote for the Okinawans. The United
States said nothing of its official commitment to self-determination,
which meant, obviously, endorsement of pro-United States self-
determination. Baldwin drafted a number of purely civil-liberties
recommendations and General Donald P. Booth, the sympathetic
High Commissioner, promised to encourage the fullest possible
self-government as soon as the Okinawans could take over. But
he was almost at the end of his two-year tour of duty and his successors reverted to established practices.

Such minor reforms as the army conceded satisfied no one.
Above all the Okinawans wanted to be reunited with Japan; they
evinced a certain skepticism of American insistence that we had
not fought their compatriots in order to acquire property. In 1960
they formed the Ryukyuan Civil Liberties Union to cooperate with
the American and Japanese Unions and to press for the elimination of the penal code's curbs on freedom of speech, press and
communication (even though, fortunately, these were not invoked), the ill defined political limitations on travel to and from Japan and the constraints on higher judicial appointments. In 1962
an executive order modified the army rule, appointing a civilian
as administrator responsible to the High Commissioner, granting
the majority party in the Legislature the right to nominate a
chief executive and increasing cooperation with Japan. Twice the
Japanese prime ministers visiting Washington have brought up
Okinawa. President Kennedy granted a request for the display
of the Japanese flag on public buildings as a symbol of ultimate
sovereignty, the actuality of which he pledged again, and issued
the 1962 executive order. Johnson encouraged greater Japanese
participation in Okinawan affairs through a joint commission.
But the army's High Commissioner remains the supreme authority in both military and civilian affairs. The Union has continued
to fight for free travel, the separation of military and civilian au-

thority, and the clarification of the confused jurisdictions of local and American courts. The major result for the Union has been the Mikado's award of his highest civilian order, the Rising Sun, to Baldwin in 1962 in recognition of the Union's persistent efforts. The United States has done nothing to prove either its commitment to self-determination or its disinterest in taking territory from former enemies.

Planned Union activity in the field of international civil liberties began even before the war ended: in 1944 the Union wisely set up its Committee on International Civil Liberties to study the problems to be anticipated after the war with respect to control of foreign territories, as well as reciprocal relations with other nations in matters of communications, travel and the protection of refugees. Early in 1945 the committee began to collaborate with the State Department and with the American delegates to the United Nations' organising conference in San Francisco on an "international bill of rights," which was to become the Universal Declaration of the Rights of Man, adopted by the General Assembly on December 10, 1948, and ignored since by its signatories. In essence the Declaration embraces all the guaranties of the American Bill of Rights and goes farther to prohibit slavery, pledge due process, affirm the right to a nationality and its change, as well as to asylum, and assert economic and civil rights of every character in specific terms. In conclusion, however, the Declaration denies to governments the "right to engage in any activity or to perform any act aimed at the destruction of any of the rights and freedoms set forth herein."

While the Declaration was under study, the directors of the Union published a number of policy statements concerning the postwar world, primarily from a purely American but not parochial point of view. The Union was to note exclusions of American journalists from foreign countries and to seek periodically to convoke leaders of the communications industries and Government officials to formulate international agreements for the free flow of opinion and news in all media of expression. The Union's executive director was to notify his board of instances in which pressure should be exerted on foreign governments to obtain such freedom. He was also to direct the board's attention to all efforts by the UN or other international agencies to obtain protection for minorities and the right of asylum; corollarily, he was to inform the board of every American denial of a passport except refusals based on efforts to escape legal process—the Union feared the United States might exert pressure on other countries to deny visas to Americans on the bases of race, color, religion or opinion. The board was also to be apprised of any denial of fair treatment to Americans in criminal proceedings abroad, though it was stipulated that the only question here for the Union would be whether American consular officials acted discriminatorily or without due diligence to extend the protection and assistance that were their obligation. The Union saw no proper occasion for it to express itself on proposed UN trusteeships of former enemy territory except to use its influence for civilian rather than military control by all trustee nations. The directors saw no issues for the Union in American military occupation or control of foreign territory (a view that was, most properly, to be drastically revised) or in fiscal arrangements under which the United States might be a party to the collection of debts owed to its nationals.

The Union had to put some of these policies into execution almost at once. By way of the State Department it intervened, with varying results, on behalf of American journalists excluded from or censored by Yugoslavia, various eastern European countries, China and parts of the British Empire. Pressure was exerted on both the State and War Departments for the full reopening of the mails with Germany and Japan. The Union was scathing in its excoriation of the American Military Government's decision in Germany, where we were supposed to be giving object lessons in democracy, to confiscate and destroy all Nazi publications.

By 1950 the UN had submitted for its members' ratification not only the Declaration of the Rights of Man but a convention outlawing genocide. Neither had yet been ratified by the United States, though the Union was pressing for such action in the Senate (none was needed in the House). The Union was also working with the UN on the proposed convention on the status of women. But the fate of all such conventions was threatened by the introduction of the Bricker Amendment: Senator John Bricker of Ohio proposed that all treaties be required to be ratified by both Houses and that none be approved if it interfered with states' rights or the rights of American citizens. The patriots, the know-nothings and the exploiters of states' rights supported Bricker enthusiastically, but the Union helped to defeat his amendment, which was hardly necessary in the light of the parochialism already dominant in the Senate.

Union attack was also directed against United States Government imposition of security clearance on Americans seeking or holding posts with the UN or any of its agencies and against inquiries—by their own Government, of course: the UN did not stoop so low—into the beliefs and associations of such Americans. The ACLU pledged itself to defend their rights, including that of resort to UN tribunals for reinstatement if their Government procured their dismissals on political grounds. The pledge was marred, however, by the Union's exception of investigations of possible subversion: the United States, after all, owes its existence to eighteenth-century subversion. The UN itself, to avoid antagonising its chief financial support, discharged the Americans accused by their own Government, and the Union supported their appeals to an international tribunal to approve their claims for damages. The General Assembly changed its rules on the matter to meet most of the Union's objections, making subversive activities, rather than beliefs or associations, the ground for discharge, narrowing the Secretary General's discretion, widening that of its appeals tribunal and authorising a special tribunal headed by an appointee of the International Court to pass on all allegations of subversion. In Congress the Union helped to defeat a bill to make it a crime for any American to take employment in any international public agency without prior clearance by the Attorney General; but the Union lost its fight against the State Department's refusal of passports to Americans traveling on UN business without clearance by the President's Loyalty Board.

The United States was and remains the only nation this side of the Iron Curtain to set loyalty tests for its nationals in UN work: the Union held, rightly, that international civil servants were beyond any state's jurisdiction. The Union criticised Henry Cabot Lodge Jr., American Ambassador to the UN, for rebuking the American director of the UNESCO who refused to discharge American employes defying orders to appear before the Presidential board in Paris, the agency's headquarters, and for frightening the UNESCO man into reversing himself and dismissing seven people. Corollarily the Government tightened its curbs, despite Union protests, on aliens admitted on special permission of the Attorney General for UN business: ultimately a frightened Government allowed these foreigners to travel as much as twenty-five miles from the UN Secretariat, and in any direction they chose.

In substantive matters the Union has spent ten years vainly trying to persuade the United States to live up to its responsibilities. Though the Bricker Amendment was defeated in 1953, the State Department long refused to submit any of the UN conventions—genocide, women's rights, exchange of cultural and scientific materials—to the Senate. Pressured by labor unions, the United States finally agreed to participate in the drafting of the convention against forced labor; but, when it was completed and submitted to the Senate in 1959, both the Labor and the State Departments indicated that its provisions were matters not for federal but for state action! Of course it was not ratified. Finally, in 1963, the State Department nerved itself to face the Senate with three UN conventions concerning human rights: one on the political rights of women, the International Labor Office's convention on forced labor, and a set of amendments to the 1926 slavery convention that the United States had ratified. In sum, American participation in the basic work of the UN was still prevented by the opposition to the conventions in the Senate and the fear that these conventions would actually strengthen civil liberties, override unjust but highly favored federal laws and invade the sacrosanct "states' rights."

A further obstacle to American participation in the rest of the civilised world was the infamous Connally Amendment, which made the United States the sole judge as to those disputes involving this nation that might be "domestic" and hence kept out of the International Court of Justice. Eisenhower, Nixon and even Dulles urged the repeal of the Amendment, and Senator Hubert Humphrey introduced a bill for its repeal, but petty nationalism, as usual, was paramount to international concord and justice.

The American Bar Association had joined the Union's support of the repeal drive, but the votes of members of both organisations totaled so many fewer than those of Legionnaires, Daughters of the American Revolution and other "real" Americans that the august and dedicated Senators harkened, naturally, to those who got there loudest with the mostest.

Within the UN the American delegates have played the State Department's game with one eye on the Senate and the enemies of the UN and the other on the holy battle to contain Communism; sometimes one or the other eye, but rarely both, focuses on principle. The game has been a hypocritical one in which the denial of human rights by Communist states has been ringingly denounced while the same denial by allies and friendly nations has been solemnly condoned. Lofty expressions of loyalty to the purposes of the United Nations' Charter parallel the silent suppression of the truth that what really concerns the United States is not world order but American power, undiluted sovereignty and the defeat of Communism. No one bothers to recall John Kennedy's admonition that the real enemies are poverty, war and tyranny. Human contemptibility is never so glaring as when it is projected to a national level.

22

In Sum...

Not since the First World War, Norman Thomas told the board of directors of the Union on November 23, 1964, after a tour of all the continental states and Hawaii, had he seen such organised persecution of the heterodox—printed and broadcast propaganda by letter and telephone, anonymous and otherwise, and by such devices as the sending of hearses to the homes of the heretical— or such sustained hysteria. He was particularly perturbed—as are thoughtful people of a later generation than his, who were young in the 1920's and 1930's—by the tremendous *rôle* played in the persecutions and the hysteria by those who in all other countries are the advance, not the rear, guard of society: the young. But ten-year surveys of high-school and college students completed in 1960 showed steady declines in the proportion that endorsed freedom of speech and the press, that believed foreigners entitled to the rights of Americans, that disapproved police brutality, that upheld the separation of religion and education. Censorship, discrimination, the deprivation of due process and infiltration by the churches were overwhelmingly supported by the leaders of tomorrow.

It would be easy to conclude that the forty-five years of the

424

American Civil Liberties Union's work had been wasted and that the principles of freedom, common decency, human dignity and individual privacy for which it stands had not been advanced by a millimeter in that time. Such a conclusion would be as superficial and as fallacious as it would be easy. The principles for which the Union has fought, though they may be heartbreakingly seldom enforced in the Bible Belt and not much more often put into execution in the self-styled citadels of "liberalism," have largely become incorporated into law, chiefly by court decision but sometimes even by statute; to some extent they have become usage through less formal procedures. Even statistically the lie is given to the unqualified pessimist: in 1920 the Union had 1000 members in a population of 120,000,000 and today, though the population has not even doubled, the Union's membership has increased 7500 per cent. Granted there cannot be jubilation over the fact that in a population of 193,000,000 exactly 75,000 people care enough about unqualified freedom to do something about it—and that most of the 75,000 do no more than pay their annual dues and commiserate with one another over the velocity with which the world is going to hell in a hydramatic hack. There was a time when the world was traveling the same road on two roughly rounded stones, and it has never changed direction since, whatever the method of transport; but the road is long and the end of it seems constantly to recede. That this is so is in large measure the achievement of small, stubborn democratic *élites* like those 75,000 members of the American Civil Liberties Union.

Why has this nucleus multiplied itself seventy-five times in a half-century marked not only by two world wars but by unprecedented efforts at mass enslavement side by side with equally unprecedented achievements in the liberation of individuals, peoples and territories and with history's first real attempt to achieve world organisation and peace by reason rather than by force of arms and military controls? In part the answer is to be found in the intensity of the drive toward tyranny and the compulsion to conform, for this combination of outer and inner pressures, though it has taken a frightful toll, has also, necessarily, caused many to revise their thinking and many more to think for the first time: it is highly significant that the Union's membership doubled in one of the

first years of the rampant repressions of the 1950's. In at least e-
qual part the answer is to be found in the Union itself.

The American Civil Liberties Union has two outstanding characteristics that account for its growth. The first is its scrupulous
rejection of partisan interest: pure principle will always exert a powerful attraction on independent minds; and the Union's only goal
is equal justice and equal freedom for all, including its mockers and
its opponents. The second aspect of the Union that has contributed
to its growth is its successes—and every action undertaken by the
Union, whatever its immediate practical outcome, has been in the
larger sense a success because it has reinforced, by the mere fact
of its having been undertaken, the concepts of freedom, justice
and equality. The Union has lost many battles but it has won far
more in the perpetual war against injustice, tyranny and bigotry,
and even the battles lost have been milestones toward a war won.
When the Union came into being in 1920, it was legally impossible,
for example, for an alien conscientious objector to become an
American citizen; for a workman who refused a yellow-dog contract to resist dismissal; for a criminal defendant to prevent or
remedy a trial in which he had had no representation by counsel;
for a naturalised American to remain outside the country more
than three years without losing his citizenship; for a dismissed Government employe to compel the confrontation and cross-examination of his accusers; for a sectarian pupil to refuse on religious
grounds to salute the flag without penalty; for a union to prevent
the breaking of its strike by injunction; for a teacher to combat
dismissal for political activity or utterance; for a Negro to claim
the rights of first-class citizenship; for an insurgent union member
to protect his membership and his job.

In the ensuing forty-five years the millennium has not arrived.
But it is beyond dispute that in 1965, despite the setbacks of the
McCarthy-McCarran period and the unabated hysteria of what is
called the cold war, the guaranties of the Bill of Rights have come
out of the archives into the streets, the schools, the courts, the legislatures and even, to some degree, the police stations. Corollarily,
however, the unquestionable advances in civil liberties for minorities and for dissenters that have been ratified by courts and less
often by legislatures have inevitably stimulated new resistances—

but, whereas in 1920 the primary source of resistance was most often governmental, in 1965 government is to be found more and more often on the side of freedom, despite the unsupportable restrictions on radical activity, the political police of J. Edgar Hoover, the unjustifiable restrictions on travel by Americans and immigration by others, the rejection of the Constitution and of federal law by a large part of the nation, the intolerable sumptuary laws regulating private sexual conduct. By far the greatest resistance comes from public prejudices; almost as much arises out of public apathy, which may well be no more, in many cases, than a flight from the fears that in other instances arm the bigotries. For every convert to freedom made by a civil-liberties endeavor there is at least one matching enemy alarmed by the prospect of change, if by nothing more selfish.

Nonetheless progress toward a free society by judicial decision and legislative enactment is an undeniable fact. The strike-breaking detective squads and the suborned militias of the 1920's have become past history. The film censor has been ordered to prove his charges before he may act. The municipal satrap has been stripped of his authority to muzzle and deport. The lyncher has been virtually forced out of business and the vigilante has been legally, if not always effectually, forbidden to coerce his neighbors and his elected employes. The racist has lost the legal guardianship that for so long tolerated, when it did not foster, his bigotries. The policeman is losing his privilege of breaking the laws, or some of them. Statutes and judgments in favor of civil liberty grow in number with every year.

One of the strengths of the ACLU, which has contributed so largely to the visible progress in courtroom and legislative chamber, is its incessant alertness to safeguard and extend the victories. If the Union, through its thirty-five affiliates and its local correspondents, were not constantly alert to observe, to report and to contest every obscure effort to flout appellate rulings or statutory commands and prohibitions, neither the decisions nor the laws would have much practical value: they would be little more than historical exhibits. But it is precisely this constant *qui-vive* of the ACLU and its affiliates and correspondents, their readiness to investigate and combat every violation of the rights guaranteed to every resident of this country, that makes its enemies as well as its friends so much the less liable to arrest without a warrant, to suppression of their right to meet and to speak and to publish.

It would be fatuous to attribute every gain in freedom to the ACLU or to pretend that it has always been unhelped; it has in fact been not infrequently the more or less obscure collaborator of some other organisation or organisations, whether in litigation, in lobbying or in such educational activities as pamphleteering, conferences and forums. When, in the two decades between the wars, the Union often found itself cooperating with the Communists— as in the Scottsboro trial, the Herndon case and the innumerable free-speech prosecutions directed at the left—its opponents immediately branded it Communist by association; yet somehow they never noticed when the Union worked with equal diligence in cooperation with the National Council of Churches or the American Bar Association. Despite this astigmatism, the fact remains that in defending freedom against attack or in advancing its frontiers—goals that have been pursued variously, as circumstances indicated best, by litigation, by opposing or advocating legislation, by private negotiation, by public protest—the Union has never hesitated to cooperate with any organisation, regardless of its political, religious or racial affiliations, that was genuinely concerned with a civil-liberties issue. It has worked with labor unions, with church groups, with Catholic, Protestant and Jewish lay bodies, with racial-rights organisations and with such professional entities as bar associations and teachers' organisations.

What the Union's enemies assiduously omit to note is the fact that the ACLU scrupulously avoids embracing any political or partisan cause in its dedication to furthering the Constitutional rights of all. But its adversaries still seek, because it has always defended the rights of Communists, to identify the Union with Communism. It would be, on such reasoning, equally possible to contend that, because the Union has defended the American Nazi Party or the Christian Nationalist Crusade against invasions of Constitutional rights, the ACLU is a Fascist organisation—"action" or "front." What has largely contributed to the esteem that the Union has gained from both government and the enlightened public is its utter lack of partisanship and its concentration on principle.

But its reputation for being impossible either to buy or to intimidate has been almost as important.

As it has attracted, it has repelled; some who were once repelled and antagonised have come to respect and even to endorse the Union, whether because of changing circumstances or of growing understanding of its purposes and its character. Its board of directors and its committees have included hundreds of distinguished Americans of every religion and none, of a variety of national and racial origins, from the arts, labor, the professions, government and business. The names of a few appear in this history (it would require a chapter of nothing but names to record them all); the 1965 board of directors and national committee, listed in Appendix II, are only a sampling of the leaders who have been and are associated with the ACLU.

Its adversaries have been sometimes distinguished, sometimes notorious, often neither. In its earlier years the Union had virtually no friends in the press; at one time or another almost every major newspaper condemned it in terms varying from mere rebuke to execration, but today there is hardly a responsible newspaper in the United States that does not regard the Union as an essential and valuable force in American life. It has been denounced, however, by labor leaders like Samuel Gompers (when he was president of the American Federation of Labor) and John L. Lewis (when it criticised lawlessness by his United Mine Workers); by the Communist Party (even when the party was glad to have its help: what angered the Communists was the Union's insistence that their opponents were entitled to the same rights and the same assistance); by most of the professional patriots (though at rare times the American Legion and the Union have been on the same side, and many individual Legionnaires have publicly disassociated themselves from their organisation's diatribes); by a few such former Union directors as Corliss Lamont, a confused leftist who contended that the Union began to decay when it defended the rights of causes and persons that he found antipathetic; by virtually all the American extreme right; by the religious fundamentalists and by a large part of the Catholic establishment, angered by the Union's policies on censorship and birth control; and by innumerable police chiefs, prosecutors and municipal officials whose abuses it challenges.

The major attacks on the Union have all been made on the untenable ground of Communism or Communist sympathies. During most of its first twenty years the Union was almost exclusively preoccupied with the problems of labor and radicals— both of which, after all, were the major targets of oppression in that period, when the right was virtually unmolested—but at no time could it justly be accused of favoring Communists despite the tendentious conclusions drawn by those who have looked for —and therefore "found"—what they have been pleased to call proof of Communist infiltration. What is true of this early period is the sad fact that the Union, because of its preconceived and not wholly accurate notion that civil liberties were primarily based on political and economic problems, did neglect the vast jungle of police lawlessness and judicial abuse, which was virtually sanctified by usage through the excesses of Prohibition enforcement. In the years since the Second World War, for all its valiant struggle on behalf of the individual victimised by calculating panic-mongers exploiting a national paranoia, the Union has been derelict in an equally important area of individual liberty, the right to be let alone and to be protected against prurient prying; and this is not unrelated to the Union's firm stand for the closed shop and against any qualification of the suffrage. Each represents a predilection, no doubt born of the preoccupation with collective values common to both east and west, for public or majority rights over those of the individual and for a theoretical doctrine inherently dangerous to both freedom and justice.

At the same time it is impossible not to deplore the attack on its own principles implicit in the Union's insistence on two kinds of treatment for the Communist, dependent on whether he acts as a member of a political party or as an instrument of a foreign conspiracy. Civil liberties should not be governed by teleology, in the first place; the accuracy of the dichotomised view of the Communist is at least questionable, in the second place. The continuation of such a policy by an organisation as influential as the ACLU can only encourage Government excesses that will create a host of new civil-liberties tasks.

One of the most immediate problems of the Union, therefore, should be recognised as the revision of this ambiguous policy and the restoration of a true civil-liberties attitude toward the Communist. Otherwise the Union, in its own way, will be reinforcing the hypocrisy of the United States Government, which, claiming the leadership of the more or less democratic world, practices imperialism on at least three continents under the guise of "containing Communism"—itself far from an unchallengeable function of this Government outside its borders, if indeed a "Communist menace" and not merely a rival imperialism exists. In its endeavors on behalf of true racial equality in the United States, the Union has for the future one of its most important tasks, if only to strive to make American pretensions to democratic leadership more tenable and American exhortations to other sinners more palatable.

An at least equally important task facing the Union is the consolidation of the gains already made against the threat represented by the growth in repressivism among the generation that will be the voters of the next few decades. But the most effective means of educating the public to the meaning and necessity of civil liberties lies in practical civil-liberties action—not only the methods that have become traditional for the Union but, in addition to these "reactive" measures, "initiative" action in the form of positive work both prophylactic and therapeutic, with all the publicity consistent with maximum results. By this is meant the drafting and presentation of, and lobbying for, legislation designed to strengthen civil liberties in their various aspects, as well as administrative regulations and practices—for example, those of the police, or of regulatory agencies—required for the same end. Every concrete action, even if it does not succeed, is worth a ton of pamphlets and speeches; but one does not intend to imply that these should be skimped.

Both the reactive and the initiative, in at least one field, can be particularly furthered by the affiliates and their chapters. The police and the minor judiciary will always be the source of innumerable invasions of civil liberties—political and non-political. The organisation of observer teams among the thousands of ACLU volunteer workers, functioning on regular schedule as reporters of what goes on in courtrooms, is far more useful to the cause of civil liberties than a season of seminars and earnest garden parties: the reports of these observers provide the means of publicising abuses and hence of initiating not only remedial but preventative action. It is submitted that the Union's work would be expedited and its usefulness would be made even greater by a clear division of work jurisdiction between the affiliate and the national office.

The function of the affiliate, it seems to me, is not only to act as the local scout and agent of the national office but, above all, to concentrate on the problems of police lawlessness, judicial abuse, vigilantism on behalf of censorship, the freedoms of teachers and students, the rights of the indigent not only in court but elsewhere, the invasions of civil liberties incidental to the administration of public welfare, and other local issues, leaving the national office free to concentrate its full effort on major fundamental problems. Frequently the two will overlap and the affiliate and the national will of course be mutually useful; but it seems a mistake, quite analogous to the folly of states' rights, to allow local organisations to wander from local problems when in fact it is those organisations that can be most effective in attacking them under a national policy and when fundamental national problems demand resources and perspectives not available on a local level. It would be difficult to exaggerate the value of this kind of affiliate work not only for the immediate but for the foreseeable future. For, if the Union is to continue and increase its already considerable contribution to American freedoms, it must redouble its vigilance at the very bottom of the structure. Whatever influence the United States is to have on the advance of equal rights everywhere must depend almost wholly on its own example, toward the improvement of which the Union can do, as it already has done, so much. "No civil-liberties victory," to reiterate Roger Baldwin's aphorism, "ever stays won."

Acknowledgments

First of all I must attempt to express my appreciation for the patience of my wife, Marianne, in allowing the completion of this book to take precedence over the inauguration of our marriage, as well as for her help in preparing the manuscript for publication.

Alan Reitman, Associate Director of the American Civil Liberties Union, has rendered so much and such constructive assistance that I can fairly say that without his stimulating friendship, his encouragement and his conscientious abstention from influence or censorship of any kind the book could never have been undertaken. To him and to Roger Baldwin I am grateful, too, for their correction of the inevitable errors of fact; I must also acknowledge my great debt to Mr. Baldwin for his innumerable helpful indications of sources, his always cheerful cooperation and the sheer pleasure of consultation with him. George Rundquist, recently retired as executive director of the New York Civil Liberties Union, provided a wealth of information and perceptive insights.

John de J. Pemberton Jr., executive director of the Union, was constantly of assistance, always available for questions and discussion and inexhaustibly patient with intrusions on the premises and facilities of the Union. Mrs. Louise C. Floyd, administrative assistant; Edward Lewin, chief of research, and Leanne G. Katz, executive assistant, suffered constant interruptions of their work with cordiality and (for me) profit. Melvin Wulf, legal director; Lawrence Speiser, executive director of the Washington office; Gordon Haskell, membership and development director; Luther Knight Macnair, executive director of the Civil Liberties Union of Massachusetts; Fred Barbaro, executive director of the ACLU of New Jersey; David Carliner, chairman of the National Capital Area Civil Liberties Union, and Spencer Coxe, executive director of the ACLU of Pennsylvania, deserve special thanks for their availability for consultation and for their assistance in research. The chairmen and executive directors of all the other affiliates, too numerous to mention and too distant to visit, are asked to accept this inadequate recognition of the invaluable assistance rendered by their prompt and comprehensive attention to questions and correspondence—including that chairman who was moved by my queries to inform me that the only foreseeable problem of the Union was "how we can prevent it from taking fools [like myself] to its bosom."

My thanks are due too to all those who sacrificed time from the demands of professions and institutions to aid my research: Ernest Angell, Dr. Allan Knight Chalmers, Edward J. Ennis, Morris L. Ernst, Osmond K. Fraenkel, Walter Frank, Jeffrey Fuller, the Honorable Frank Graham, Professor Louis M. Hacker, August Heckscher, Quincy Howe, the Honorable Dorothy Kenyon, the Honorable John V. Lindsay, Will Maslow, Mrs. Harriet Pilpel, Elmer Rice, Whitney North Seymour, Norman Thomas and Raymond Young. If any names have been omitted through the customary auctorial inadvertence, both thanks and apologies go to their owners.

No list of acknowledgments would be complete if it excluded Miss Anne Strickland, secretary to Mr. Pemberton, and Mrs. Maria Reteguiz, secretary to Mr. Reitman, as well as the devoted support of my agent, James F. Seligmann.

Bibliography

Roger Nash Baldwin, *The Reminiscences of Roger Nash Baldwin*. Unpublished document of the Columbia University Oral History Research Office. (New York, 1953-4).

Barton Bean, *Pressure for Freedom*—The American Civil Liberties Union. Unpublished thesis presented to the Graduate School of Cornell University for the degree of Doctor of Philosophy. (Ithaca, 1954).

Myron Brenton, *The Privacy Invaders*. (New York, 1964).

Fred J. Cook, *The FBI Nobody Knows*. (New York, 1964).

John Dollard, *Caste and Class in a Southern Town*. (New York, 1937).

John Henry Faulk, *Fear on Trial*. (New York, 1964).

Osmond K. Fraenkel, *The Supreme Court and Civil Liberties*. Introduction by Joseph O'Meara. (Dobbs Ferry, 1963).

Osmond K. Fraenkel, *ACLU Diaries*, 1933-57. Unpublished.

Donald Johnson, *The Challenge to American Freedoms*. (University of Kentucky, 1963).

Corliss Lamont, *Freedom Is As Freedom Does*. (New York, 1956).

Anthony Lewis, *Gideon's Trumpet*. (New York, 1964).

Charles Lam Markmann and Mark Sherwin, *John F. Kennedy: A Sense of Purpose.* (New York, 1961).

Lucille Milner, *Education of an American Liberal.* Introduction by Alvin Johnson. (New York, 1954).

Walter Nelles, *A Liberal in Wartime*: The Education of Albert DeSilver. Edited by Lewis Gannett. Introduction by Roger N. Baldwin. (New York, 1940).

John P. Roche, *The Quest for the Dream.* (New York, 1963).

Mark Sherwin, *The Extremists.* (New York, 1962).

Mark Sherwin and Charles Lam Markmann, *One Week in March.* (New York, 1961).

Joseph Tanenhaus, "The American Civil Liberties Union and the Communist Movement: 1920-1954." *In* John P. Roche, editor, *Studies in Infiltration.* (Ithaca, 1965).

Norman Thomas, *The Conscientious Objector In America.* Introduction by Robert M. La Follette. (New York, 1923).

Warren Commission: *Report of the Warren Commission.* (New York, 1964).

The publications of the American Civil Liberties Union.

Special acknowledgement is due to the authors of the unpublished material for their permission to consult and draw on it; thanks are also offered to Professors Roche and Tanenhaus for access before publication to Professor Tanenhaus' contribution to Professor Roche's study.

Appendix I: The Bill of Rights

Passed by Congress, September 25, 1789;
ratified by the States, December 15, 1791.

First Amendment

Congress shall make no law respecting an establishment of religion, or prohibiting the free exercise thereof; or abridging the freedom of speech, or of the press; or the right of the people peaceably to assemble and to petition the Government for a redress of grievances.

Second Amendment

A well regulated Militia, being necessary to the security of a free State, the right of the people to keep and bear Arms, shall not be infringed.

Third Amendment

No Soldier shall, in time of peace be quartered in any house, without the consent of the Owner, nor in time of war, but in a manner to be prescribed by law.

Fourth Amendment

The right of the people to be secure in their persons, houses, papers, and effects, against unreasonable searches and seizures, shall not be violated, and no Warrants shall issue, but upon probable cause, supported by Oath or affirmation, and particularly describing the place to be searched, and the persons or things to be seized.

Fifth Amendment

No person shall be held to answer for a capital, or otherwise infamous crime, unless on a presentment or indictment of a Grand Jury, except in cases arising in the land or naval forces, or in the Militia, when in actual service in time of War or public danger; nor shall any person be subject for the same offense to be twice put in jeopardy of life or limb; nor shall be compelled in any criminal case to be a witness against himself, nor be deprived of life, liberty, or property, without due process of law; nor shall private property be taken for public use, without just compensation.

Sixth Amendment

In all criminal prosecutions, the accused shall enjoy the right to a speedy and public trial, by an impartial jury of the State and district wherein the crime shall have been committed, which district shall have been previously ascertained by law, and to be informed of the nature and cause of the accusation; to be confronted with the witnesses against him; to have compulsory process for obtaining witnesses in his favor, and to have the Assistance of counsel for his defence.

Seventh Amendment

In suits at common law, where the value in controversy shall exceed twenty dollars, the right of trial by jury shall be preserved, and no fact tried by jury shall be otherwise reexamined in any Court of the United States, than according to the rules of the common law.

Eighth Amendment

Excessive bail shall not be required, nor excessive fines imposed, nor cruel and unusual punishment inflicted.

Ninth Amendment

The enumeration in the Constitution, of certain rights, shall not be construed to deny or disparage others retained by the people.

Tenth Amendment

The powers not delegated to the United States by the Constitution, nor prohibited by it to the States, are reserved to the States respectively, or to the people.

LATER AMENDMENTS
AFFECTING CIVIL LIBERTIES

Thirteenth Amendment

Neither slavery nor involuntary servitude, except as a punishment for crime whereof the party shall have been duly convicted, shall exist within the United States, or any place subject to their jurisdiction.

Fourteenth Amendment

All persons born or naturalized in the United States, and subject to the jurisdiction thereof, are citizens of the United States and of the State wherein they reside. No State shall make or enforce any law which shall abridge the privileges or immunities of citizens of the United States; nor shall any State deprive any person of life, liberty, or property, without due process of law; nor deny to any person within its jurisdiction the equal protection of the laws.

Fifteenth Amendment

The right of citizens of the United States to vote shall not be denied or abridged by the United States or by any State on account of race, color, or previous condition of servitude.

Nineteenth Amendment

The right of citizens of the United States to vote shall not be denied or abridged by the United States or by any State on account of sex.

Twenty-fourth Amendment

Section 1: The right of citizens of the United States to vote in any primary or other election for President or Vice President, or for Senator or Representative in Congress, shall not be denied or abridged by the United States or any State by reason of failure to pay any poll tax or other tax.

Section 2: The Congress shall have power to enforce this article by appropriate legislation.

Provisions of Article I in the Original Constitution Affecting Civil Liberties

The privilege of the Writ of Habeas Corpus shall not be suspended, unless when in Cases of Rebellion or Invasion the public Safety may require it.

No Bill of Attainder or ex post facto Law shall be passed.

Appendix II: Who and Where

THE BOARD OF DIRECTORS OF THE

AMERICAN CIVIL LIBERTIES UNION

Ernest Angell, *Chairman*

Irving Achtenberg
Raymond E. Balcomb
Edward J. Barshak
Dr. Robert Bierstedt
Algernon D. Black
Emmett Bondurant
Professor Ralph S. Brown
George Buchalter
David Carliner
Bruce Clayton
Robert L. Crowell
Professor Norman Dorsen
Professor Thomas I. Emerson
Edward J. Ennis
Dr. Luther H. Evans
James Farmer
Osmond K. Fraenkel
Walter Frank
Howard Friedman
Lewis Galantière
Victor S. Gettner
The Reverend Hugh Gillilan
Julian Goldberg
Professor Louis M. Hacker
Professor Franklyn S. Haiman
Michael Harrington
Patricia Roberts Harris
W. Edward Harris
August Heckscher
Sophia Yarnall Jacobs
Professor Marvin Karlin
Judge Dorothy Kenyon
Arthur Kling

William Kunstler
Dan Lacy
Richard Lipsitz
Joseph Losos
The Reverend Brandoch Lovely
Will Maslow
Dr. Henry C. Meserve
The Reverend Edward O. Miller
Walter Millis
The Reverend Irving R. Murray
Mrs. Louise Noun
Rolland O'Hare
The Reverend John Papandrew
Paul H. Phillips
Gerard Piel
Harriet Pilpel
Herbert Prashker
James Lee Rankin
Elmer Rice
Dr. Robert G. Risk
Steven H. Rubin
Leonard W. Schroeter
Harry Seyler
George Slaff
George Soll
Dr. Matthew Stark
Oscar H. Steiner
Glenn S. Visher
Stephen Vladeck
Judge J. Waties Waring
Professor Alan Westin
Waldo Wetmore
Howard Whiteside

440

THE NATIONAL COMMITTEE

Francis Biddle, *Chairman;* Pearl S. Buck, Howard F. Burns, Albert Sprague Coolidge, Lloyd K. Garrison, Frank P. Graham, Palmer Hoyt, Karl Menninger, Loren Miller, Morris Rubin and Lillian E. Smith, *Vice Chairmen.*

Sadie Alexander
J. Garner Anthony
Thurman Arnold
Clarence Ayres
Roger N. Baldwin
Alan Barth
Sarah Gibson Blanding
Catherine Drinker Bowen
Julian P. Boyd
John Mason Brown
Robert K. Carr
Dr. Allan Knight Chalmers
Stuart Chase
Grenville Clark
Rufus E. Clement
Henry Steele Commager
Giovanni Costigan
George S. Counts
Robert E. Cushman
Melvyn Douglas
Thomas H. Eliot
Victor Fischer
Walter T. Fisher
James Lawrence Fly
Dr. Erich Fromm
Ralph F. Fuchs
Willard E. Goslin
Mark De W. Howe
Quincy Howe
Dr. Robert M. Hutchins

Gerald W. Johnson
Mordecai W. Johnson
James Kerney, Jr.
Benjamin H. Kizer
Milton R. Konvitz
Agnes Brown Leach
Max Lerner
Louis Lusky
Robert S. Lynd
Robert Mathews
Wesley H. Maurer
Emil Mezey
Millicent C. McIntosh
Sylvan Meyer
Donald R. Murphy
Frank C. Newman
J. Robert Oppenheimer
John B. Orr, Jr.
James G. Patton
A. Philip Randolph
Elmo Roper
Arthur Schlesinger, Jr.
Edward J. Sparling
George R. Stewart
Mrs. Dorothy Tilly
José Trias Monge
William L. White
Thornton Wilder
Marion Wright
Benjamin Youngdahl

The national office of the Union is at 156 Fifth Avenue, New York 10010. Its officers are:

John de J. Pemberton, Jr., *Executive Director*
Alan Reitman, *Associate Director*
Melvin Wulf, *Legal Director*

The Washington office, directed by Lawrence Speiser, is in the Warner Building at 1101 Vermont Avenue, N.W. The addresses of the affiliates follow:
Alabama — 1006 Thirty-second Street, Birmingham 35205.
Arizona — Southern Area, P.O. Box 17010, Tucson; Northern Area, P.O. Box 7421, Phoenix.
California — Northern California, 503 Market Street, San Francisco 5; Southern California, 323 West Fifth Street, Room 202, Los Angeles 13.
Colorado — 1452 Pennsylvania Street, Denver 3.
Connecticut — Room 207, 18 Asylum Street, Hartford.
District of Columbia — Suite 803, 1101 Vermont Avenue, N.W., Washington 5.

Florida — 502 Olympia Building, Miami 33132.
Georgia — 4655 Jett Road, N.W., Atlanta 30327.
Illinois — 19 South LaSalle Street, Chicago 3.
Indiana — 423 Board of Trade Building, Indianapolis.
Kansas — 1014 West Twentieth Street, Lawrence.
Iowa — 3865 East Thirty-eighth Street, Des Moines.
Kentucky — c/o Mrs. Samuel Fulkerson, Route 2, Jeffersontown.
Louisiana — 7312 Maple Street, New Orleans 70118.
Maryland — First Unitarian Church, Charles & Franklin Streets, Baltimore 1.
Massachusetts — Room 4, 3 Joy Street, Boston.
Michigan — 1600 Washington Boulevard Building, Detroit 48226
Minnesota — 516 New York Building, St. Paul.
Missouri — Greater Kansas City Civil Liberties Union, 5100 Rockhill Road, Kansas City; St. Louis Civil Liberties Committee, 933 Jay Road, St. Louis 63124.
New Jersey — 31 Central Avenue, Newark.
New Mexico — First National Bank Building, Albuquerque.
New York — New York City Civil Liberties Union, 156 Fifth Avenue, New York 10010; Upstate New York Division, 952 Main Street, Buffalo 14202.
Ohio — 354 Hippodrome Building Annex, 715 Prospect Avenue, Cleveland 44115.
Oklahoma — First Presbyterian Church, Norman.
Oregon — 124 Northwest Hermosa Boulevard, Portland.
Pennsylvania — 260 South Fifteenth Street, Philadelphia 19102.
Rhode Island — Box 1904, Brown Station, Providence 02912.
Texas — 205 May Building, 308 West Eleventh Street, Austin 78701.
Utah — First Unitarian Church, 569 South Thirteenth East, Salt Lake City.
Washington — 2120 Smith Tower, Seattle 4.
Wisconsin — 324 South Hamilton Street, Madison 53703.

Index